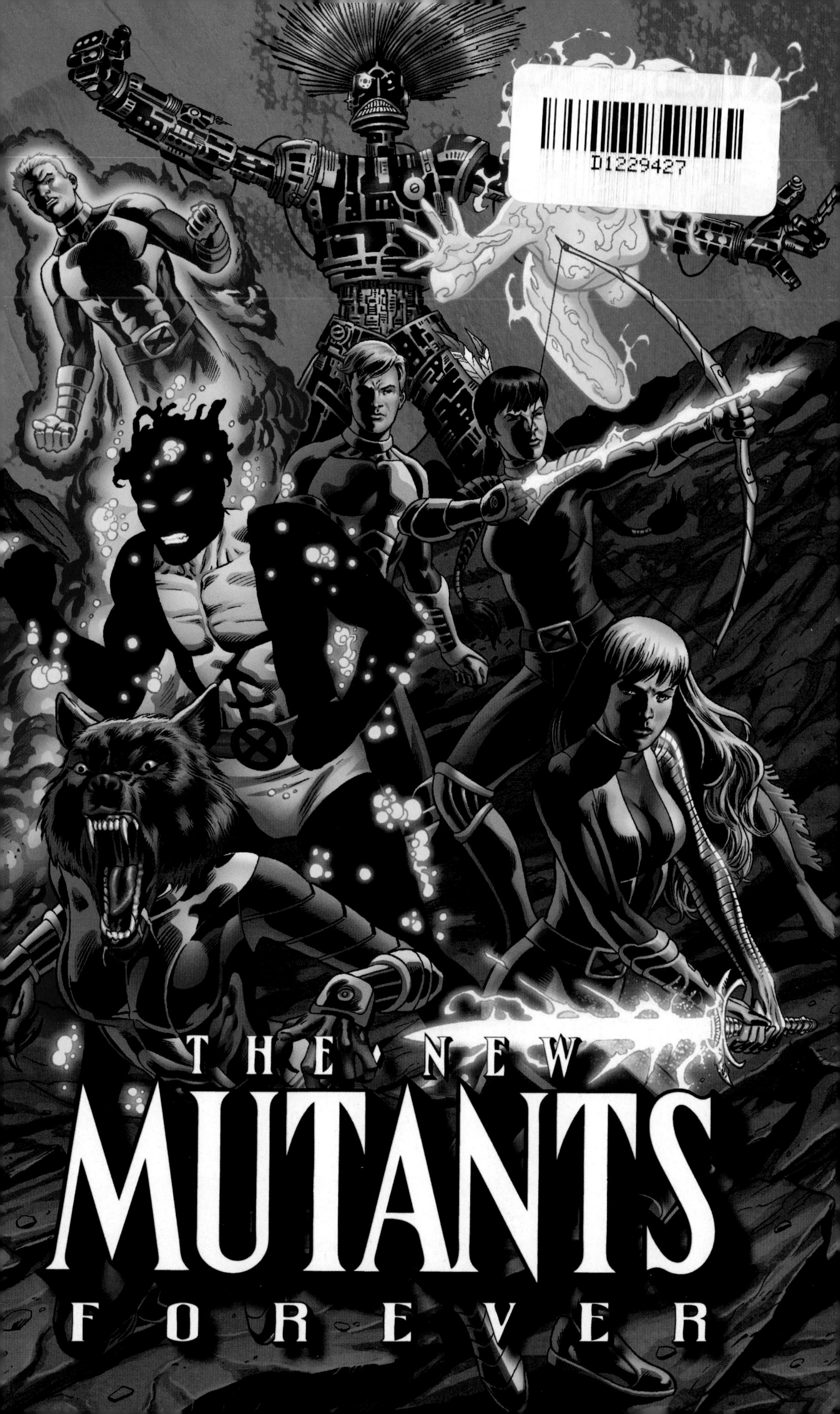
D1229427
THE NEW
MUTANTS
FOREVER

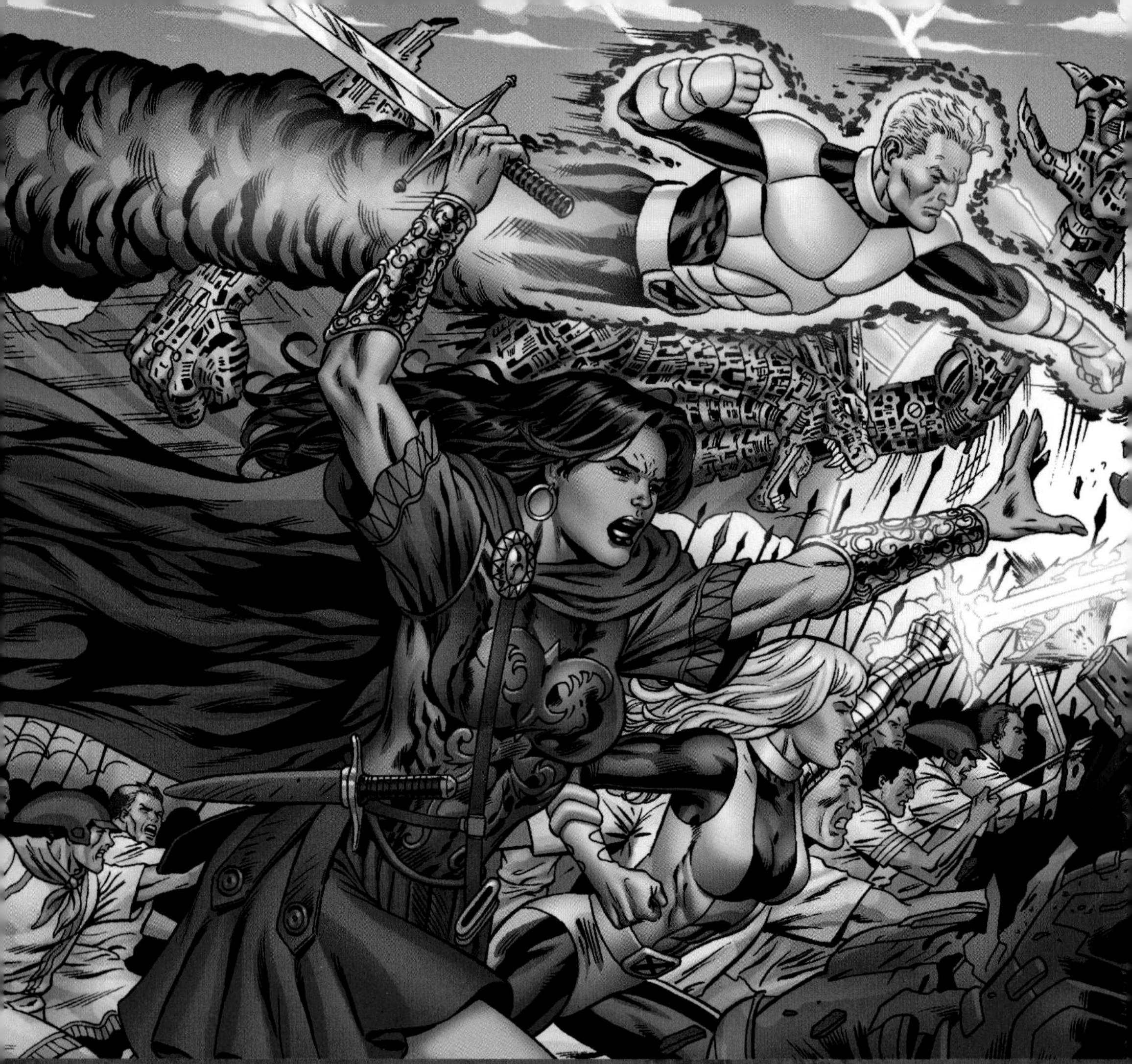

**"The Fall of Nova Roma"**
Writer: **CHRIS CLAREMONT**
Penciler: **AL RIO**
Inker: **BOB MCLEOD**
Colorist: **GURU EFX**
Letterer: **TOM ORZECHOWSKI**
Cover Artists: **AL RIO** with **GURU EFX** (Issues #1, 3 & 5)
& **ARTHUR ADAMS** with **PETER STEIGERWALD** (Issues #2 & 4)
Assistant Editor: **MICHAEL HORWITZ**
Editor: **JORDAN WHITE**
Senior Editor: **MARK PANICCIA**

**"Seduced and Abandoned" (from *New Mutants #53*)**
Writer: **CHRIS CLAREMONT**
Penciler: **RICK LEONARDI**
Inker: **TERRY AUSTIN**
Colorist: **GLYNIS OLIVER**
Letterer: **TOM ORZECHOWSKI**
Editor: **ANN NOCENTI**

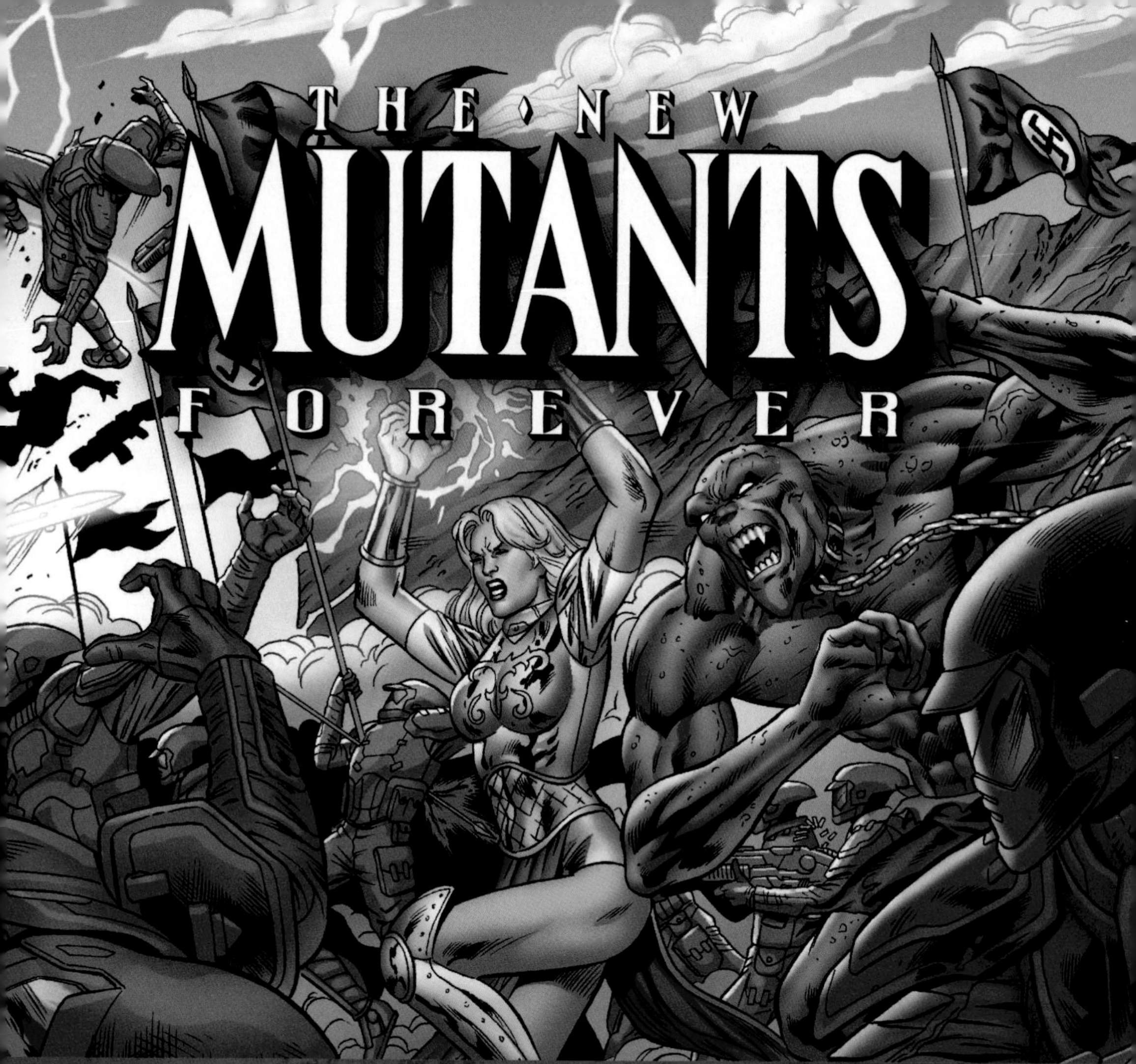
THE NEW
MUTANTS
FOREVER

**"Ratrace!" (from *New Mutants #54*)**
Writer: **CHRIS CLAREMONT**
Penciler: **SAL BUSCEMA**
Inker: **TERRY AUSTIN**
Colorist: **GLYNIS OLIVER**
Letterer: **TOM ORZECHOWSKI**
Editor: **ANN NOCENTI**

Collection Editor: **CORY LEVINE**
Editorial Assistants: **JAMES EMMETT** & **JOE HOCHSTEIN**
Assistant Editors: **MATT MASDEU, ALEX STARBUCK** & **NELSON RIBEIRO**
Editors, Special Projects: **JENNIFER GRÜNWALD** & **MARK D. BEAZLEY**
Senior Editor, Special Projects: **JEFF YOUNGQUIST**
Senior Vice President of Sales: **DAVID GABRIEL**
Color Reconstruction: **DIGIKORE**
Book Design: **ARLENE SO**

Editor in Chief: **JOE QUESADA**
Publisher: **DAN BUCKLEY**
Executive Producer: **ALAN FINE**

#1

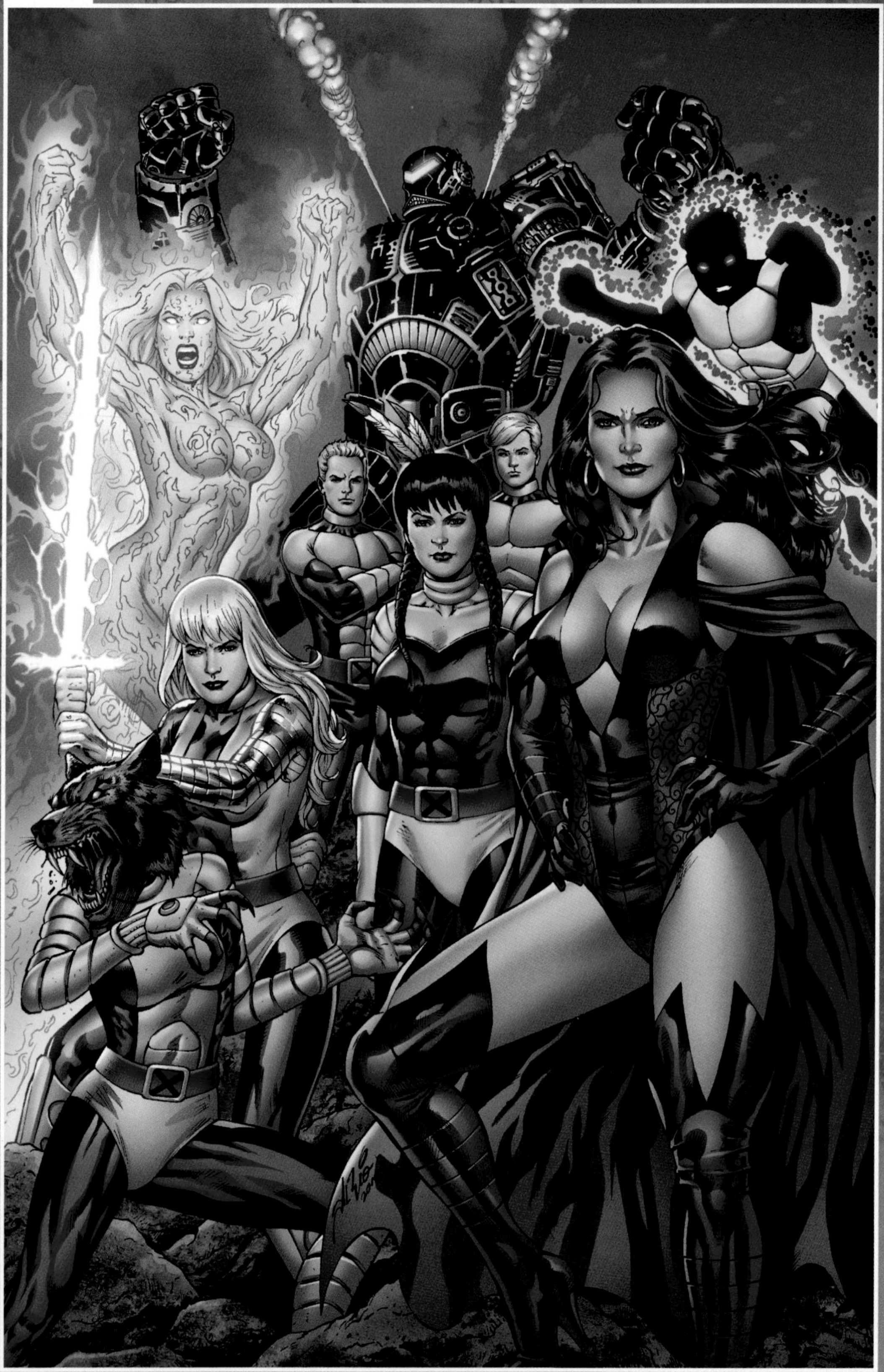

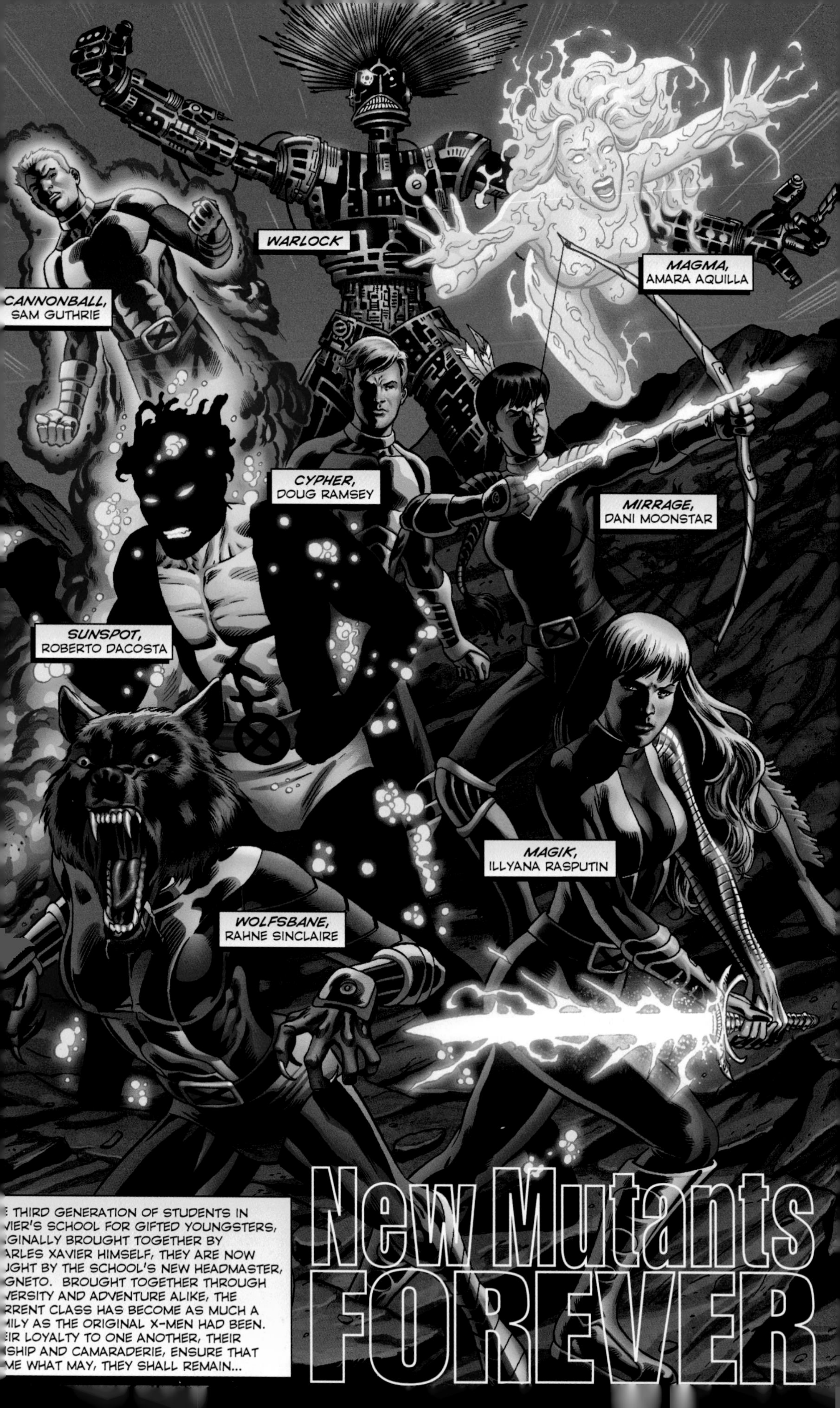
WARLOCK
MAGMA, AMARA AQUILLA
CANNONBALL, SAM GUTHRIE
CYPHER, DOUG RAMSEY
MIRRAGE, DANI MOONSTAR
SUNSPOT, ROBERTO DACOSTA
MAGIK, ILLYANA RASPUTIN
WOLFSBANE, RAHNE SINCLAIRE
E THIRD GENERATION OF STUDENTS IN VIER'S SCHOOL FOR GIFTED YOUNGSTERS, IGINALLY BROUGHT TOGETHER BY ARLES XAVIER HIMSELF, THEY ARE NOW UGHT BY THE SCHOOL'S NEW HEADMASTER, GNETO. BROUGHT TOGETHER THROUGH VERSITY AND ADVENTURE ALIKE, THE RRENT CLASS HAS BECOME AS MUCH A MILY AS THE ORIGINAL X-MEN HAD BEEN. EIR LOYALTY TO ONE ANOTHER, THEIR SHIP AND CAMARADERIE, ENSURE THAT ME WHAT MAY, THEY SHALL REMAIN...
New Mutants FOREVER

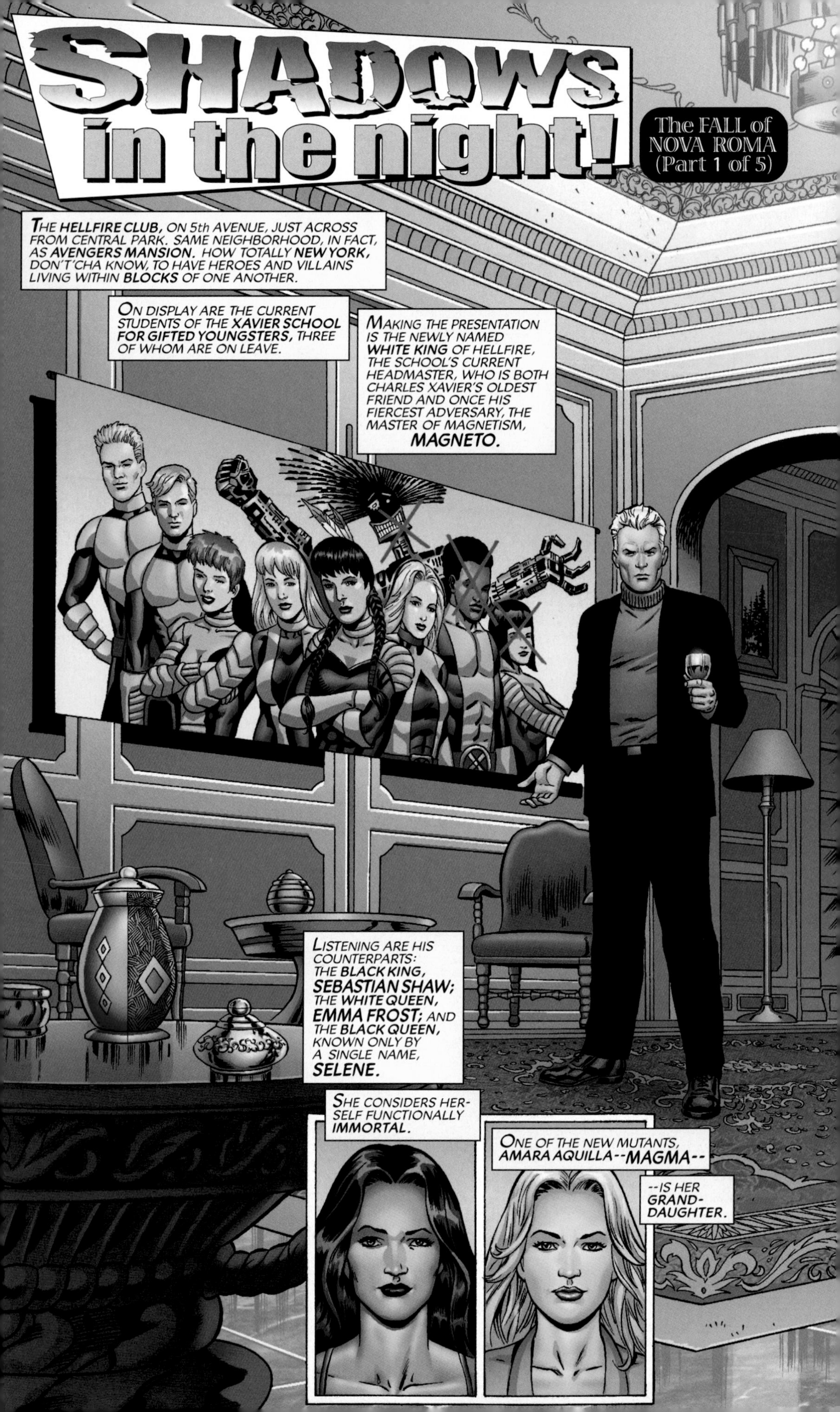
SHADOWS in the night!
The FALL of NOVA ROMA (Part 1 of 5)
THE HELLFIRE CLUB, ON 5th AVENUE, JUST ACROSS FROM CENTRAL PARK. SAME NEIGHBORHOOD, IN FACT, AS AVENGERS MANSION. HOW TOTALLY NEW YORK, DON'T'CHA KNOW, TO HAVE HEROES AND VILLAINS LIVING WITHIN BLOCKS OF ONE ANOTHER.
ON DISPLAY ARE THE CURRENT STUDENTS OF THE XAVIER SCHOOL FOR GIFTED YOUNGSTERS, THREE OF WHOM ARE ON LEAVE.
MAKING THE PRESENTATION IS THE NEWLY NAMED WHITE KING OF HELLFIRE, THE SCHOOL'S CURRENT HEADMASTER, WHO IS BOTH CHARLES XAVIER'S OLDEST FRIEND AND ONCE HIS FIERCEST ADVERSARY, THE MASTER OF MAGNETISM, MAGNETO.
LISTENING ARE HIS COUNTERPARTS: THE BLACK KING, SEBASTIAN SHAW; THE WHITE QUEEN, EMMA FROST; AND THE BLACK QUEEN, KNOWN ONLY BY A SINGLE NAME, SELENE.
SHE CONSIDERS HER-SELF FUNCTIONALLY IMMORTAL.
ONE OF THE NEW MUTANTS, AMARA AQUILLA--MAGMA--
--IS HER GRAND-DAUGHTER.

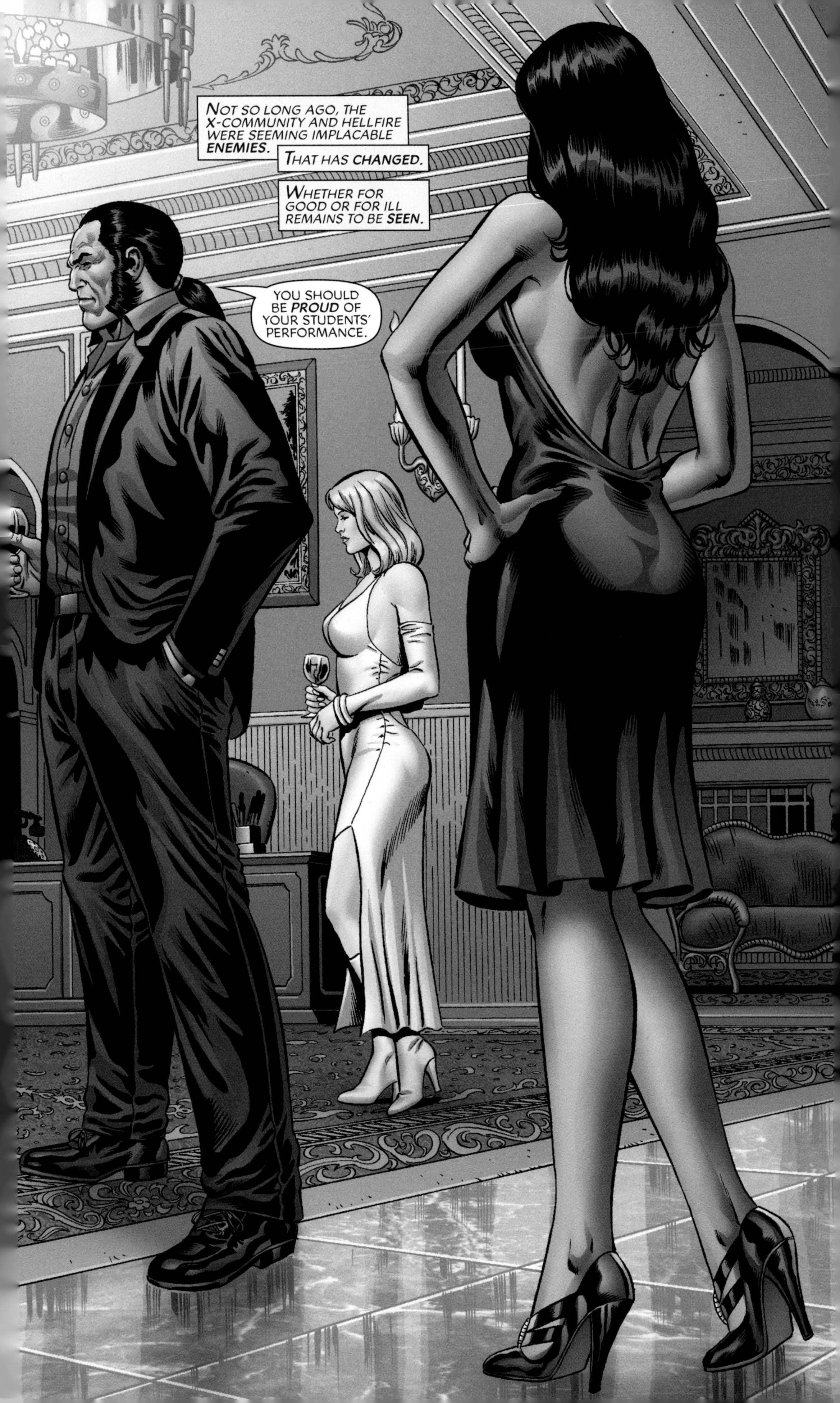
NOT SO LONG AGO, THE X-COMMUNITY AND HELLFIRE WERE SEEMING IMPLACABLE ENEMIES.
THAT HAS CHANGED.
WHETHER FOR GOOD OR FOR ILL REMAINS TO BE SEEN.
YOU SHOULD BE PROUD OF YOUR STUDENTS' PERFORMANCE.

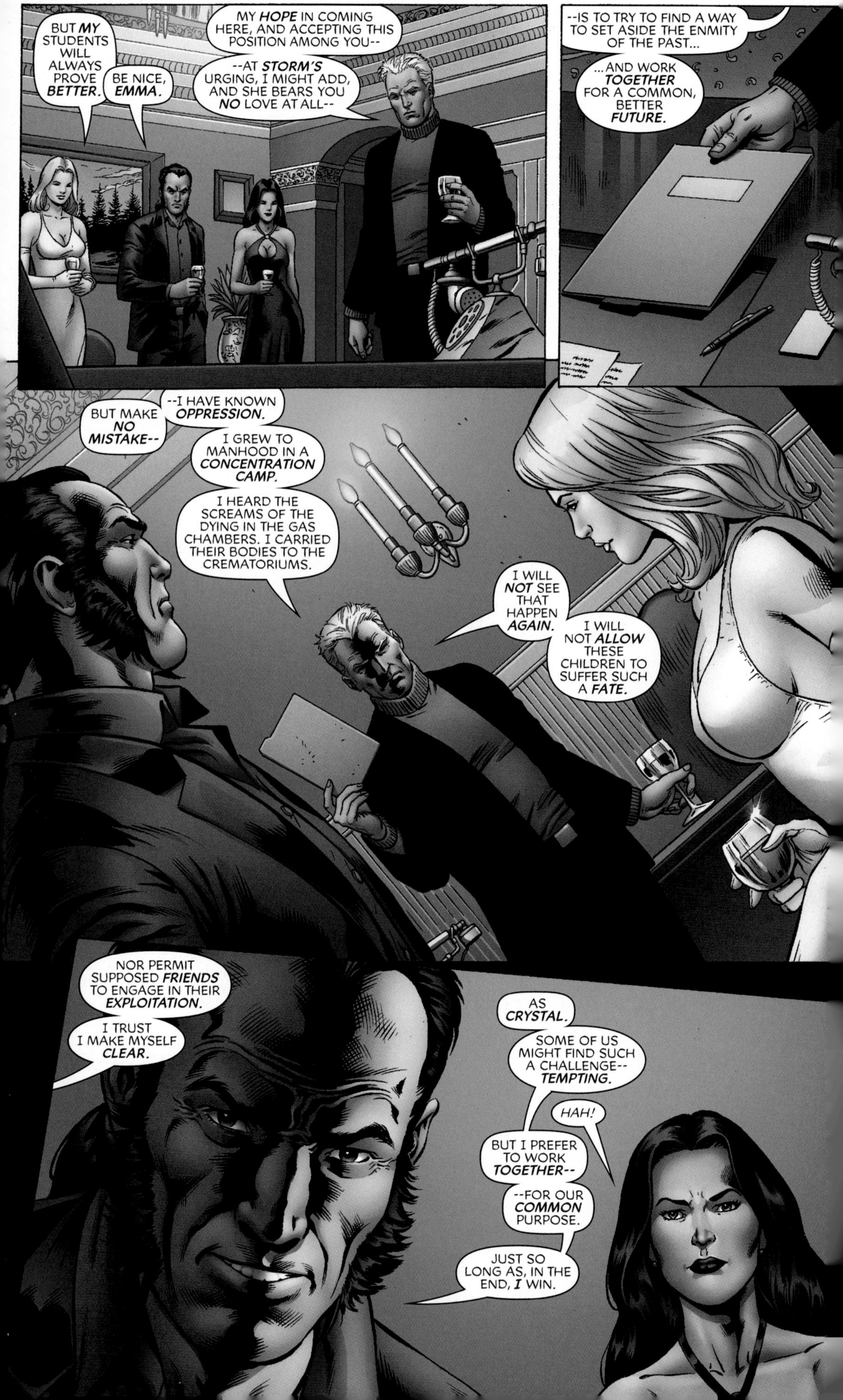

MY HOPE IN COMING HERE, AND ACCEPTING THIS POSITION AMONG YOU--
BUT MY STUDENTS WILL ALWAYS PROVE BETTER.
BE NICE, EMMA.
--AT STORM'S URGING, I MIGHT ADD, AND SHE BEARS YOU NO LOVE AT ALL--
--IS TO TRY TO FIND A WAY TO SET ASIDE THE ENMITY OF THE PAST...
...AND WORK TOGETHER FOR A COMMON, BETTER FUTURE.
BUT MAKE NO MISTAKE--
--I HAVE KNOWN OPPRESSION.
I GREW TO MANHOOD IN A CONCENTRATION CAMP.
I HEARD THE SCREAMS OF THE DYING IN THE GAS CHAMBERS. I CARRIED THEIR BODIES TO THE CREMATORIUMS.
I WILL NOT SEE THAT HAPPEN AGAIN.
I WILL NOT ALLOW THESE CHILDREN TO SUFFER SUCH A FATE.
NOR PERMIT SUPPOSED FRIENDS TO ENGAGE IN THEIR EXPLOITATION.
I TRUST I MAKE MYSELF CLEAR.
AS CRYSTAL.
SOME OF US MIGHT FIND SUCH A CHALLENGE-- TEMPTING.
HAH!
BUT I PREFER TO WORK TOGETHER--
--FOR OUR COMMON PURPOSE.
JUST SO LONG AS, IN THE END, I WIN.

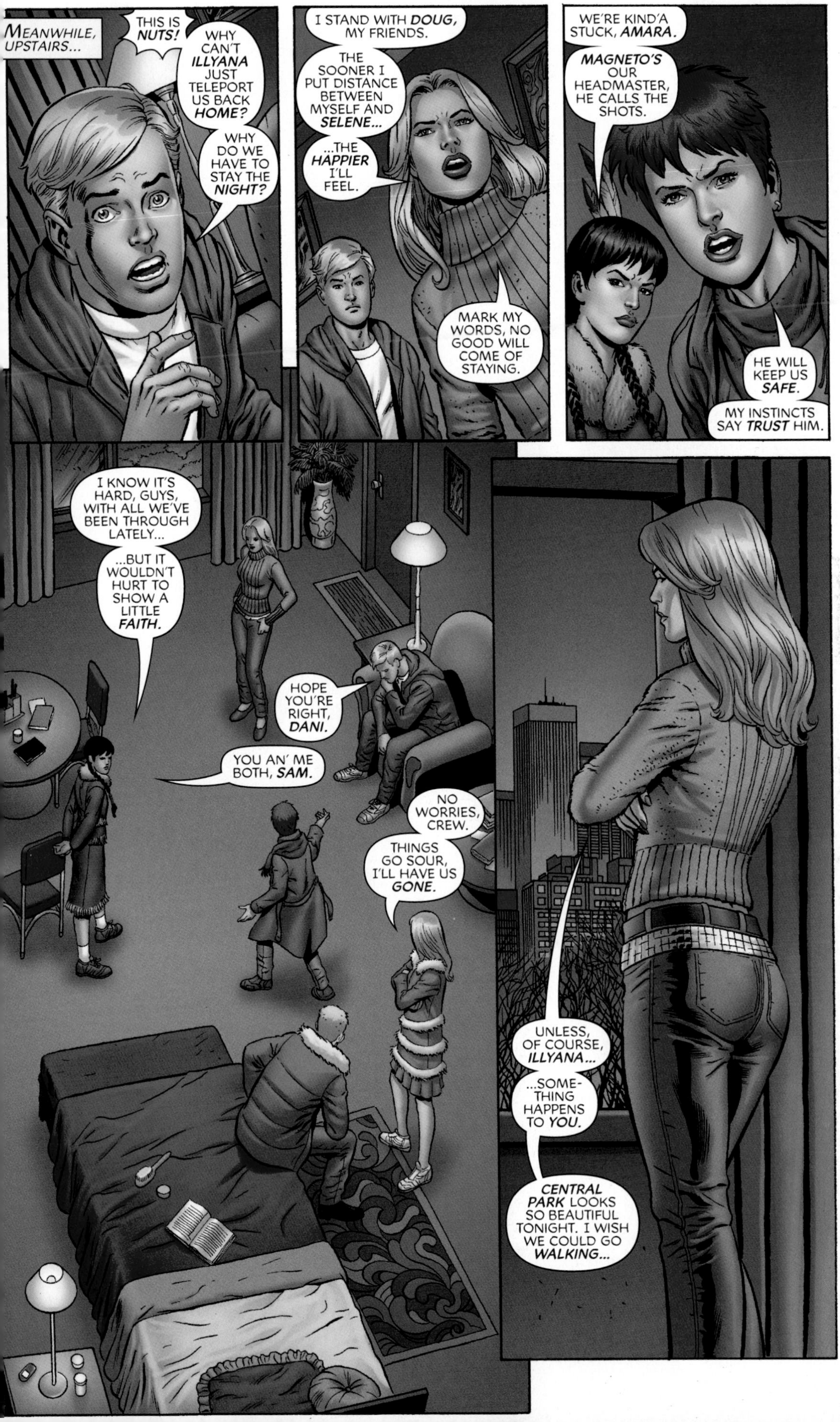
MEANWHILE, UPSTAIRS...
THIS IS NUTS!
WHY CAN'T ILLYANA JUST TELEPORT US BACK HOME?
WHY DO WE HAVE TO STAY THE NIGHT?
I STAND WITH DOUG, MY FRIENDS.
THE SOONER I PUT DISTANCE BETWEEN MYSELF AND SELENE...
...THE HAPPIER I'LL FEEL.
MARK MY WORDS, NO GOOD WILL COME OF STAYING.
WE'RE KIND'A STUCK, AMARA.
MAGNETO'S OUR HEADMASTER, HE CALLS THE SHOTS.
HE WILL KEEP US SAFE.
MY INSTINCTS SAY TRUST HIM.
I KNOW IT'S HARD, GUYS, WITH ALL WE'VE BEEN THROUGH LATELY...
...BUT IT WOULDN'T HURT TO SHOW A LITTLE FAITH.
HOPE YOU'RE RIGHT, DANI.
YOU AN' ME BOTH, SAM.
NO WORRIES, CREW.
THINGS GO SOUR, I'LL HAVE US GONE.
UNLESS, OF COURSE, ILLYANA...
...SOMETHING HAPPENS TO YOU.
CENTRAL PARK LOOKS SO BEAUTIFUL TONIGHT. I WISH WE COULD GO WALKING...

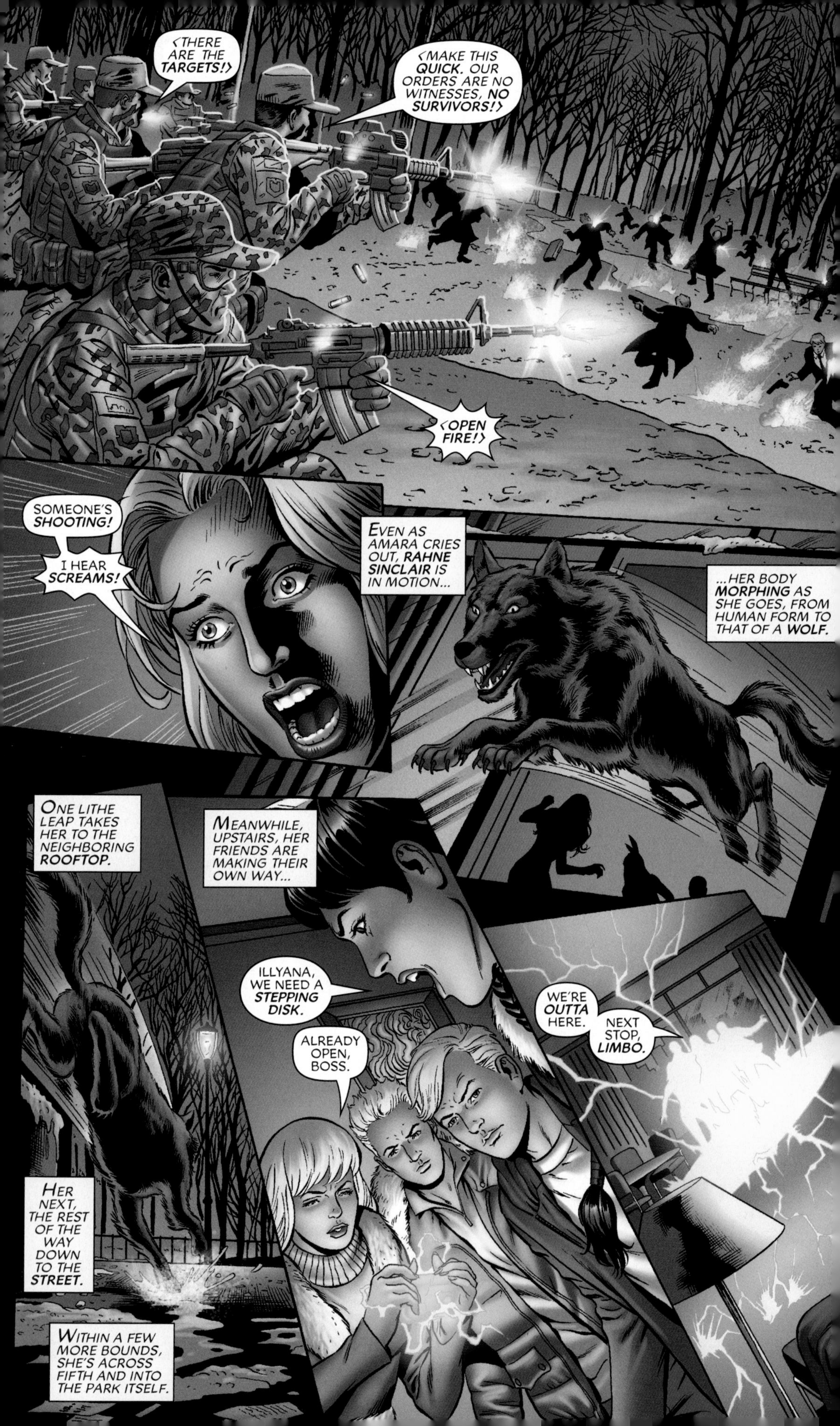

<THERE ARE THE TARGETS!>
<MAKE THIS QUICK. OUR ORDERS ARE NO WITNESSES, NO SURVIVORS!>
<OPEN FIRE!>
SOMEONE'S SHOOTING!
I HEAR SCREAMS!
EVEN AS AMARA CRIES OUT, RAHNE SINCLAIR IS IN MOTION...
...HER BODY MORPHING AS SHE GOES, FROM HUMAN FORM TO THAT OF A WOLF.
ONE LITHE LEAP TAKES HER TO THE NEIGHBORING ROOFTOP.
MEANWHILE, UPSTAIRS, HER FRIENDS ARE MAKING THEIR OWN WAY...
ILLYANA, WE NEED A STEPPING DISK.
ALREADY OPEN, BOSS.
WE'RE OUTTA HERE.
NEXT STOP, LIMBO.
HER NEXT, THE REST OF THE WAY DOWN TO THE STREET.
WITHIN A FEW MORE BOUNDS, SHE'S ACROSS FIFTH AND INTO THE PARK ITSELF.

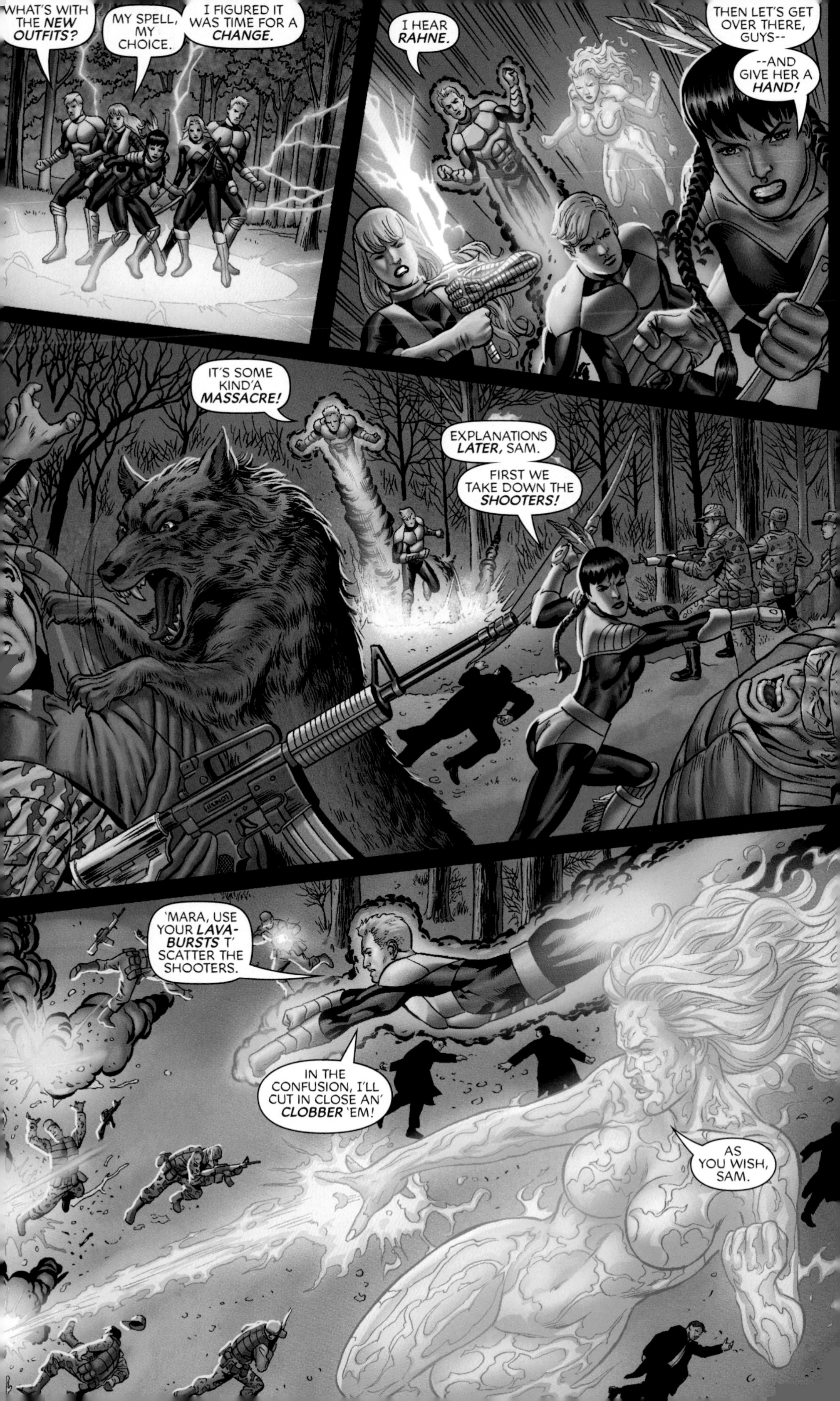
WHAT'S WITH THE *NEW OUTFITS?*
MY SPELL, MY CHOICE.
I FIGURED IT WAS TIME FOR A *CHANGE.*
I HEAR *RAHNE.*
THEN LET'S GET OVER THERE, GUYS--
--AND GIVE HER A *HAND!*
IT'S SOME KIND'A *MASSACRE!*
EXPLANATIONS *LATER,* SAM.
FIRST WE TAKE DOWN THE *SHOOTERS!*
'MARA, USE YOUR *LAVA-BURSTS* T' SCATTER THE SHOOTERS.
IN THE CONFUSION, I'LL CUT IN CLOSE AN' *CLOBBER* 'EM!
AS YOU WISH, SAM.

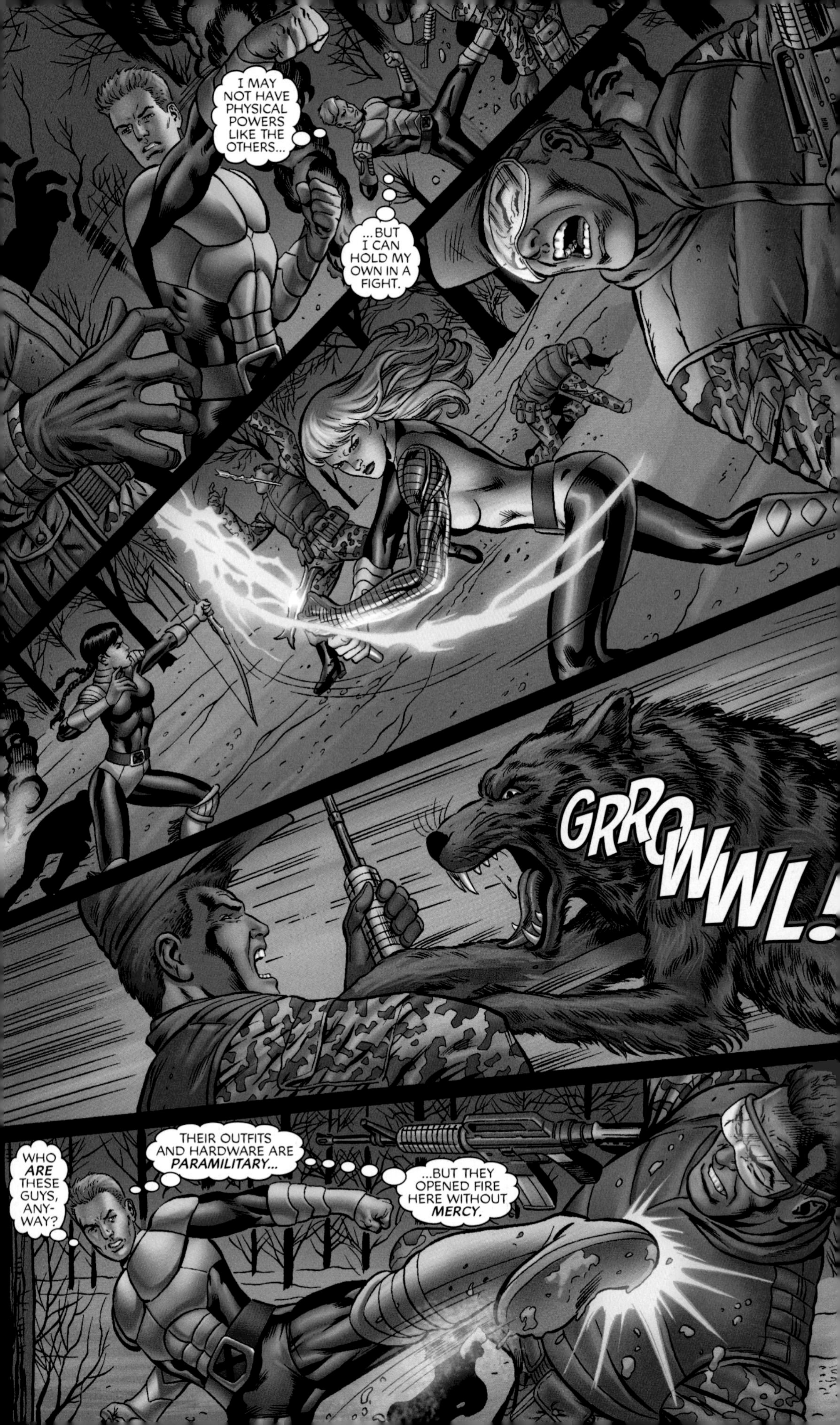

I MAY NOT HAVE PHYSICAL POWERS LIKE THE OTHERS...
...BUT I CAN HOLD MY OWN IN A FIGHT.
GRROWWL!!
WHO *ARE* THESE GUYS, ANY-WAY?
THEIR OUTFITS AND HARDWARE ARE *PARAMILITARY*...
...BUT THEY OPENED FIRE HERE WITHOUT *MERCY*.

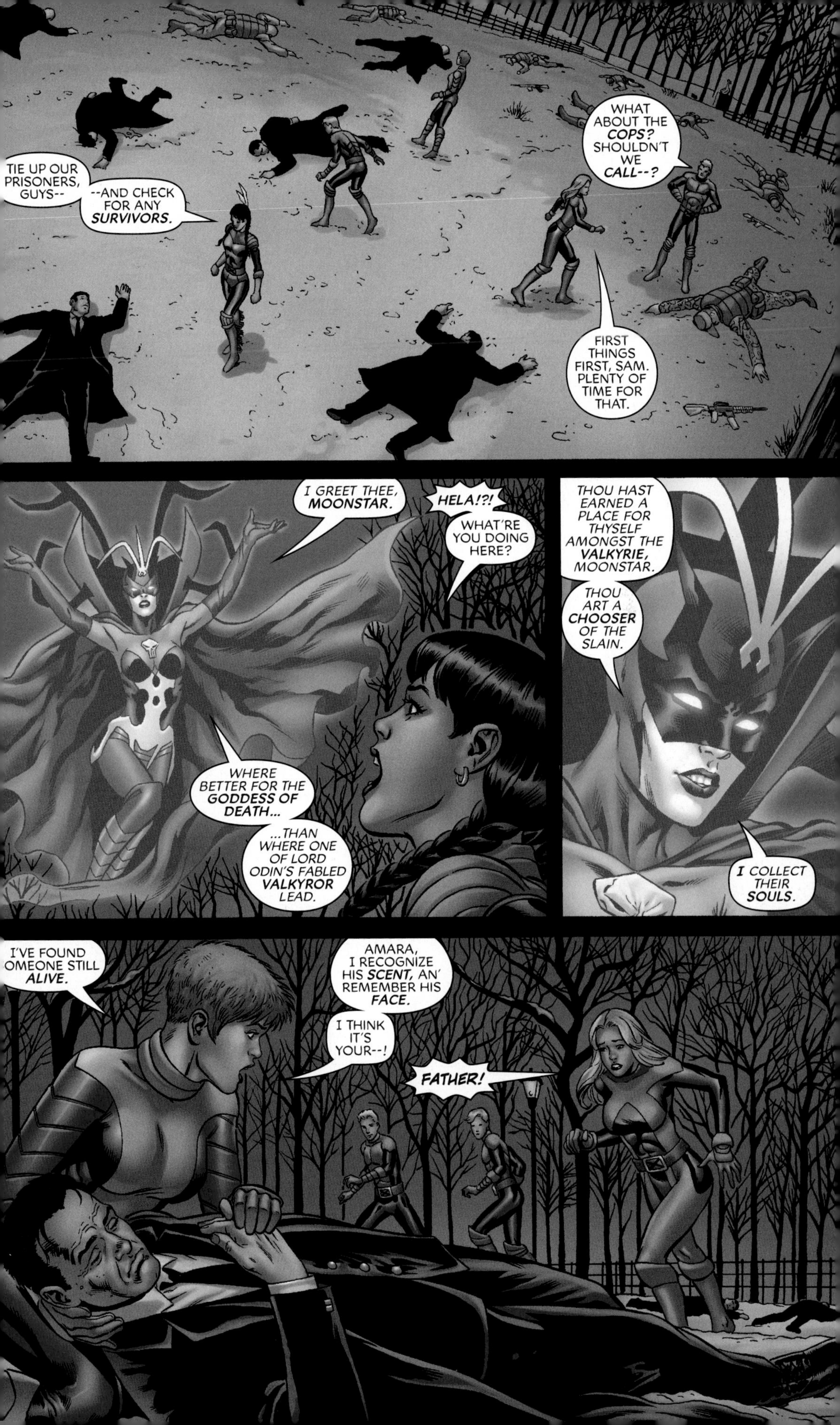
TIE UP OUR PRISONERS, GUYS--
--AND CHECK FOR ANY SURVIVORS.
WHAT ABOUT THE COPS? SHOULDN'T WE CALL--?
FIRST THINGS FIRST, SAM. PLENTY OF TIME FOR THAT.
I GREET THEE, MOONSTAR.
HELA!?!
WHAT'RE YOU DOING HERE?
WHERE BETTER FOR THE GODDESS OF DEATH...
...THAN WHERE ONE OF LORD ODIN'S FABLED VALKYROR LEAD.
THOU HAST EARNED A PLACE FOR THYSELF AMONGST THE VALKYRIE, MOONSTAR.
THOU ART A CHOOSER OF THE SLAIN.
I COLLECT THEIR SOULS.
I'VE FOUND OMEONE STILL ALIVE.
AMARA, I RECOGNIZE HIS SCENT, AN' REMEMBER HIS FACE.
I THINK IT'S YOUR--!
FATHER!

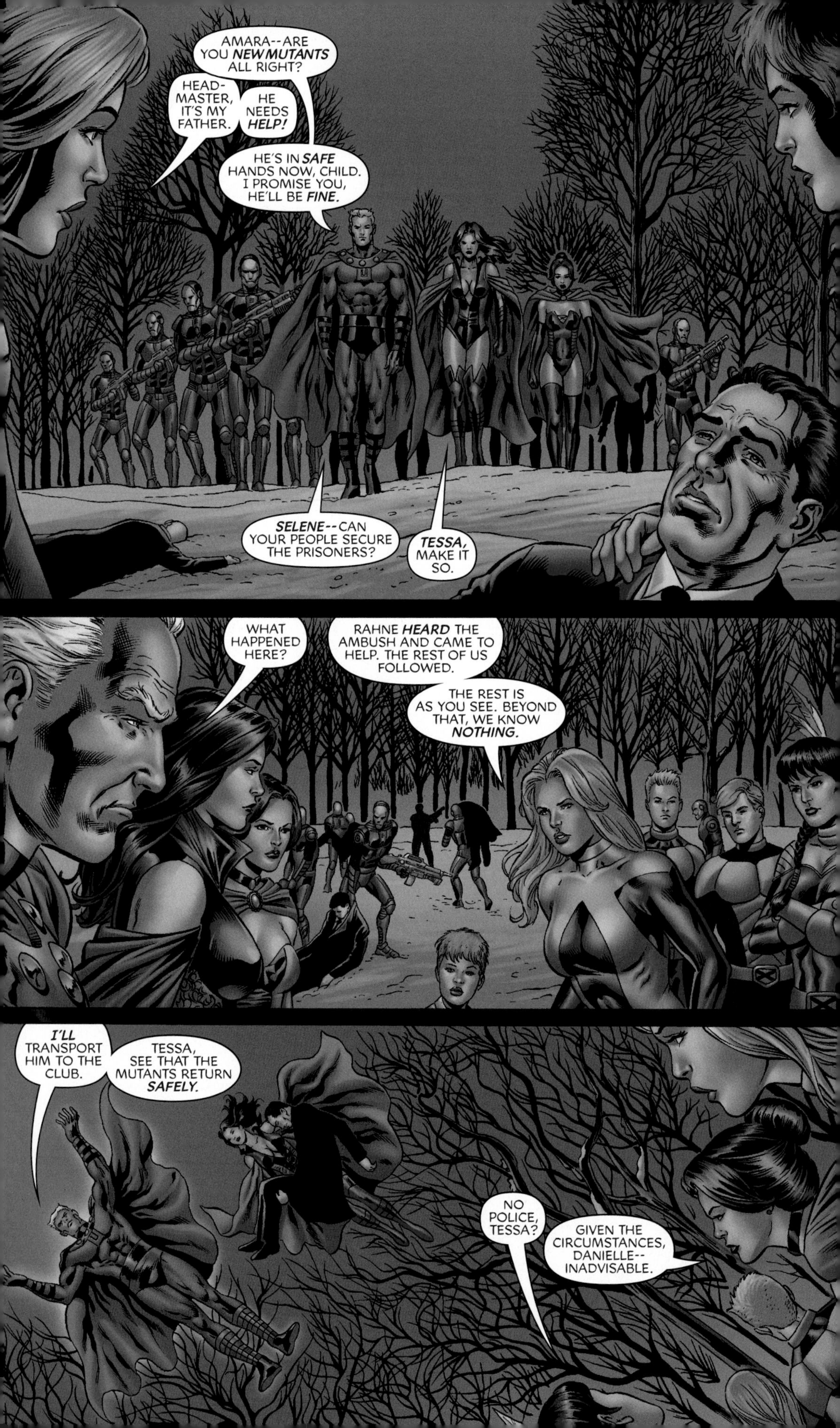

AMARA--ARE YOU NEW MUTANTS ALL RIGHT?
HEAD-MASTER, IT'S MY FATHER.
HE NEEDS HELP!
HE'S IN SAFE HANDS NOW, CHILD. I PROMISE YOU, HE'LL BE FINE.
SELENE--CAN YOUR PEOPLE SECURE THE PRISONERS?
TESSA, MAKE IT SO.
WHAT HAPPENED HERE?
RAHNE HEARD THE AMBUSH AND CAME TO HELP. THE REST OF US FOLLOWED.
THE REST IS AS YOU SEE. BEYOND THAT, WE KNOW NOTHING.
I'LL TRANSPORT HIM TO THE CLUB.
TESSA, SEE THAT THE MUTANTS RETURN SAFELY.
NO POLICE, TESSA?
GIVEN THE CIRCUMSTANCES, DANIELLE--INADVISABLE.

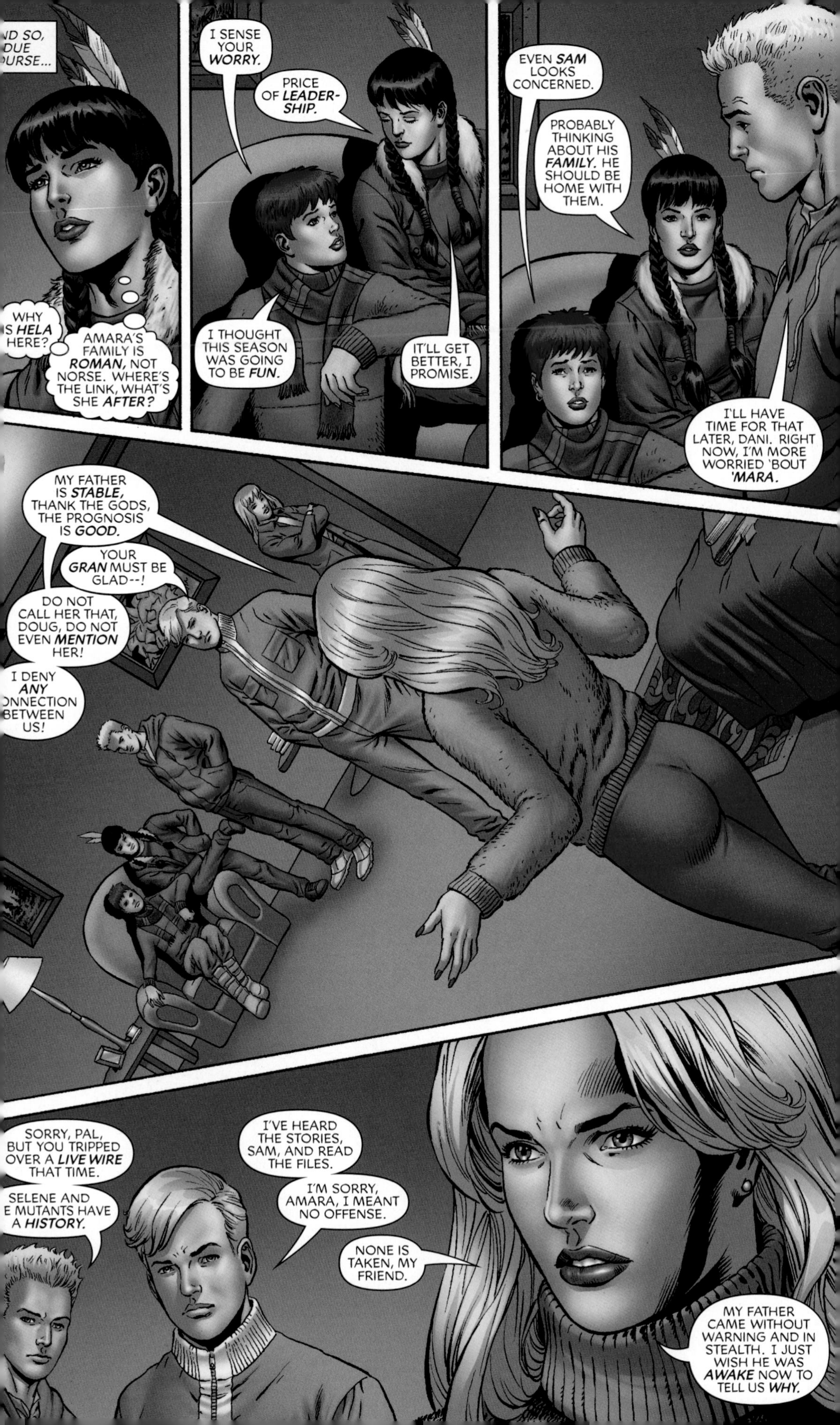

ND SO, DUE OURSE...
WHY S HELA HERE?
AMARA'S FAMILY IS ROMAN, NOT NORSE. WHERE'S THE LINK, WHAT'S SHE AFTER?
I SENSE YOUR WORRY.
PRICE OF LEADER-SHIP.
I THOUGHT THIS SEASON WAS GOING TO BE FUN.
IT'LL GET BETTER, I PROMISE.
EVEN SAM LOOKS CONCERNED.
PROBABLY THINKING ABOUT HIS FAMILY. HE SHOULD BE HOME WITH THEM.
I'LL HAVE TIME FOR THAT LATER, DANI. RIGHT NOW, I'M MORE WORRIED 'BOUT 'MARA.
MY FATHER IS STABLE, THANK THE GODS, THE PROGNOSIS IS GOOD.
YOUR GRAN MUST BE GLAD--!
DO NOT CALL HER THAT, DOUG, DO NOT EVEN MENTION HER!
I DENY ANY ONNECTION BETWEEN US!
SORRY, PAL, BUT YOU TRIPPED OVER A LIVE WIRE THAT TIME.
SELENE AND E MUTANTS HAVE A HISTORY.
I'VE HEARD THE STORIES, SAM, AND READ THE FILES.
I'M SORRY, AMARA, I MEANT NO OFFENSE.
NONE IS TAKEN, MY FRIEND.
MY FATHER CAME WITHOUT WARNING AND IN STEALTH. I JUST WISH HE WAS AWAKE NOW TO TELL US WHY.

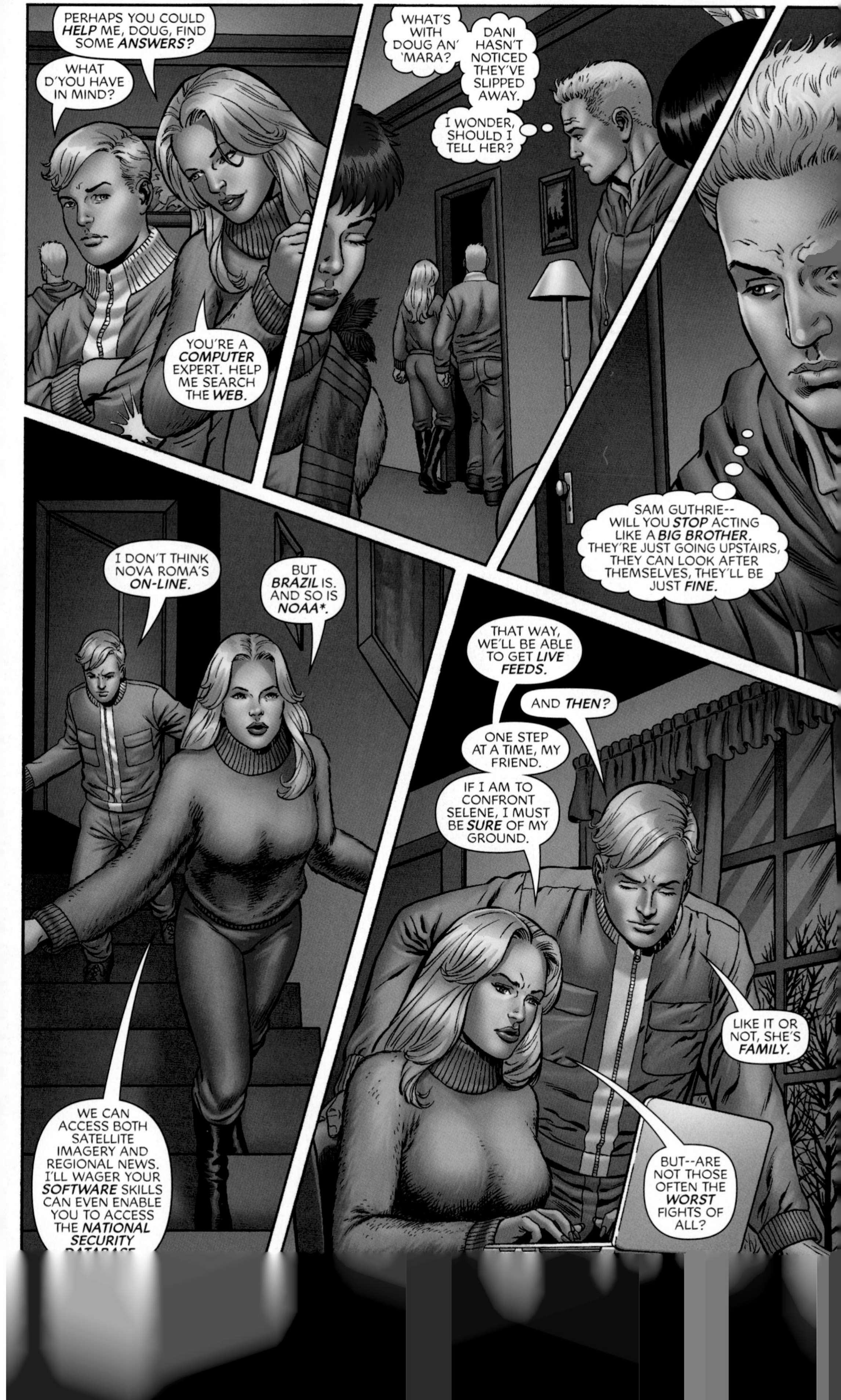
PERHAPS YOU COULD HELP ME, DOUG, FIND SOME ANSWERS?
WHAT D'YOU HAVE IN MIND?
YOU'RE A COMPUTER EXPERT. HELP ME SEARCH THE WEB.
WHAT'S WITH DOUG AN' 'MARA?
DANI HASN'T NOTICED THEY'VE SLIPPED AWAY.
I WONDER, SHOULD I TELL HER?
SAM GUTHRIE-- WILL YOU STOP ACTING LIKE A BIG BROTHER. THEY'RE JUST GOING UPSTAIRS, THEY CAN LOOK AFTER THEMSELVES, THEY'LL BE JUST FINE.
I DON'T THINK NOVA ROMA'S ON-LINE.
BUT BRAZIL IS. AND SO IS NOAA*.
WE CAN ACCESS BOTH SATELLITE IMAGERY AND REGIONAL NEWS. I'LL WAGER YOUR SOFTWARE SKILLS CAN EVEN ENABLE YOU TO ACCESS THE NATIONAL SECURITY
THAT WAY, WE'LL BE ABLE TO GET LIVE FEEDS.
AND THEN?
ONE STEP AT A TIME, MY FRIEND.
IF I AM TO CONFRONT SELENE, I MUST BE SURE OF MY GROUND.
LIKE IT OR NOT, SHE'S FAMILY.
BUT--ARE NOT THOSE OFTEN THE WORST FIGHTS OF ALL?

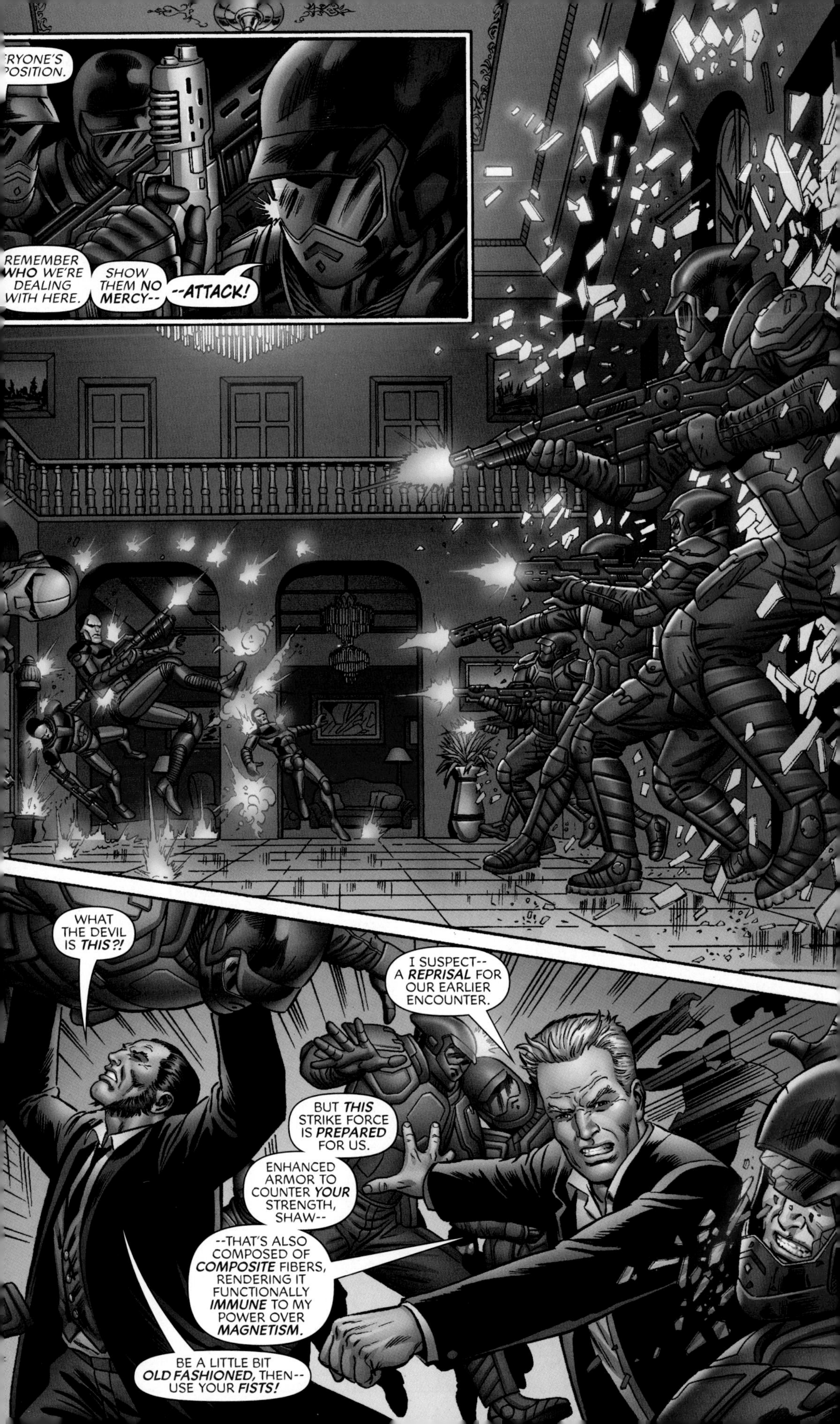

...RYONE'S POSITION.
REMEMBER WHO WE'RE DEALING WITH HERE.
SHOW THEM NO MERCY--
--ATTACK!
WHAT THE DEVIL IS THIS?!
I SUSPECT-- A REPRISAL FOR OUR EARLIER ENCOUNTER.
BUT THIS STRIKE FORCE IS PREPARED FOR US.
ENHANCED ARMOR TO COUNTER YOUR STRENGTH, SHAW--
--THAT'S ALSO COMPOSED OF COMPOSITE FIBERS, RENDERING IT FUNCTIONALLY IMMUNE TO MY POWER OVER MAGNETISM.
BE A LITTLE BIT OLD FASHIONED, THEN-- USE YOUR FISTS!

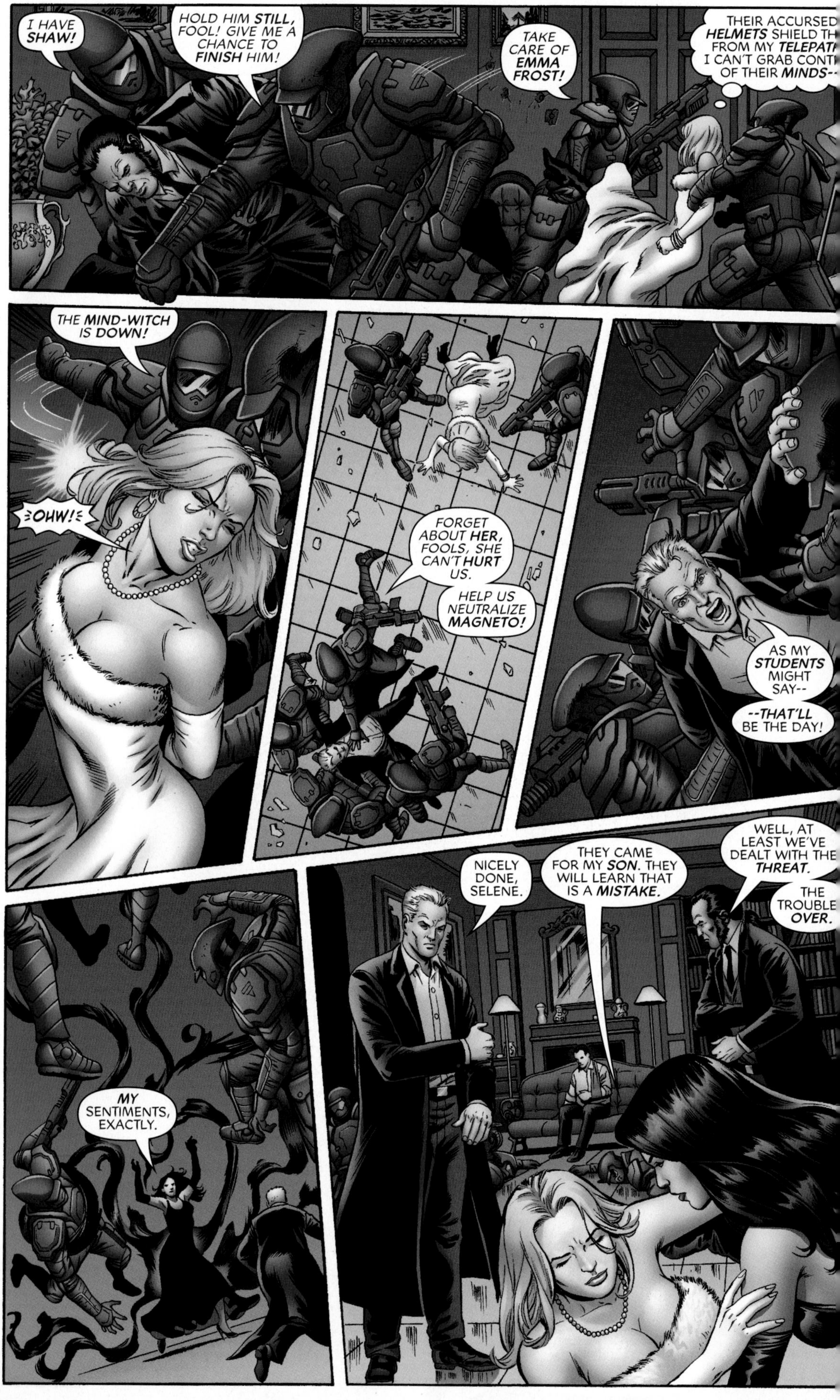
I HAVE SHAW!
HOLD HIM STILL, FOOL! GIVE ME A CHANCE TO FINISH HIM!
TAKE CARE OF EMMA FROST!
THE MIND-WITCH IS DOWN!
OHW!
FORGET ABOUT HER, FOOLS, SHE CAN'T HURT US.
HELP US NEUTRALIZE MAGNETO!
AS MY STUDENTS MIGHT SAY--
--THAT'LL BE THE DAY!
MY SENTIMENTS, EXACTLY.
NICELY DONE, SELENE.
THEY CAME FOR MY SON. THEY WILL LEARN THAT IS A MISTAKE.

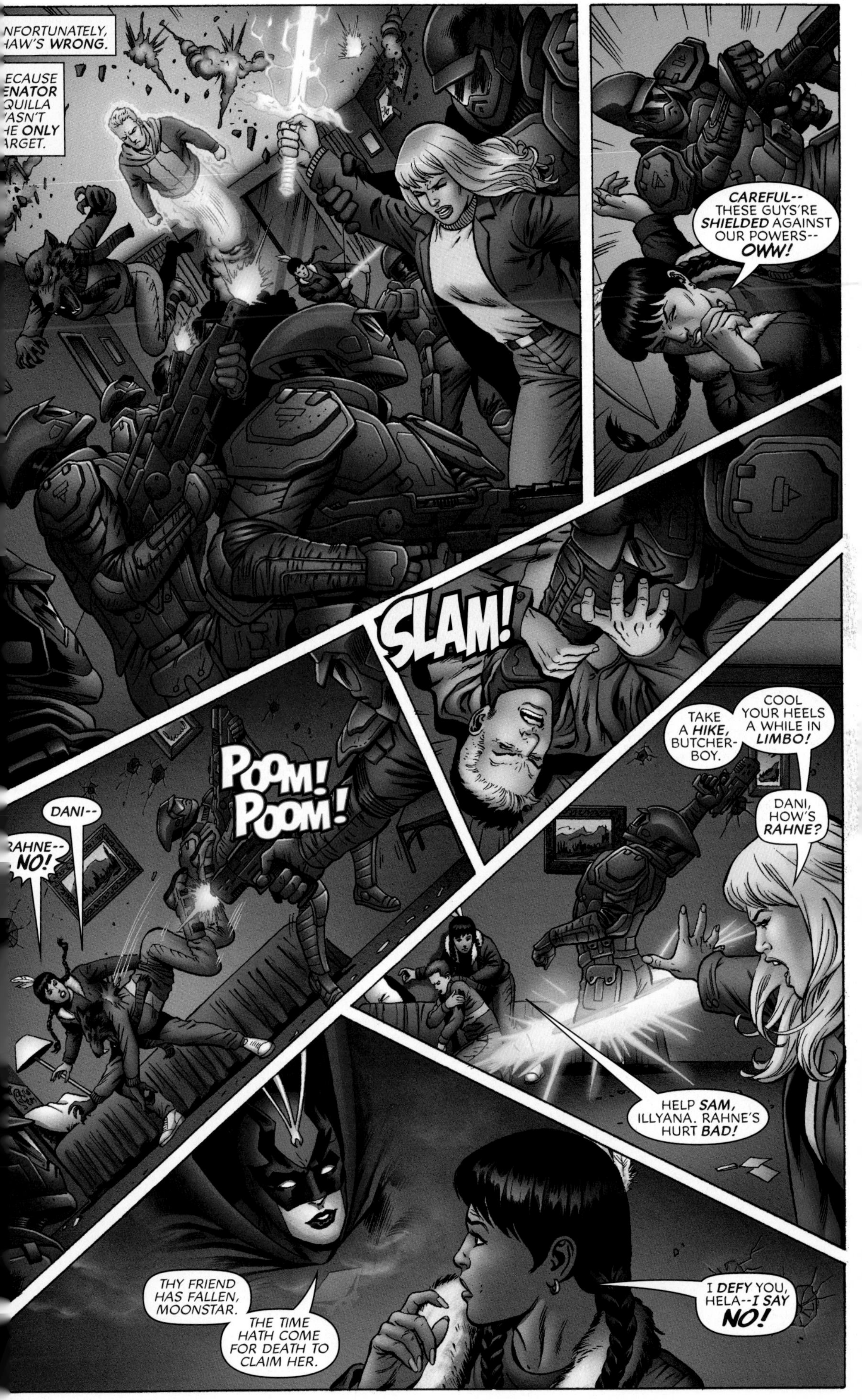

NFORTUNATELY, HAW'S WRONG.
ECAUSE ENATOR QUILLA VASN'T HE ONLY ARGET.
CAREFUL-- THESE GUYS'RE SHIELDED AGAINST OUR POWERS-- OWW!
SLAM!
POOM! POOM!
DANI--
RAHNE-- NO!
TAKE A HIKE, BUTCHER-BOY.
COOL YOUR HEELS A WHILE IN LIMBO!
DANI, HOW'S RAHNE?
HELP SAM, ILLYANA. RAHNE'S HURT BAD!
THY FRIEND HAS FALLEN, MOONSTAR.
THE TIME HATH COME FOR DEATH TO CLAIM HER.
I DEFY YOU, HELA--I SAY NO!

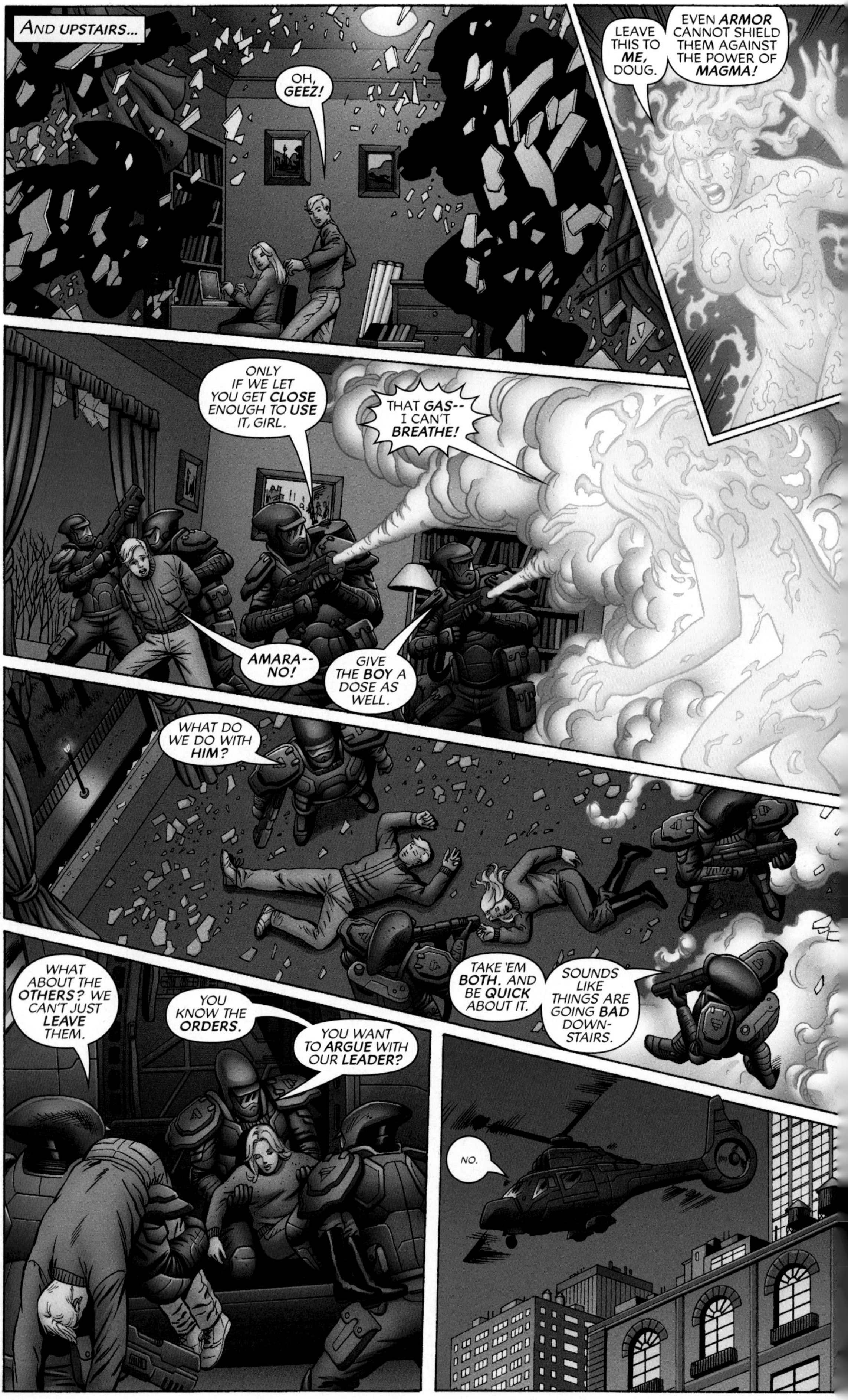

AND UPSTAIRS...
OH, GEEZ!
LEAVE THIS TO ME, DOUG.
EVEN ARMOR CANNOT SHIELD THEM AGAINST THE POWER OF MAGMA!
ONLY IF WE LET YOU GET CLOSE ENOUGH TO USE IT, GIRL.
THAT GAS-- I CAN'T BREATHE!
AMARA-- NO!
GIVE THE BOY A DOSE AS WELL.
WHAT DO WE DO WITH HIM?
TAKE 'EM BOTH. AND BE QUICK ABOUT IT.
SOUNDS LIKE THINGS ARE GOING BAD DOWN-STAIRS.
WHAT ABOUT THE OTHERS? WE CAN'T JUST LEAVE THEM.
YOU KNOW THE ORDERS.
YOU WANT TO ARGUE WITH OUR LEADER?
NO.

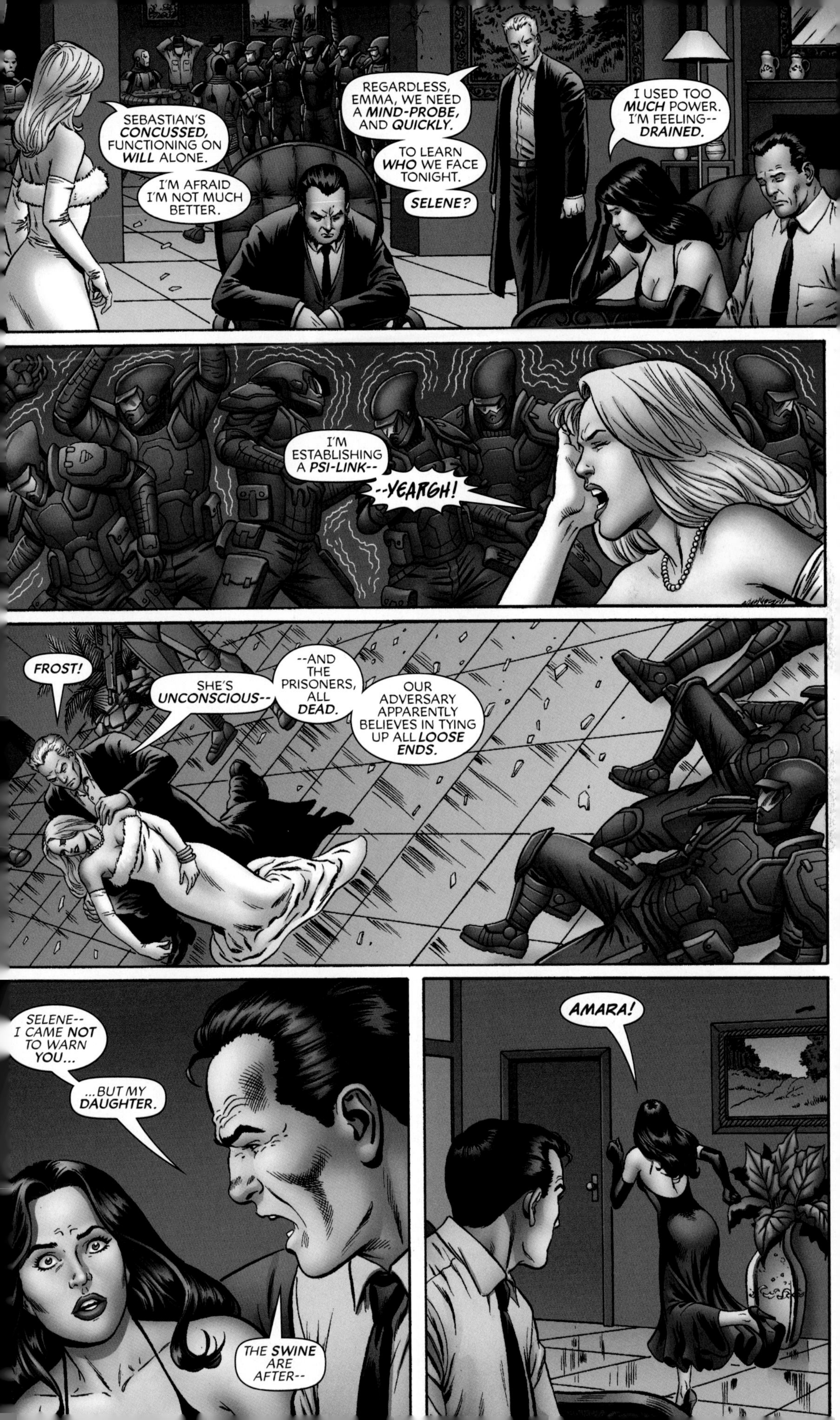
SEBASTIAN'S CONCUSSED, FUNCTIONING ON WILL ALONE.
I'M AFRAID I'M NOT MUCH BETTER.
REGARDLESS, EMMA, WE NEED A MIND-PROBE, AND QUICKLY.
TO LEARN WHO WE FACE TONIGHT.
SELENE?
I USED TOO MUCH POWER. I'M FEELING-- DRAINED.
I'M ESTABLISHING A PSI-LINK--
--YEARGH!
FROST!
SHE'S UNCONSCIOUS--
--AND THE PRISONERS, ALL DEAD.
OUR ADVERSARY APPARENTLY BELIEVES IN TYING UP ALL LOOSE ENDS.
SELENE-- I CAME NOT TO WARN YOU...
...BUT MY DAUGHTER.
THE SWINE ARE AFTER--
AMARA!

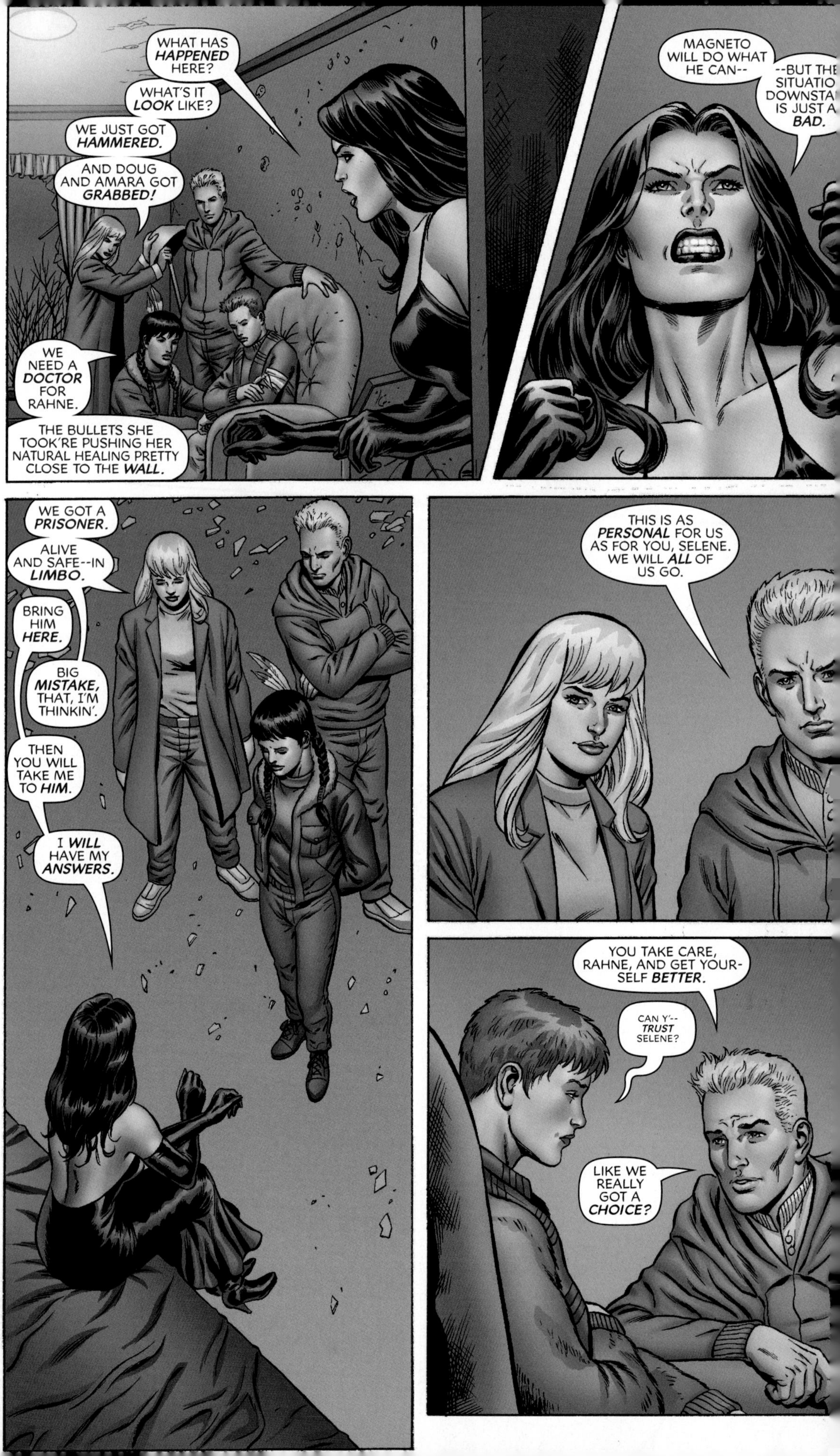
WHAT HAS HAPPENED HERE?
WHAT'S IT LOOK LIKE?
WE JUST GOT HAMMERED.
AND DOUG AND AMARA GOT GRABBED!
WE NEED A DOCTOR FOR RAHNE.
THE BULLETS SHE TOOK'RE PUSHING HER NATURAL HEALING PRETTY CLOSE TO THE WALL.
MAGNETO WILL DO WHAT HE CAN--
--BUT THE SITUATIO DOWNSTA IS JUST A BAD.
WE GOT A PRISONER.
ALIVE AND SAFE--IN LIMBO.
BRING HIM HERE.
BIG MISTAKE, THAT, I'M THINKIN'.
THEN YOU WILL TAKE ME TO HIM.
I WILL HAVE MY ANSWERS.
THIS IS AS PERSONAL FOR US AS FOR YOU, SELENE. WE WILL ALL OF US GO.
YOU TAKE CARE, RAHNE, AND GET YOUR-SELF BETTER.
CAN Y'--TRUST SELENE?
LIKE WE REALLY GOT A CHOICE?

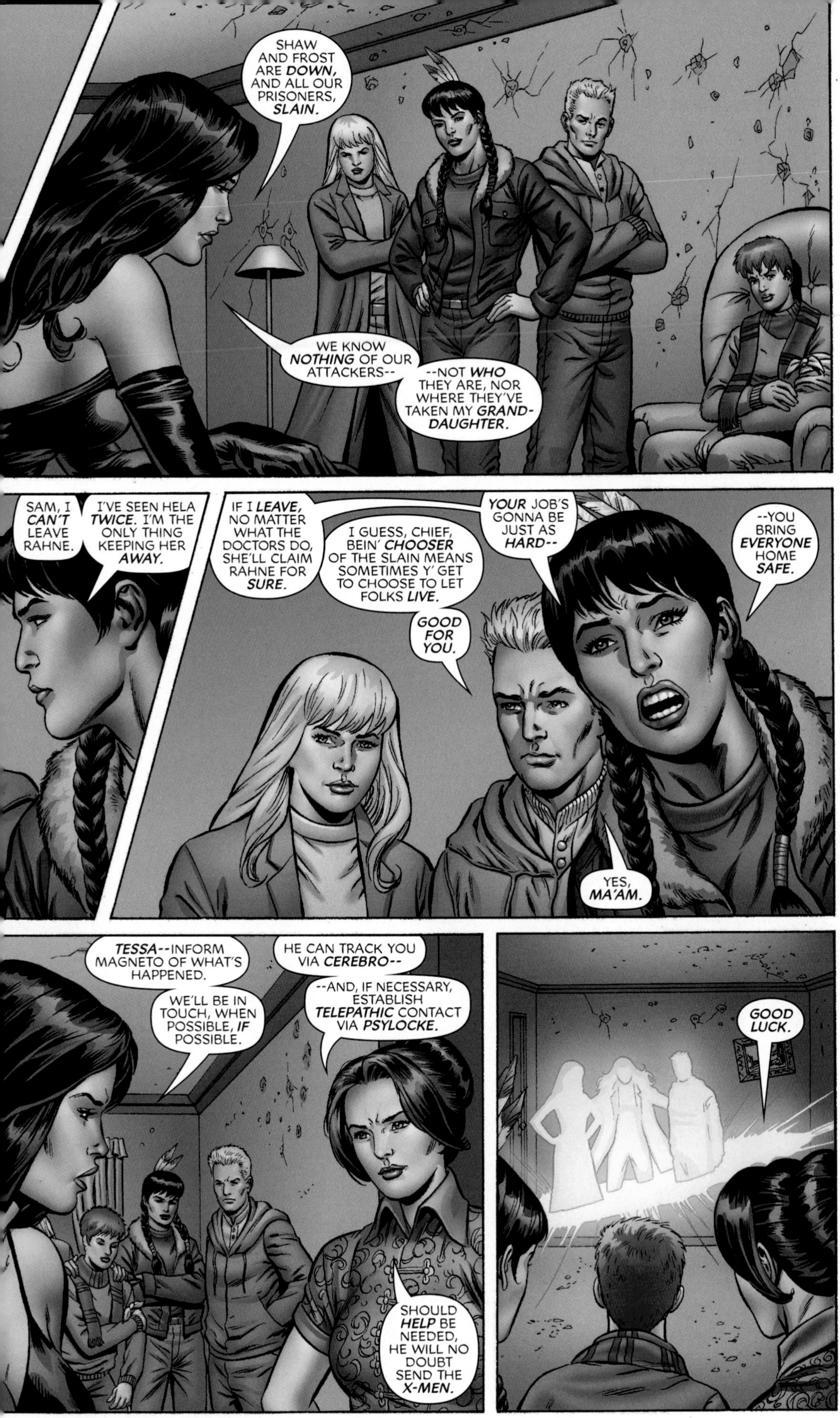
SHAW AND FROST ARE DOWN, AND ALL OUR PRISONERS, SLAIN.
WE KNOW NOTHING OF OUR ATTACKERS--
--NOT WHO THEY ARE, NOR WHERE THEY'VE TAKEN MY GRAND-DAUGHTER.
SAM, I CAN'T LEAVE RAHNE.
I'VE SEEN HELA TWICE. I'M THE ONLY THING KEEPING HER AWAY.
IF I LEAVE, NO MATTER WHAT THE DOCTORS DO, SHE'LL CLAIM RAHNE FOR SURE.
I GUESS, CHIEF, BEIN' CHOOSER OF THE SLAIN MEANS SOMETIMES Y' GET TO CHOOSE TO LET FOLKS LIVE.
GOOD FOR YOU.
YOUR JOB'S GONNA BE JUST AS HARD--
--YOU BRING EVERYONE HOME SAFE.
YES, MA'AM.
TESSA--INFORM MAGNETO OF WHAT'S HAPPENED.
WE'LL BE IN TOUCH, WHEN POSSIBLE, IF POSSIBLE.
HE CAN TRACK YOU VIA CEREBRO--
--AND, IF NECESSARY, ESTABLISH TELEPATHIC CONTACT VIA PSYLOCKE.
SHOULD HELP BE NEEDED, HE WILL NO DOUBT SEND THE X-MEN.
GOOD LUCK.

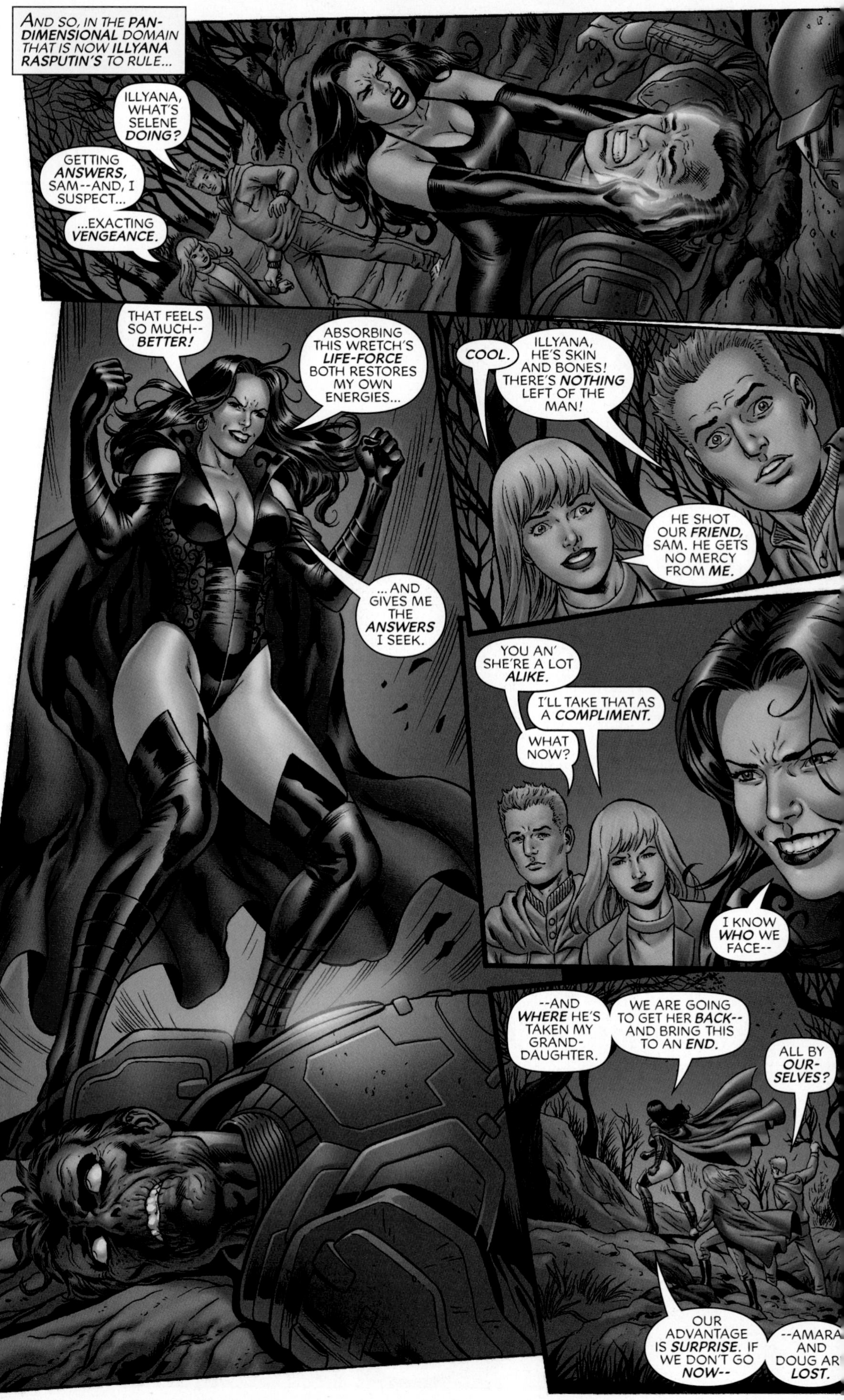

AND SO, IN THE PAN-DIMENSIONAL DOMAIN THAT IS NOW ILLYANA RASPUTIN'S TO RULE...
ILLYANA, WHAT'S SELENE DOING?
GETTING ANSWERS, SAM--AND, I SUSPECT...
...EXACTING VENGEANCE.
THAT FEELS SO MUCH--BETTER!
ABSORBING THIS WRETCH'S LIFE-FORCE BOTH RESTORES MY OWN ENERGIES...
...AND GIVES ME THE ANSWERS I SEEK.
COOL.
ILLYANA, HE'S SKIN AND BONES! THERE'S NOTHING LEFT OF THE MAN!
HE SHOT OUR FRIEND, SAM. HE GETS NO MERCY FROM ME.
YOU AN' SHE'RE A LOT ALIKE.
I'LL TAKE THAT AS A COMPLIMENT.
WHAT NOW?
I KNOW WHO WE FACE--
--AND WHERE HE'S TAKEN MY GRAND-DAUGHTER.
WE ARE GOING TO GET HER BACK--AND BRING THIS TO AN END.
ALL BY OUR-SELVES?
OUR ADVANTAGE IS SURPRISE. IF WE DON'T GO NOW--
--AMARA AND DOUG AR LOST.

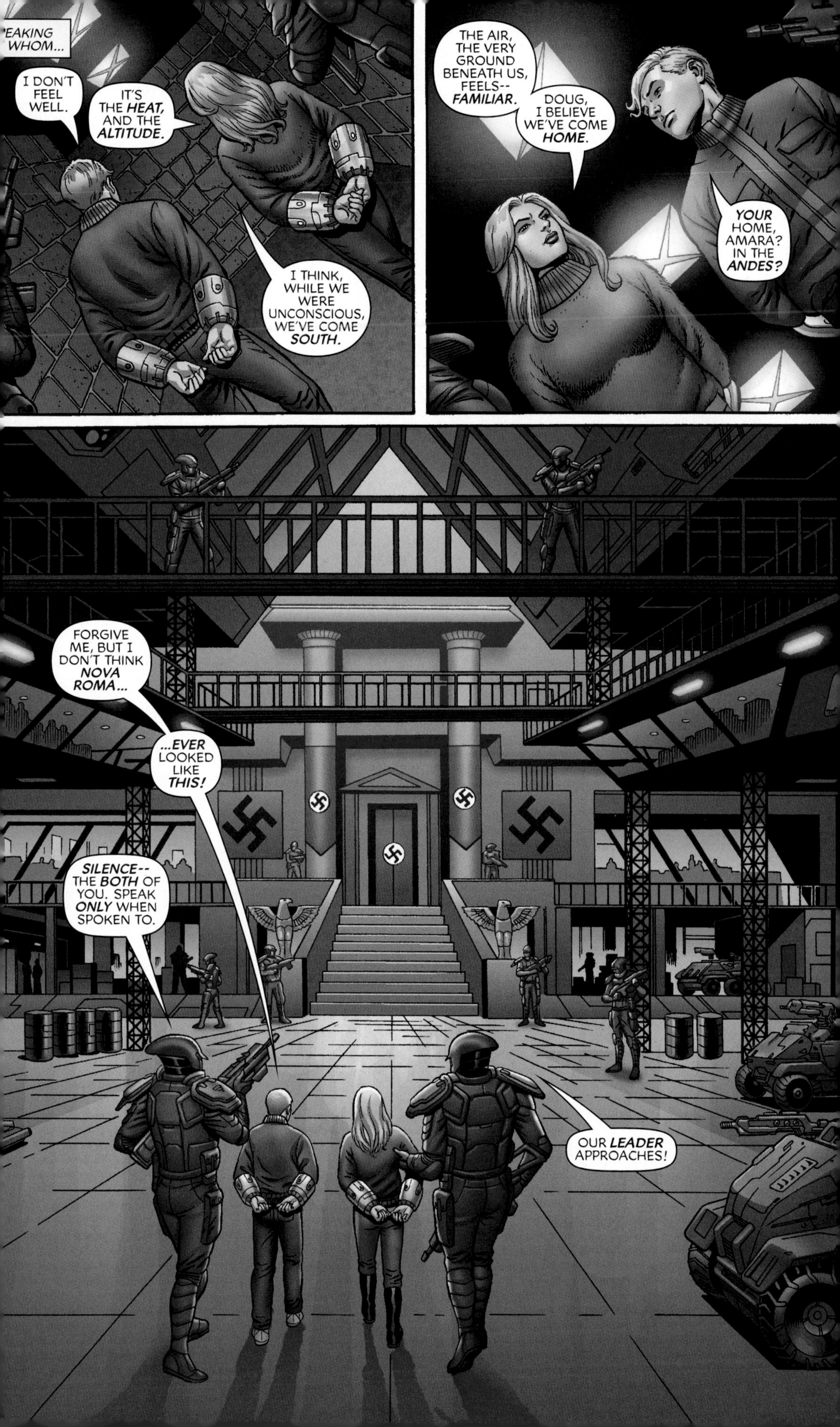

EAKING WHOM...
I DON'T FEEL WELL.
IT'S THE HEAT, AND THE ALTITUDE.
I THINK, WHILE WE WERE UNCONSCIOUS, WE'VE COME SOUTH.
THE AIR, THE VERY GROUND BENEATH US, FEELS-- FAMILIAR.
DOUG, I BELIEVE WE'VE COME HOME.
YOUR HOME, AMARA? IN THE ANDES?
FORGIVE ME, BUT I DON'T THINK NOVA ROMA...
...EVER LOOKED LIKE THIS!
SILENCE-- THE BOTH OF YOU. SPEAK ONLY WHEN SPOKEN TO.
OUR LEADER APPROACHES!

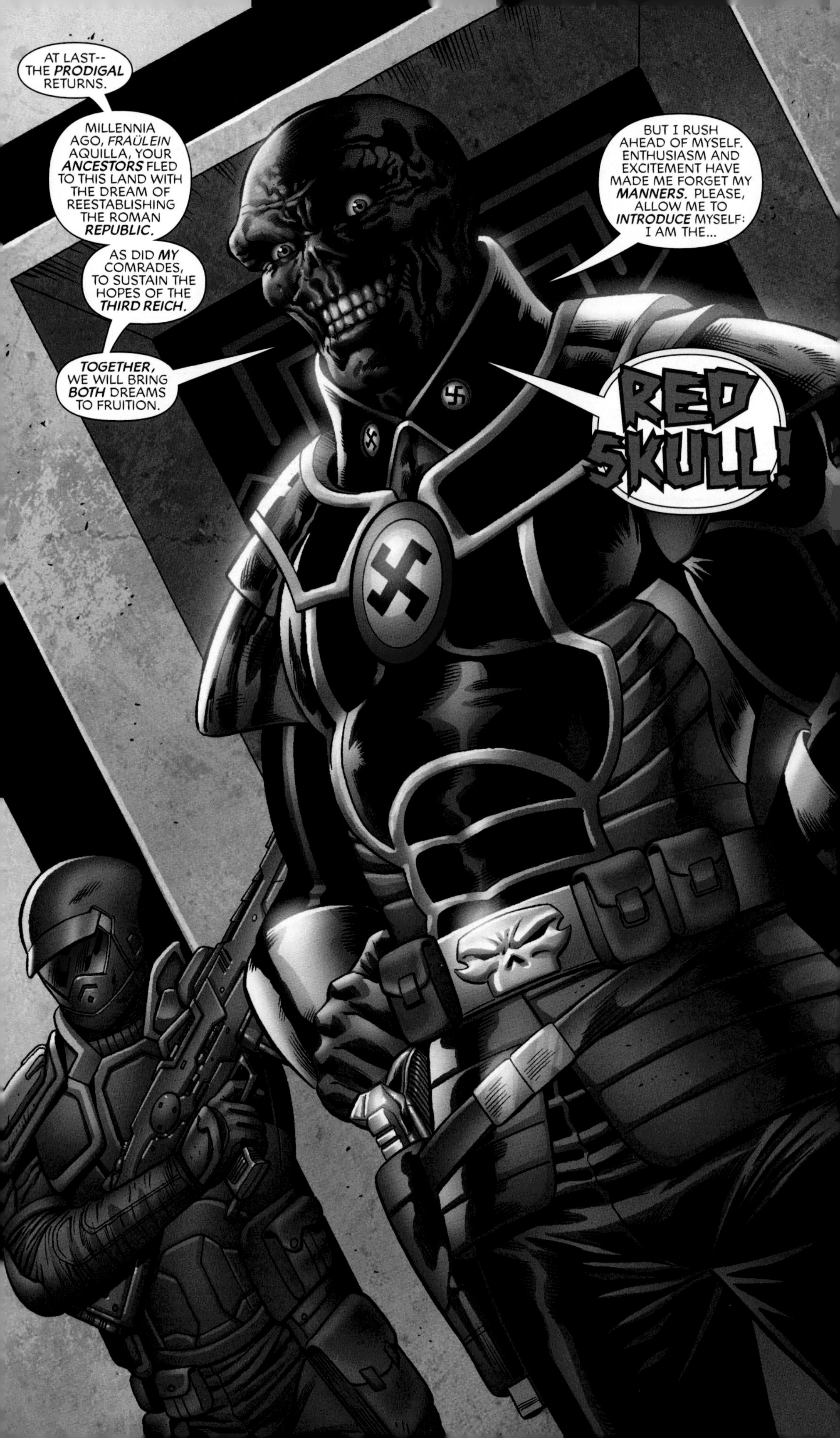
AT LAST-- THE *PRODIGAL* RETURNS.
MILLENNIA AGO, *FRAÜLEIN* AQUILLA, YOUR ***ANCESTORS*** FLED TO THIS LAND WITH THE DREAM OF REESTABLISHING THE ROMAN ***REPUBLIC.***
AS DID ***MY*** COMRADES, TO SUSTAIN THE HOPES OF THE ***THIRD REICH.***
***TOGETHER,*** WE WILL BRING ***BOTH*** DREAMS TO FRUITION.
BUT I RUSH AHEAD OF MYSELF. ENTHUSIASM AND EXCITEMENT HAVE MADE ME FORGET MY ***MANNERS.*** PLEASE, ALLOW ME TO ***INTRODUCE*** MYSELF: I AM THE...
RED SKULL!

#2

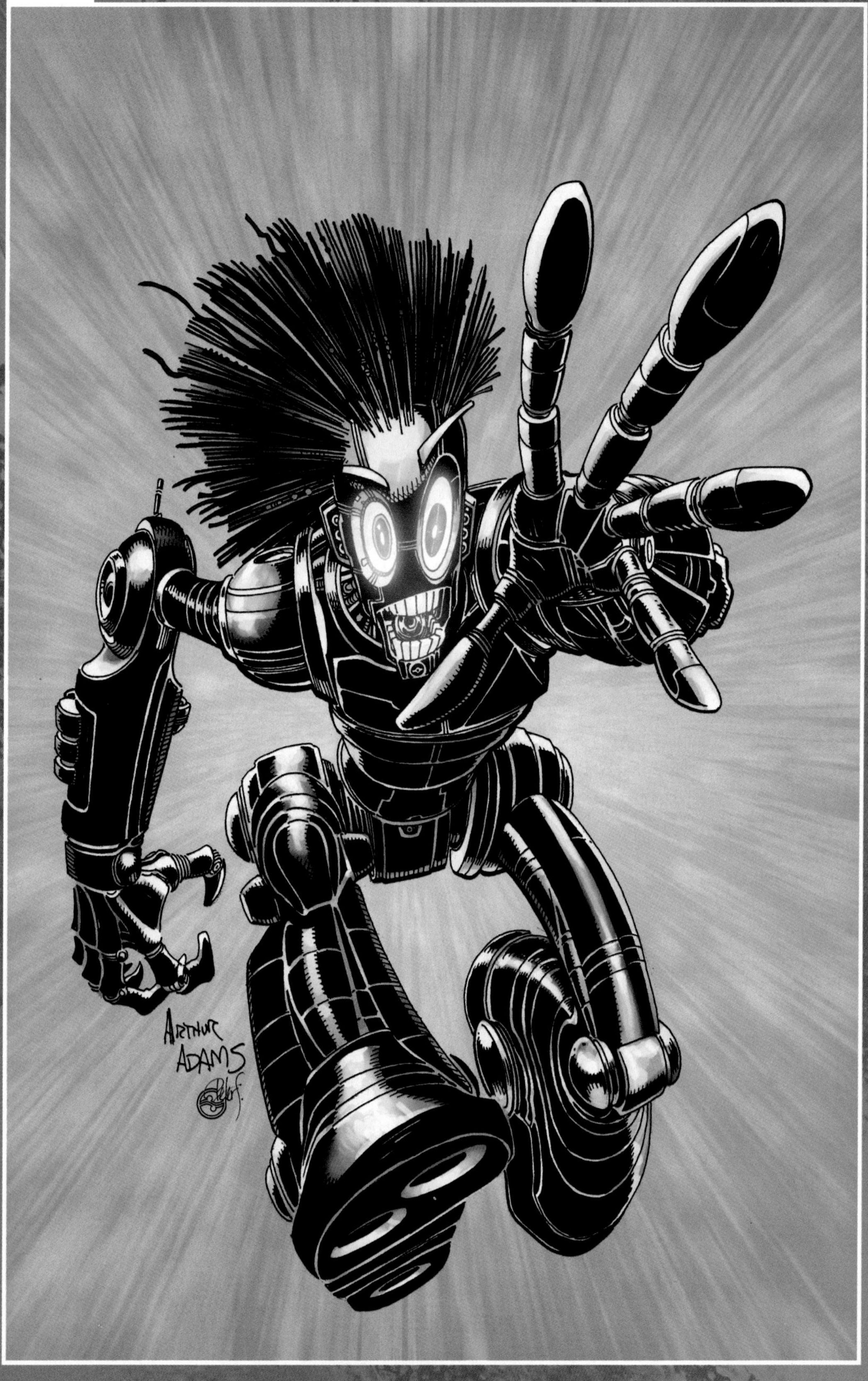
ARTHUR ADAMS

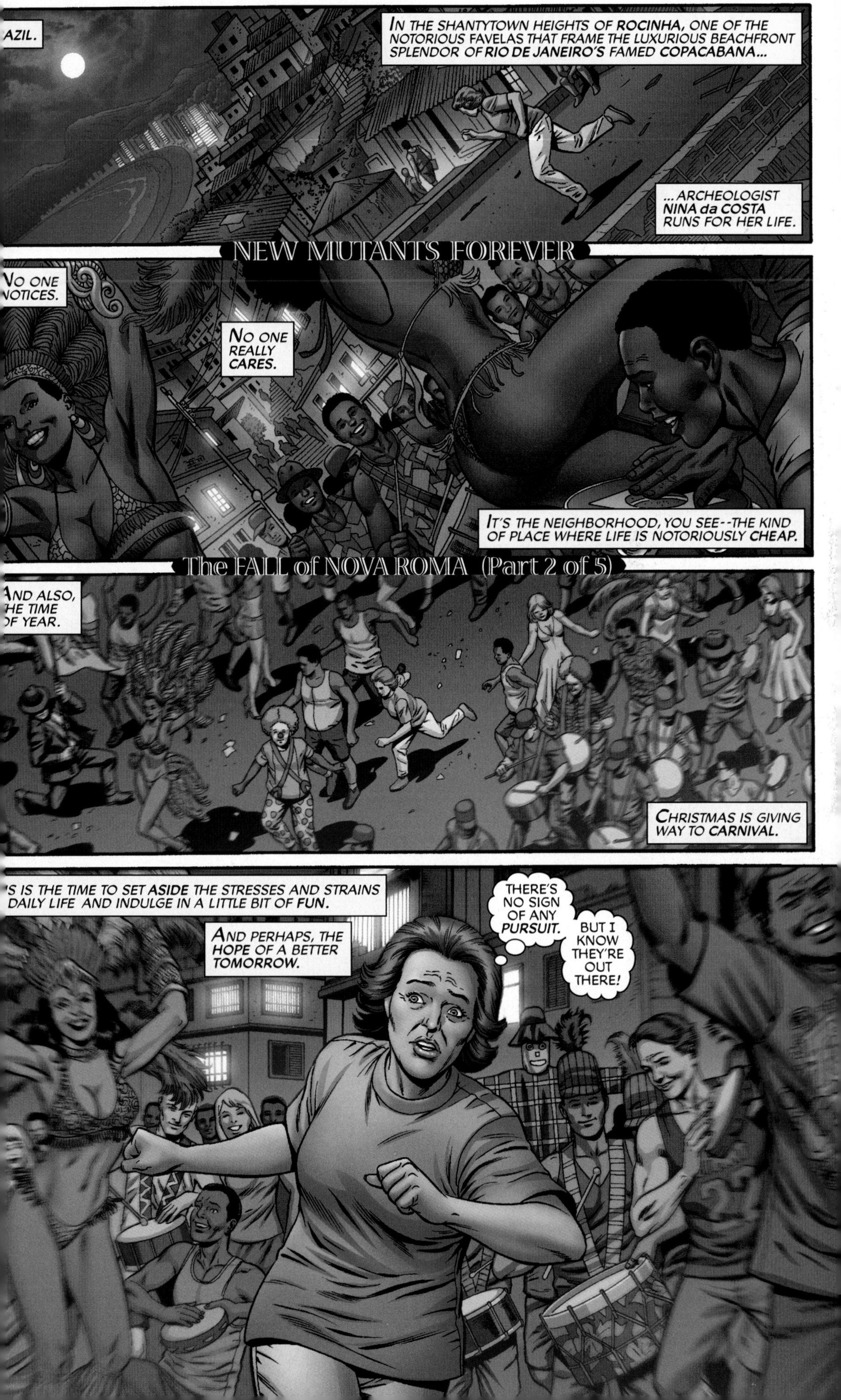

AZIL.
IN THE SHANTYTOWN HEIGHTS OF ROCINHA, ONE OF THE NOTORIOUS FAVELAS THAT FRAME THE LUXURIOUS BEACHFRONT SPLENDOR OF RIO DE JANEIRO'S FAMED COPACABANA...
...ARCHEOLOGIST NINA da COSTA RUNS FOR HER LIFE.
NEW MUTANTS FOREVER
NO ONE NOTICES.
NO ONE REALLY CARES.
IT'S THE NEIGHBORHOOD, YOU SEE--THE KIND OF PLACE WHERE LIFE IS NOTORIOUSLY CHEAP.
The FALL of NOVA ROMA (Part 2 of 5)
AND ALSO, THE TIME OF YEAR.
CHRISTMAS IS GIVING WAY TO CARNIVAL.
'S IS THE TIME TO SET ASIDE THE STRESSES AND STRAINS DAILY LIFE AND INDULGE IN A LITTLE BIT OF FUN.
AND PERHAPS, THE HOPE OF A BETTER TOMORROW.
THERE'S NO SIGN OF ANY PURSUIT.
BUT I KNOW THEY'RE OUT THERE!

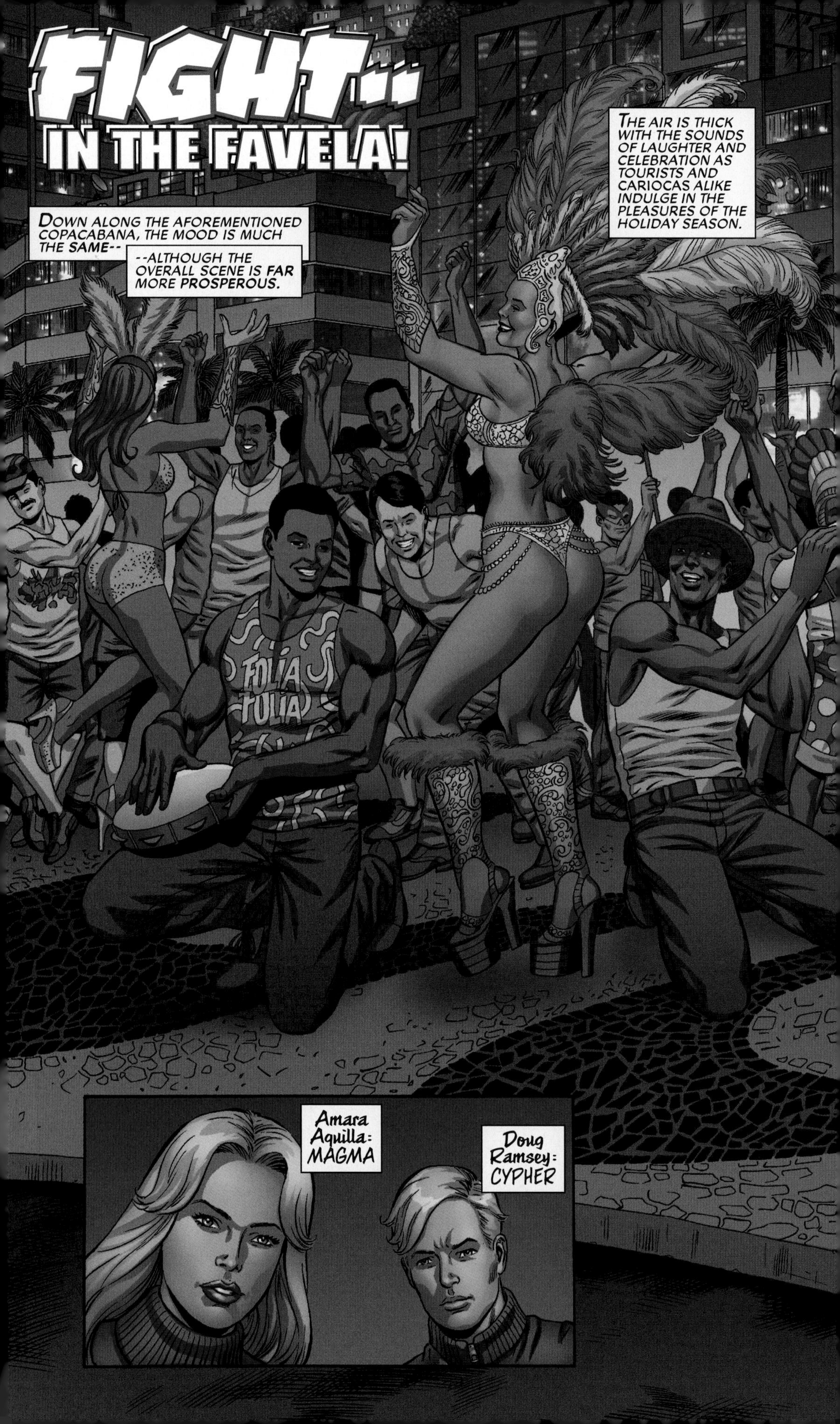
FIGHT... IN THE FAVELA!
DOWN ALONG THE AFOREMENTIONED COPACABANA, THE MOOD IS MUCH THE SAME--
--ALTHOUGH THE OVERALL SCENE IS FAR MORE PROSPEROUS.
THE AIR IS THICK WITH THE SOUNDS OF LAUGHTER AND CELEBRATION AS TOURISTS AND CARIOCAS ALIKE INDULGE IN THE PLEASURES OF THE HOLIDAY SEASON.
FOLIA FOLIA
Amara Aquilla: MAGMA
Doug Ramsey: CYPHER

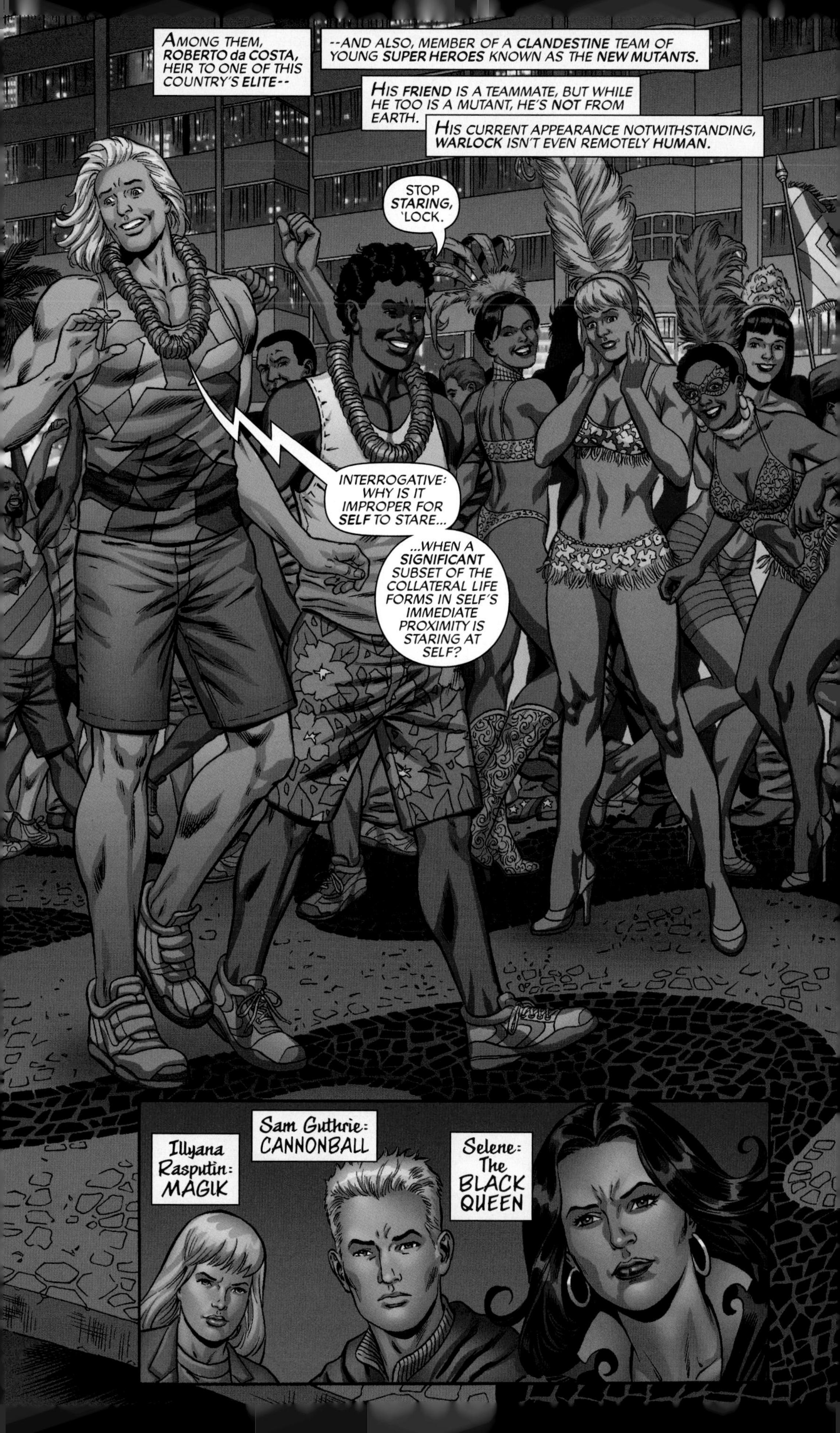
AMONG THEM, ROBERTO da COSTA, HEIR TO ONE OF THIS COUNTRY'S ELITE--
--AND ALSO, MEMBER OF A CLANDESTINE TEAM OF YOUNG SUPER HEROES KNOWN AS THE NEW MUTANTS.
HIS FRIEND IS A TEAMMATE, BUT WHILE HE TOO IS A MUTANT, HE'S NOT FROM EARTH.
HIS CURRENT APPEARANCE NOTWITHSTANDING, WARLOCK ISN'T EVEN REMOTELY HUMAN.
STOP STARING, 'LOCK.
INTERROGATIVE: WHY IS IT IMPROPER FOR SELF TO STARE...
...WHEN A SIGNIFICANT SUBSET OF THE COLLATERAL LIFE FORMS IN SELF'S IMMEDIATE PROXIMITY IS STARING AT SELF?
Illyana Rasputin: MAGIK
Sam Guthrie: CANNONBALL
Selene: The BLACK QUEEN

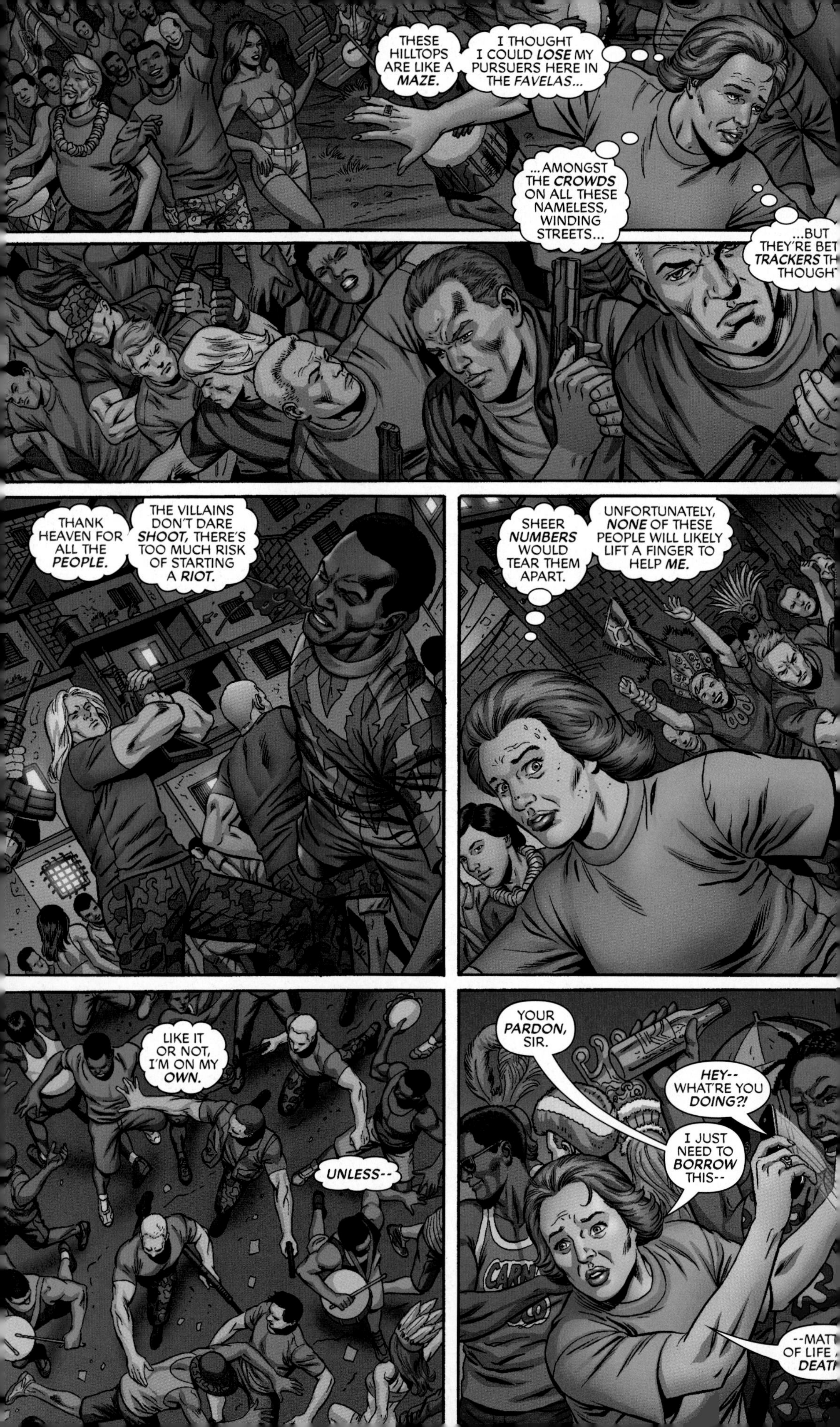
THESE HILLTOPS ARE LIKE A MAZE.
I THOUGHT I COULD LOSE MY PURSUERS HERE IN THE FAVELAS...
...AMONGST THE CROWDS ON ALL THESE NAMELESS, WINDING STREETS...
...BUT THEY'RE BET TRACKERS TH THOUGHT
THANK HEAVEN FOR ALL THE PEOPLE.
THE VILLAINS DON'T DARE SHOOT, THERE'S TOO MUCH RISK OF STARTING A RIOT.
SHEER NUMBERS WOULD TEAR THEM APART.
UNFORTUNATELY, NONE OF THESE PEOPLE WILL LIKELY LIFT A FINGER TO HELP ME.
LIKE IT OR NOT, I'M ON MY OWN.
UNLESS--
YOUR PARDON, SIR.
HEY-- WHAT'RE YOU DOING?!
I JUST NEED TO BORROW THIS--
--MAT OF LIFE DEAT

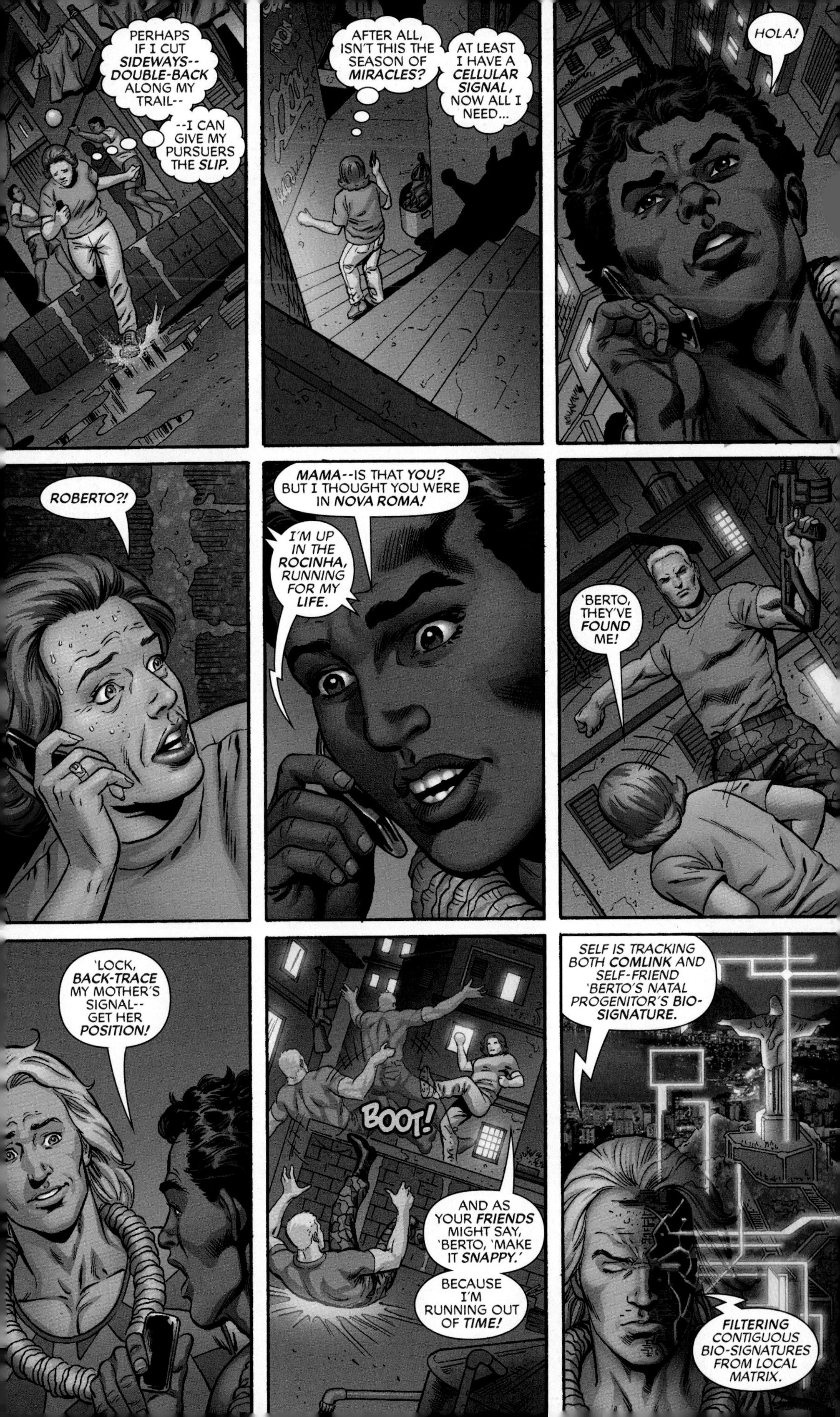
PERHAPS IF I CUT SIDEWAYS--DOUBLE-BACK ALONG MY TRAIL--
--I CAN GIVE MY PURSUERS THE SLIP.
AFTER ALL, ISN'T THIS THE SEASON OF MIRACLES?
AT LEAST I HAVE A CELLULAR SIGNAL, NOW ALL I NEED...
HOLA!
ROBERTO?!
MAMA--IS THAT YOU? BUT I THOUGHT YOU WERE IN NOVA ROMA!
I'M UP IN THE ROCINHA, RUNNING FOR MY LIFE.
'BERTO, THEY'VE FOUND ME!
'LOCK, BACK-TRACE MY MOTHER'S SIGNAL--GET HER POSITION!
BOOT!
AND AS YOUR FRIENDS MIGHT SAY, 'BERTO, 'MAKE IT SNAPPY.'
BECAUSE I'M RUNNING OUT OF TIME!
SELF IS TRACKING BOTH COMLINK AND SELF-FRIEND 'BERTO'S NATAL PROGENITOR'S BIO-SIGNATURE.
FILTERING CONTIGUOUS BIO-SIGNATURES FROM LOCAL MATRIX.

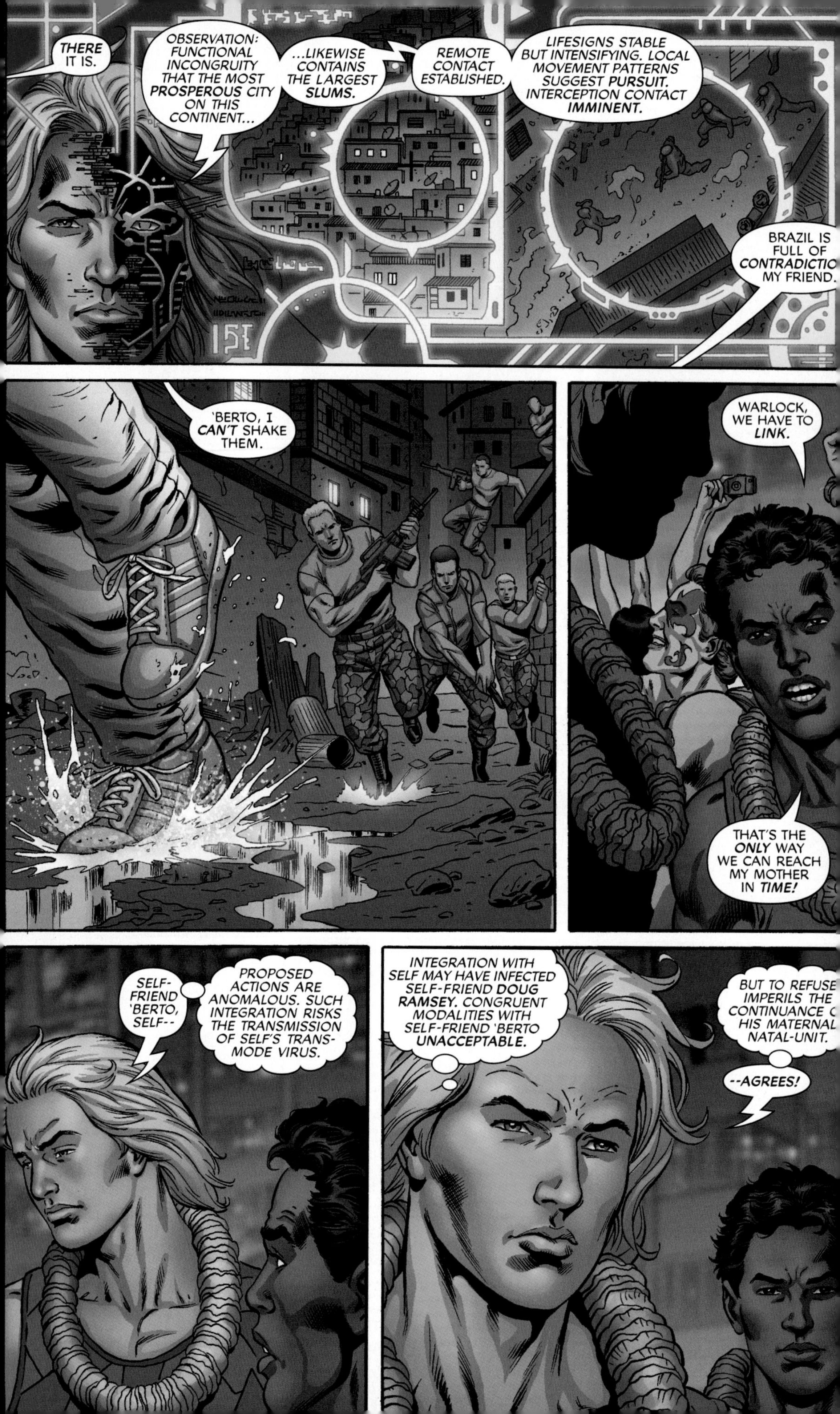
THERE IT IS.
OBSERVATION: FUNCTIONAL INCONGRUITY THAT THE MOST PROSPEROUS CITY ON THIS CONTINENT...
...LIKEWISE CONTAINS THE LARGEST SLUMS.
REMOTE CONTACT ESTABLISHED.
LIFESIGNS STABLE BUT INTENSIFYING. LOCAL MOVEMENT PATTERNS SUGGEST PURSUIT. INTERCEPTION CONTACT IMMINENT.
BRAZIL IS FULL OF CONTRADICTIO MY FRIEND.
'BERTO, I CAN'T SHAKE THEM.
WARLOCK, WE HAVE TO LINK.
THAT'S THE ONLY WAY WE CAN REACH MY MOTHER IN TIME!
SELF-FRIEND 'BERTO, SELF--
PROPOSED ACTIONS ARE ANOMALOUS. SUCH INTEGRATION RISKS THE TRANSMISSION OF SELF'S TRANS-MODE VIRUS.
INTEGRATION WITH SELF MAY HAVE INFECTED SELF-FRIEND DOUG RAMSEY. CONGRUENT MODALITIES WITH SELF-FRIEND 'BERTO UNACCEPTABLE.
BUT TO REFUSE IMPERILS THE CONTINUANCE C HIS MATERNAL NATAL-UNIT.
--AGREES!

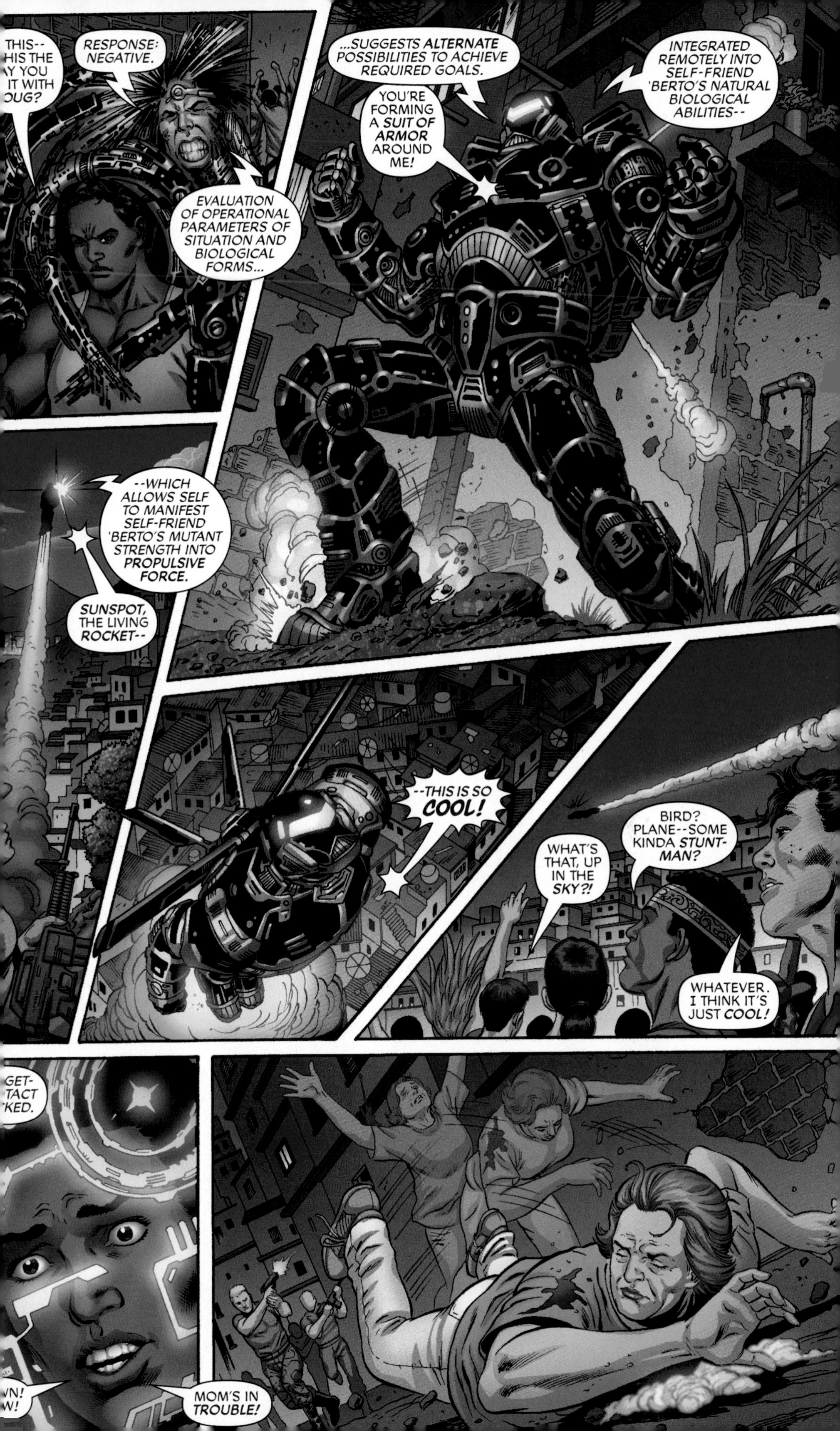
THIS--
HIS THE
Y YOU
IT WITH
OUG?
RESPONSE: NEGATIVE.
EVALUATION OF OPERATIONAL PARAMETERS OF SITUATION AND BIOLOGICAL FORMS...
...SUGGESTS ALTERNATE POSSIBILITIES TO ACHIEVE REQUIRED GOALS.
YOU'RE FORMING A SUIT OF ARMOR AROUND ME!
INTEGRATED REMOTELY INTO SELF-FRIEND 'BERTO'S NATURAL BIOLOGICAL ABILITIES--
--WHICH ALLOWS SELF TO MANIFEST SELF-FRIEND 'BERTO'S MUTANT STRENGTH INTO PROPULSIVE FORCE.
SUNSPOT, THE LIVING ROCKET--
--THIS IS SO COOL!
WHAT'S THAT, UP IN THE SKY?!
BIRD? PLANE--SOME KINDA STUNT-MAN?
WHATEVER. I THINK IT'S JUST COOL!
GET-
TACT
KED.
N!
W!
MOM'S IN TROUBLE!

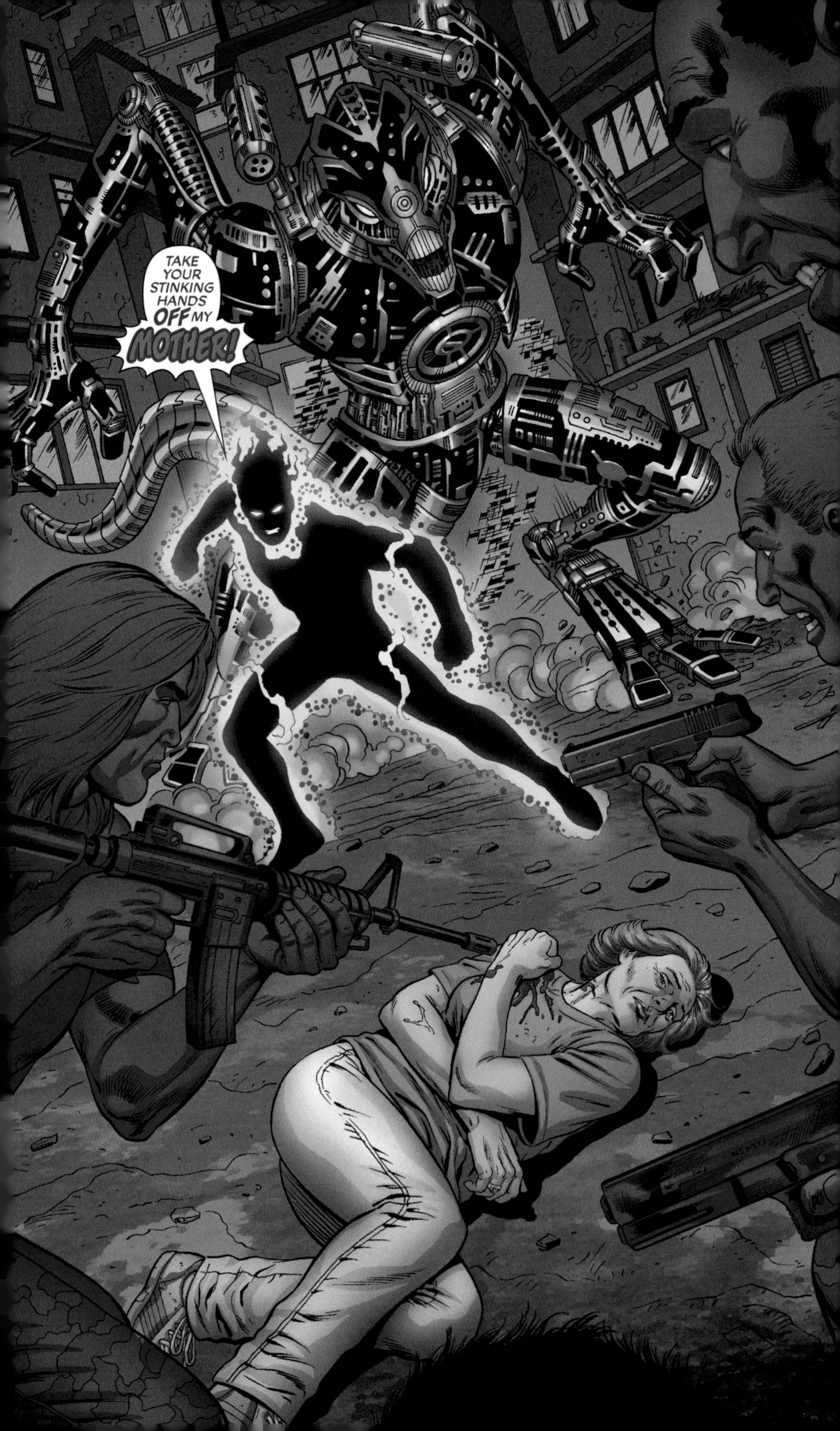
TAKE YOUR STINKING HANDS OFF MY MOTHER!

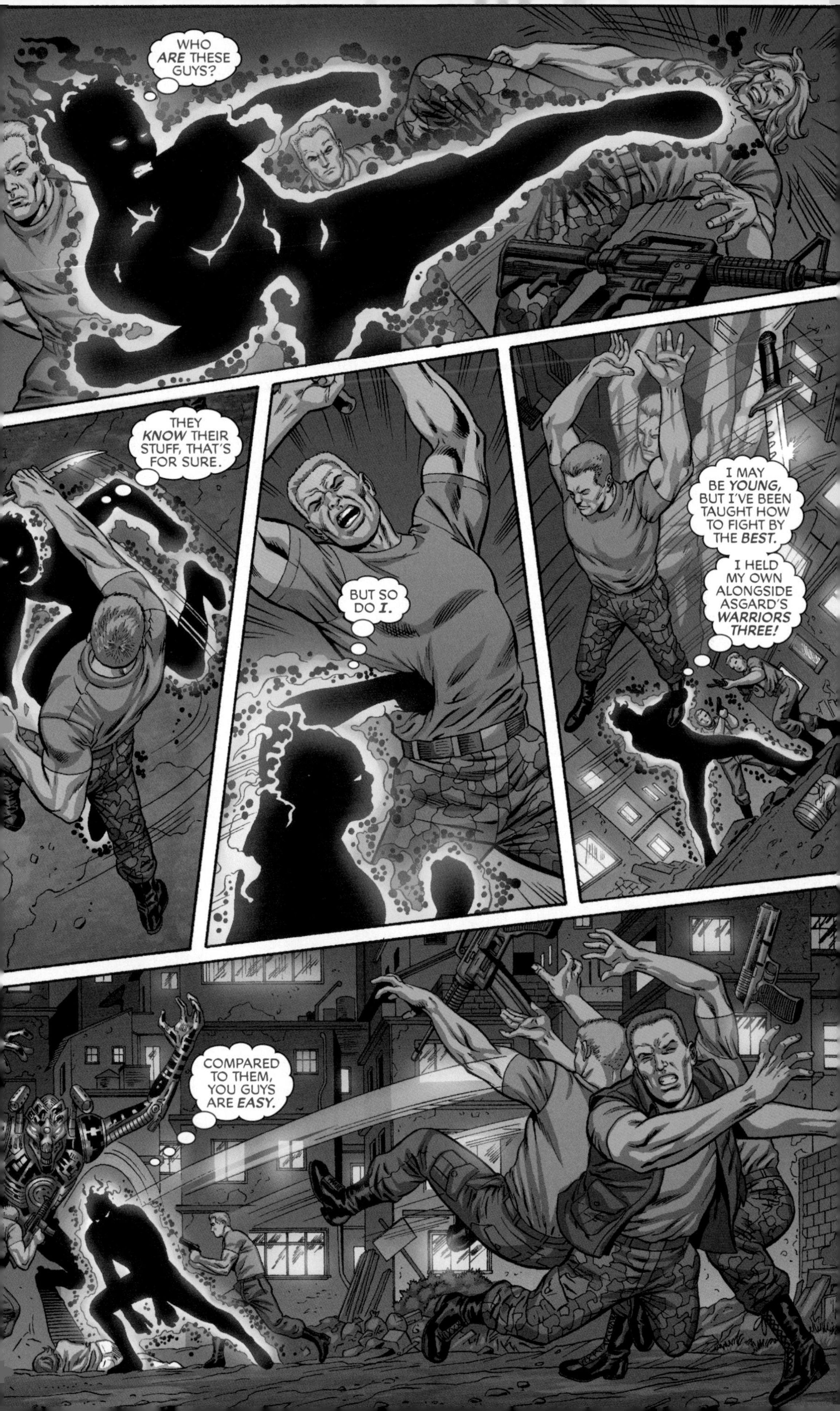
WHO ARE THESE GUYS?
THEY KNOW THEIR STUFF, THAT'S FOR SURE.
BUT SO DO I.
I MAY BE YOUNG, BUT I'VE BEEN TAUGHT HOW TO FIGHT BY THE BEST.
I HELD MY OWN ALONGSIDE ASGARD'S WARRIORS THREE!
COMPARED TO THEM, YOU GUYS ARE EASY.

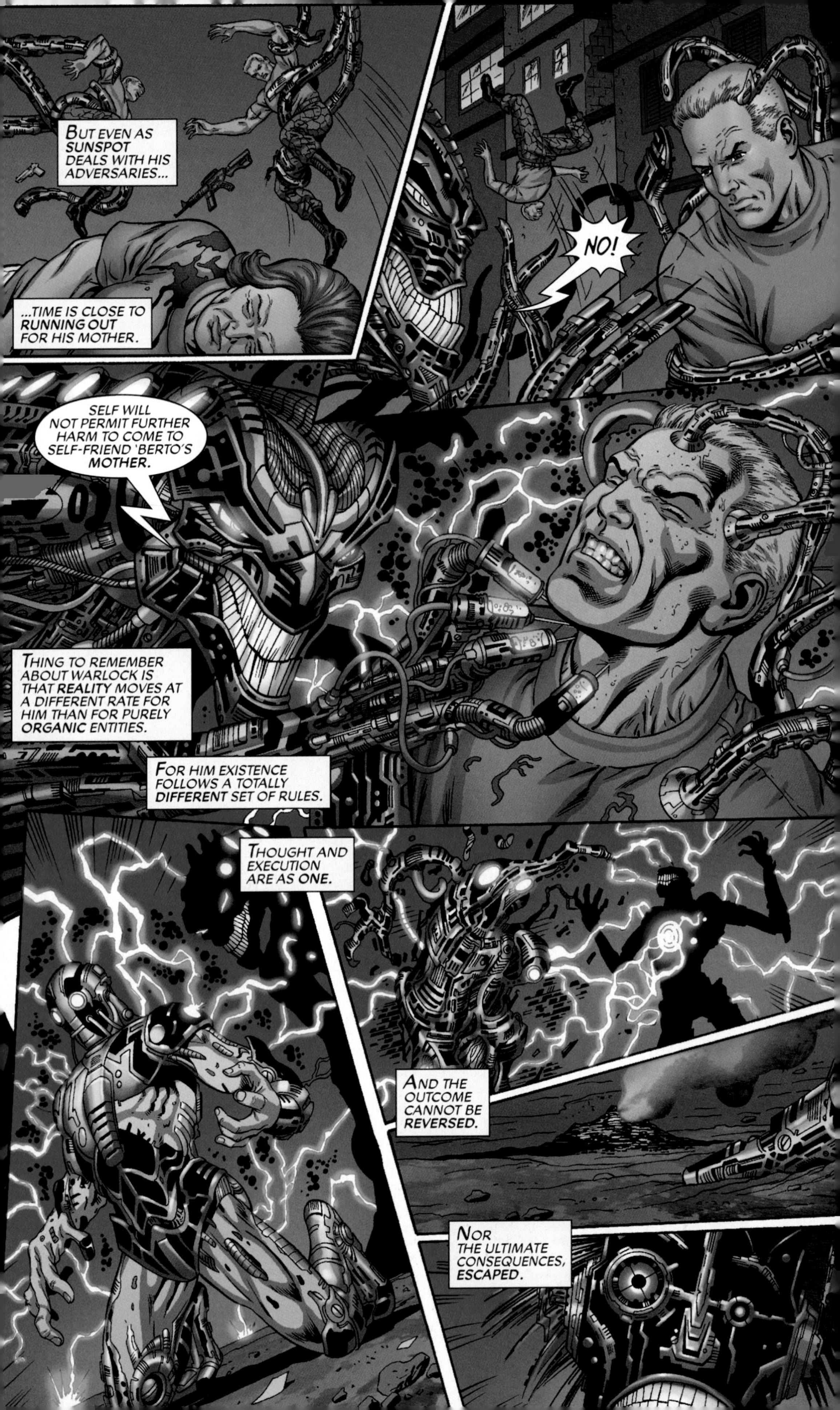

BUT EVEN AS SUNSPOT DEALS WITH HIS ADVERSARIES...
...TIME IS CLOSE TO RUNNING OUT FOR HIS MOTHER.
NO!
SELF WILL NOT PERMIT FURTHER HARM TO COME TO SELF-FRIEND 'BERTO'S MOTHER.
THING TO REMEMBER ABOUT WARLOCK IS THAT REALITY MOVES AT A DIFFERENT RATE FOR HIM THAN FOR PURELY ORGANIC ENTITIES.
FOR HIM EXISTENCE FOLLOWS A TOTALLY DIFFERENT SET OF RULES.
THOUGHT AND EXECUTION ARE AS ONE.
AND THE OUTCOME CANNOT BE REVERSED.
NOR THE ULTIMATE CONSEQUENCES, ESCAPED.

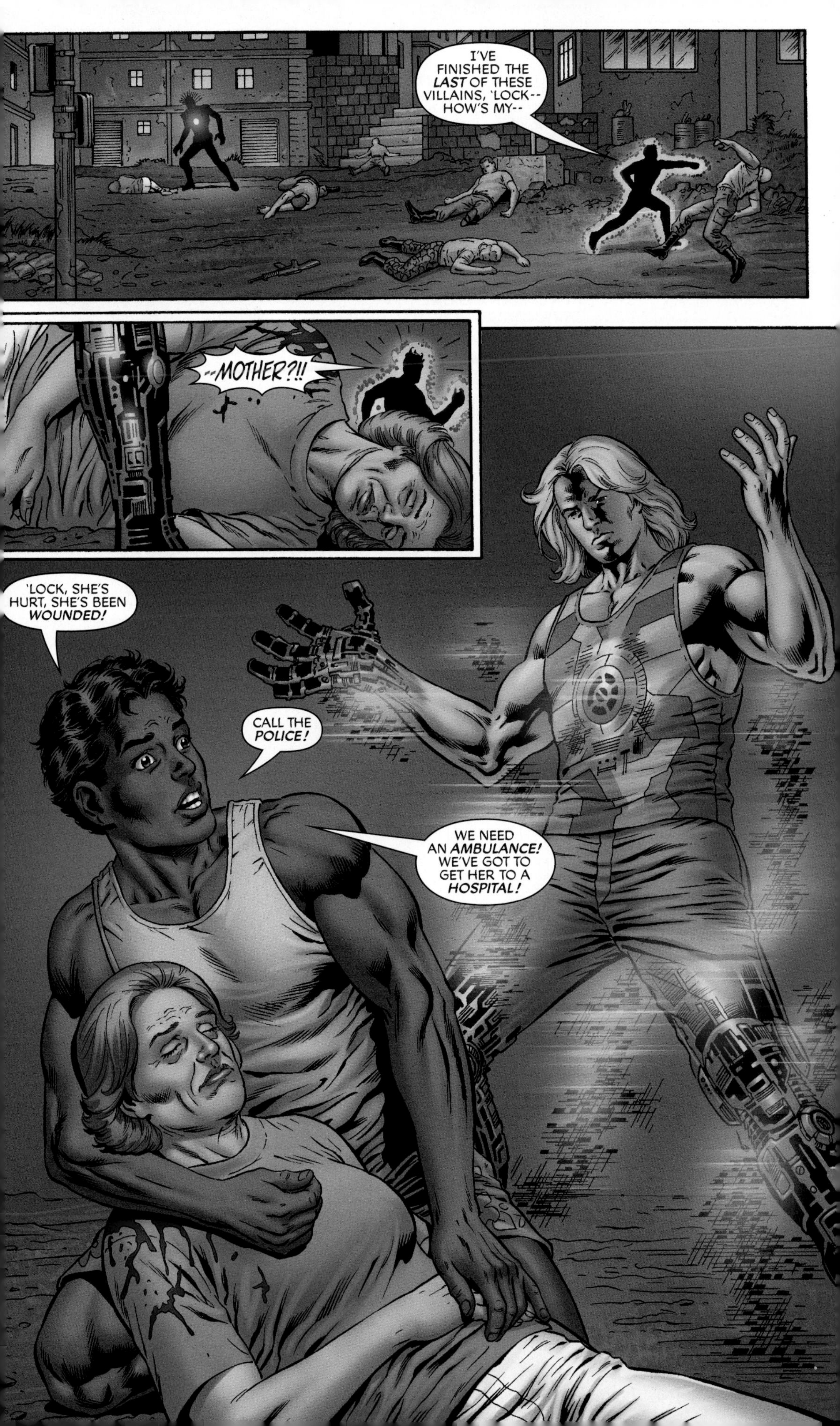
I'VE FINISHED THE LAST OF THESE VILLAINS, 'LOCK-- HOW'S MY--
--MOTHER?!!
'LOCK, SHE'S HURT, SHE'S BEEN WOUNDED!
CALL THE POLICE!
WE NEED AN AMBULANCE! WE'VE GOT TO GET HER TO A HOSPITAL!

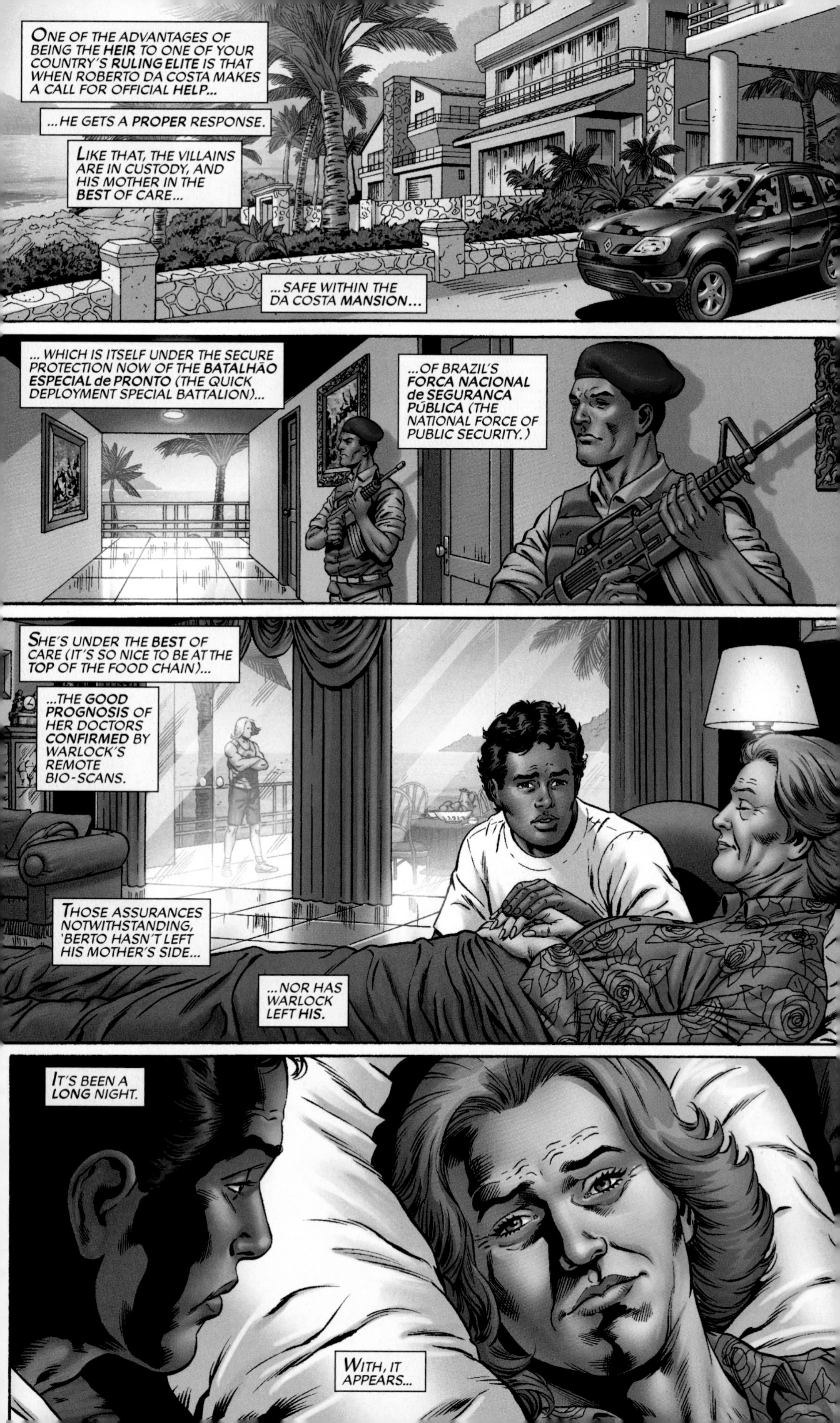
ONE OF THE ADVANTAGES OF BEING THE HEIR TO ONE OF YOUR COUNTRY'S RULING ELITE IS THAT WHEN ROBERTO DA COSTA MAKES A CALL FOR OFFICIAL HELP...
...HE GETS A PROPER RESPONSE.
LIKE THAT, THE VILLAINS ARE IN CUSTODY, AND HIS MOTHER IN THE BEST OF CARE...
...SAFE WITHIN THE DA COSTA MANSION...
... WHICH IS ITSELF UNDER THE SECURE PROTECTION NOW OF THE BATALHÃO ESPECIAL de PRONTO (THE QUICK DEPLOYMENT SPECIAL BATTALION)...
...OF BRAZIL'S FORCA NACIONAL de SEGURANCA PÚBLICA (THE NATIONAL FORCE OF PUBLIC SECURITY.)
SHE'S UNDER THE BEST OF CARE (IT'S SO NICE TO BE AT THE TOP OF THE FOOD CHAIN)...
...THE GOOD PROGNOSIS OF HER DOCTORS CONFIRMED BY WARLOCK'S REMOTE BIO-SCANS.
THOSE ASSURANCES NOTWITHSTANDING, 'BERTO HASN'T LEFT HIS MOTHER'S SIDE...
...NOR HAS WARLOCK LEFT HIS.
IT'S BEEN A LONG NIGHT.
WITH, IT APPEARS...

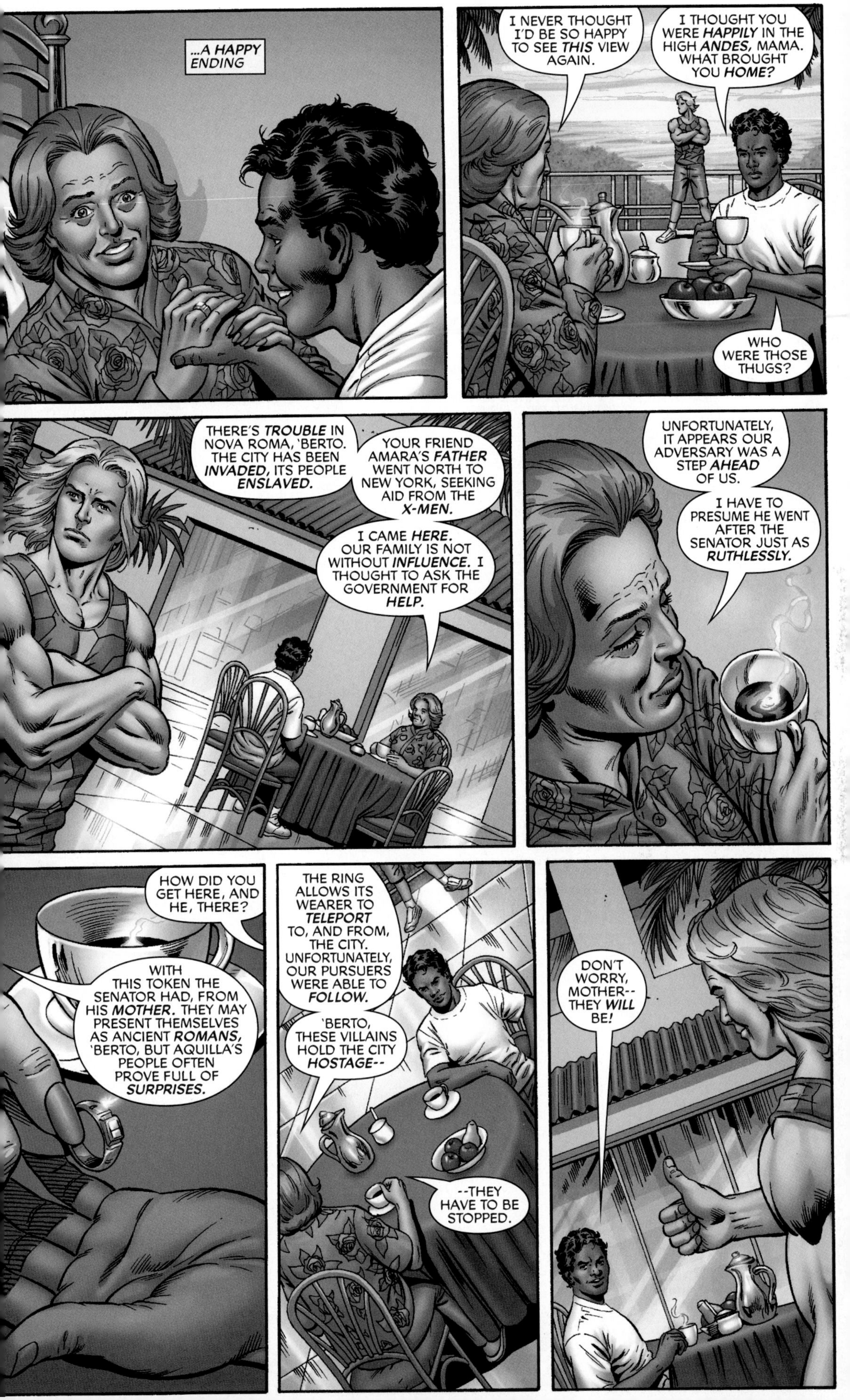
...A HAPPY ENDING
I NEVER THOUGHT I'D BE SO HAPPY TO SEE THIS VIEW AGAIN.
I THOUGHT YOU WERE HAPPILY IN THE HIGH ANDES, MAMA. WHAT BROUGHT YOU HOME?
WHO WERE THOSE THUGS?
THERE'S TROUBLE IN NOVA ROMA, 'BERTO. THE CITY HAS BEEN INVADED, ITS PEOPLE ENSLAVED.
YOUR FRIEND AMARA'S FATHER WENT NORTH TO NEW YORK, SEEKING AID FROM THE X-MEN.
I CAME HERE. OUR FAMILY IS NOT WITHOUT INFLUENCE. I THOUGHT TO ASK THE GOVERNMENT FOR HELP.
UNFORTUNATELY, IT APPEARS OUR ADVERSARY WAS A STEP AHEAD OF US.
I HAVE TO PRESUME HE WENT AFTER THE SENATOR JUST AS RUTHLESSLY.
HOW DID YOU GET HERE, AND HE, THERE?
WITH THIS TOKEN THE SENATOR HAD, FROM HIS MOTHER. THEY MAY PRESENT THEMSELVES AS ANCIENT ROMANS, 'BERTO, BUT AQUILLA'S PEOPLE OFTEN PROVE FULL OF SURPRISES.
THE RING ALLOWS ITS WEARER TO TELEPORT TO, AND FROM, THE CITY. UNFORTUNATELY, OUR PURSUERS WERE ABLE TO FOLLOW.
'BERTO, THESE VILLAINS HOLD THE CITY HOSTAGE--
--THEY HAVE TO BE STOPPED.
DON'T WORRY, MOTHER-- THEY WILL BE!

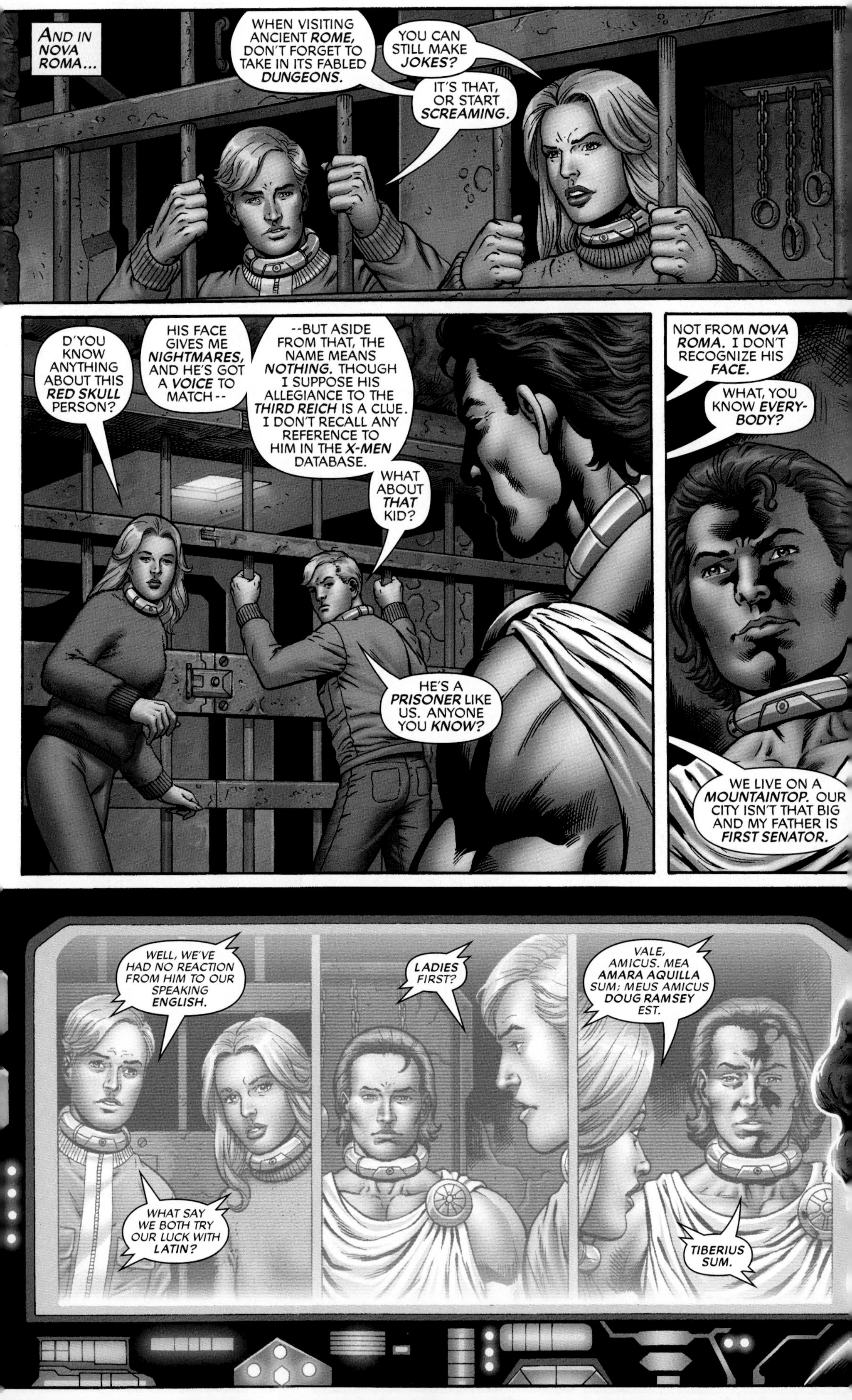
AND IN NOVA ROMA...
WHEN VISITING ANCIENT ROME, DON'T FORGET TO TAKE IN ITS FABLED DUNGEONS.
YOU CAN STILL MAKE JOKES?
IT'S THAT, OR START SCREAMING.
D'YOU KNOW ANYTHING ABOUT THIS RED SKULL PERSON?
HIS FACE GIVES ME NIGHTMARES, AND HE'S GOT A VOICE TO MATCH--
--BUT ASIDE FROM THAT, THE NAME MEANS NOTHING. THOUGH I SUPPOSE HIS ALLEGIANCE TO THE THIRD REICH IS A CLUE. I DON'T RECALL ANY REFERENCE TO HIM IN THE X-MEN DATABASE.
WHAT ABOUT THAT KID?
HE'S A PRISONER LIKE US. ANYONE YOU KNOW?
NOT FROM NOVA ROMA. I DON'T RECOGNIZE HIS FACE.
WHAT, YOU KNOW EVERY-BODY?
WE LIVE ON A MOUNTAINTOP. OUR CITY ISN'T THAT BIG AND MY FATHER IS FIRST SENATOR.
WELL, WE'VE HAD NO REACTION FROM HIM TO OUR SPEAKING ENGLISH.
WHAT SAY WE BOTH TRY OUR LUCK WITH LATIN?
LADIES FIRST?
VALE, AMICUS. MEA AMARA AQUILLA SUM; MEUS AMICUS DOUG RAMSEY EST.
TIBERIUS SUM.

I HAVE BEEN THE SKULL'S CAPTIVE FOR AS LONG AS I CAN REMEMBER.

OF MY LIFE BEFORE THAT, NOTHING IS CLEAR.

HE SEEKS THE RESTORATION OF SOMEONE HE CALLS HIS "FÜHRER."

BUT WHY COME HERE?

THE SKULL DOES NOT CONFIDE IN CAPTIVES.

I WOULD ASSUME THERE IS SOMETHING HERE OF VALUE-- PERHAPS TO USE IT AS A BASE?

HIS STORY SOUNDS LEGIT.

SO WHY CAN'T I SHAKE THE FEELING THAT SOMETHING ABOUT THIS GUY FEELS TOTALLY-- WRONG?

DOESN'T HELP THAT 'MARA SEEMS TO LIKE HIM.

HARDLY SURPRISING, THE GUY HAS MAJOR CHARM.

TIBERIUS, YOU SAID SENATOR AQUILLA ESCAPED.

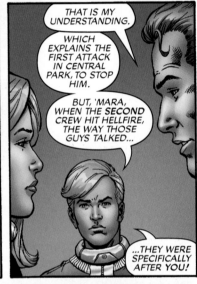

THAT IS MY UNDERSTANDING.

WHICH EXPLAINS THE FIRST ATTACK IN CENTRAL PARK, TO STOP HIM.

BUT, 'MARA, WHEN THE SECOND CREW HIT HELLFIRE, THE WAY THOSE GUYS TALKED...

...THEY WERE SPECIFICALLY AFTER YOU!

AN INSIGHTFUL OBSERVATION, BOY.

YOU ARE TO BE COMMENDED.

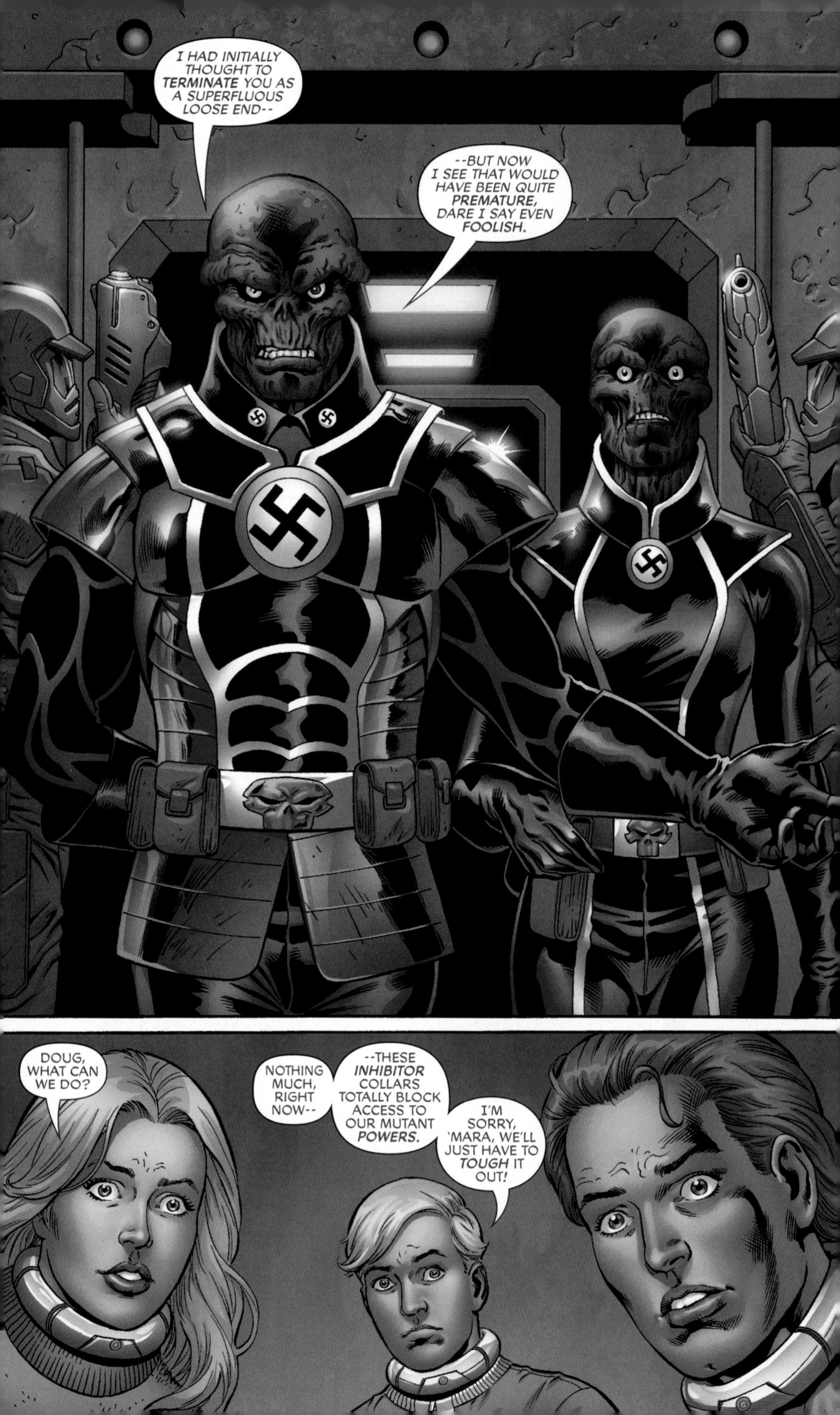
I HAD INITIALLY THOUGHT TO TERMINATE YOU AS A SUPERFLUOUS LOOSE END--
--BUT NOW I SEE THAT WOULD HAVE BEEN QUITE PREMATURE, DARE I SAY EVEN FOOLISH.
DOUG, WHAT CAN WE DO?
NOTHING MUCH, RIGHT NOW--
--THESE INHIBITOR COLLARS TOTALLY BLOCK ACCESS TO OUR MUTANT POWERS.
I'M SORRY, 'MARA, WE'LL JUST HAVE TO TOUGH IT OUT!

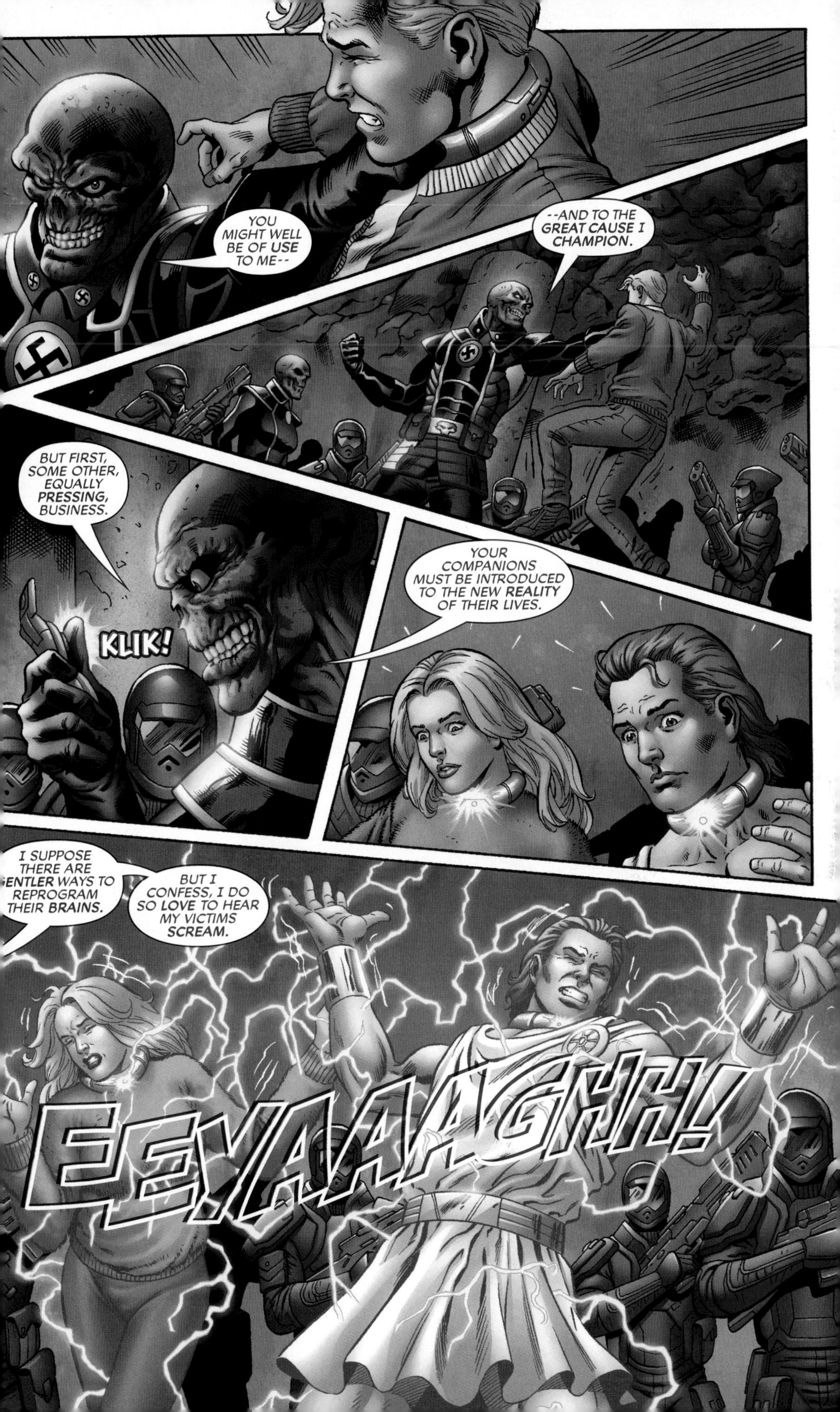
YOU MIGHT WELL BE OF USE TO ME--
--AND TO THE GREAT CAUSE I CHAMPION.
BUT FIRST, SOME OTHER, EQUALLY PRESSING, BUSINESS.
KLIK!
YOUR COMPANIONS MUST BE INTRODUCED TO THE NEW REALITY OF THEIR LIVES.
I SUPPOSE THERE ARE GENTLER WAYS TO REPROGRAM THEIR BRAINS.
BUT I CONFESS, I DO SO LOVE TO HEAR MY VICTIMS SCREAM.
EEYAAAGHH!

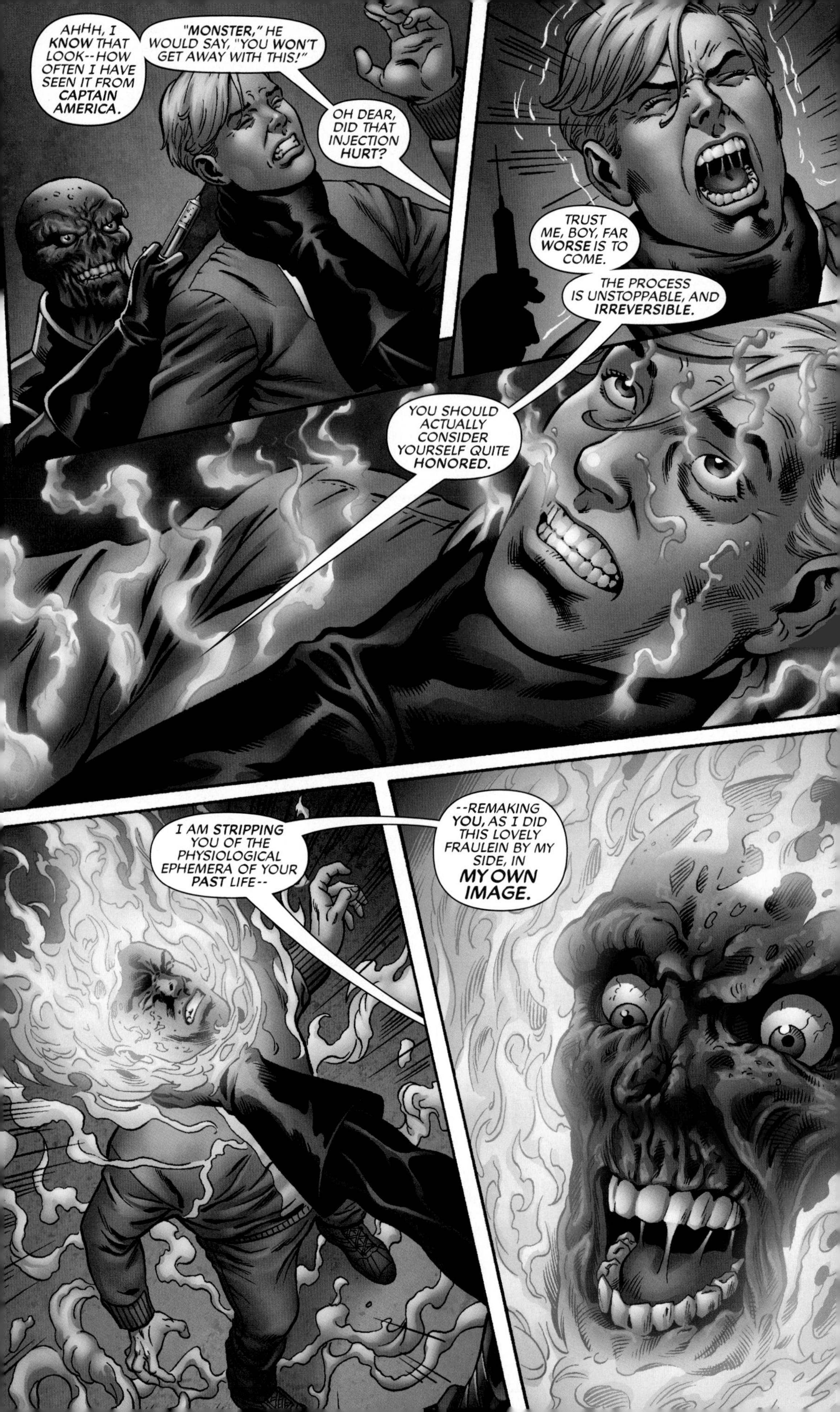
AHHH, I KNOW THAT LOOK--HOW OFTEN I HAVE SEEN IT FROM CAPTAIN AMERICA.
"MONSTER," HE WOULD SAY, "YOU WON'T GET AWAY WITH THIS!"
OH DEAR, DID THAT INJECTION HURT?
TRUST ME, BOY, FAR WORSE IS TO COME.
THE PROCESS IS UNSTOPPABLE, AND IRREVERSIBLE.
YOU SHOULD ACTUALLY CONSIDER YOURSELF QUITE HONORED.
I AM STRIPPING YOU OF THE PHYSIOLOGICAL EPHEMERA OF YOUR PAST LIFE--
--REMAKING YOU, AS I DID THIS LOVELY FRAULEIN BY MY SIDE, IN MY OWN IMAGE.

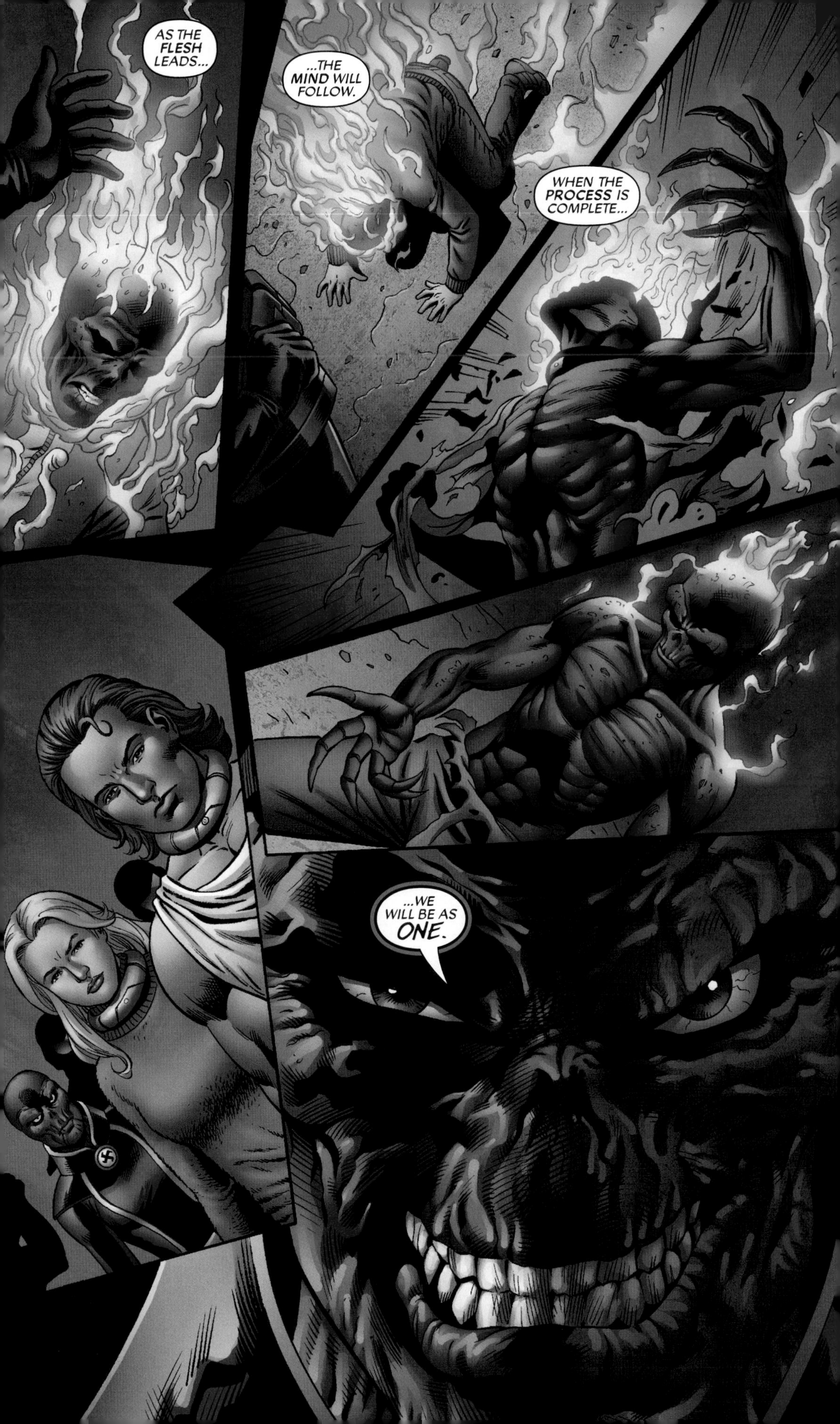
AS THE FLESH LEADS...
...THE MIND WILL FOLLOW.
WHEN THE PROCESS IS COMPLETE...
...WE WILL BE AS ONE.

ROUGHLY 2,000 YEARS AGO, A REFUGEE SHIPLOAD OF ROMAN REPUBLICANS FLED THAT ANCIENT CITY IN THE AFTERMATH OF THE CIVIL WAR THAT FOLLOWED THE DEATH OF JULIUS CAESAR.

THE RISE OF OCTAVIAN MEANT AN END TO THE ROME THEY CHERISHED. THEIR HOPE WAS TO FORGE THEIR WAY TO ANOTHER LAND AND START ANEW.

WINDS AND FATE--AND PERHAPS THE CAPRICES OF THE GODS THEMSELVES-- BROUGHT THEM ACROSS THE ATLANTIC AND UP THE AMAZON, WHERE THEY BUILT THEIR NEW HOME AT THE VERY CREST OF THE ANDES, THEIR CULTURE MERGING WITH THOSE OF THE EQUALLY VENERABLE INCA.

FOR GENERATIONS, THEY REMAINED UNDISCOVERED. AND WITH THAT ISOLATION CAME THEIR ONGOING SAFETY.

SADLY, THE WORLD'S GROWN A WHOLE LOT SMALLER NOW.

NOWHERE ON EARTH IS AS ISOLATED--AND UNREACHABLE-- AS ONCE IT WAS.

EVERYONE OFF THE LIMBO EXPRESS TO--

LOOKS LIKE THAT RING DID THE--

?!? ?! ?!

WHAT'RE YOU DOING HERE?!?

MY MOM WAS ATTACKED IN RIO!

WE WERE ATTACKED IN NEW YORK.

AMARA AND DOUG WERE KIDNAPPED!

INTERROGATIVE REGARDING CURRENT STATUS OF SELF-FRIEND DOUG AND TEAMMATE AMARA!

WE DUNNO 'LOCK, I SORRY

TH W HO TH

RES TH

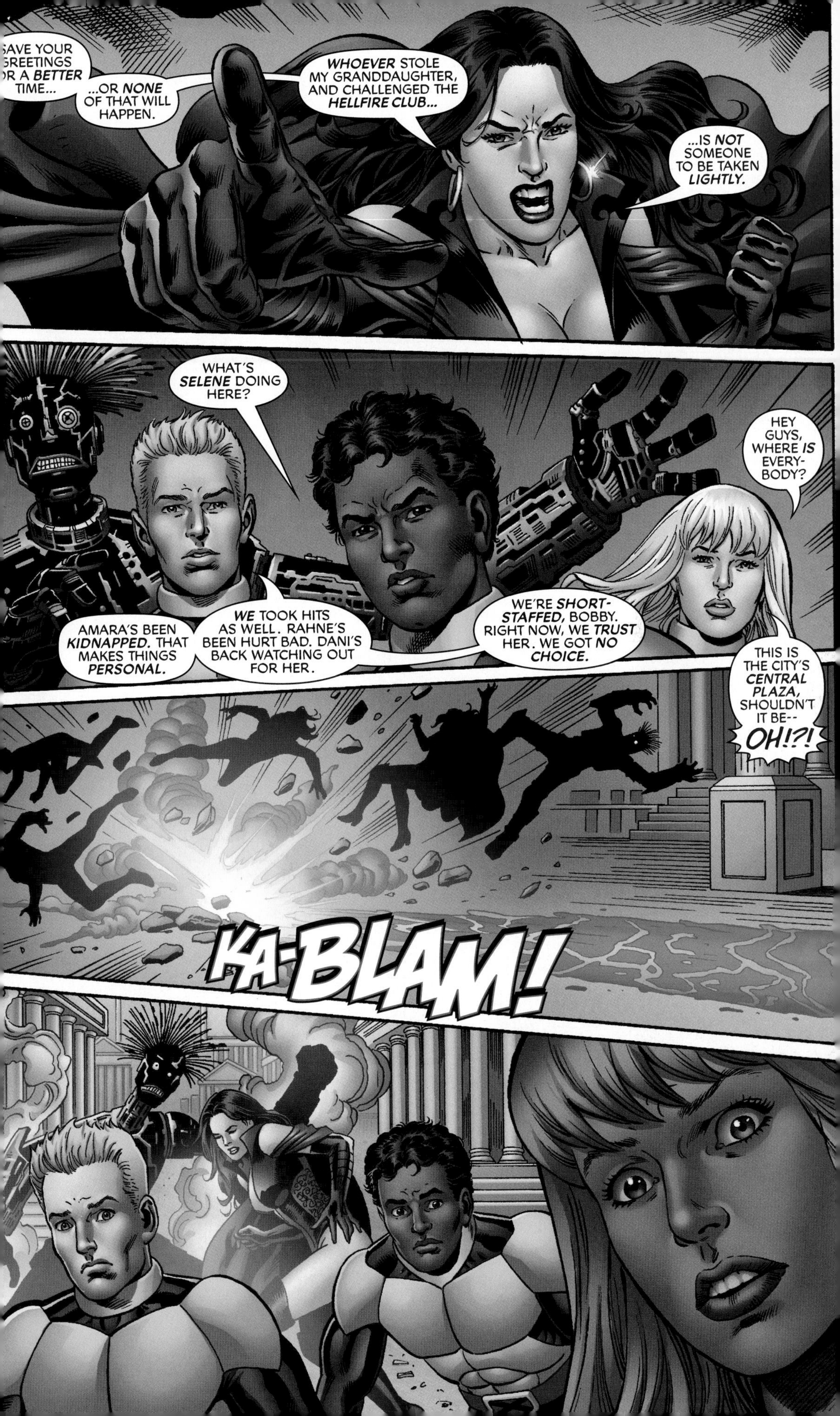

SAVE YOUR GREETINGS FOR A BETTER TIME...
...OR NONE OF THAT WILL HAPPEN.
WHOEVER STOLE MY GRANDDAUGHTER, AND CHALLENGED THE HELLFIRE CLUB...
...IS NOT SOMEONE TO BE TAKEN LIGHTLY.
WHAT'S SELENE DOING HERE?
HEY GUYS, WHERE IS EVERY-BODY?
AMARA'S BEEN KIDNAPPED. THAT MAKES THINGS PERSONAL.
WE TOOK HITS AS WELL. RAHNE'S BEEN HURT BAD. DANI'S BACK WATCHING OUT FOR HER.
WE'RE SHORT-STAFFED, BOBBY. RIGHT NOW, WE TRUST HER. WE GOT NO CHOICE.
THIS IS THE CITY'S CENTRAL PLAZA, SHOULDN'T IT BE--
OH!?!
KA-BLAM!

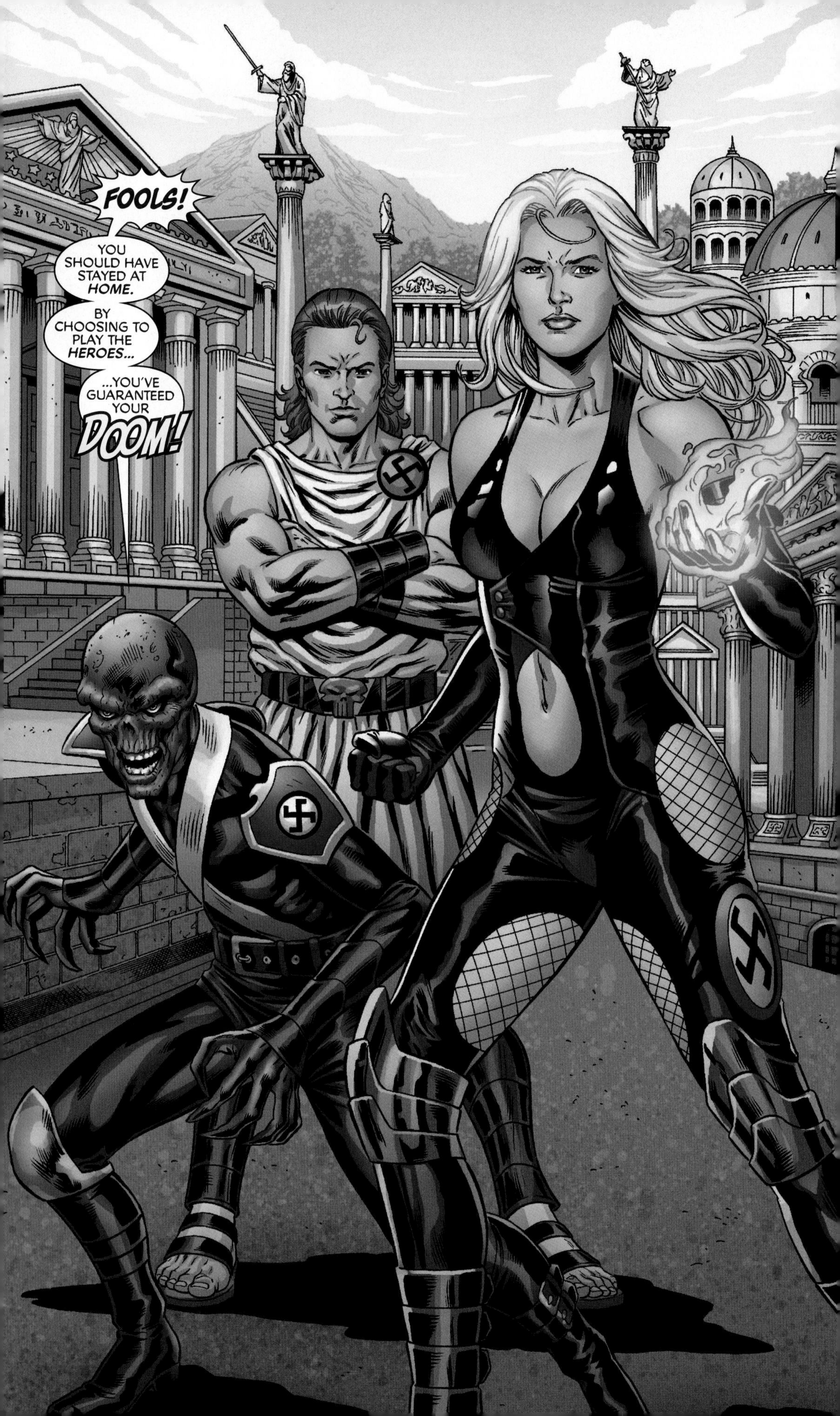
FOOLS!
YOU SHOULD HAVE STAYED AT HOME.
BY CHOOSING TO PLAY THE HEROES...
...YOU'VE GUARANTEED YOUR
DOOM!

#3

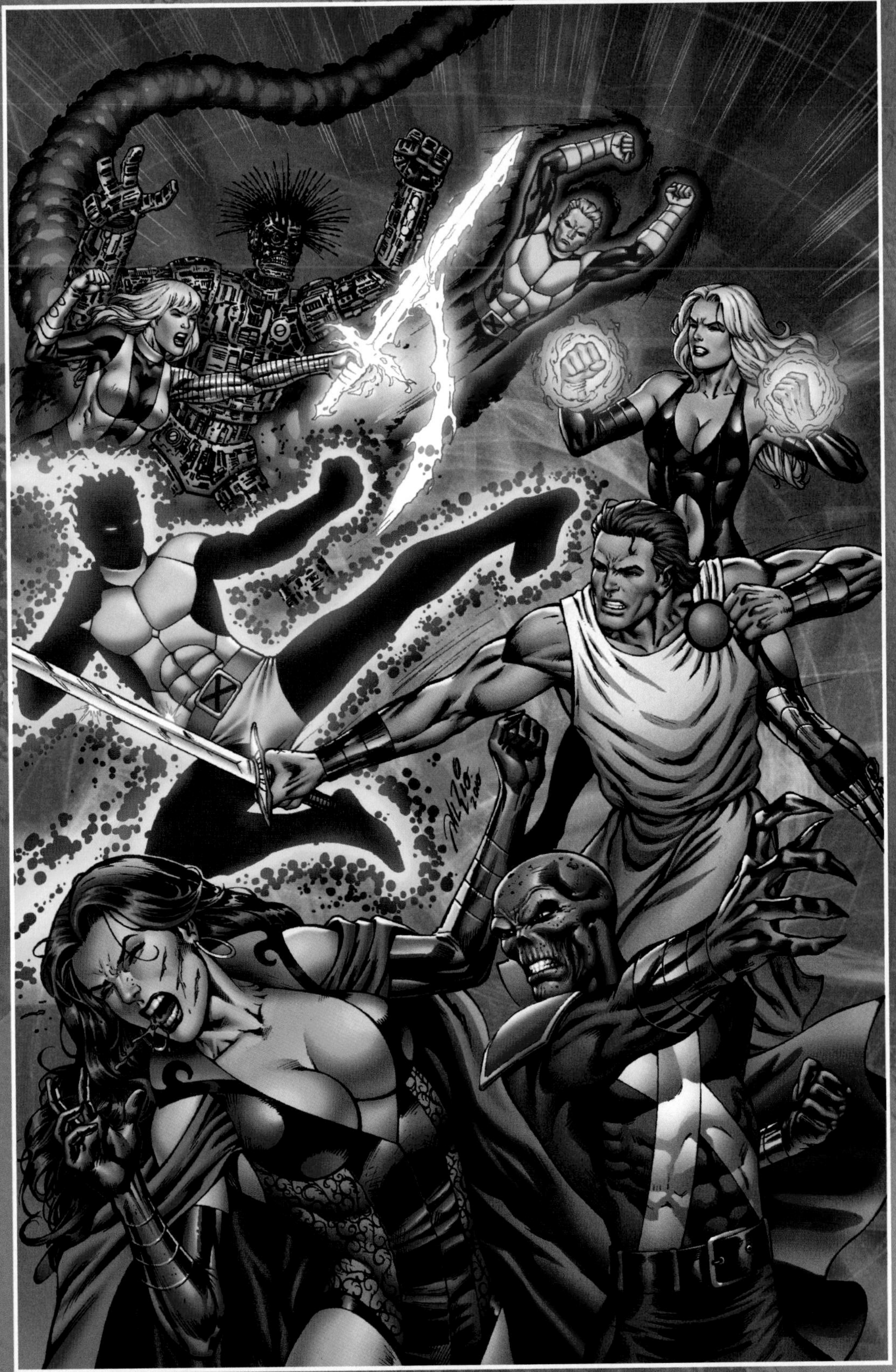

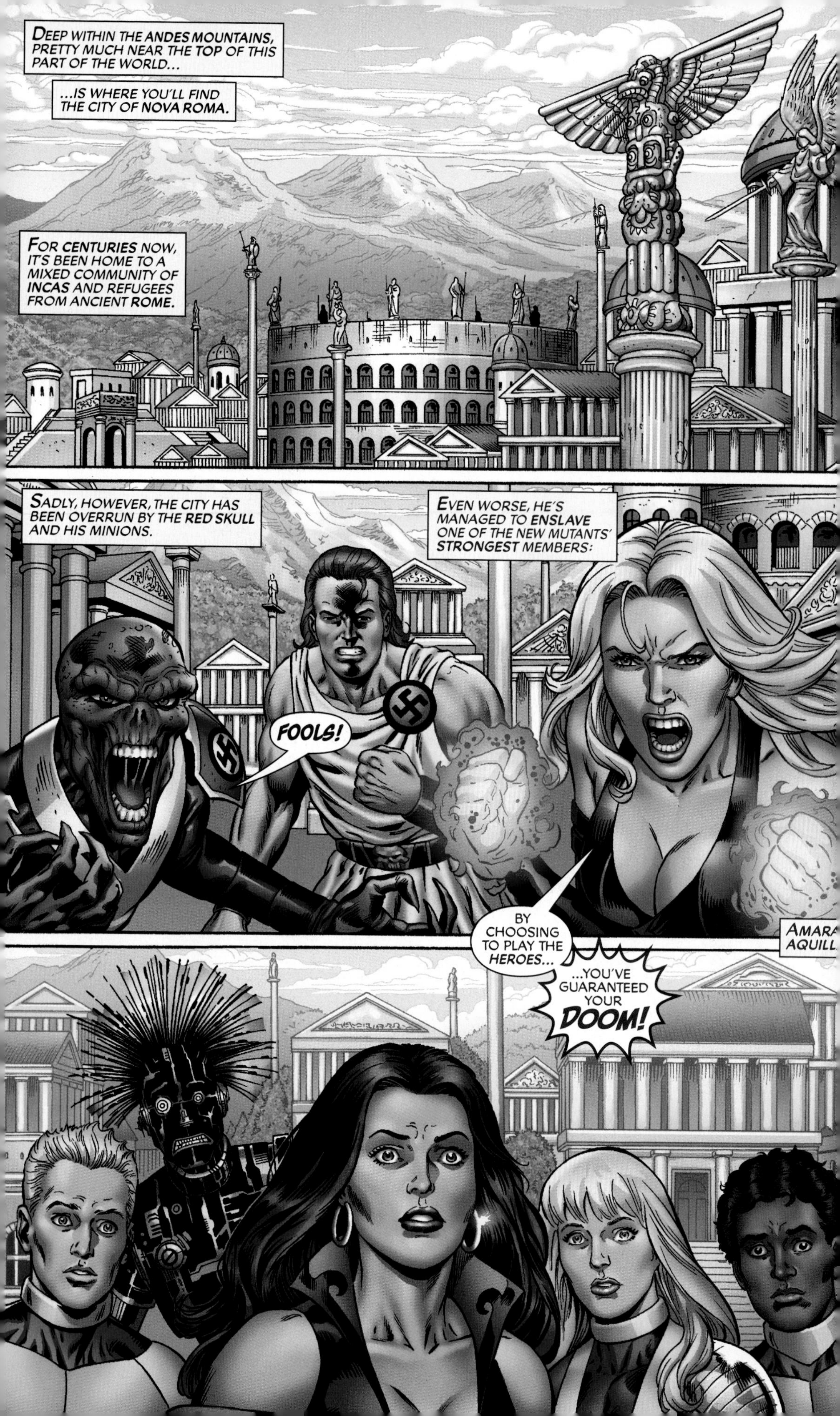
DEEP WITHIN THE ANDES MOUNTAINS, PRETTY MUCH NEAR THE TOP OF THIS PART OF THE WORLD...
...IS WHERE YOU'LL FIND THE CITY OF NOVA ROMA.
FOR CENTURIES NOW, IT'S BEEN HOME TO A MIXED COMMUNITY OF INCAS AND REFUGEES FROM ANCIENT ROME.
SADLY, HOWEVER, THE CITY HAS BEEN OVERRUN BY THE RED SKULL AND HIS MINIONS.
EVEN WORSE, HE'S MANAGED TO ENSLAVE ONE OF THE NEW MUTANTS' STRONGEST MEMBERS:
FOOLS!
BY CHOOSING TO PLAY THE HEROES...
...YOU'VE GUARANTEED YOUR DOOM!

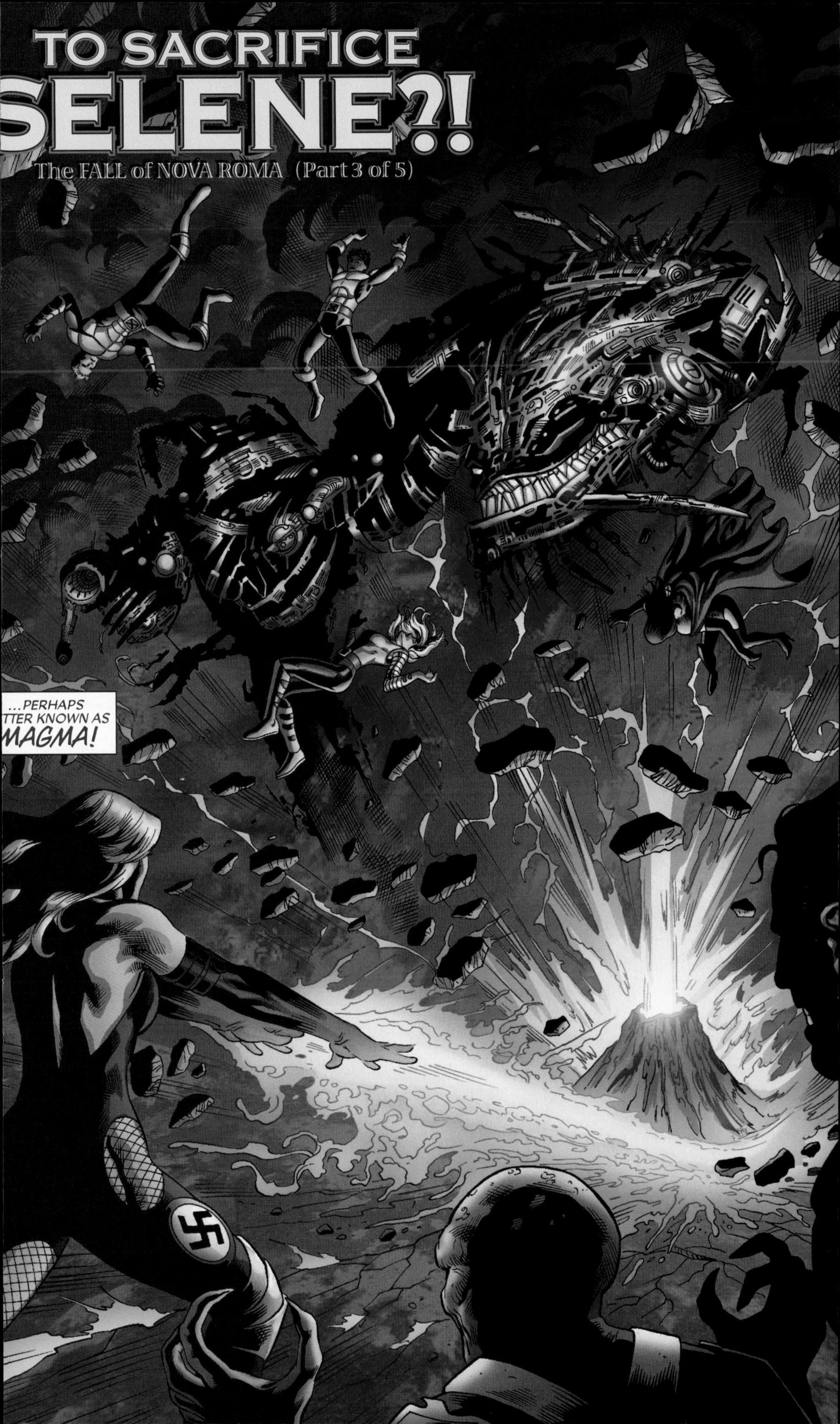

TO SACRIFICE
SELENE?!
The FALL of NOVA ROMA (Part 3 of 5)
...PERHAPS
TTER KNOWN AS
MAGMA!

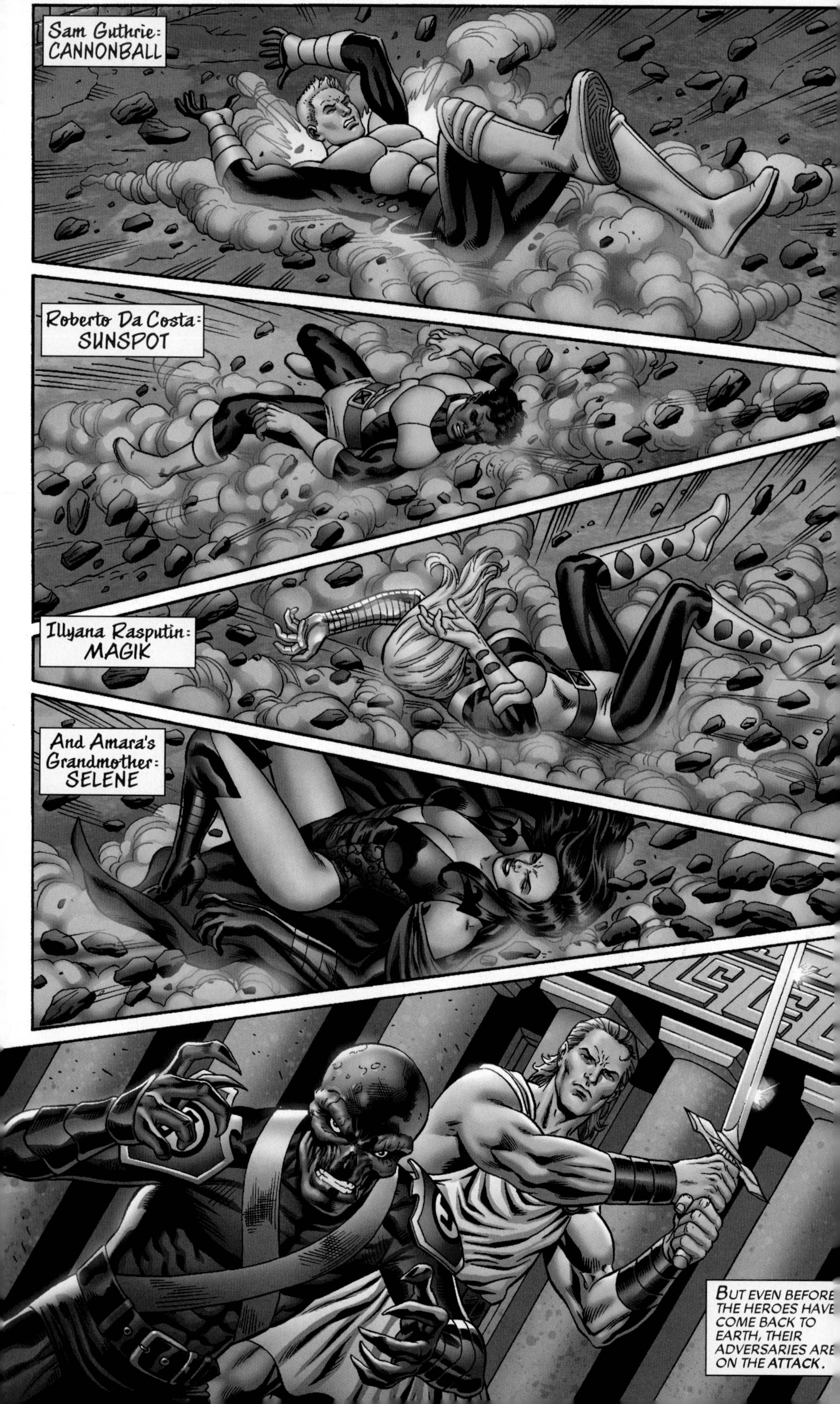
Sam Guthrie: CANNONBALL
Roberto Da Costa: SUNSPOT
Illyana Rasputin: MAGIK
And Amara's Grandmother: SELENE
BUT EVEN BEFORE THE HEROES HAVE COME BACK TO EARTH, THEIR ADVERSARIES ARE ON THE ATTACK.

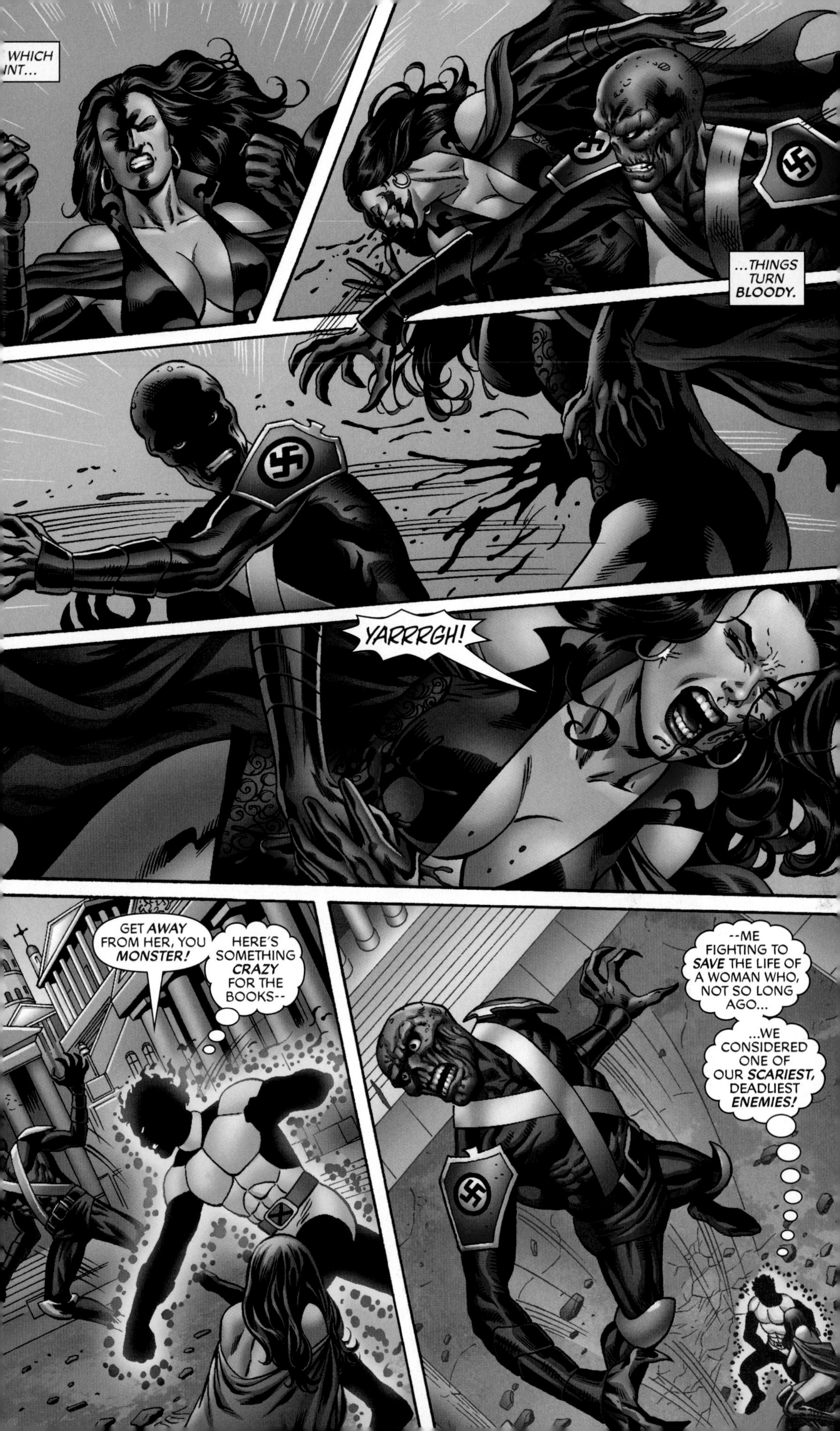
WHICH
INT...
...THINGS TURN BLOODY.
YARRRGH!
GET AWAY FROM HER, YOU MONSTER!
HERE'S SOMETHING CRAZY FOR THE BOOKS--
--ME FIGHTING TO SAVE THE LIFE OF A WOMAN WHO, NOT SO LONG AGO...
...WE CONSIDERED ONE OF OUR SCARIEST, DEADLIEST ENEMIES!

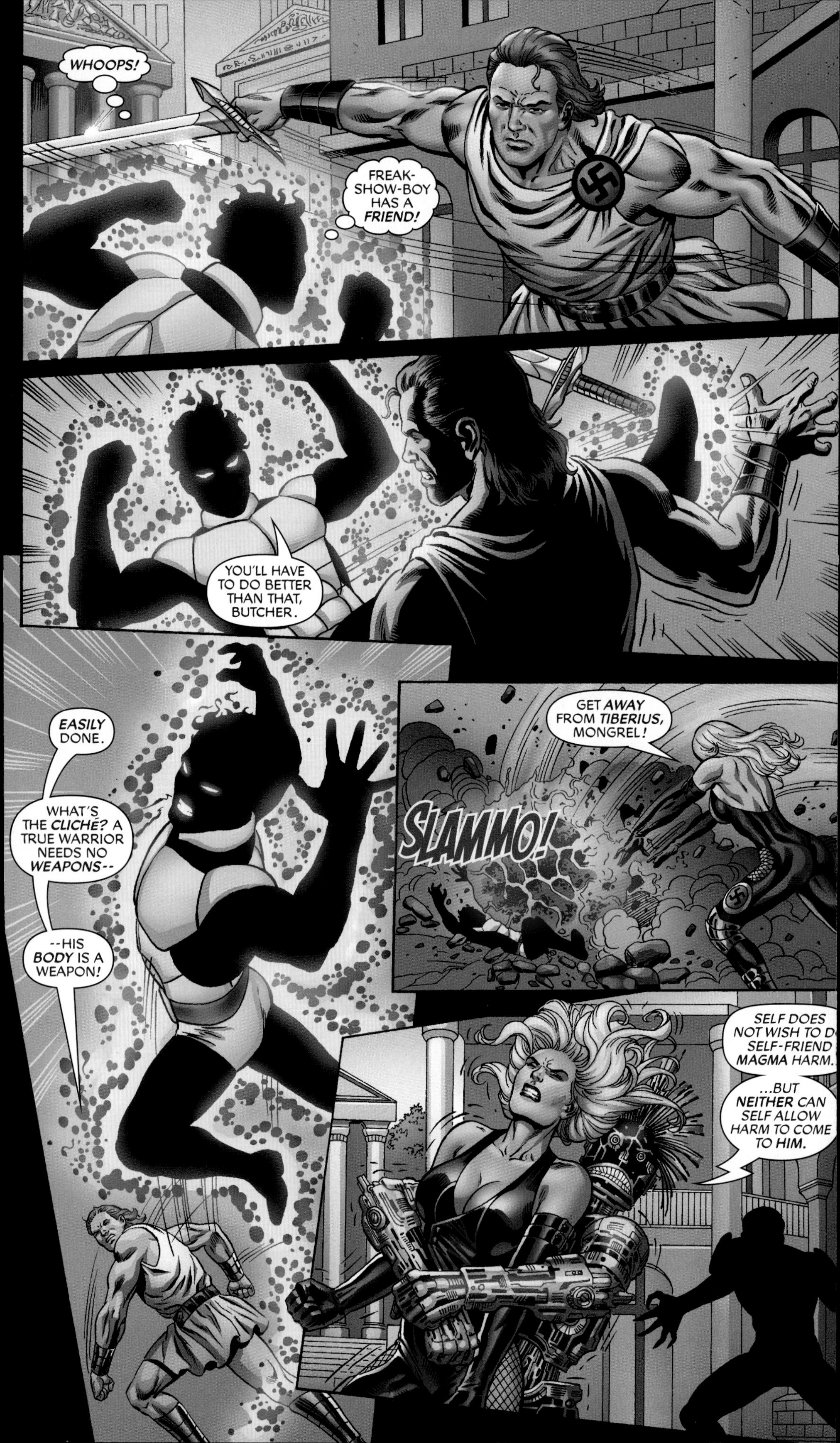
WHOOPS!
FREAK-SHOW-BOY HAS A FRIEND!
YOU'LL HAVE TO DO BETTER THAN THAT, BUTCHER.
EASILY DONE.
WHAT'S THE CLICHÉ? A TRUE WARRIOR NEEDS NO WEAPONS--
--HIS BODY IS A WEAPON!
GET AWAY FROM TIBERIUS, MONGREL!
SLAMMO!
SELF DOES NOT WISH TO DO SELF-FRIEND MAGMA HARM.
...BUT NEITHER CAN SELF ALLOW HARM TO COME TO HIM.

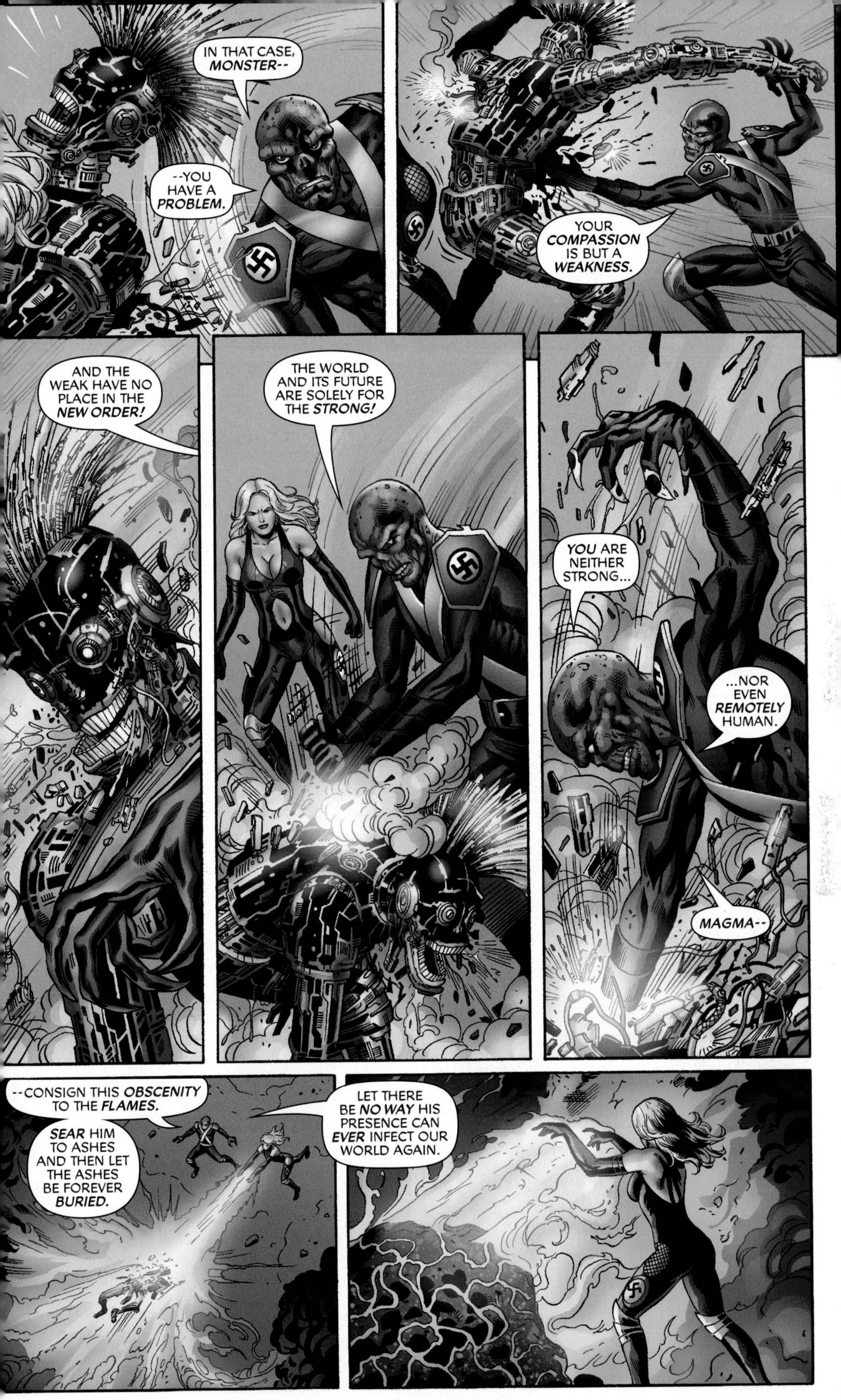
IN THAT CASE, MONSTER--
--YOU HAVE A PROBLEM.
YOUR COMPASSION IS BUT A WEAKNESS.
AND THE WEAK HAVE NO PLACE IN THE NEW ORDER!
THE WORLD AND ITS FUTURE ARE SOLELY FOR THE STRONG!
YOU ARE NEITHER STRONG...
...NOR EVEN REMOTELY HUMAN.
MAGMA--
--CONSIGN THIS OBSCENITY TO THE FLAMES.
SEAR HIM TO ASHES AND THEN LET THE ASHES BE FOREVER BURIED.
LET THERE BE NO WAY HIS PRESENCE CAN EVER INFECT OUR WORLD AGAIN.

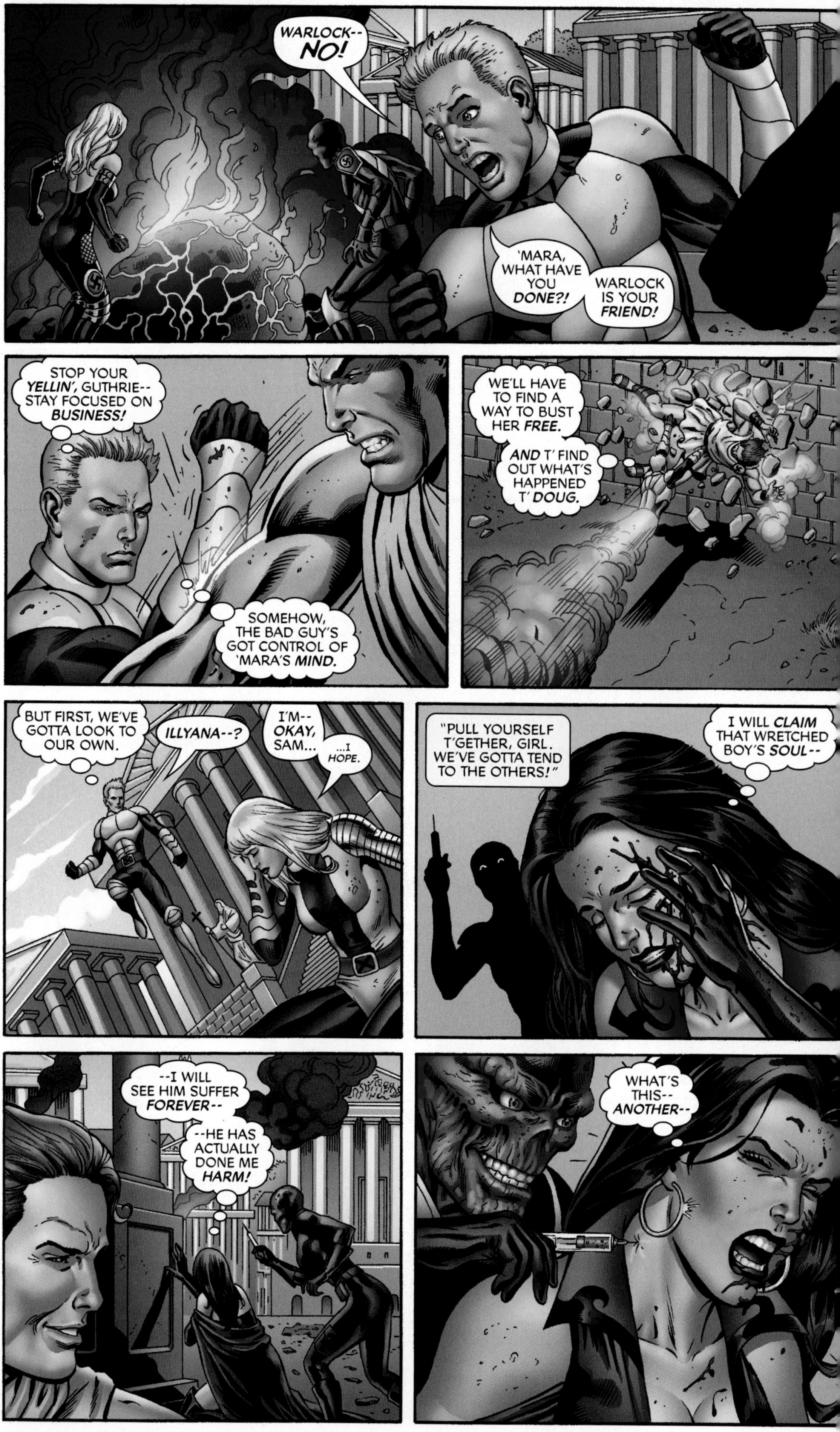
WARLOCK-- NO!
'MARA, WHAT HAVE YOU DONE?!
WARLOCK IS YOUR FRIEND!
STOP YOUR YELLIN', GUTHRIE-- STAY FOCUSED ON BUSINESS!
SOMEHOW, THE BAD GUY'S GOT CONTROL OF 'MARA'S MIND.
WE'LL HAVE TO FIND A WAY TO BUST HER FREE.
AND T' FIND OUT WHAT'S HAPPENED T' DOUG.
BUT FIRST, WE'VE GOTTA LOOK TO OUR OWN.
ILLYANA--?
I'M-- OKAY, SAM...
...I HOPE.
"PULL YOURSELF T'GETHER, GIRL. WE'VE GOTTA TEND TO THE OTHERS!"
I WILL CLAIM THAT WRETCHED BOY'S SOUL--
--I WILL SEE HIM SUFFER FOREVER--
--HE HAS ACTUALLY DONE ME HARM!
WHAT'S THIS-- ANOTHER--

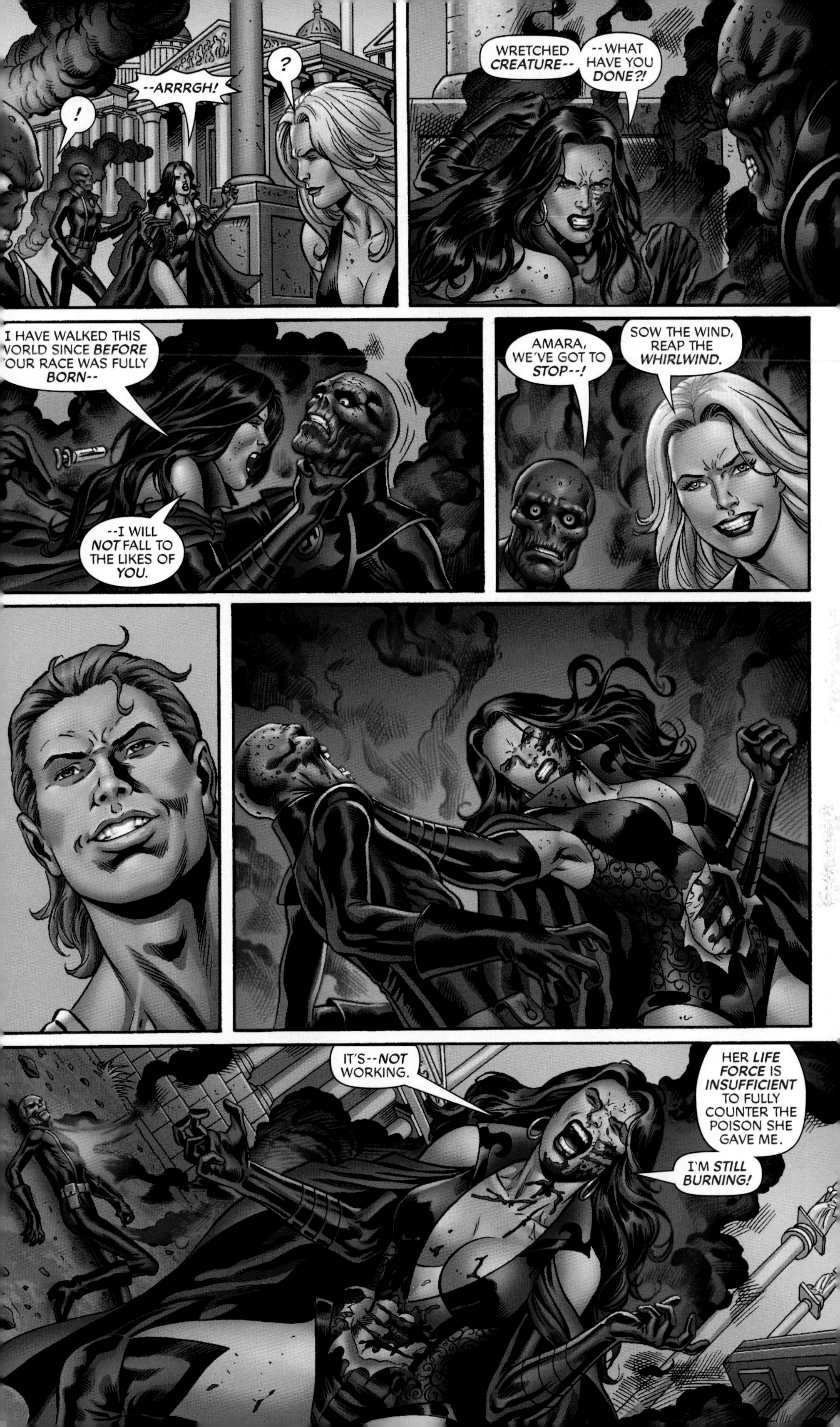
!
--ARRRGH!
?
WRETCHED CREATURE--
--WHAT HAVE YOU DONE?!
I HAVE WALKED THIS WORLD SINCE BEFORE YOUR RACE WAS FULLY BORN--
--I WILL NOT FALL TO THE LIKES OF YOU.
AMARA, WE'VE GOT TO STOP--!
SOW THE WIND, REAP THE WHIRLWIND.
IT'S--NOT WORKING.
HER LIFE FORCE IS INSUFFICIENT TO FULLY COUNTER THE POISON SHE GAVE ME.
I'M STILL BURNING!

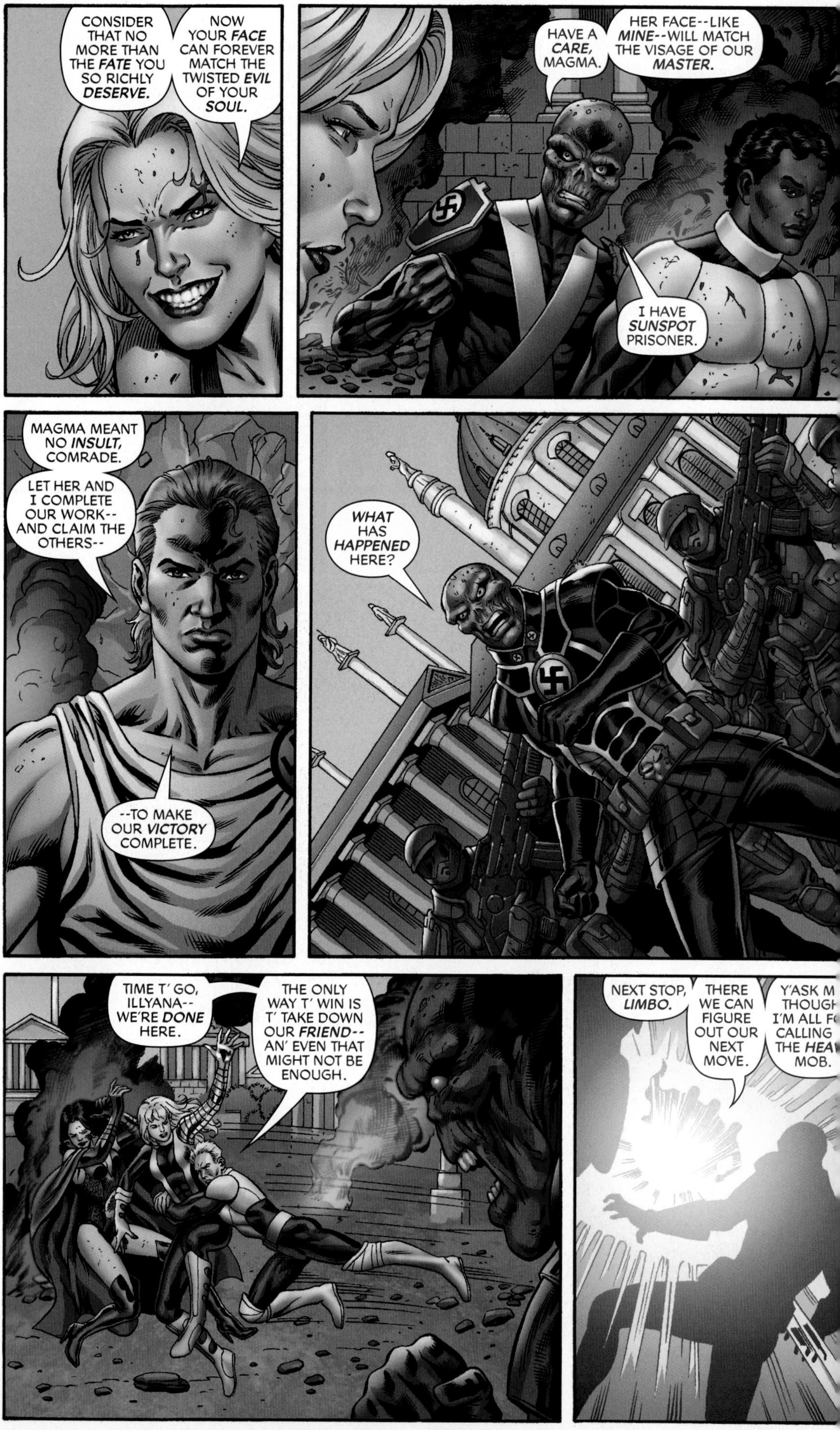
CONSIDER THAT NO MORE THAN THE *FATE* YOU SO RICHLY *DESERVE.*
NOW YOUR *FACE* CAN FOREVER MATCH THE TWISTED *EVIL* OF YOUR *SOUL.*
HAVE A *CARE,* MAGMA.
HER FACE--LIKE *MINE*--WILL MATCH THE VISAGE OF OUR *MASTER.*
I HAVE *SUNSPOT* PRISONER.
MAGMA MEANT NO *INSULT,* COMRADE.
LET HER AND I COMPLETE OUR WORK--AND CLAIM THE OTHERS--
--TO MAKE OUR *VICTORY* COMPLETE.
*WHAT* HAS *HAPPENED* HERE?
TIME T' GO, ILLYANA--WE'RE *DONE* HERE.
THE ONLY WAY T' WIN IS T' TAKE DOWN OUR *FRIEND*--AN' EVEN THAT MIGHT NOT BE ENOUGH.
NEXT STOP, *LIMBO.*
THERE WE CAN FIGURE OUT OUR NEXT MOVE.
Y'ASK M THOUGH I'M ALL F CALLING THE HEA MOB.

I EXPECTED-- *BETTER.*

I DID NOT EXPECT-- *CASUALTIES.*

BUT THAT IS THE NATURE OF *WAR.*

THE *BEST* OF BATTLES DEMAND THEIR SHARE OF *BLOOD.*

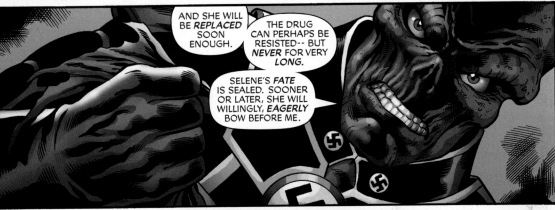

AND SHE WILL BE *REPLACED* SOON ENOUGH.

THE DRUG CAN PERHAPS BE RESISTED-- BUT *NEVER* FOR VERY *LONG.*

*SELENE'S FATE* IS SEALED. SOONER OR LATER, SHE WILL WILLINGLY, *EAGERLY* BOW BEFORE ME.

AS WILL *YOU,* MONGREL.

I WILL NOT PERMIT YOU TO *SHARE* MY VISAGE, BUT REST ASSURED, AN APPRO-PRIATE PLACE WILL BE FOUND FOR YOU TO *SERVE.*

*NOTHING* IN THE WORLD CAN *SAVE* YOU--

--OR YOUR *FRIENDS.*

LIMBO.

ILLYANA SPENT MOST OF HER YOUNG LIFETIME HERE, AFTER BEING KIDNAPPED BY THE DEMON-LORD BELASCO.

AFTER HIS "DEATH," SHE TOOK OVER.

CREEPY THING IS, EVEN THOUGH SHE'S HAPPY TO BE WITH THE X-COMMUNITY...

...THIS IS THE PLACE THAT TO HER FEELS LIKE HOME.

SELENE LOOKS PRETTY AWFUL.

IS THERE ANYTHING WE CAN DO TO HELP, ILLYANA?

SOME KIND OF SPELL OR ENCHANTMENT?

FIRST PROBLEM, SAM--HER TRANSFORMATION'S BEING CAUSED BY SCIENCE, NOT MAGIC.

EVEN IF I HAD A SPELL THAT MIGHT WORK, IT WOULDN'T HAVE ANY EFFECT OUTSIDE OF HERE.

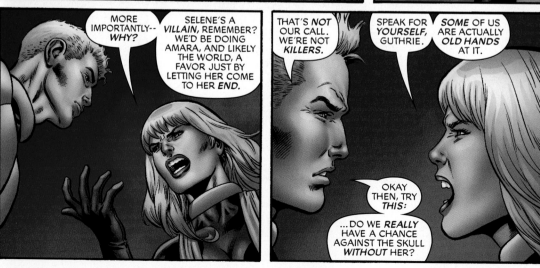

MORE IMPORTANTLY-- WHY?

SELENE'S A VILLAIN, REMEMBER? WE'D BE DOING AMARA, AND LIKELY THE WORLD, A FAVOR JUST BY LETTING HER COME TO HER END.

THAT'S NOT OUR CALL. WE'RE NOT KILLERS.

SPEAK FOR YOURSELF, GUTHRIE.

SOME OF US ARE ACTUALLY OLD HANDS AT IT.

OKAY THEN, TRY THIS:

...DO WE REALLY HAVE A CHANCE AGAINST THE SKULL WITHOUT HER?

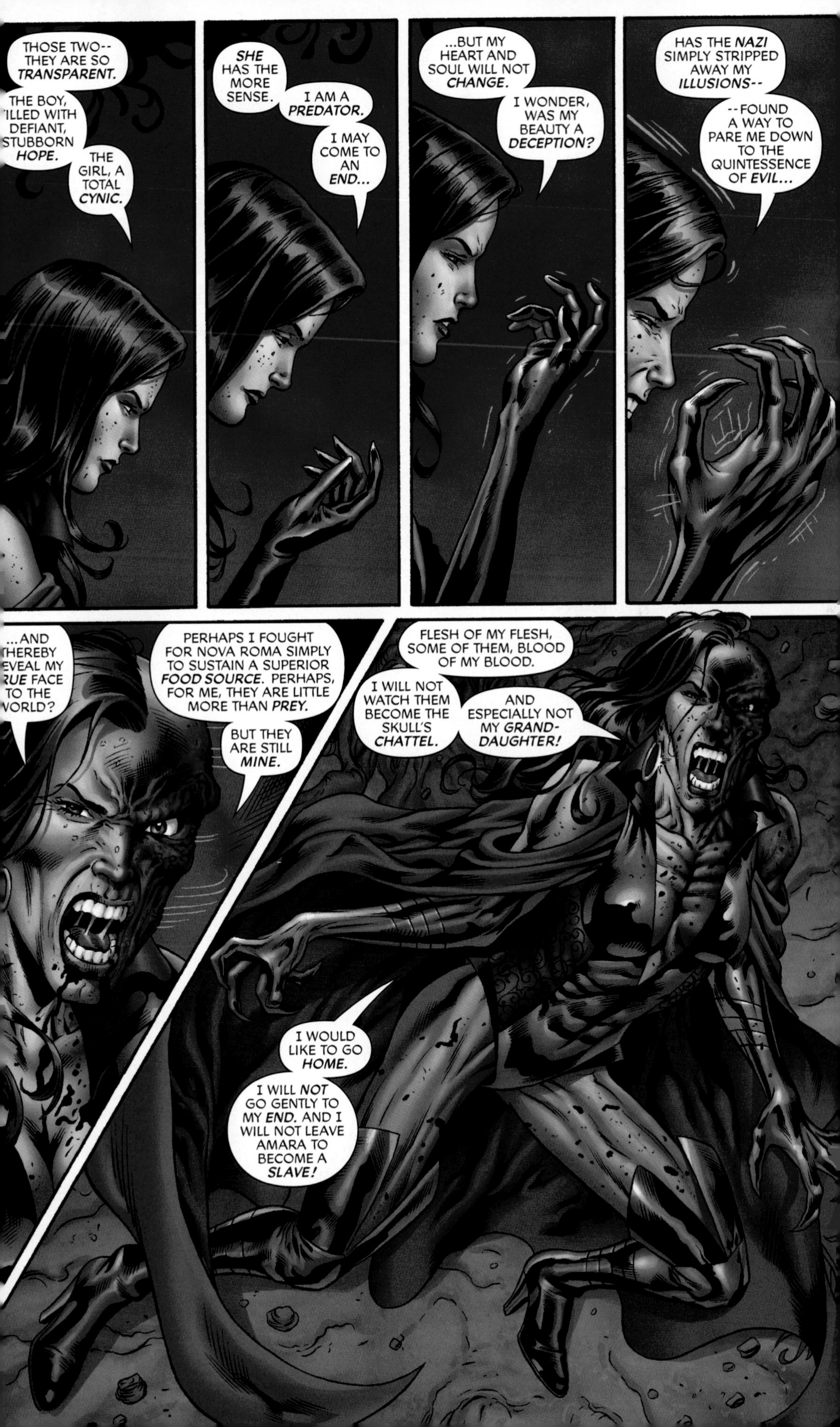
THOSE TWO-- THEY ARE SO TRANSPARENT.
THE BOY, ILLED WITH DEFIANT, STUBBORN HOPE.
THE GIRL, A TOTAL CYNIC.
SHE HAS THE MORE SENSE.
I AM A PREDATOR.
I MAY COME TO AN END...
...BUT MY HEART AND SOUL WILL NOT CHANGE.
I WONDER, WAS MY BEAUTY A DECEPTION?
HAS THE NAZI SIMPLY STRIPPED AWAY MY ILLUSIONS--
--FOUND A WAY TO PARE ME DOWN TO THE QUINTESSENCE OF EVIL...
...AND THEREBY EVEAL MY RUE FACE TO THE ORLD?
PERHAPS I FOUGHT FOR NOVA ROMA SIMPLY TO SUSTAIN A SUPERIOR FOOD SOURCE. PERHAPS, FOR ME, THEY ARE LITTLE MORE THAN PREY.
BUT THEY ARE STILL MINE.
FLESH OF MY FLESH, SOME OF THEM, BLOOD OF MY BLOOD.
I WILL NOT WATCH THEM BECOME THE SKULL'S CHATTEL.
AND ESPECIALLY NOT MY GRAND-DAUGHTER!
I WOULD LIKE TO GO HOME.
I WILL NOT GO GENTLY TO MY END. AND I WILL NOT LEAVE AMARA TO BECOME A SLAVE!

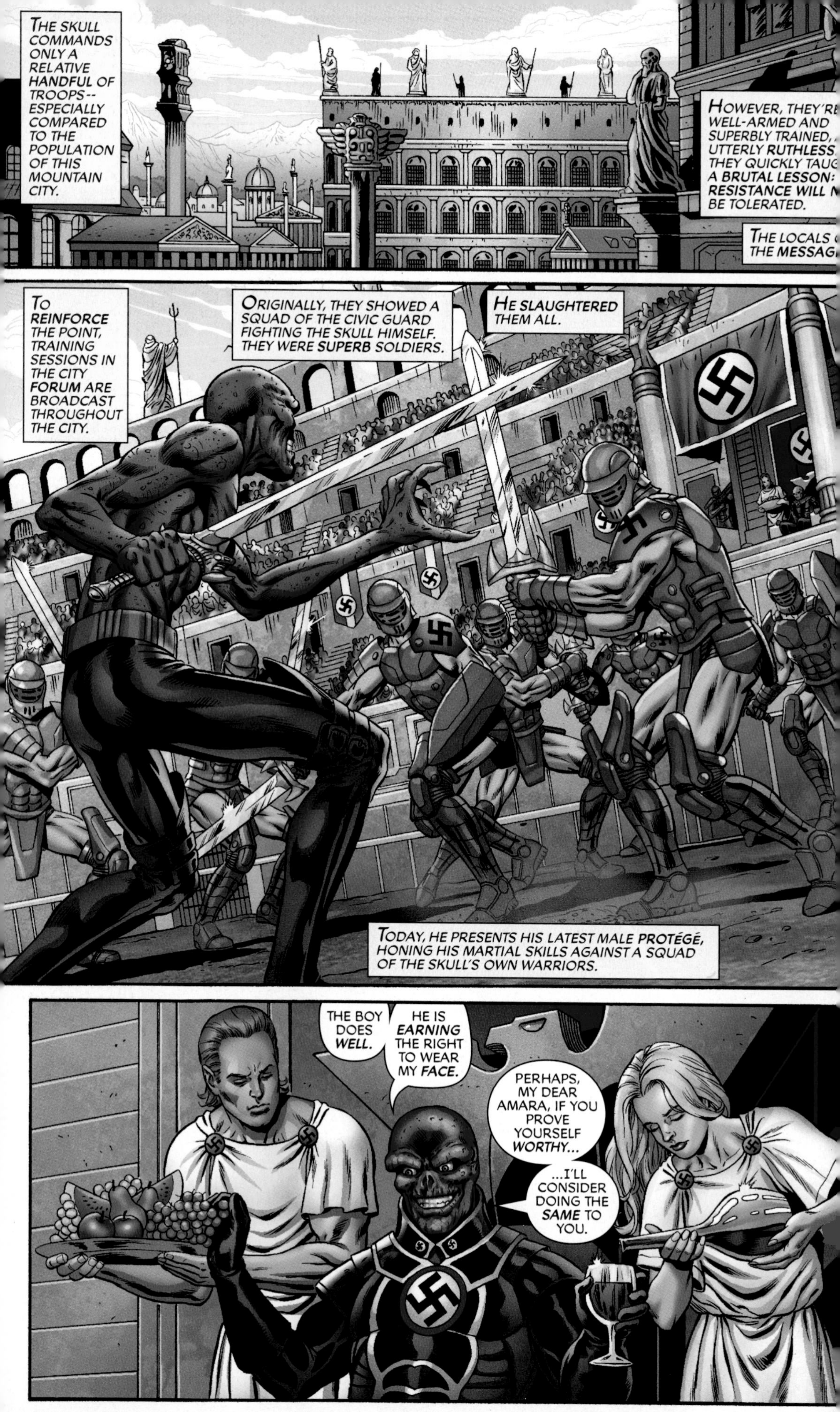

THE SKULL COMMANDS ONLY A RELATIVE HANDFUL OF TROOPS-- ESPECIALLY COMPARED TO THE POPULATION OF THIS MOUNTAIN CITY.
HOWEVER, THEY'RE WELL-ARMED AND SUPERBLY TRAINED, UTTERLY RUTHLESS. THEY QUICKLY TAUG A BRUTAL LESSON: RESISTANCE WILL N BE TOLERATED.
THE LOCALS THE MESSAG
TO REINFORCE THE POINT, TRAINING SESSIONS IN THE CITY FORUM ARE BROADCAST THROUGHOUT THE CITY.
ORIGINALLY, THEY SHOWED A SQUAD OF THE CIVIC GUARD FIGHTING THE SKULL HIMSELF. THEY WERE SUPERB SOLDIERS.
HE SLAUGHTERED THEM ALL.
TODAY, HE PRESENTS HIS LATEST MALE PROTÉGÉ, HONING HIS MARTIAL SKILLS AGAINST A SQUAD OF THE SKULL'S OWN WARRIORS.
THE BOY DOES WELL.
HE IS EARNING THE RIGHT TO WEAR MY FACE.
PERHAPS, MY DEAR AMARA, IF YOU PROVE YOURSELF WORTHY...
...I'LL CONSIDER DOING THE SAME TO YOU.

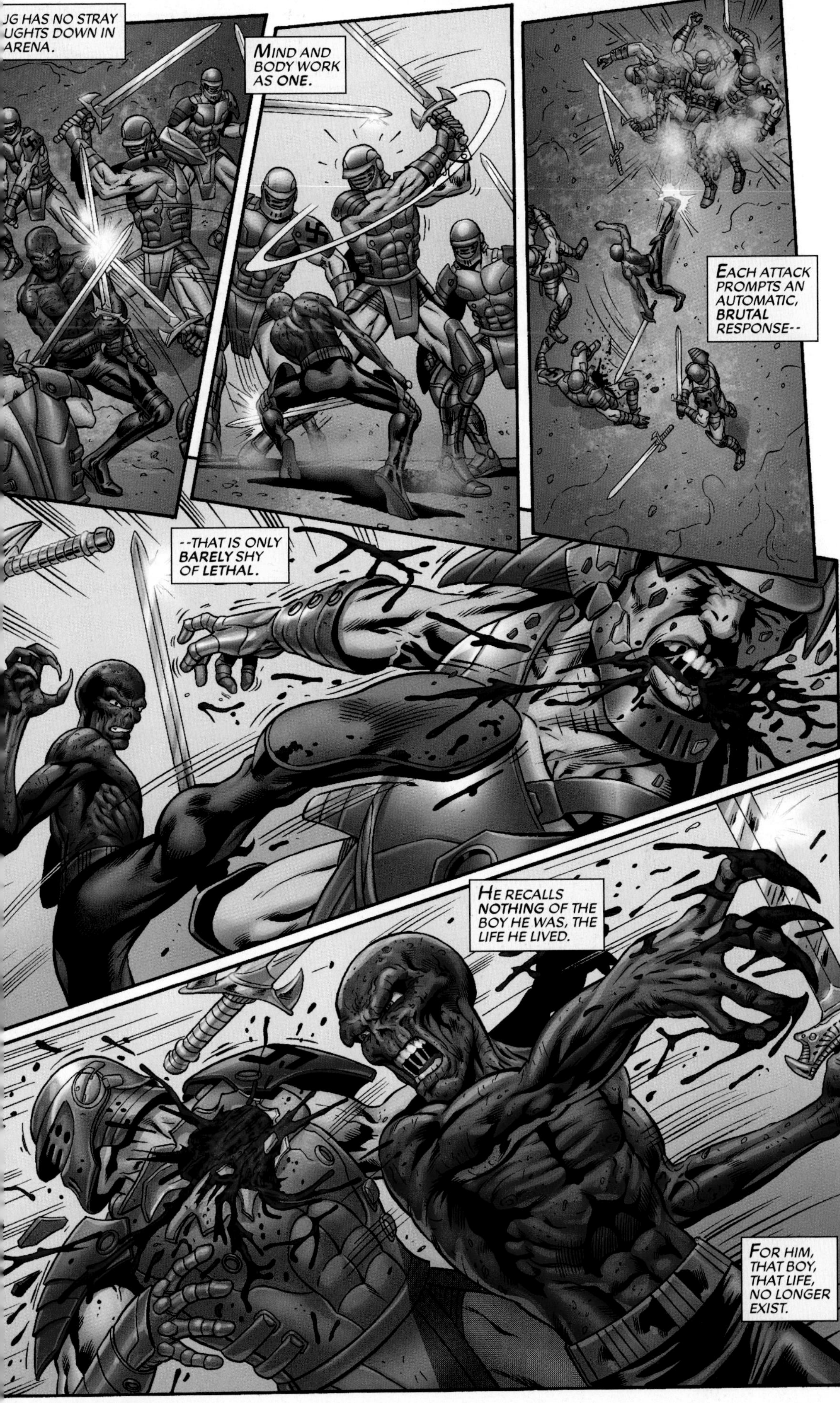
JG HAS NO STRAY
UGHTS DOWN IN
ARENA.
MIND AND BODY WORK AS ONE.
EACH ATTACK PROMPTS AN AUTOMATIC, BRUTAL RESPONSE--
--THAT IS ONLY BARELY SHY OF LETHAL.
HE RECALLS NOTHING OF THE BOY HE WAS, THE LIFE HE LIVED.
FOR HIM, THAT BOY, THAT LIFE, NO LONGER EXIST.

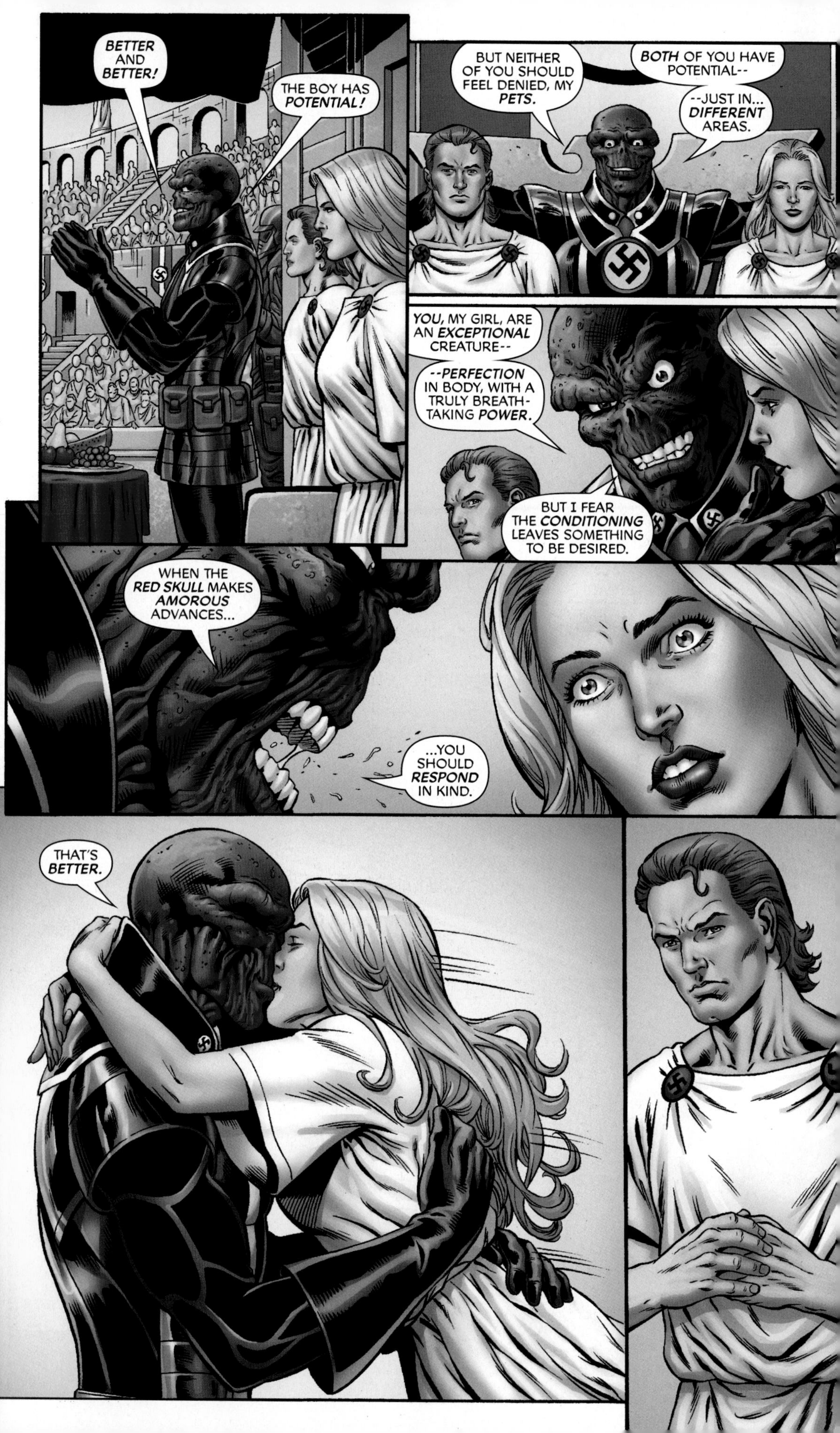
BETTER AND BETTER!
THE BOY HAS POTENTIAL!
BUT NEITHER OF YOU SHOULD FEEL DENIED, MY PETS.
BOTH OF YOU HAVE POTENTIAL--
--JUST IN... DIFFERENT AREAS.
YOU, MY GIRL, ARE AN EXCEPTIONAL CREATURE--
--PERFECTION IN BODY, WITH A TRULY BREATH-TAKING POWER.
BUT I FEAR THE CONDITIONING LEAVES SOMETHING TO BE DESIRED.
WHEN THE RED SKULL MAKES AMOROUS ADVANCES...
...YOU SHOULD RESPOND IN KIND.
THAT'S BETTER.

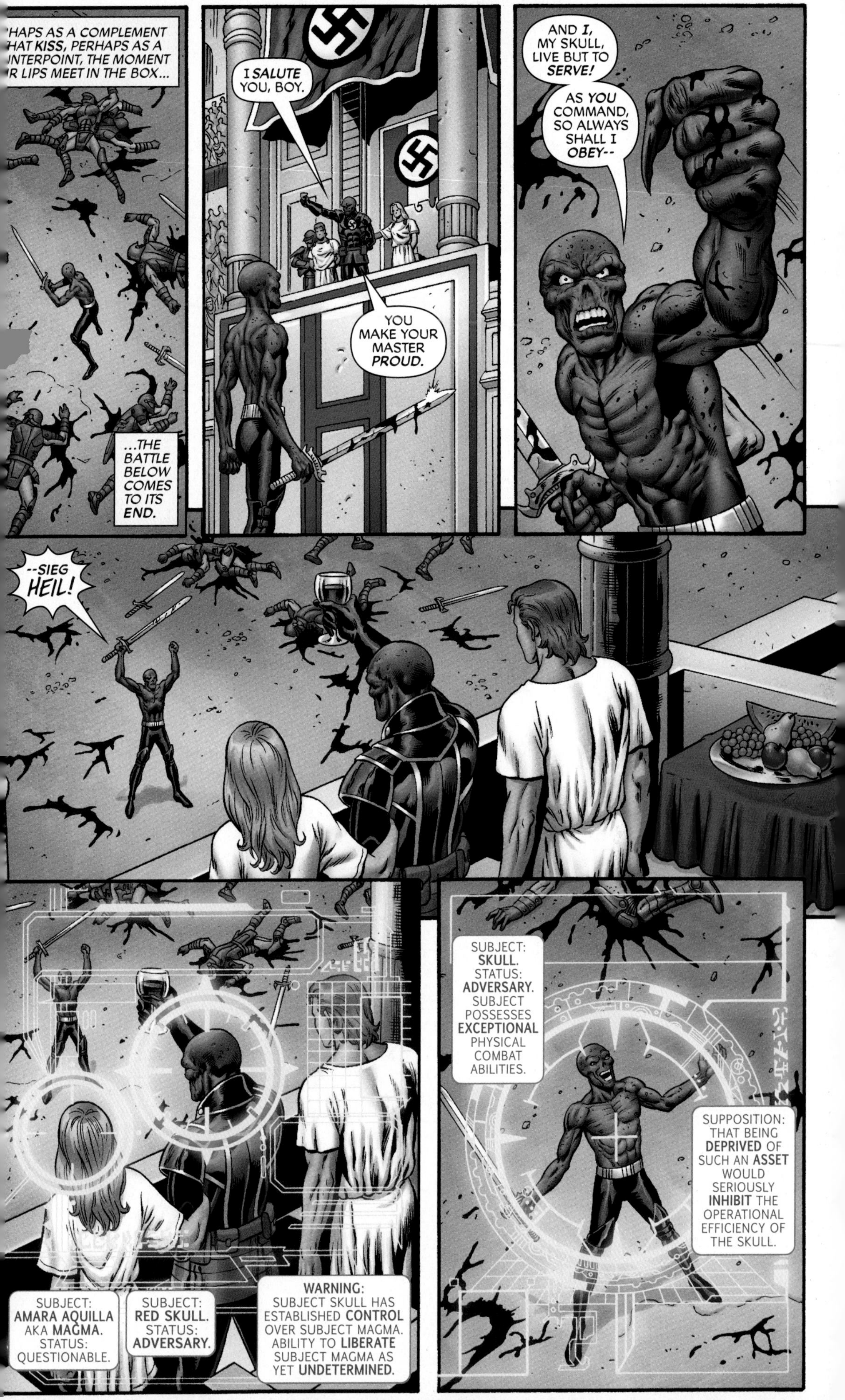
'HAPS AS A COMPLEMENT
'HAT KISS, PERHAPS AS A
INTERPOINT, THE MOMENT
'R LIPS MEET IN THE BOX...
...THE BATTLE BELOW COMES TO ITS END.
I SALUTE YOU, BOY.
YOU MAKE YOUR MASTER PROUD.
AND I, MY SKULL, LIVE BUT TO SERVE!
AS YOU COMMAND, SO ALWAYS SHALL I OBEY--
--SIEG HEIL!
SUBJECT: AMARA AQUILLA AKA MAGMA. STATUS: QUESTIONABLE.
SUBJECT: RED SKULL. STATUS: ADVERSARY.
WARNING: SUBJECT SKULL HAS ESTABLISHED CONTROL OVER SUBJECT MAGMA. ABILITY TO LIBERATE SUBJECT MAGMA AS YET UNDETERMINED.
SUBJECT: SKULL. STATUS: ADVERSARY. SUBJECT POSSESSES EXCEPTIONAL PHYSICAL COMBAT ABILITIES.
SUPPOSITION: THAT BEING DEPRIVED OF SUCH AN ASSET WOULD SERIOUSLY INHIBIT THE OPERATIONAL EFFICIENCY OF THE SKULL.

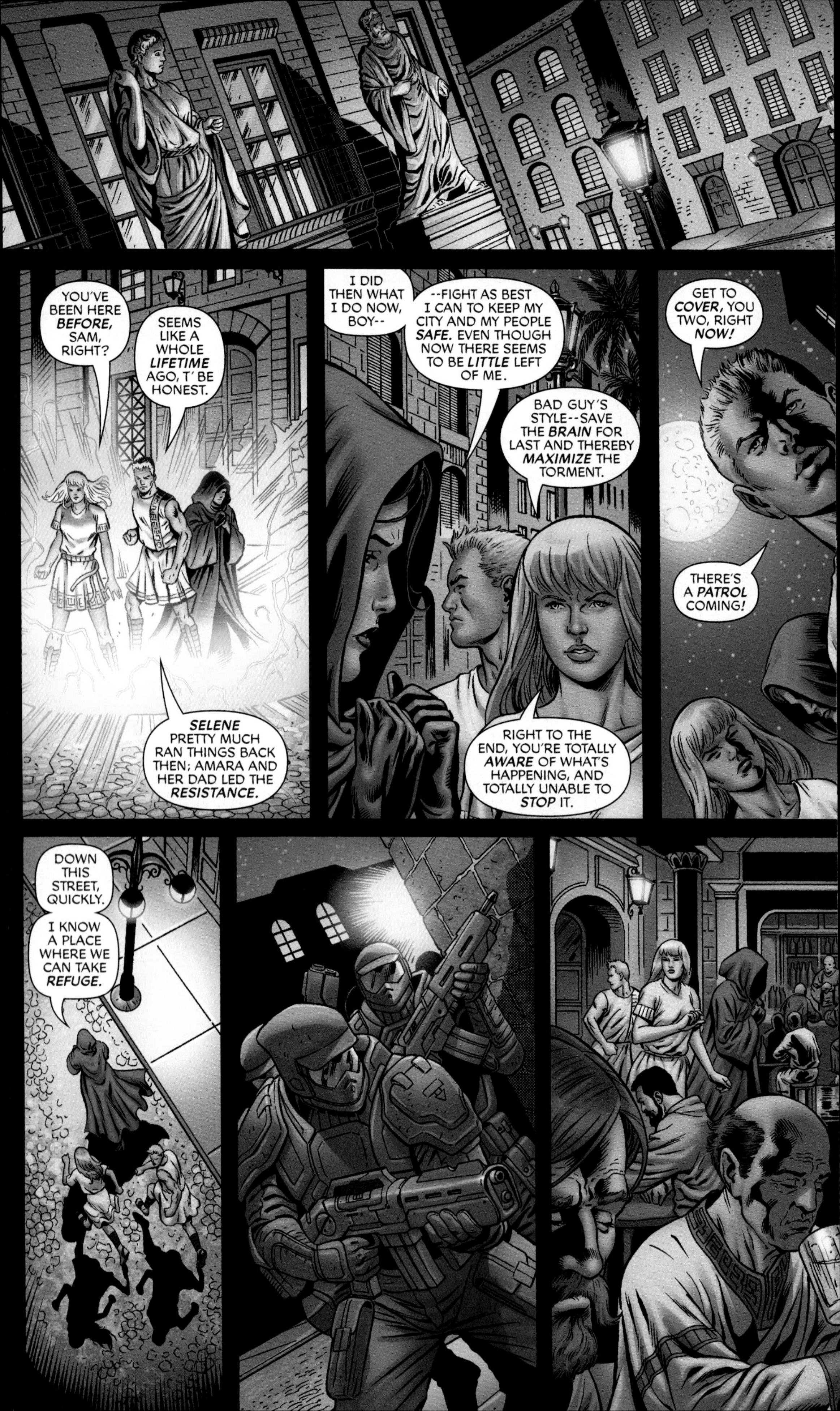
YOU'VE BEEN HERE BEFORE, SAM, RIGHT?
SEEMS LIKE A WHOLE LIFETIME AGO, T' BE HONEST.
SELENE PRETTY MUCH RAN THINGS BACK THEN; AMARA AND HER DAD LED THE RESISTANCE.
I DID THEN WHAT I DO NOW, BOY--
--FIGHT AS BEST I CAN TO KEEP MY CITY AND MY PEOPLE SAFE. EVEN THOUGH NOW THERE SEEMS TO BE LITTLE LEFT OF ME.
BAD GUY'S STYLE--SAVE THE BRAIN FOR LAST AND THEREBY MAXIMIZE THE TORMENT.
RIGHT TO THE END, YOU'RE TOTALLY AWARE OF WHAT'S HAPPENING, AND TOTALLY UNABLE TO STOP IT.
GET TO COVER, YOU TWO, RIGHT NOW!
THERE'S A PATROL COMING!
DOWN THIS STREET, QUICKLY.
I KNOW A PLACE WHERE WE CAN TAKE REFUGE.

NOBODY SEEMS TO NOTICE WE'RE HERE.

YOU'D RATHER THEY *REACT*?

COUNT YOUR BLESSINGS, SAM-- AND HOPE WE STAY *INVISIBLE*.

...KE IT BACK--*EVERY* ...E IN THE PLACE IS ON US.

...FIGURE ...EY'RE BIDING ...HEIR TIME, THE COAST IS CLEAR ...OUTSIDE.

WORST COMES TO WORST, I'LL *PORT* US BACK TO *LIMBO*.

*NO*. THIS IS MY *HOME*.

THE *TRANSFORMATION* IS PICKING UP SPEED, I CAN NO LONGER *RESIST* IT.

I WILL NOT BECOME THE RED SKULL'S *SLAVE*-- BETTER BY FAR AN *HONORABLE DEATH*.

*FINE* BY *ME*.

*ILLYANA*-- PUT AWAY YOUR *SOUL-SWORD*!

YOU GOT A *BETTER* IDEA, SAM? CAN YOU SET THINGS RIGHT, CAN YOU EVEN *STOP* IT FROM HAPPENING? *TRUST* ME, PAL--

--THIS IS WAY MORE *MERCIFUL*.

...MAJESTRIX?

...BY ALL ...E GODS, ...T TRULY ...YOU?

...MERCIFUL ...VE, WHAT HAS ...APPENED?!

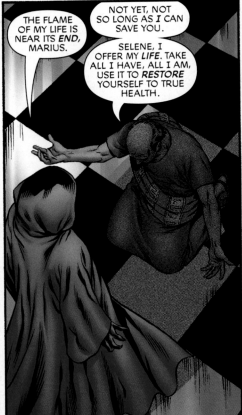

THE FLAME OF MY LIFE IS NEAR ITS *END*, MARIUS.

NOT YET, NOT SO LONG AS *I* CAN SAVE YOU.

*SELENE*, I OFFER MY *LIFE*. TAKE ALL I HAVE, ALL I AM, USE IT TO *RESTORE* YOURSELF TO TRUE HEALTH.

YOU DO ME *HONOR* WITH YOUR SACRIFICE, OLD FRIEND.

BY ALL THE GODS, I *VOW* TO PROVE MYSELF *WORTHY* OF IT.

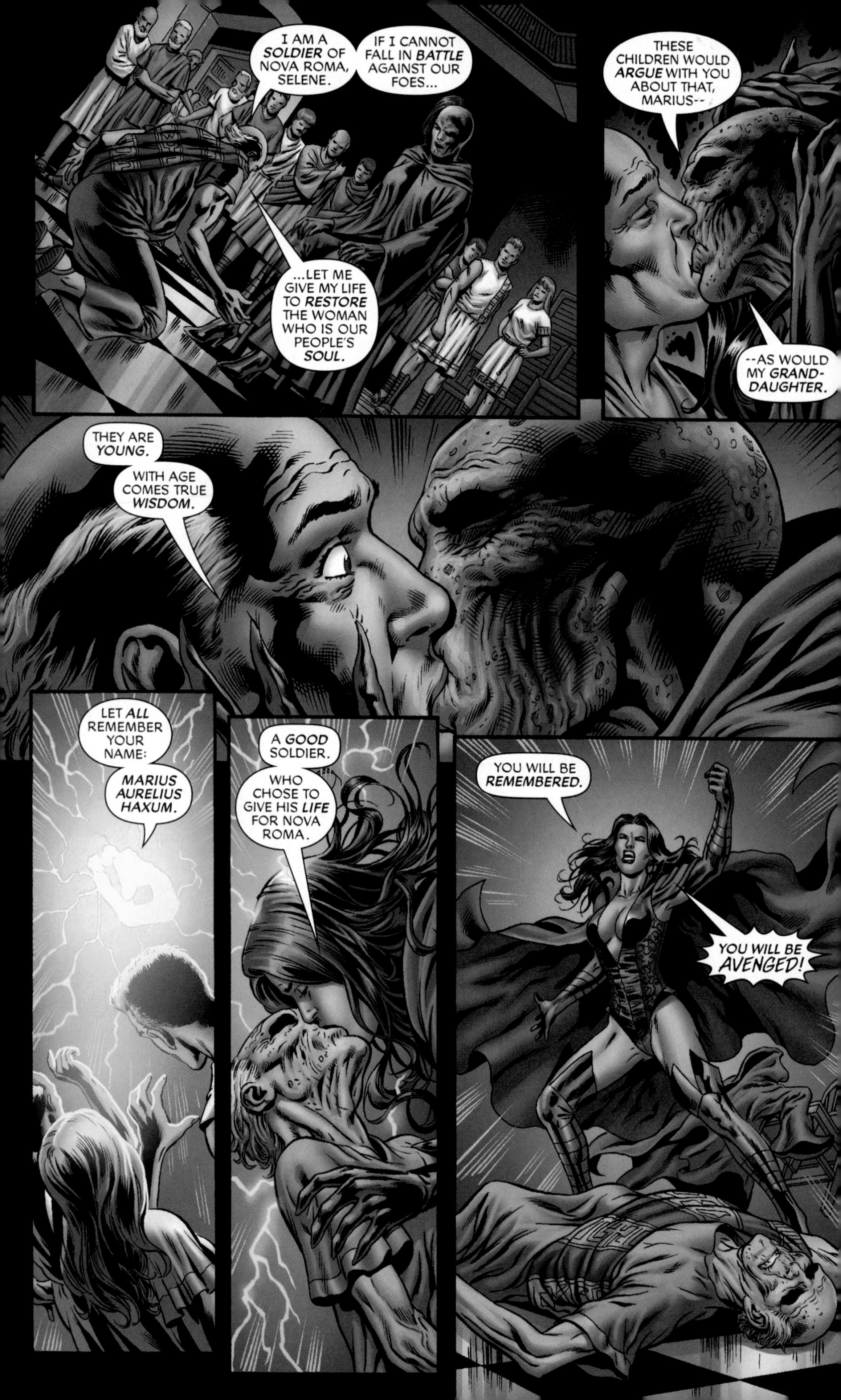
I AM A SOLDIER OF NOVA ROMA, SELENE.
IF I CANNOT FALL IN BATTLE AGAINST OUR FOES...
...LET ME GIVE MY LIFE TO RESTORE THE WOMAN WHO IS OUR PEOPLE'S SOUL.
THESE CHILDREN WOULD ARGUE WITH YOU ABOUT THAT, MARIUS--
--AS WOULD MY GRAND-DAUGHTER.
THEY ARE YOUNG.
WITH AGE COMES TRUE WISDOM.
LET ALL REMEMBER YOUR NAME:
MARIUS AURELIUS HAXUM.
A GOOD SOLDIER.
WHO CHOSE TO GIVE HIS LIFE FOR NOVA ROMA.
YOU WILL BE REMEMBERED.
YOU WILL BE AVENGED!

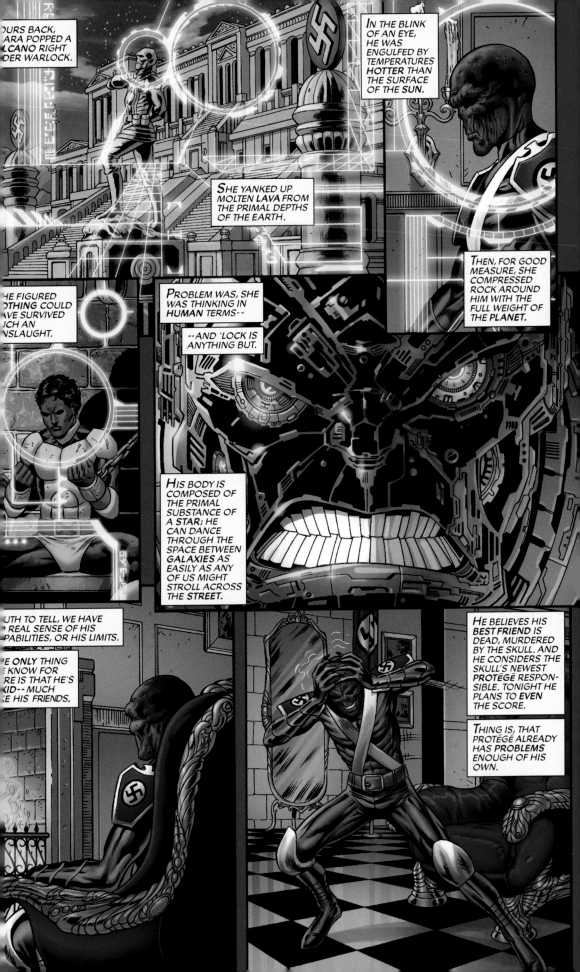

...OURS BACK, ...ARA POPPED A ...LCANO RIGHT ...DER WARLOCK.

IN THE BLINK OF AN EYE, HE WAS ENGULFED BY TEMPERATURES HOTTER THAN THE SURFACE OF THE SUN.

SHE YANKED UP MOLTEN LAVA FROM THE PRIMAL DEPTHS OF THE EARTH.

THEN, FOR GOOD MEASURE, SHE COMPRESSED ROCK AROUND HIM WITH THE FULL WEIGHT OF THE PLANET.

...HE FIGURED ...OTHING COULD ...VE SURVIVED ...CH AN ...SLAUGHT.

PROBLEM WAS, SHE WAS THINKING IN HUMAN TERMS--

--AND 'LOCK IS ANYTHING BUT.

HIS BODY IS COMPOSED OF THE PRIMAL SUBSTANCE OF A STAR; HE CAN DANCE THROUGH THE SPACE BETWEEN GALAXIES AS EASILY AS ANY OF US MIGHT STROLL ACROSS THE STREET.

...UTH TO TELL, WE HAVE ... REAL SENSE OF HIS ...PABILITIES, OR HIS LIMITS.

...E ONLY THING ... KNOW FOR ...RE IS THAT HE'S ...KID-- MUCH ...E HIS FRIENDS.

HE BELIEVES HIS BEST FRIEND IS DEAD, MURDERED BY THE SKULL. AND HE CONSIDERS THE SKULL'S NEWEST PROTÉGÉ RESPONSIBLE. TONIGHT HE PLANS TO EVEN THE SCORE.

THING IS, THAT PROTÉGÉ ALREADY HAS PROBLEMS ENOUGH OF HIS OWN.

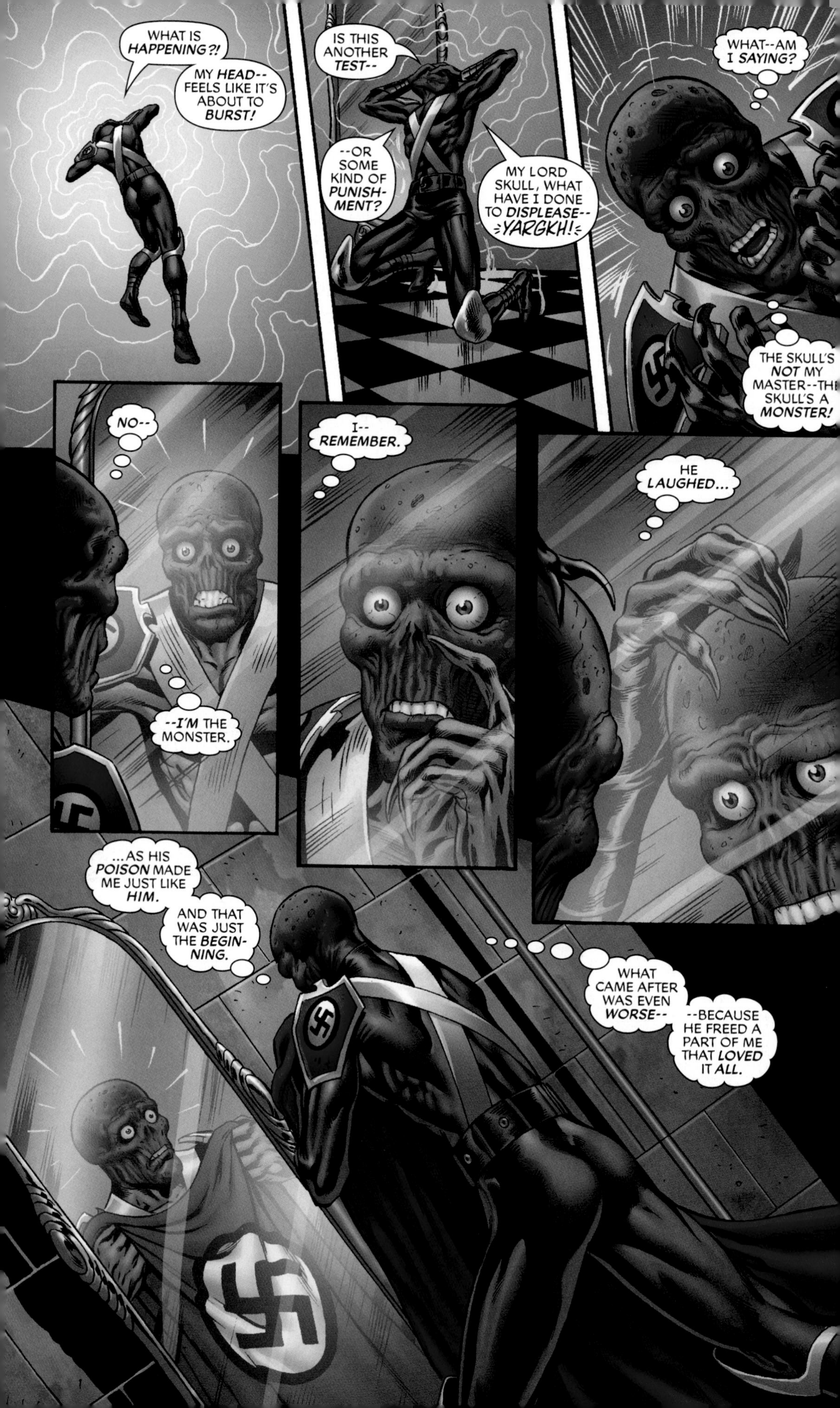
WHAT IS HAPPENING?!
MY HEAD-- FEELS LIKE IT'S ABOUT TO BURST!
IS THIS ANOTHER TEST--
--OR SOME KIND OF PUNISHMENT?
MY LORD SKULL, WHAT HAVE I DONE TO DISPLEASE-- YARGKH!
WHAT--AM I SAYING?
THE SKULL'S NOT MY MASTER--THE SKULL'S A MONSTER!
NO--
--I'M THE MONSTER.
I-- REMEMBER.
HE LAUGHED...
...AS HIS POISON MADE ME JUST LIKE HIM.
AND THAT WAS JUST THE BEGINNING.
WHAT CAME AFTER WAS EVEN WORSE--
--BECAUSE HE FREED A PART OF ME THAT LOVED IT ALL.

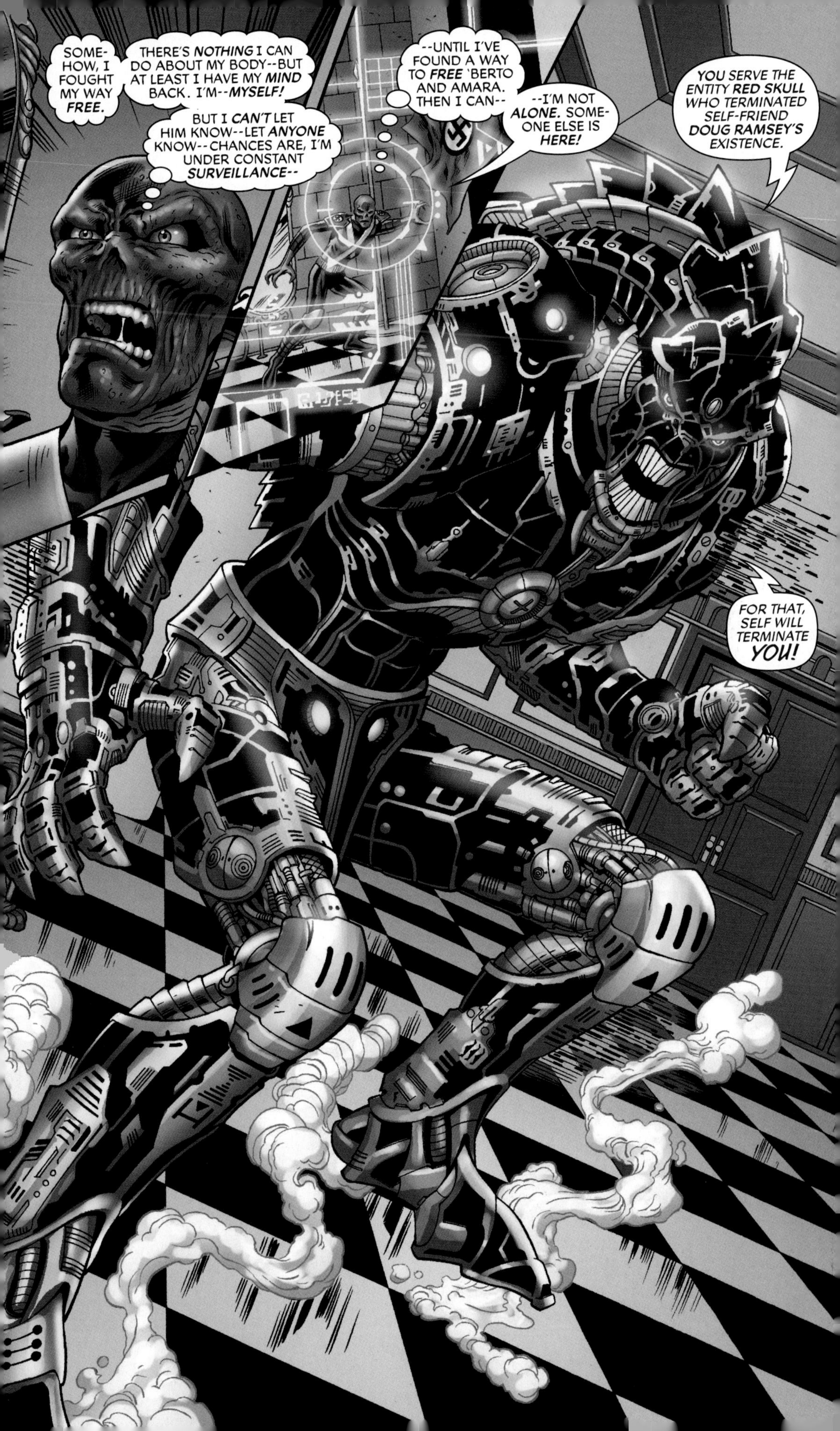
SOME-HOW, I FOUGHT MY WAY FREE.
THERE'S NOTHING I CAN DO ABOUT MY BODY--BUT AT LEAST I HAVE MY MIND BACK. I'M--MYSELF!
BUT I CAN'T LET HIM KNOW--LET ANYONE KNOW--CHANCES ARE, I'M UNDER CONSTANT SURVEILLANCE--
--UNTIL I'VE FOUND A WAY TO FREE 'BERTO AND AMARA. THEN I CAN--
--I'M NOT ALONE. SOME-ONE ELSE IS HERE!
YOU SERVE THE ENTITY RED SKULL WHO TERMINATED SELF-FRIEND DOUG RAMSEY'S EXISTENCE.
FOR THAT, SELF WILL TERMINATE YOU!

#4

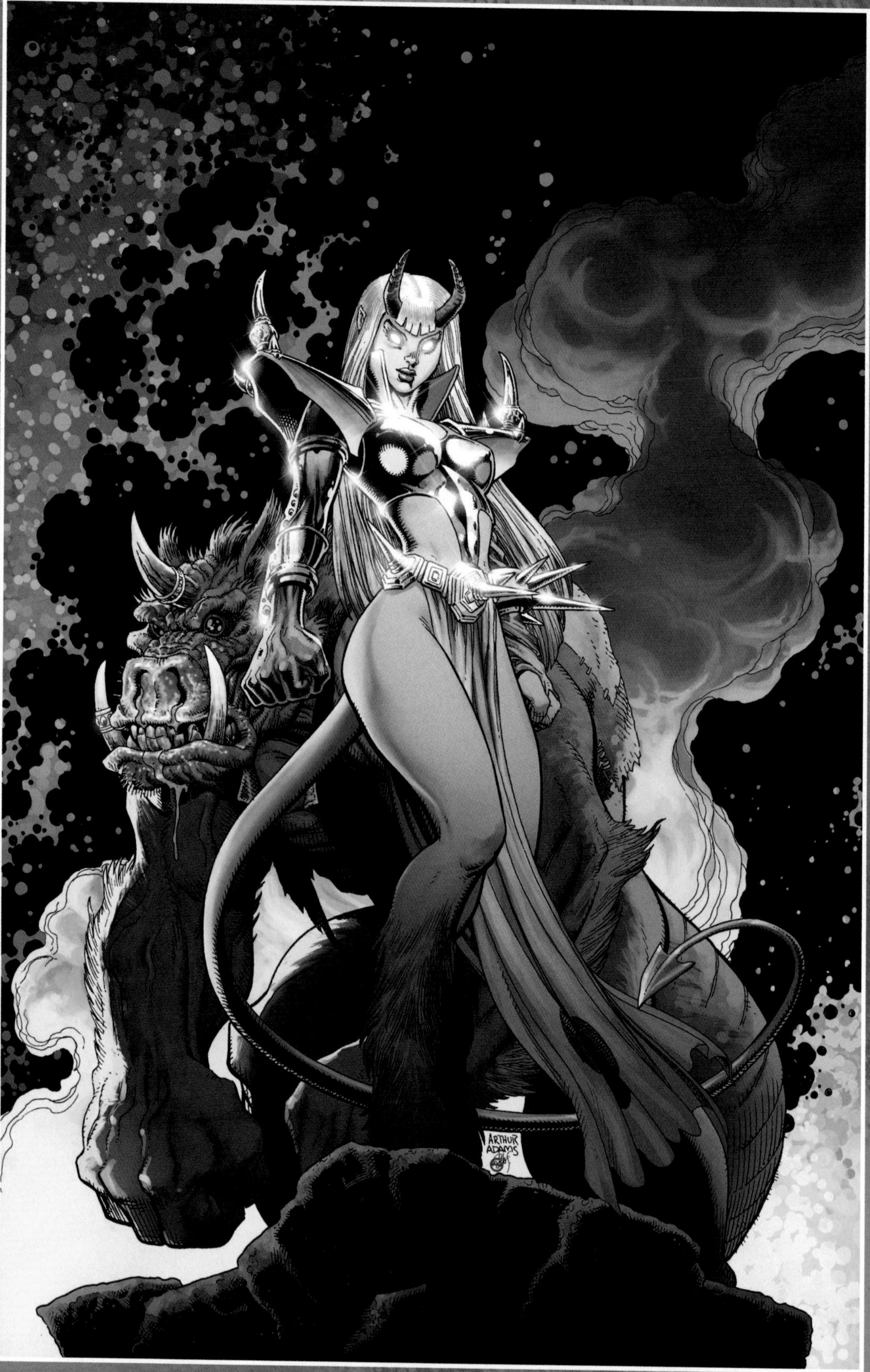
ARTHUR ADAMS

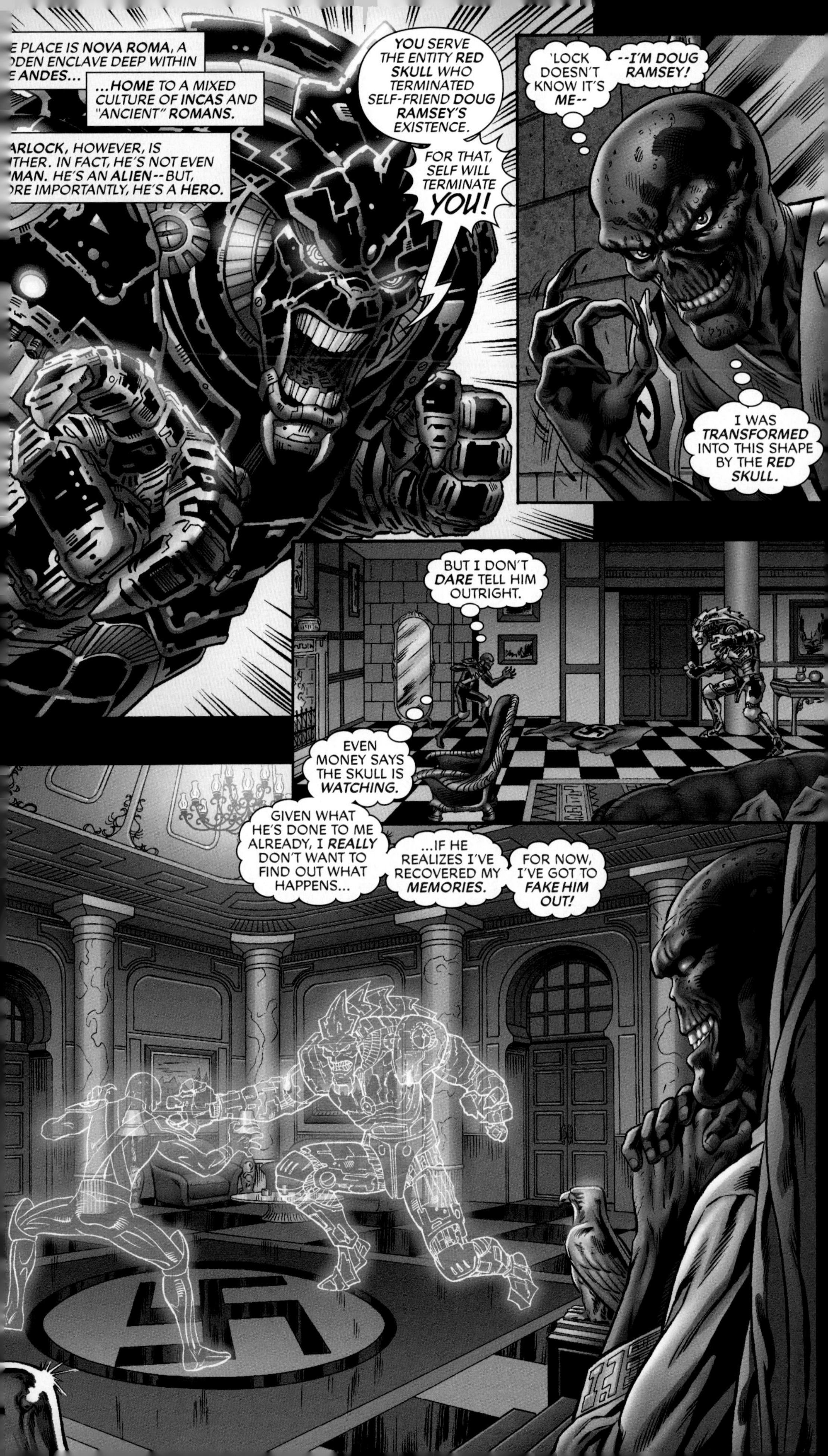

E PLACE IS NOVA ROMA, A
DDEN ENCLAVE DEEP WITHIN
E ANDES...
...HOME TO A MIXED CULTURE OF INCAS AND "ANCIENT" ROMANS.
ARLOCK, HOWEVER, IS
THER. IN FACT, HE'S NOT EVEN
MAN. HE'S AN ALIEN--BUT,
ORE IMPORTANTLY, HE'S A HERO.
YOU SERVE THE ENTITY RED SKULL WHO TERMINATED SELF-FRIEND DOUG RAMSEY'S EXISTENCE.
FOR THAT, SELF WILL TERMINATE YOU!
'LOCK DOESN'T KNOW IT'S ME--
--I'M DOUG RAMSEY!
I WAS TRANSFORMED INTO THIS SHAPE BY THE RED SKULL.
BUT I DON'T DARE TELL HIM OUTRIGHT.
EVEN MONEY SAYS THE SKULL IS WATCHING.
GIVEN WHAT HE'S DONE TO ME ALREADY, I REALLY DON'T WANT TO FIND OUT WHAT HAPPENS...
...IF HE REALIZES I'VE RECOVERED MY MEMORIES.
FOR NOW, I'VE GOT TO FAKE HIM OUT!

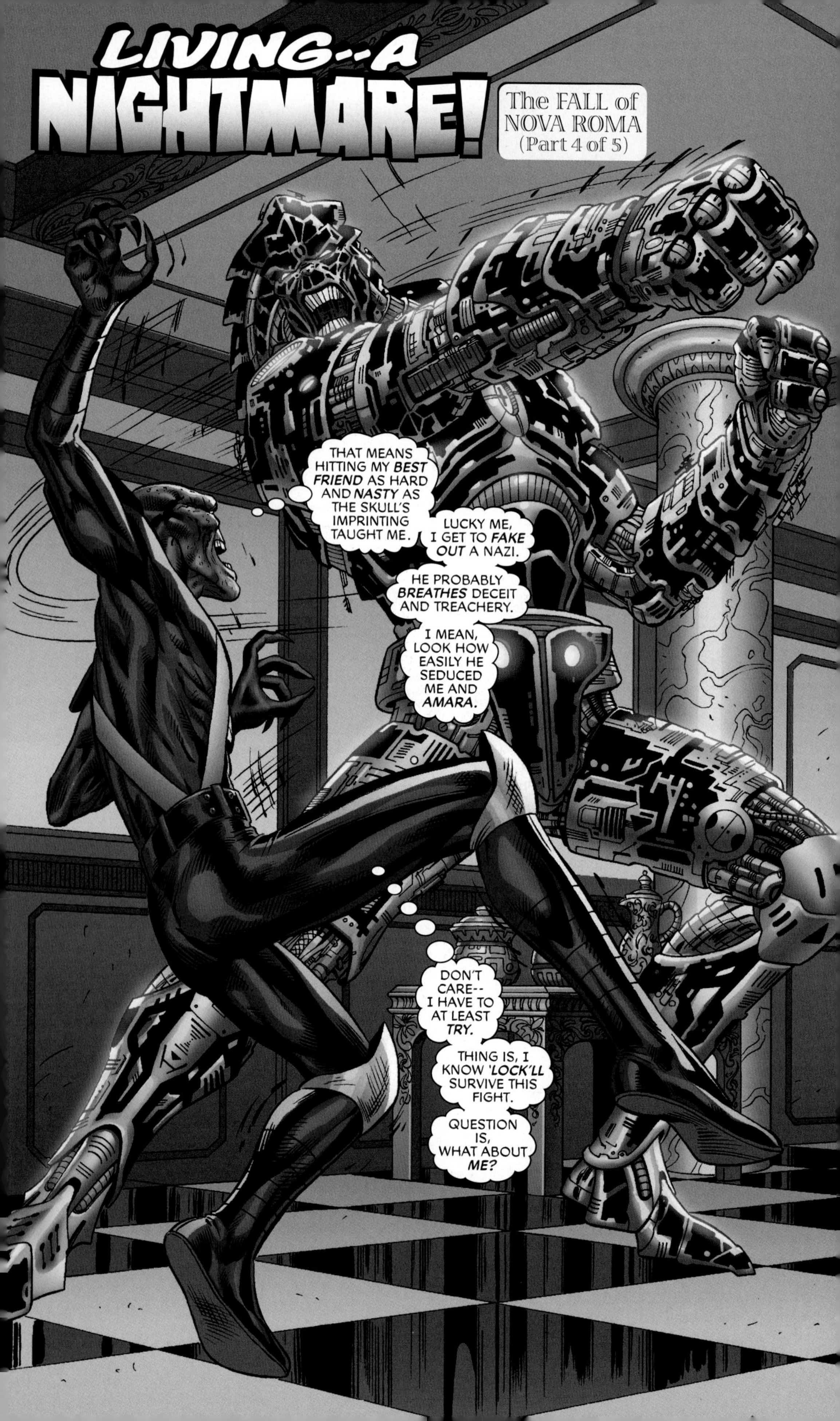

LIVING--A NIGHTMARE!
The FALL of NOVA ROMA (Part 4 of 5)
THAT MEANS HITTING MY BEST FRIEND AS HARD AND NASTY AS THE SKULL'S IMPRINTING TAUGHT ME.
LUCKY ME, I GET TO FAKE OUT A NAZI.
HE PROBABLY BREATHES DECEIT AND TREACHERY.
I MEAN, LOOK HOW EASILY HE SEDUCED ME AND AMARA.
DON'T CARE-- I HAVE TO AT LEAST TRY.
THING IS, I KNOW 'LOCK'LL SURVIVE THIS FIGHT.
QUESTION IS, WHAT ABOUT ME?

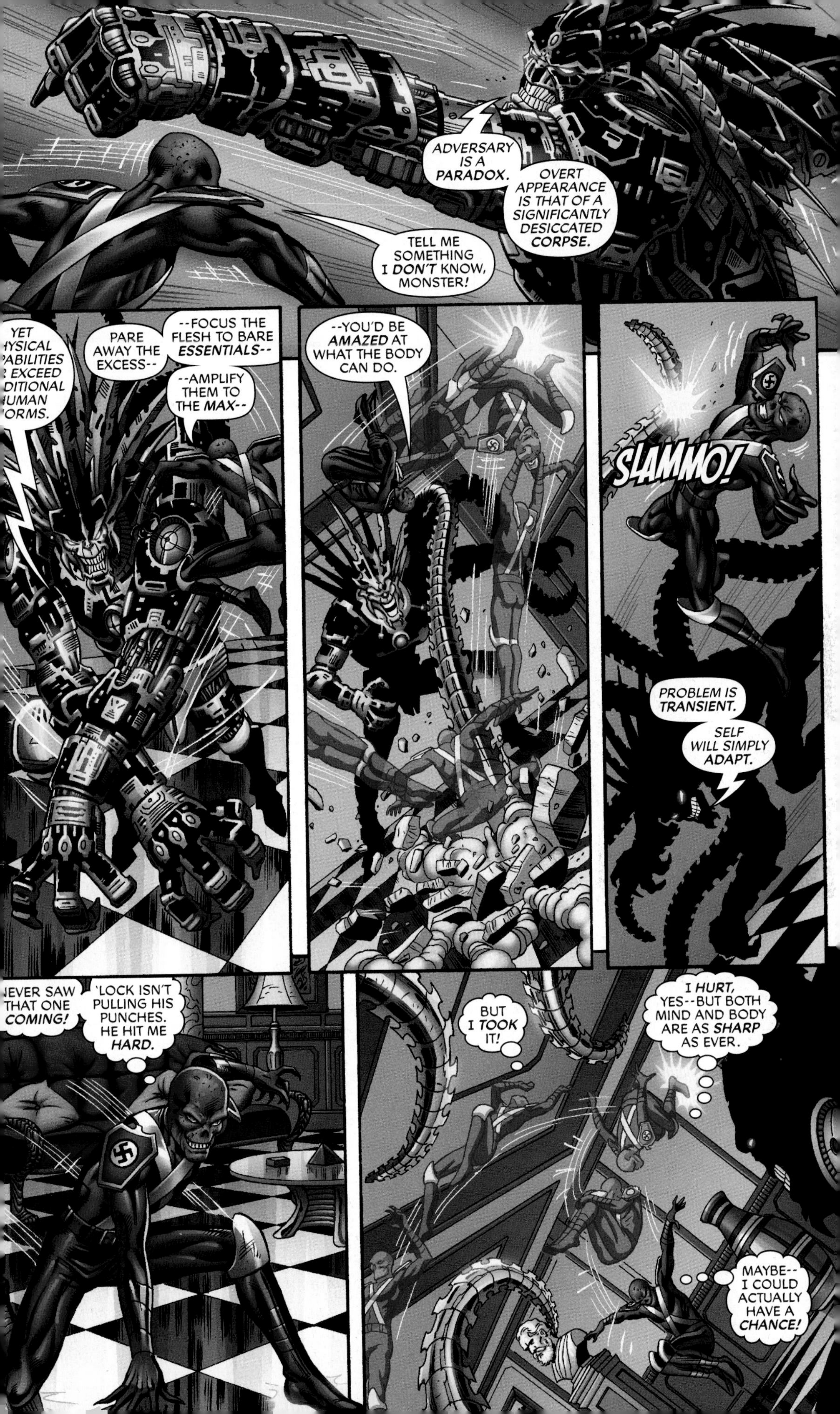
ADVERSARY IS A PARADOX.
OVERT APPEARANCE IS THAT OF A SIGNIFICANTLY DESICCATED CORPSE.
TELL ME SOMETHING I DON'T KNOW, MONSTER!
YET HYSICAL PABILITIES EXCEED DITIONAL HUMAN ORMS.
PARE AWAY THE EXCESS--
--FOCUS THE FLESH TO BARE ESSENTIALS--
--AMPLIFY THEM TO THE MAX--
--YOU'D BE AMAZED AT WHAT THE BODY CAN DO.
SLAMMO!
PROBLEM IS TRANSIENT.
SELF WILL SIMPLY ADAPT.
NEVER SAW THAT ONE COMING!
'LOCK ISN'T PULLING HIS PUNCHES. HE HIT ME HARD.
BUT I TOOK IT!
I HURT, YES--BUT BOTH MIND AND BODY ARE AS SHARP AS EVER.
MAYBE--I COULD ACTUALLY HAVE A CHANCE!

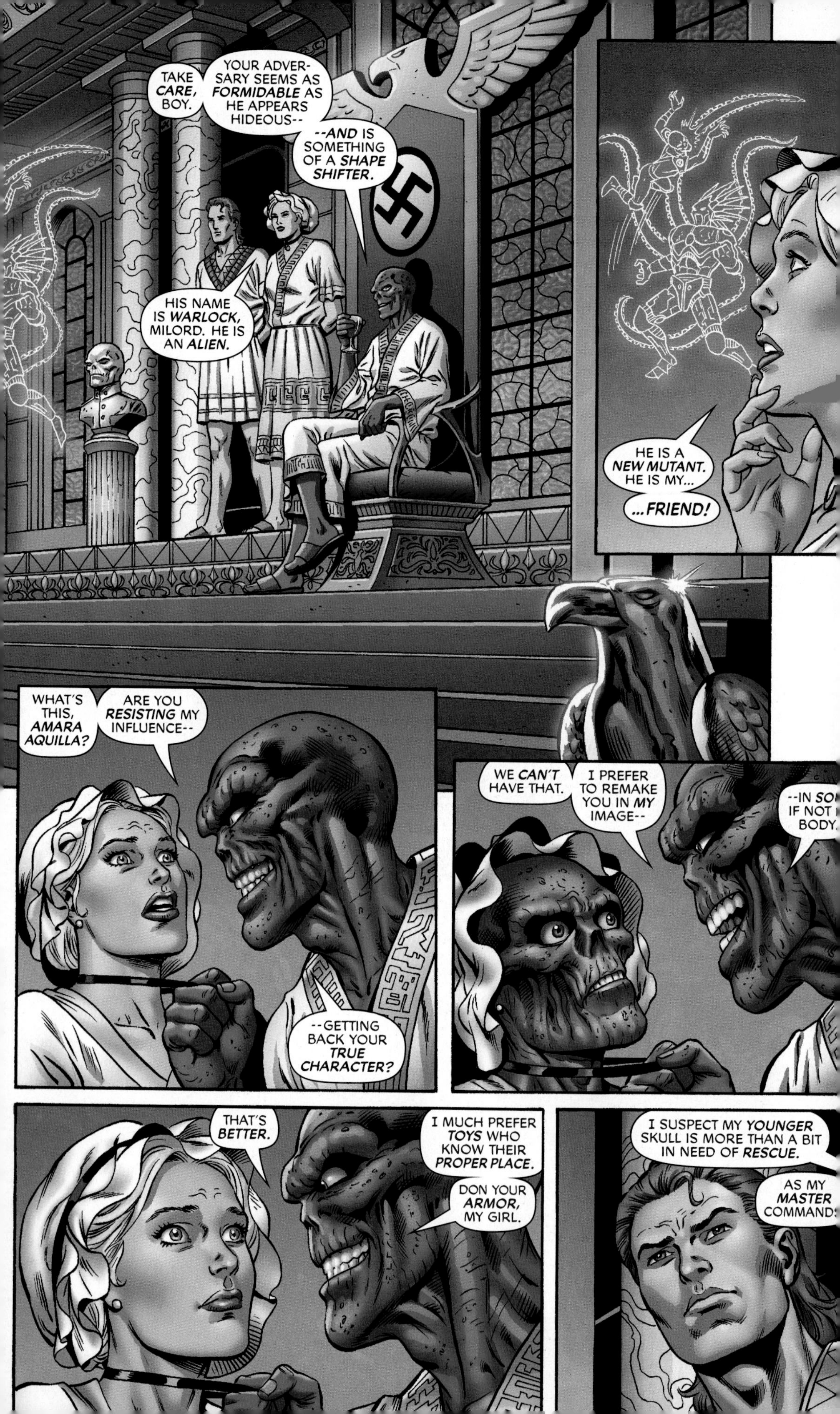

TAKE CARE, BOY.
YOUR ADVERSARY SEEMS AS FORMIDABLE AS HE APPEARS HIDEOUS--
--AND IS SOMETHING OF A SHAPE SHIFTER.
HIS NAME IS WARLOCK, MILORD. HE IS AN ALIEN.
HE IS A NEW MUTANT. HE IS MY...
...FRIEND!
WHAT'S THIS, AMARA AQUILLA?
ARE YOU RESISTING MY INFLUENCE--
--GETTING BACK YOUR TRUE CHARACTER?
WE CAN'T HAVE THAT.
I PREFER TO REMAKE YOU IN MY IMAGE--
THAT'S BETTER.
I MUCH PREFER TOYS WHO KNOW THEIR PROPER PLACE.
DON YOUR ARMOR, MY GIRL.
I SUSPECT MY YOUNGER SKULL IS MORE THAN A BIT IN NEED OF RESCUE.

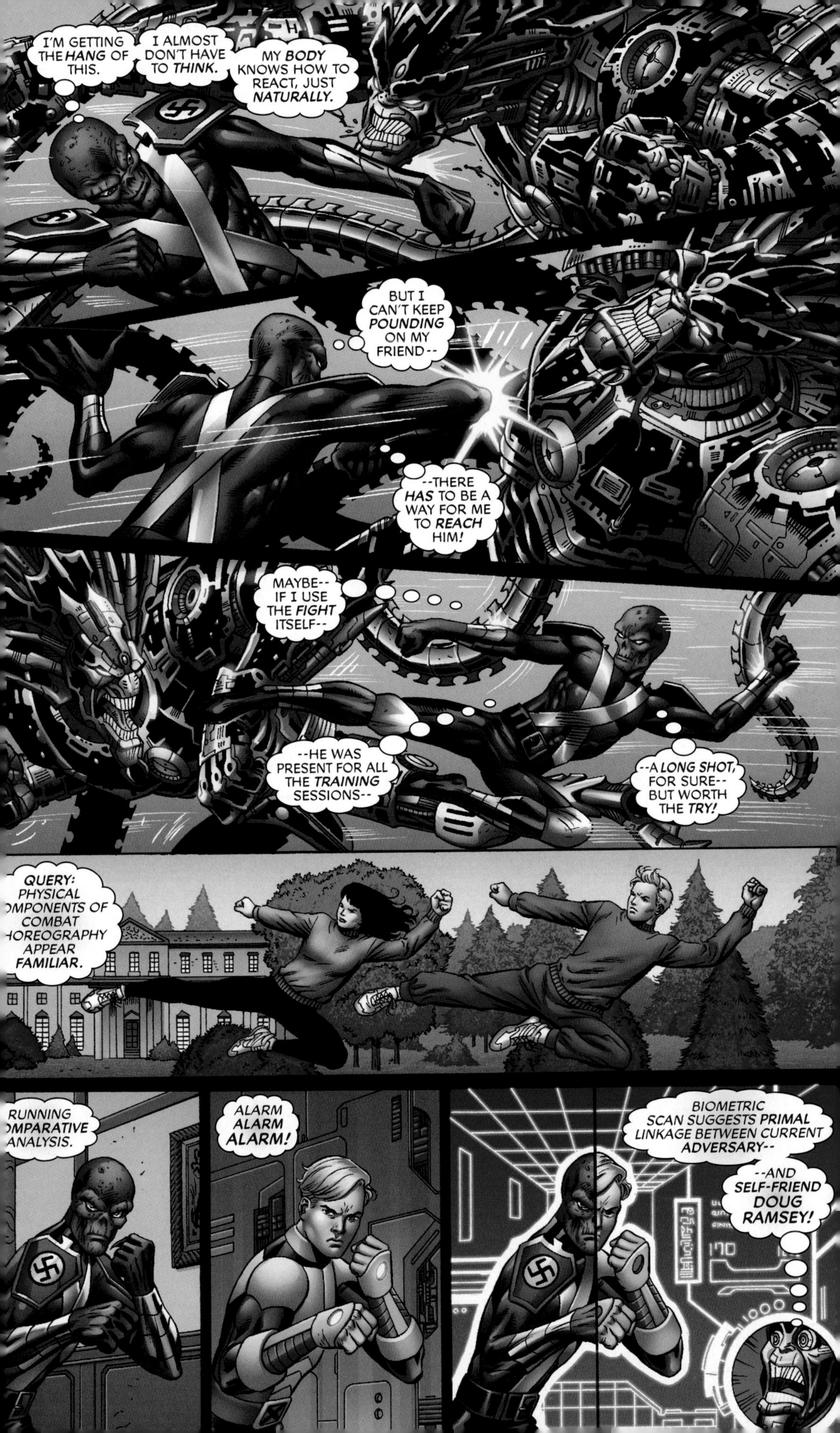
I'M GETTING THE HANG OF THIS.
I ALMOST DON'T HAVE TO THINK.
MY BODY KNOWS HOW TO REACT, JUST NATURALLY.
BUT I CAN'T KEEP POUNDING ON MY FRIEND--
--THERE HAS TO BE A WAY FOR ME TO REACH HIM!
MAYBE-- IF I USE THE FIGHT ITSELF--
--HE WAS PRESENT FOR ALL THE TRAINING SESSIONS--
--A LONG SHOT, FOR SURE-- BUT WORTH THE TRY!
QUERY: PHYSICAL OMPONENTS OF COMBAT HOREOGRAPHY APPEAR FAMILIAR.
RUNNING OMPARATIVE ANALYSIS.
ALARM ALARM ALARM!
BIOMETRIC SCAN SUGGESTS PRIMAL LINKAGE BETWEEN CURRENT ADVERSARY--
--AND SELF-FRIEND DOUG RAMSEY!

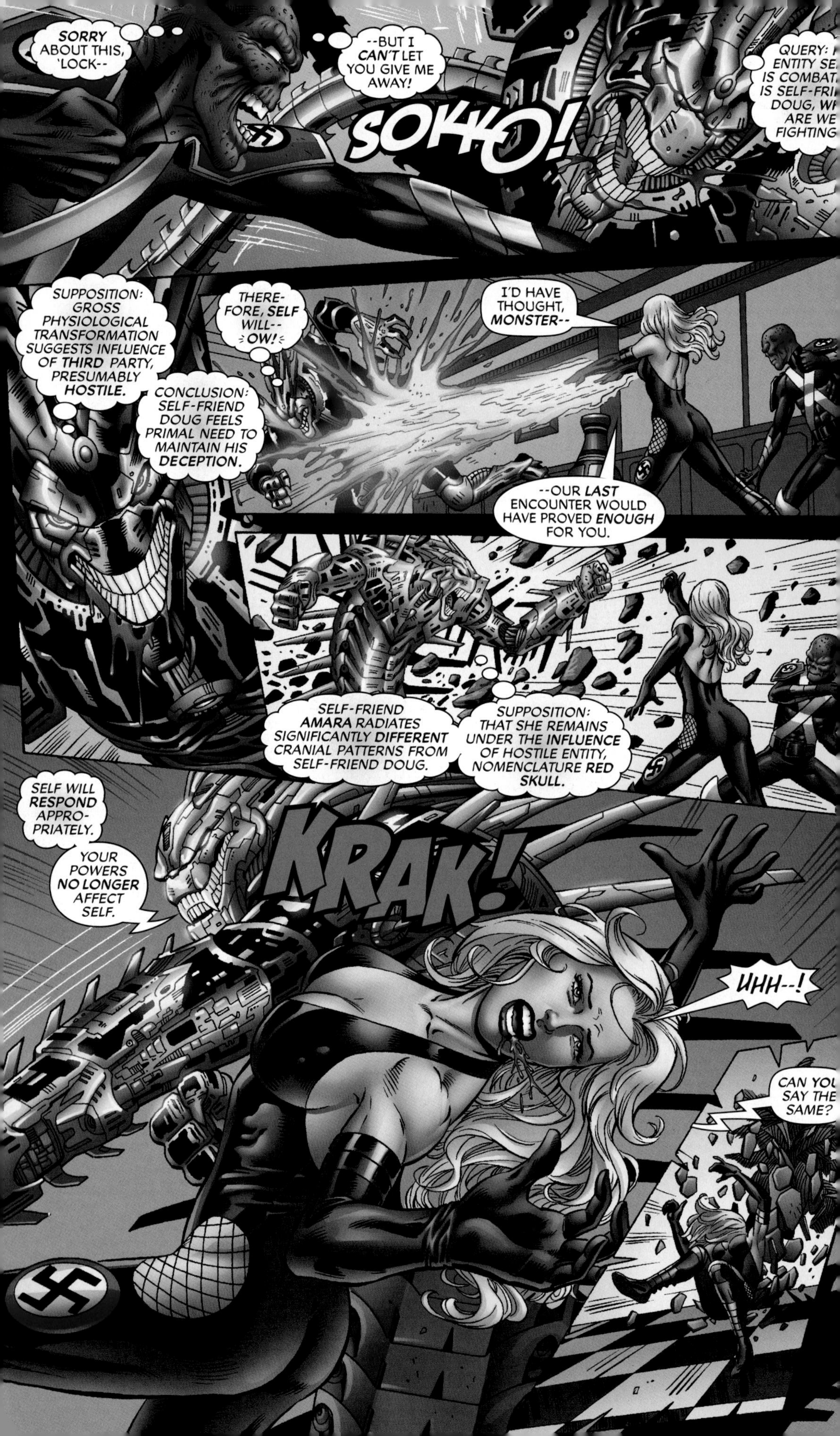
SORRY ABOUT THIS, 'LOCK--
--BUT I CAN'T LET YOU GIVE ME AWAY!
SOKKO!
QUERY: IF ENTITY SE... IS COMBAT... IS SELF-FRI... DOUG, WH... ARE WE FIGHTING
SUPPOSITION: GROSS PHYSIOLOGICAL TRANSFORMATION SUGGESTS INFLUENCE OF THIRD PARTY, PRESUMABLY HOSTILE.
THERE-FORE, SELF WILL-- OW!
I'D HAVE THOUGHT, MONSTER--
CONCLUSION: SELF-FRIEND DOUG FEELS PRIMAL NEED TO MAINTAIN HIS DECEPTION.
--OUR LAST ENCOUNTER WOULD HAVE PROVED ENOUGH FOR YOU.
SELF-FRIEND AMARA RADIATES SIGNIFICANTLY DIFFERENT CRANIAL PATTERNS FROM SELF-FRIEND DOUG.
SUPPOSITION: THAT SHE REMAINS UNDER THE INFLUENCE OF HOSTILE ENTITY, NOMENCLATURE RED SKULL.
SELF WILL RESPOND APPRO-PRIATELY.
YOUR POWERS NO LONGER AFFECT SELF.
KRAK!
UHH--!
CAN YOU SAY THE SAME?

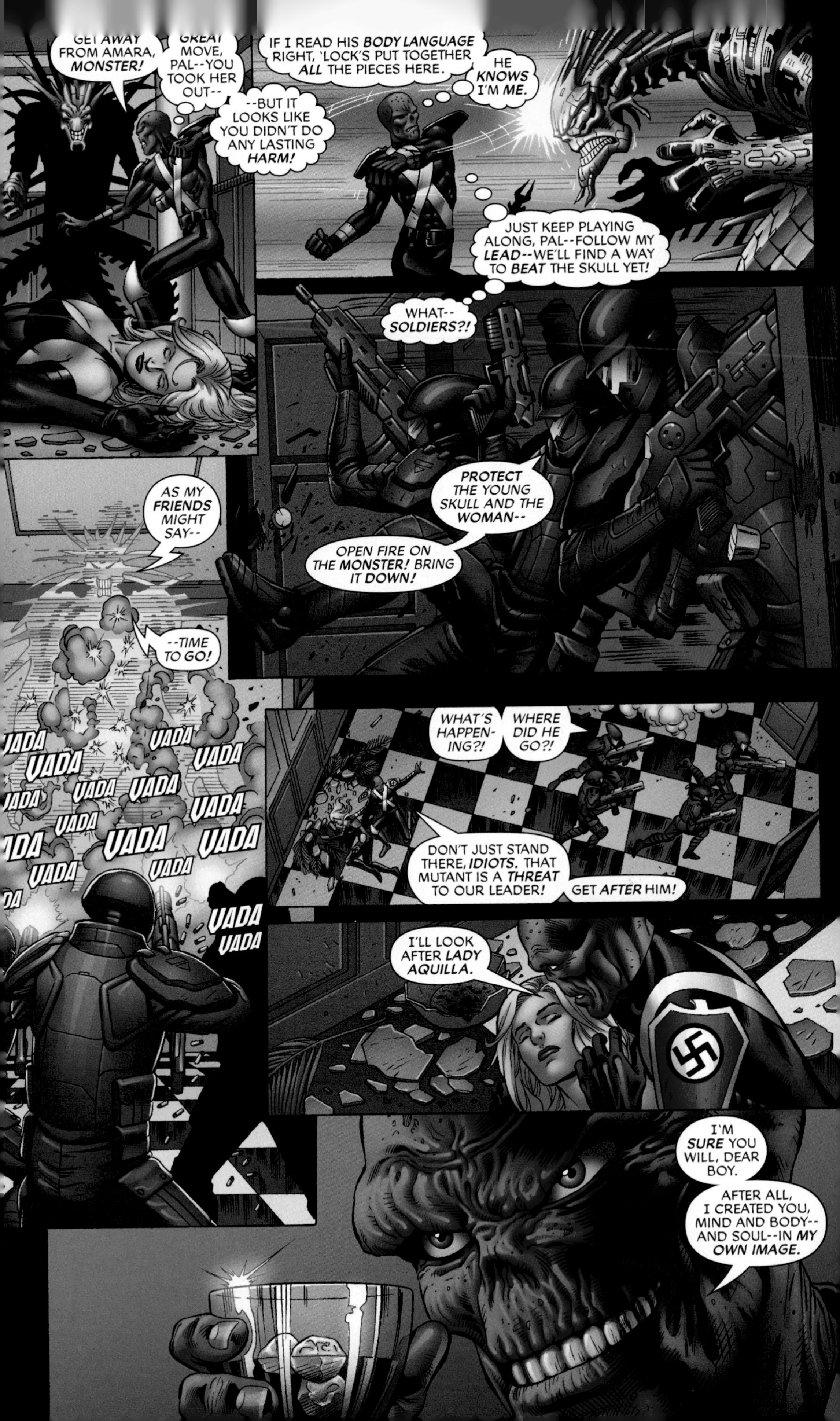
GET AWAY FROM AMARA, MONSTER!
GREAT MOVE, PAL--YOU TOOK HER OUT--
--BUT IT LOOKS LIKE YOU DIDN'T DO ANY LASTING HARM!
IF I READ HIS BODY LANGUAGE RIGHT, 'LOCK'S PUT TOGETHER ALL THE PIECES HERE.
HE KNOWS I'M ME.
JUST KEEP PLAYING ALONG, PAL--FOLLOW MY LEAD--WE'LL FIND A WAY TO BEAT THE SKULL YET!
WHAT--SOLDIERS?!
PROTECT THE YOUNG SKULL AND THE WOMAN--
OPEN FIRE ON THE MONSTER! BRING IT DOWN!
AS MY FRIENDS MIGHT SAY--
--TIME TO GO!
VADA VADA VADA VADA VADA VADA VADA VADA VADA VADA VADA VADA VADA VADA VADA VADA
WHAT'S HAPPEN-ING?!
WHERE DID HE GO?!
DON'T JUST STAND THERE, IDIOTS. THAT MUTANT IS A THREAT TO OUR LEADER!
GET AFTER HIM!
I'LL LOOK AFTER LADY AQUILLA.
I'M SURE YOU WILL, DEAR BOY.
AFTER ALL, I CREATED YOU, MIND AND BODY--AND SOUL--IN MY OWN IMAGE.

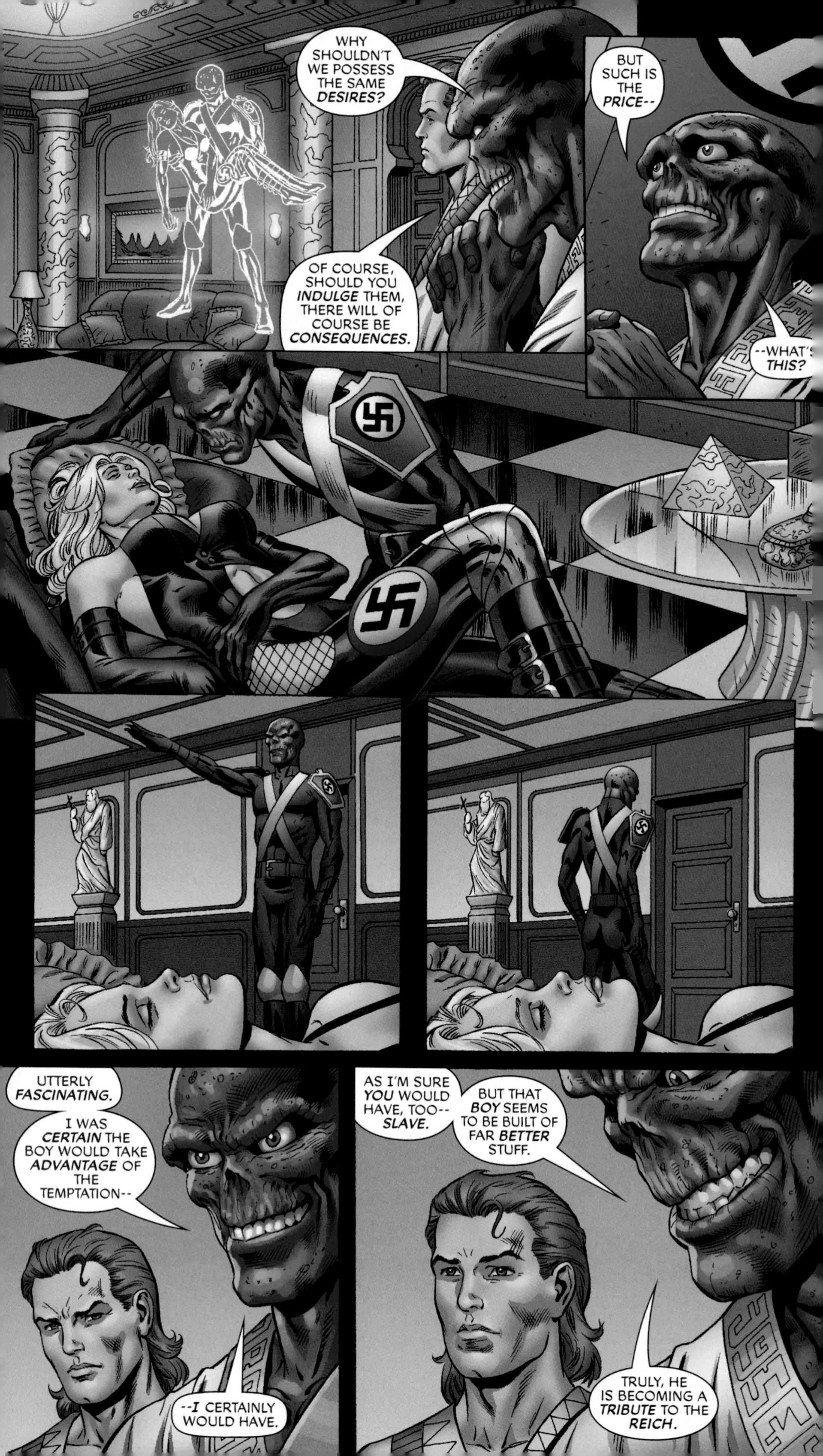
WHY SHOULDN'T WE POSSESS THE SAME DESIRES?
OF COURSE, SHOULD YOU INDULGE THEM, THERE WILL OF COURSE BE CONSEQUENCES.
BUT SUCH IS THE PRICE--
--WHAT'S THIS?
UTTERLY FASCINATING.
I WAS CERTAIN THE BOY WOULD TAKE ADVANTAGE OF THE TEMPTATION--
--I CERTAINLY WOULD HAVE.
AS I'M SURE YOU WOULD HAVE, TOO-- SLAVE.
BUT THAT BOY SEEMS TO BE BUILT OF FAR BETTER STUFF.
TRULY, HE IS BECOMING A TRIBUTE TO THE REICH.

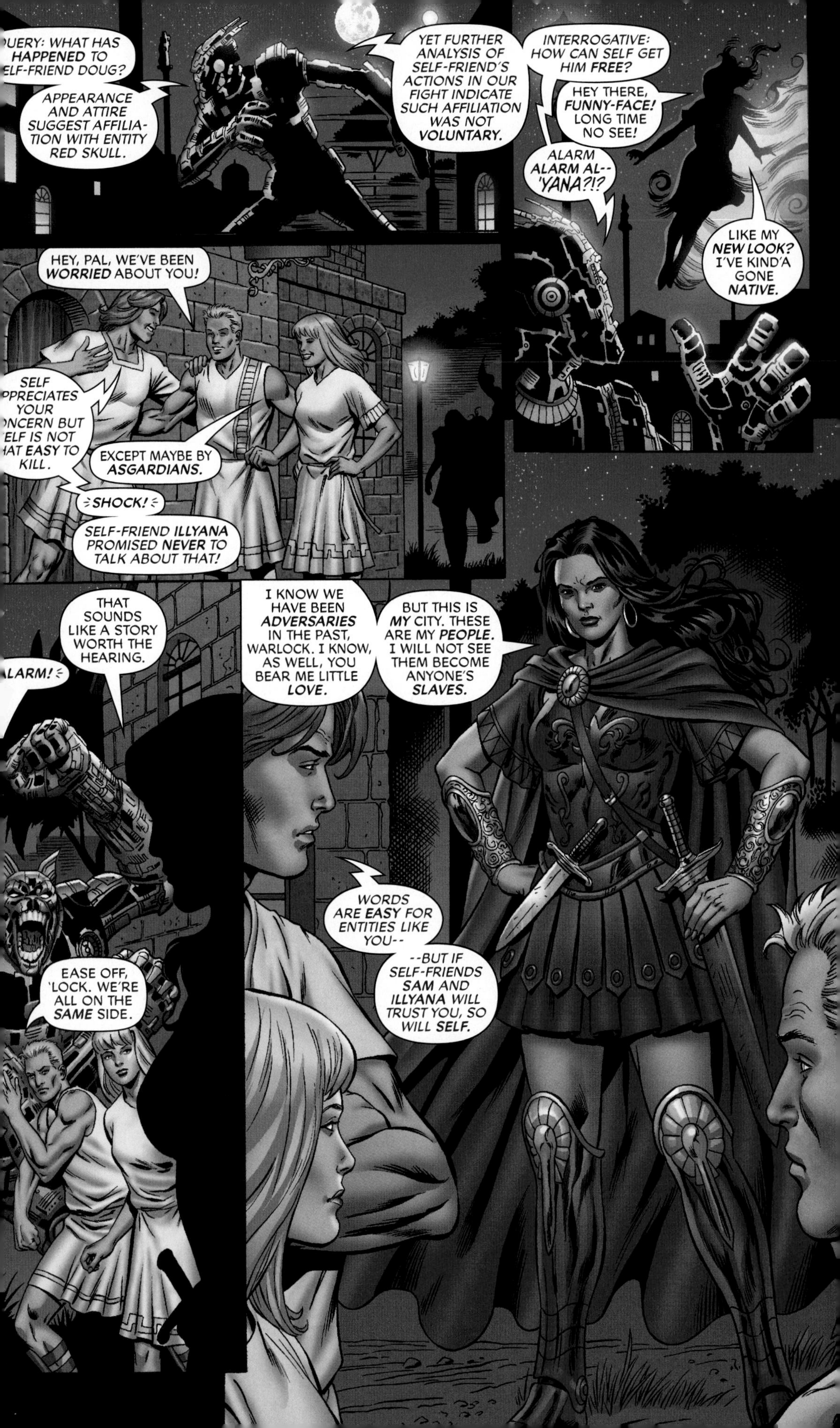
UERY: WHAT HAS HAPPENED TO ELF-FRIEND DOUG?
APPEARANCE AND ATTIRE SUGGEST AFFILIATION WITH ENTITY RED SKULL.
YET FURTHER ANALYSIS OF SELF-FRIEND'S ACTIONS IN OUR FIGHT INDICATE SUCH AFFILIATION WAS NOT VOLUNTARY.
INTERROGATIVE: HOW CAN SELF GET HIM FREE?
HEY THERE, FUNNY-FACE! LONG TIME NO SEE!
ALARM ALARM AL-- 'YANA?!?
LIKE MY NEW LOOK? I'VE KIND'A GONE NATIVE.
HEY, PAL, WE'VE BEEN WORRIED ABOUT YOU!
SELF PPRECIATES YOUR ONCERN BUT ELF IS NOT HAT EASY TO KILL.
EXCEPT MAYBE BY ASGARDIANS.
SHOCK!
SELF-FRIEND ILLYANA PROMISED NEVER TO TALK ABOUT THAT!
THAT SOUNDS LIKE A STORY WORTH THE HEARING.
LARM!
I KNOW WE HAVE BEEN ADVERSARIES IN THE PAST, WARLOCK. I KNOW, AS WELL, YOU BEAR ME LITTLE LOVE.
BUT THIS IS MY CITY. THESE ARE MY PEOPLE. I WILL NOT SEE THEM BECOME ANYONE'S SLAVES.
WORDS ARE EASY FOR ENTITIES LIKE YOU--
--BUT IF SELF-FRIENDS SAM AND ILLYANA WILL TRUST YOU, SO WILL SELF.
EASE OFF, 'LOCK. WE'RE ALL ON THE SAME SIDE.

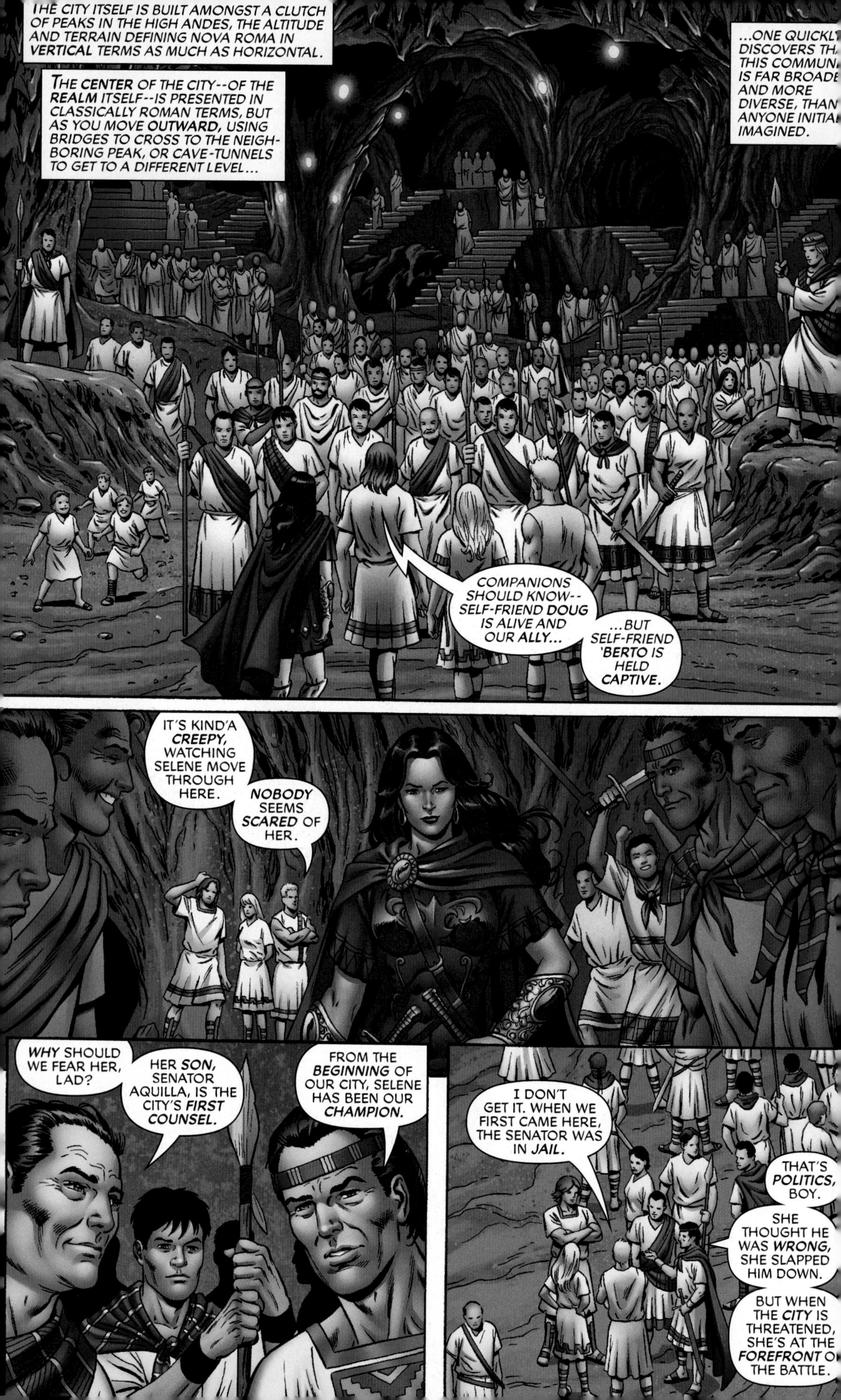
THE CITY ITSELF IS BUILT AMONGST A CLUTCH OF PEAKS IN THE HIGH ANDES, THE ALTITUDE AND TERRAIN DEFINING NOVA ROMA IN VERTICAL TERMS AS MUCH AS HORIZONTAL.
THE CENTER OF THE CITY--OF THE REALM ITSELF--IS PRESENTED IN CLASSICALLY ROMAN TERMS, BUT AS YOU MOVE OUTWARD, USING BRIDGES TO CROSS TO THE NEIGHBORING PEAK, OR CAVE-TUNNELS TO GET TO A DIFFERENT LEVEL...
...ONE QUICKLY DISCOVERS THA THIS COMMUNI IS FAR BROADE AND MORE DIVERSE, THAN ANYONE INITIA IMAGINED.
COMPANIONS SHOULD KNOW--SELF-FRIEND DOUG IS ALIVE AND OUR ALLY...
...BUT SELF-FRIEND 'BERTO IS HELD CAPTIVE.
IT'S KIND'A CREEPY, WATCHING SELENE MOVE THROUGH HERE.
NOBODY SEEMS SCARED OF HER.
WHY SHOULD WE FEAR HER, LAD?
HER SON, SENATOR AQUILLA, IS THE CITY'S FIRST COUNSEL.
FROM THE BEGINNING OF OUR CITY, SELENE HAS BEEN OUR CHAMPION.
I DON'T GET IT. WHEN WE FIRST CAME HERE, THE SENATOR WAS IN JAIL.
THAT'S POLITICS, BOY.
SHE THOUGHT HE WAS WRONG, SHE SLAPPED HIM DOWN.
BUT WHEN THE CITY IS THREATENED, SHE'S AT THE FOREFRONT O THE BATTLE.

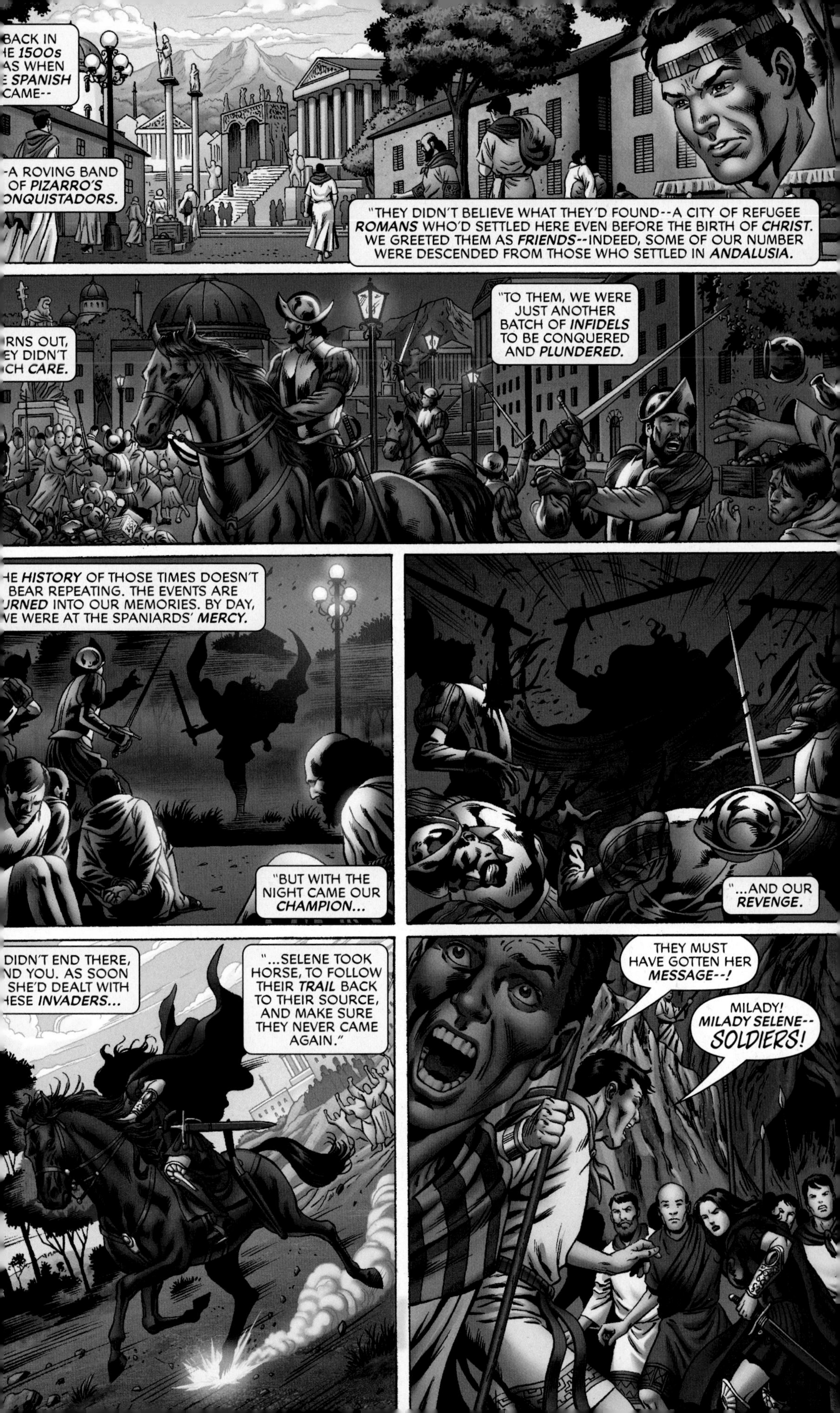

BACK IN
HE 1500s
AS WHEN
SPANISH
CAME--
-A ROVING BAND
OF PIZARRO'S
ONQUISTADORS.
"THEY DIDN'T BELIEVE WHAT THEY'D FOUND--A CITY OF REFUGEE ROMANS WHO'D SETTLED HERE EVEN BEFORE THE BIRTH OF CHRIST. WE GREETED THEM AS FRIENDS--INDEED, SOME OF OUR NUMBER WERE DESCENDED FROM THOSE WHO SETTLED IN ANDALUSIA.
RNS OUT,
EY DIDN'T
CH CARE.
"TO THEM, WE WERE JUST ANOTHER BATCH OF INFIDELS TO BE CONQUERED AND PLUNDERED.
HE HISTORY OF THOSE TIMES DOESN'T BEAR REPEATING. THE EVENTS ARE URNED INTO OUR MEMORIES. BY DAY, VE WERE AT THE SPANIARDS' MERCY.
"BUT WITH THE NIGHT CAME OUR CHAMPION...
"...AND OUR REVENGE.
DIDN'T END THERE, ND YOU. AS SOON SHE'D DEALT WITH HESE INVADERS...
"...SELENE TOOK HORSE, TO FOLLOW THEIR TRAIL BACK TO THEIR SOURCE, AND MAKE SURE THEY NEVER CAME AGAIN."
THEY MUST HAVE GOTTEN HER MESSAGE--!
MILADY! MILADY SELENE-- SOLDIERS!

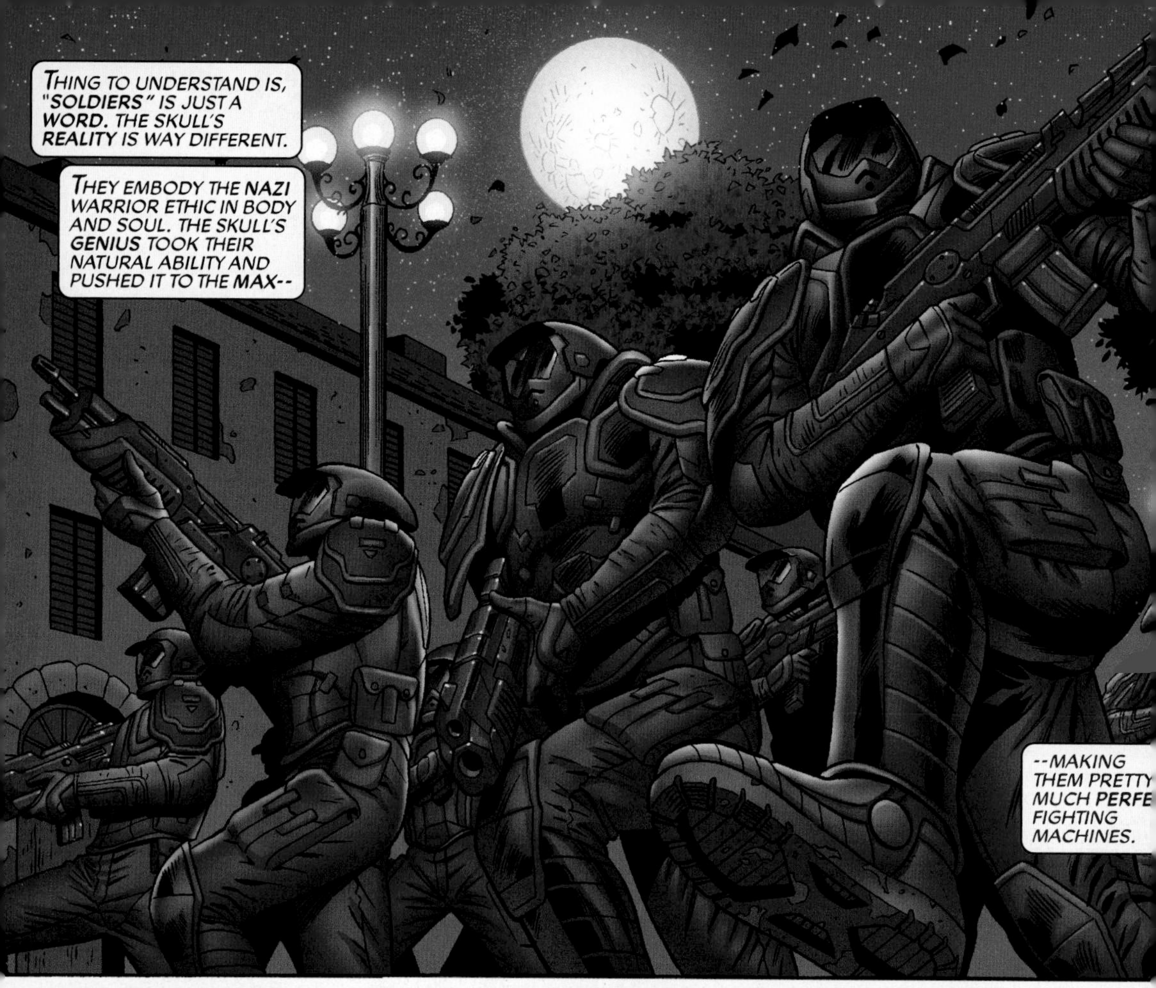
THING TO UNDERSTAND IS, "SOLDIERS" IS JUST A WORD. THE SKULL'S REALITY IS WAY DIFFERENT.
THEY EMBODY THE NAZI WARRIOR ETHIC IN BODY AND SOUL. THE SKULL'S GENIUS TOOK THEIR NATURAL ABILITY AND PUSHED IT TO THE MAX--
--MAKING THEM PRETTY MUCH PERFE FIGHTING MACHINES.

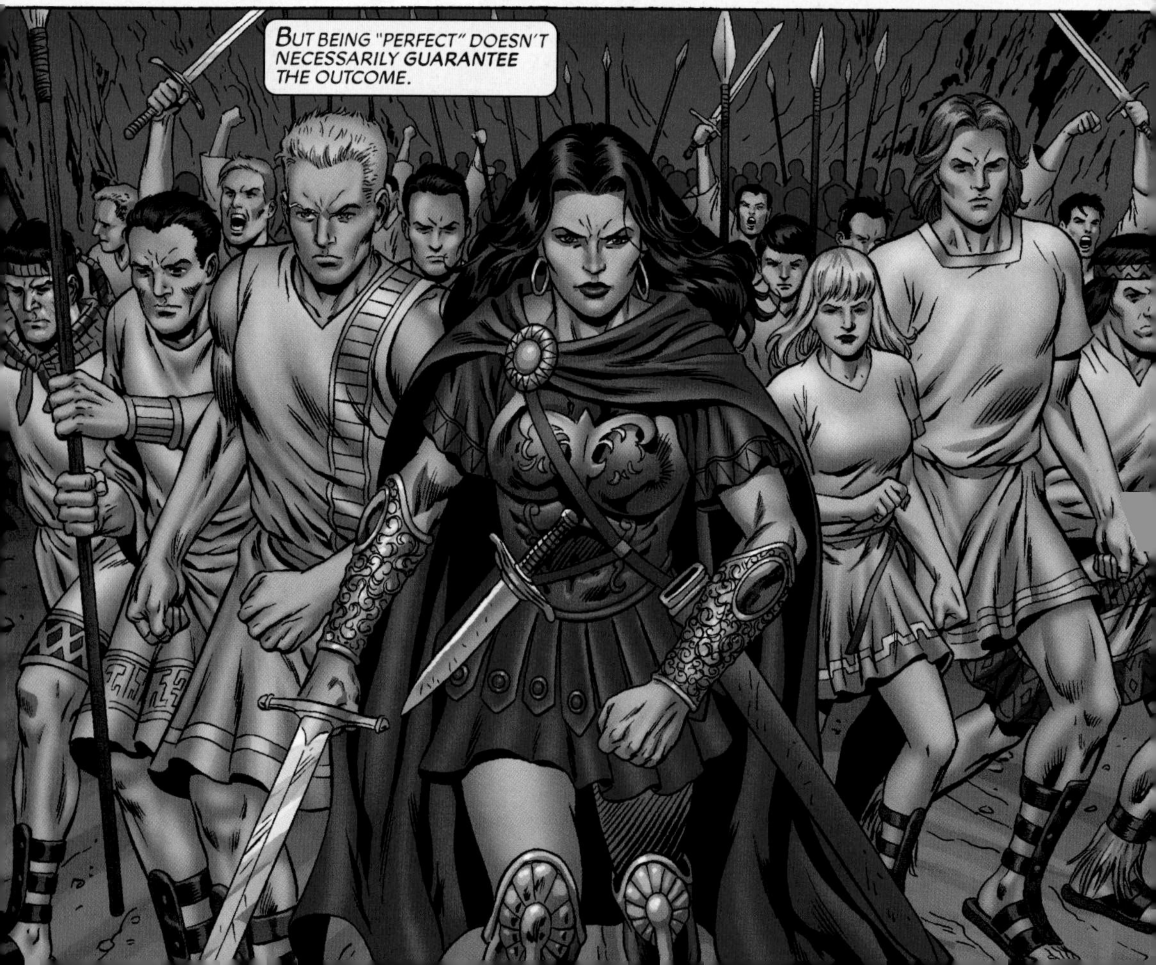
BUT BEING "PERFECT" DOESN'T NECESSARILY GUARANTEE THE OUTCOME.

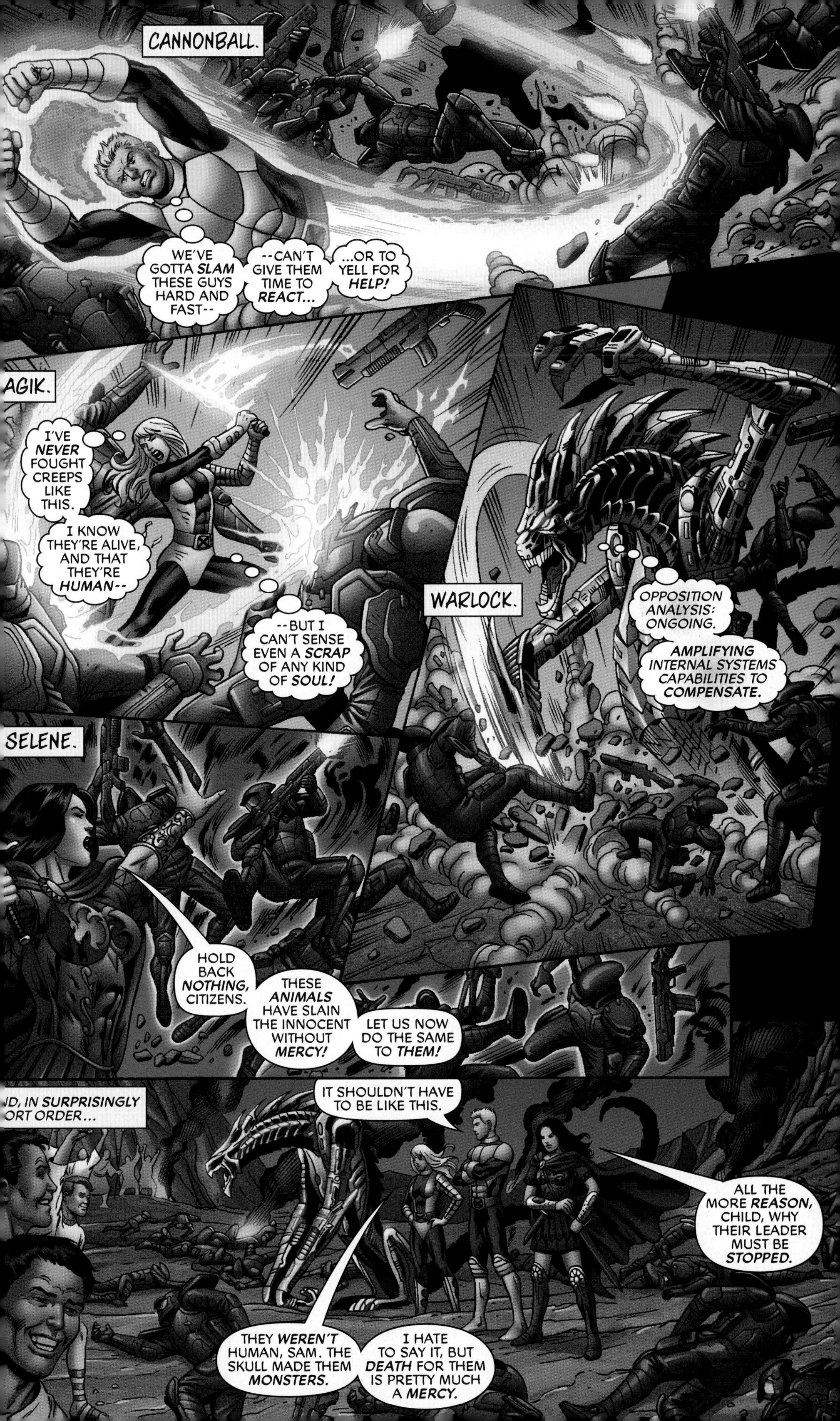
CANNONBALL.
WE'VE GOTTA SLAM THESE GUYS HARD AND FAST--
--CAN'T GIVE THEM TIME TO REACT...
...OR TO YELL FOR HELP!
AGIK.
I'VE NEVER FOUGHT CREEPS LIKE THIS.
I KNOW THEY'RE ALIVE, AND THAT THEY'RE HUMAN--
--BUT I CAN'T SENSE EVEN A SCRAP OF ANY KIND OF SOUL!
WARLOCK.
OPPOSITION ANALYSIS: ONGOING.
AMPLIFYING INTERNAL SYSTEMS CAPABILITIES TO COMPENSATE.
SELENE.
HOLD BACK NOTHING, CITIZENS.
THESE ANIMALS HAVE SLAIN THE INNOCENT WITHOUT MERCY!
LET US NOW DO THE SAME TO THEM!
D, IN SURPRISINGLY ORT ORDER...
IT SHOULDN'T HAVE TO BE LIKE THIS.
ALL THE MORE REASON, CHILD, WHY THEIR LEADER MUST BE STOPPED.
THEY WEREN'T HUMAN, SAM. THE SKULL MADE THEM MONSTERS.
I HATE TO SAY IT, BUT DEATH FOR THEM IS PRETTY MUCH A MERCY.

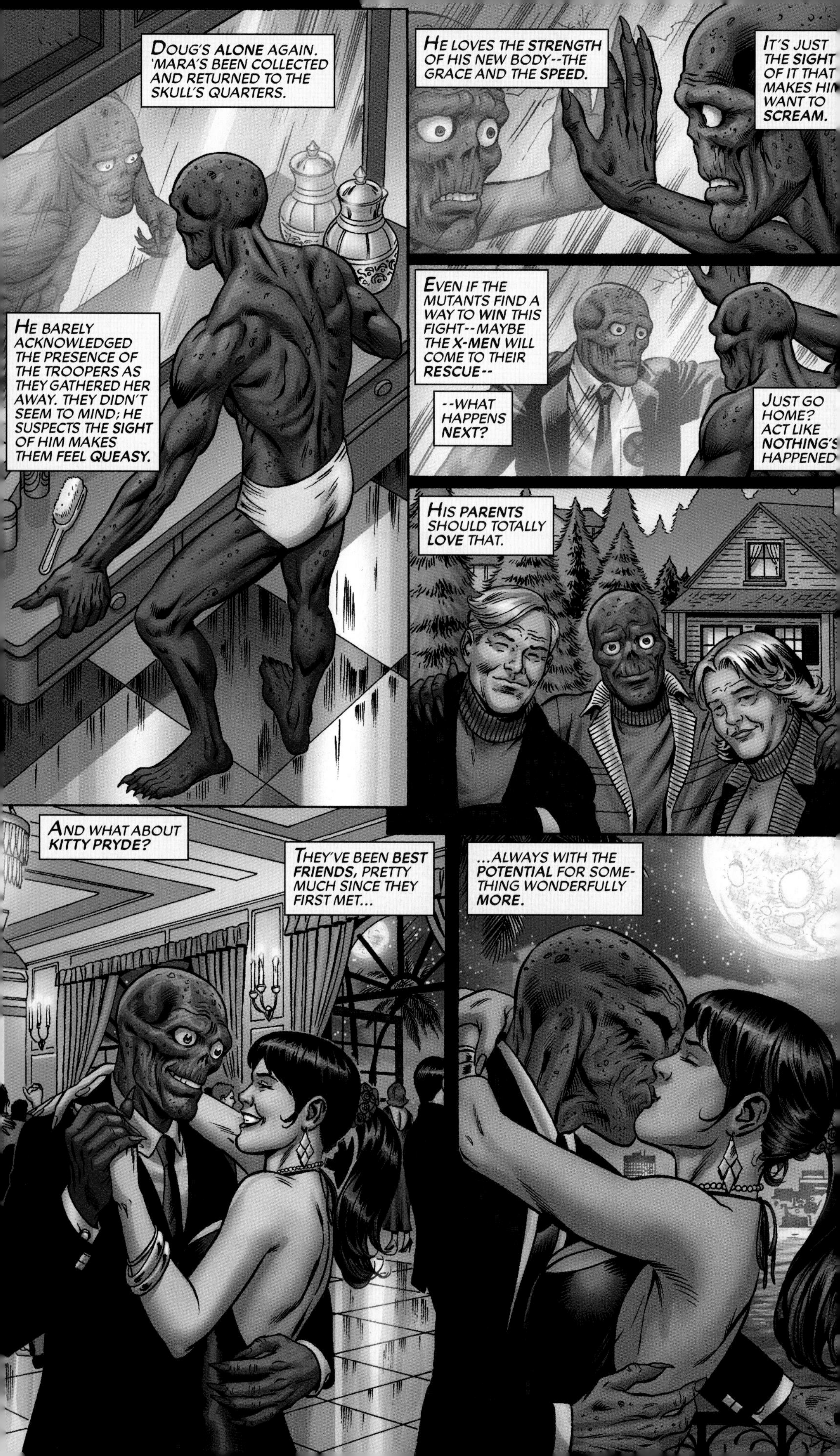
DOUG'S ALONE AGAIN. 'MARA'S BEEN COLLECTED AND RETURNED TO THE SKULL'S QUARTERS.
HE BARELY ACKNOWLEDGED THE PRESENCE OF THE TROOPERS AS THEY GATHERED HER AWAY. THEY DIDN'T SEEM TO MIND; HE SUSPECTS THE SIGHT OF HIM MAKES THEM FEEL QUEASY.
HE LOVES THE STRENGTH OF HIS NEW BODY--THE GRACE AND THE SPEED.
IT'S JUST THE SIGHT OF IT THAT MAKES HIM WANT TO SCREAM.
EVEN IF THE MUTANTS FIND A WAY TO WIN THIS FIGHT--MAYBE THE X-MEN WILL COME TO THEIR RESCUE--
--WHAT HAPPENS NEXT?
JUST GO HOME? ACT LIKE NOTHING'S HAPPENED
HIS PARENTS SHOULD TOTALLY LOVE THAT.
AND WHAT ABOUT KITTY PRYDE?
THEY'VE BEEN BEST FRIENDS, PRETTY MUCH SINCE THEY FIRST MET...
...ALWAYS WITH THE POTENTIAL FOR SOME-THING WONDERFULLY MORE.

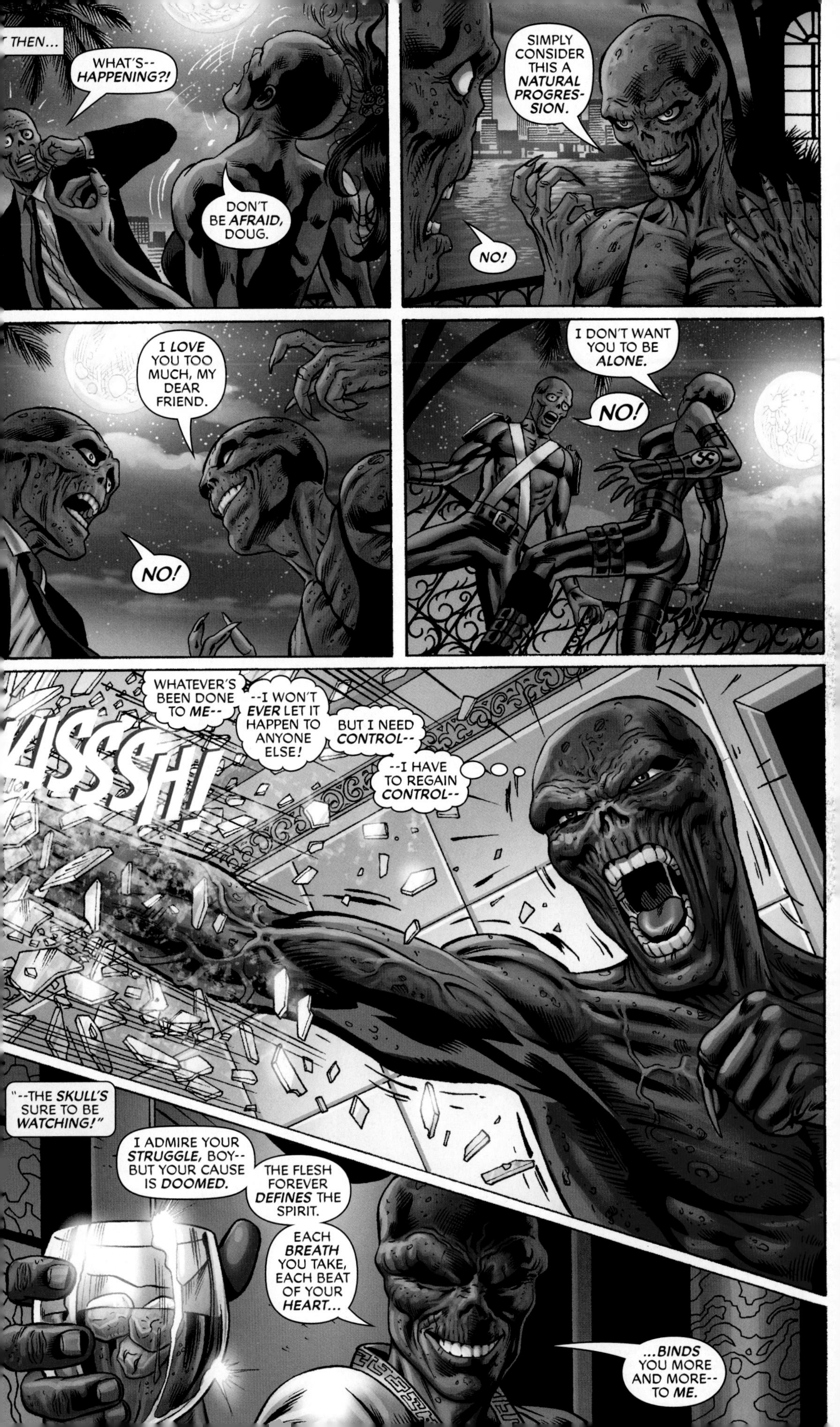
...THEN...
WHAT'S--HAPPENING?!
DON'T BE AFRAID, DOUG.
SIMPLY CONSIDER THIS A NATURAL PROGRESSION.
NO!
I LOVE YOU TOO MUCH, MY DEAR FRIEND.
NO!
I DON'T WANT YOU TO BE ALONE.
NO!
ASSSH!
WHATEVER'S BEEN DONE TO ME--
--I WON'T EVER LET IT HAPPEN TO ANYONE ELSE!
BUT I NEED CONTROL--
--I HAVE TO REGAIN CONTROL--
"--THE SKULL'S SURE TO BE WATCHING!"
I ADMIRE YOUR STRUGGLE, BOY--BUT YOUR CAUSE IS DOOMED.
THE FLESH FOREVER DEFINES THE SPIRIT.
EACH BREATH YOU TAKE, EACH BEAT OF YOUR HEART...
...BINDS YOU MORE AND MORE--TO ME.

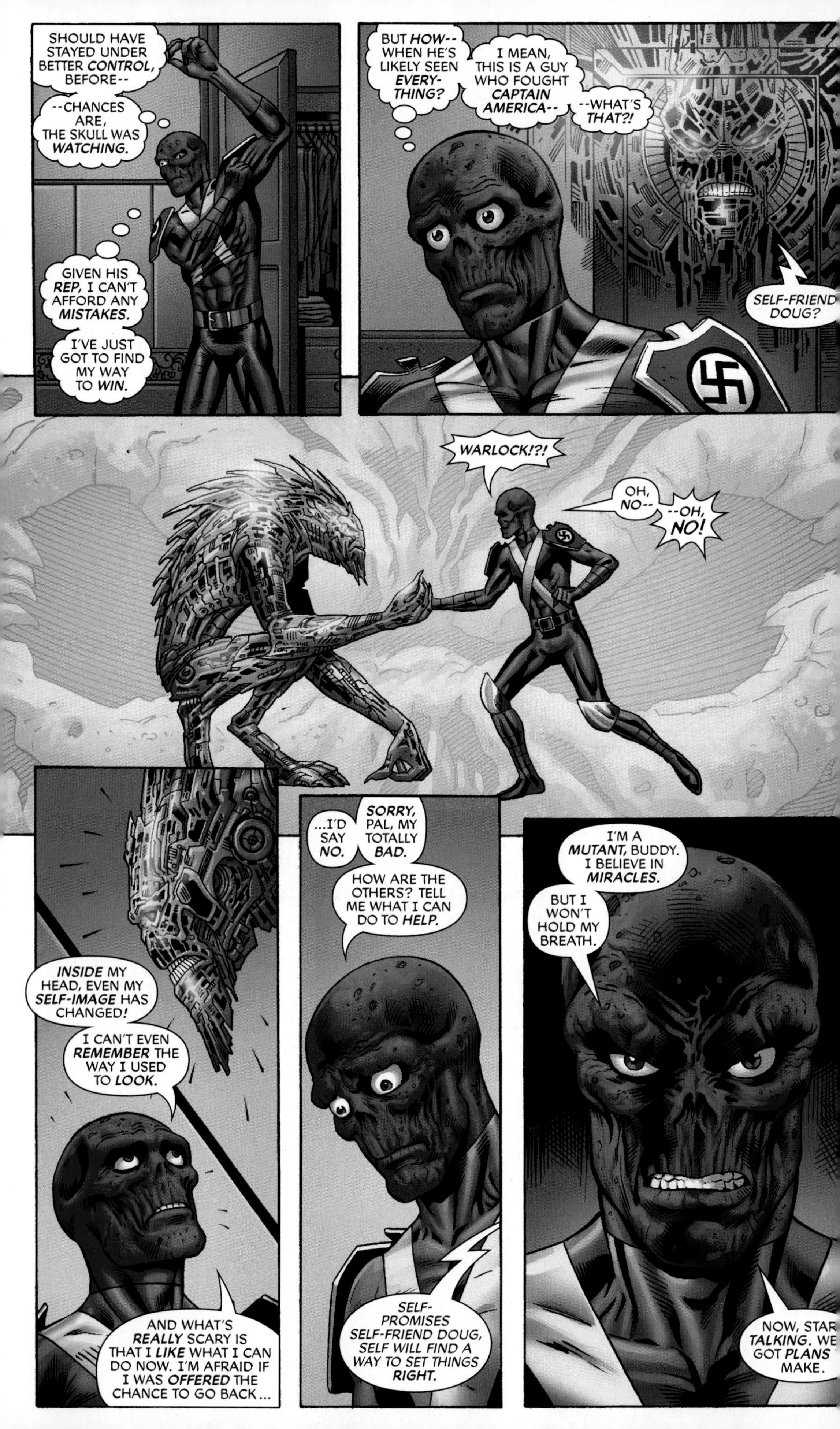
SHOULD HAVE STAYED UNDER BETTER CONTROL, BEFORE--
--CHANCES ARE, THE SKULL WAS WATCHING.
GIVEN HIS REP, I CAN'T AFFORD ANY MISTAKES.
I'VE JUST GOT TO FIND MY WAY TO WIN.
BUT HOW-- WHEN HE'S LIKELY SEEN EVERYTHING?
I MEAN, THIS IS A GUY WHO FOUGHT CAPTAIN AMERICA--
--WHAT'S THAT?!
SELF-FRIEND DOUG?
WARLOCK!?!
OH, NO--
--OH, NO!
INSIDE MY HEAD, EVEN MY SELF-IMAGE HAS CHANGED!
I CAN'T EVEN REMEMBER THE WAY I USED TO LOOK.
AND WHAT'S REALLY SCARY IS THAT I LIKE WHAT I CAN DO NOW. I'M AFRAID IF I WAS OFFERED THE CHANCE TO GO BACK...
...I'D SAY NO.
SORRY, PAL, MY TOTALLY BAD.
HOW ARE THE OTHERS? TELL ME WHAT I CAN DO TO HELP.
SELF-PROMISES SELF-FRIEND DOUG, SELF WILL FIND A WAY TO SET THINGS RIGHT.
I'M A MUTANT, BUDDY. I BELIEVE IN MIRACLES.
BUT I WON'T HOLD MY BREATH.
NOW, STAR TALKING. WE GOT PLANS MAKE.

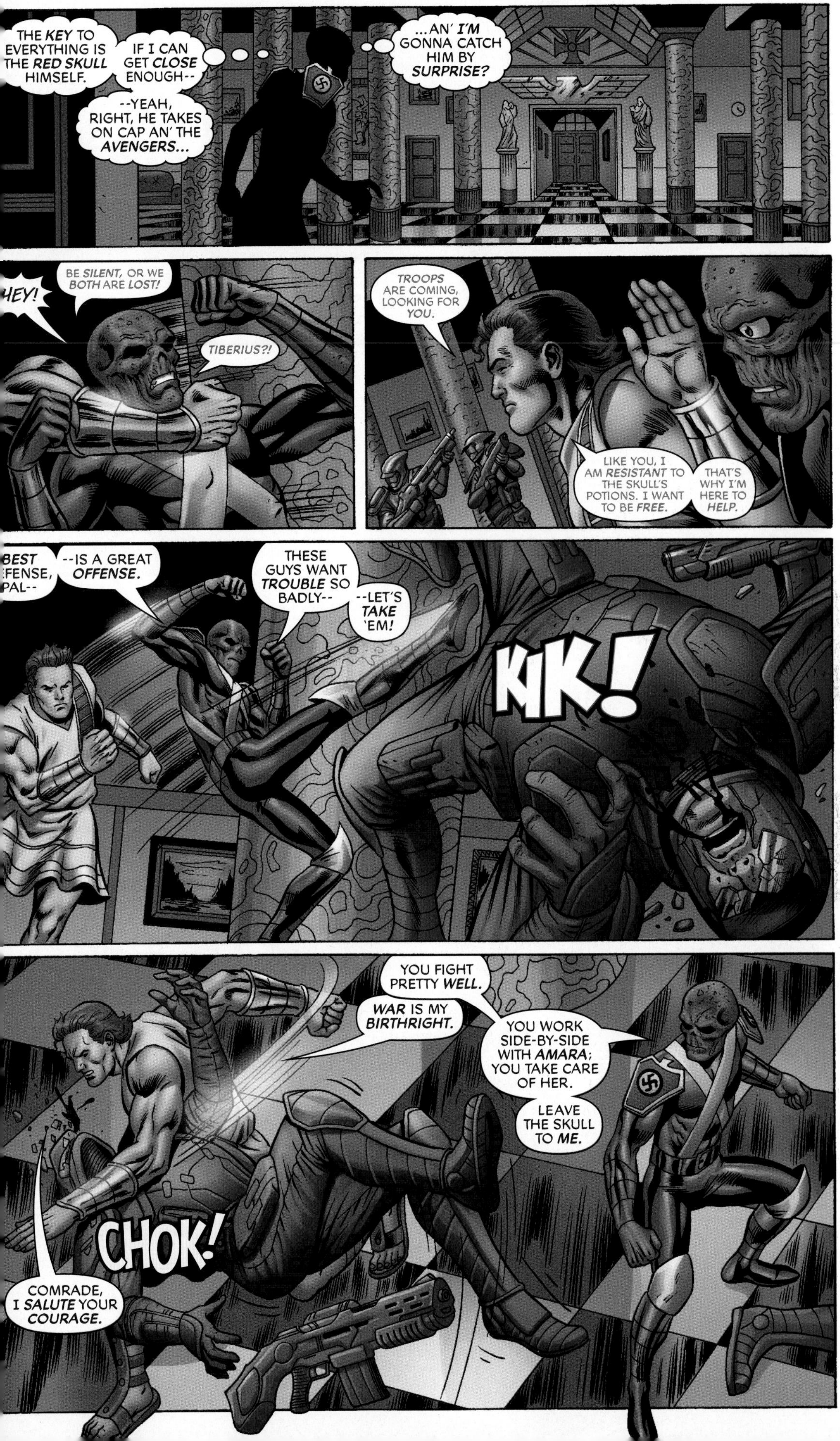

THE *KEY* TO EVERYTHING IS THE *RED SKULL* HIMSELF.
IF I CAN GET *CLOSE* ENOUGH--
--YEAH, RIGHT, HE TAKES ON CAP AN' THE *AVENGERS*...
...AN' *I'M* GONNA CATCH HIM BY *SURPRISE?*
HEY!
BE *SILENT*, OR WE *BOTH* ARE *LOST!*
TIBERIUS?!
*TROOPS* ARE COMING, LOOKING FOR *YOU*.
LIKE YOU, I AM *RESISTANT* TO THE SKULL'S POTIONS. I WANT TO BE *FREE*.
THAT'S WHY I'M HERE TO *HELP*.
BEST EFENSE, PAL--
--IS A GREAT *OFFENSE*.
THESE GUYS WANT *TROUBLE* SO BADLY--
--LET'S *TAKE* 'EM!
KIK!
YOU FIGHT PRETTY *WELL*.
*WAR* IS MY *BIRTHRIGHT*.
YOU WORK SIDE-BY-SIDE WITH *AMARA*; YOU TAKE CARE OF HER.
LEAVE THE SKULL TO *ME*.
CHOK!
COMRADE, I *SALUTE* YOUR *COURAGE*.

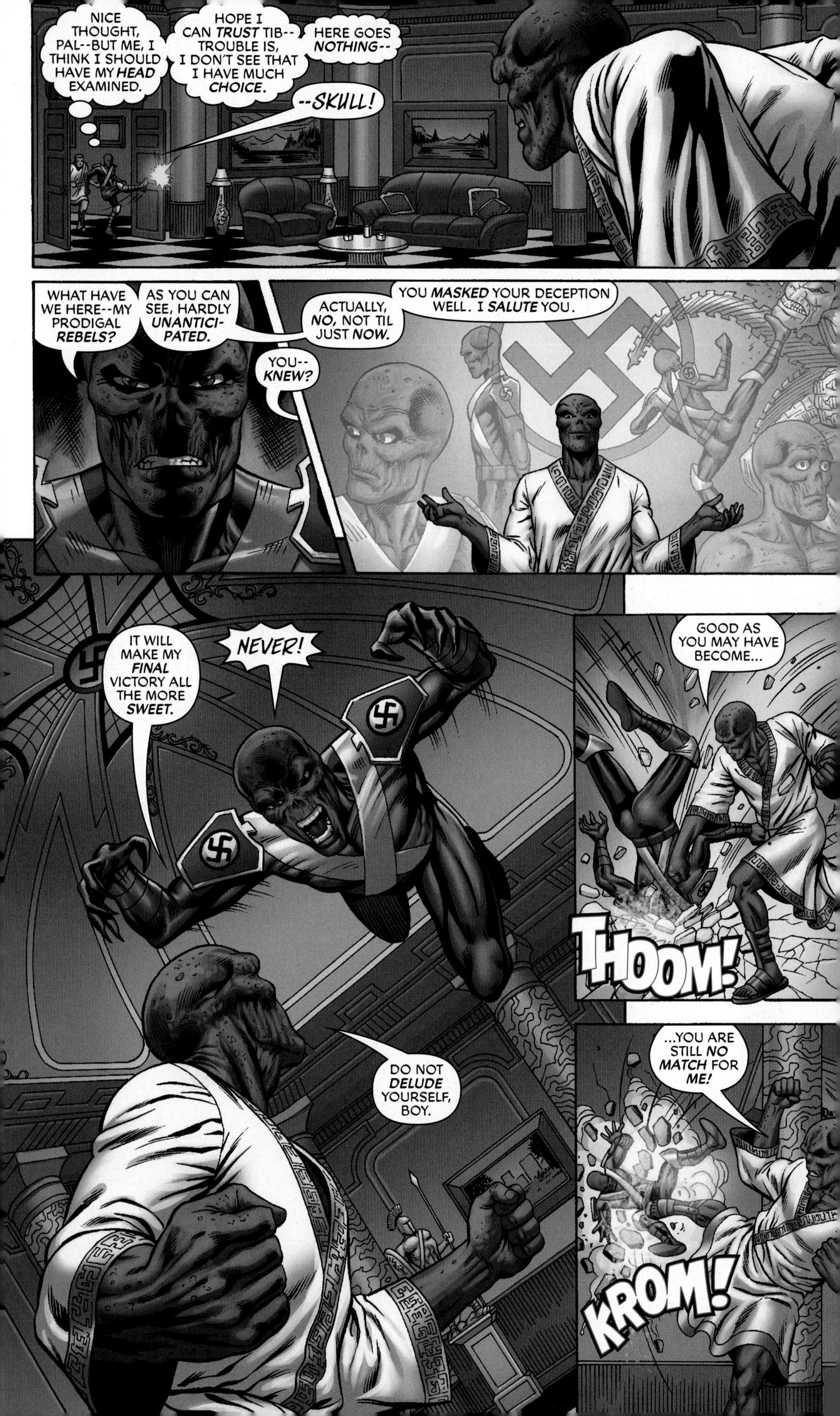

NICE THOUGHT, PAL--BUT ME, I THINK I SHOULD HAVE MY HEAD EXAMINED.
HOPE I CAN TRUST TIB-- TROUBLE IS, I DON'T SEE THAT I HAVE MUCH CHOICE.
HERE GOES NOTHING--
--SKULL!
WHAT HAVE WE HERE--MY PRODIGAL REBELS?
AS YOU CAN SEE, HARDLY UNANTICIPATED.
ACTUALLY, NO, NOT TIL JUST NOW.
YOU MASKED YOUR DECEPTION WELL. I SALUTE YOU.
YOU-- KNEW?
IT WILL MAKE MY FINAL VICTORY ALL THE MORE SWEET.
NEVER!
DO NOT DELUDE YOURSELF, BOY.
GOOD AS YOU MAY HAVE BECOME...
THOOM!
...YOU ARE STILL NO MATCH FOR ME!
KROM!

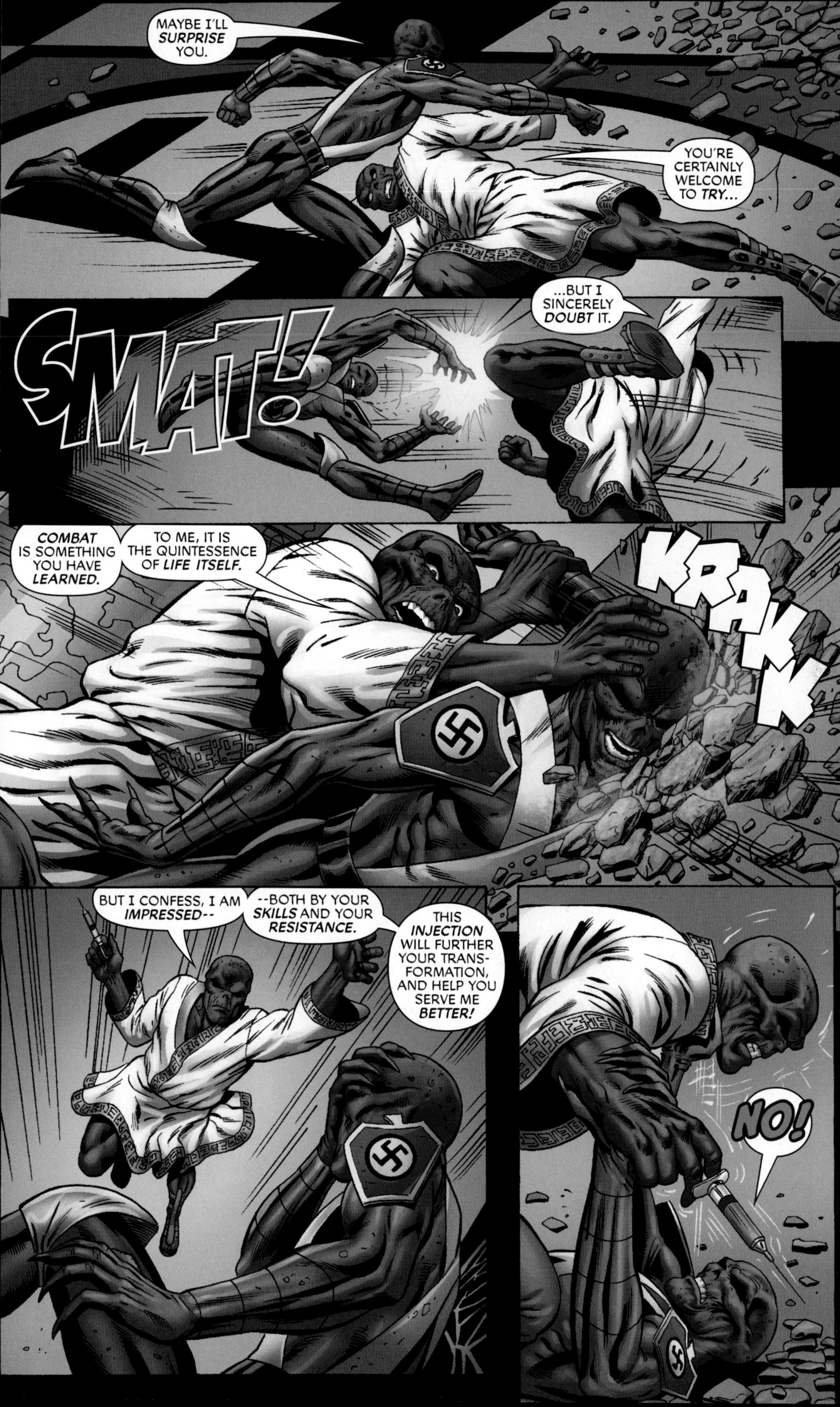

MAYBE I'LL SURPRISE YOU.
YOU'RE CERTAINLY WELCOME TO TRY...
...BUT I SINCERELY DOUBT IT.
SMAT!
COMBAT IS SOMETHING YOU HAVE LEARNED.
TO ME, IT IS THE QUINTESSENCE OF LIFE ITSELF.
KRAKK
BUT I CONFESS, I AM IMPRESSED--
--BOTH BY YOUR SKILLS AND YOUR RESISTANCE.
THIS INJECTION WILL FURTHER YOUR TRANSFORMATION, AND HELP YOU SERVE ME BETTER!
NO!

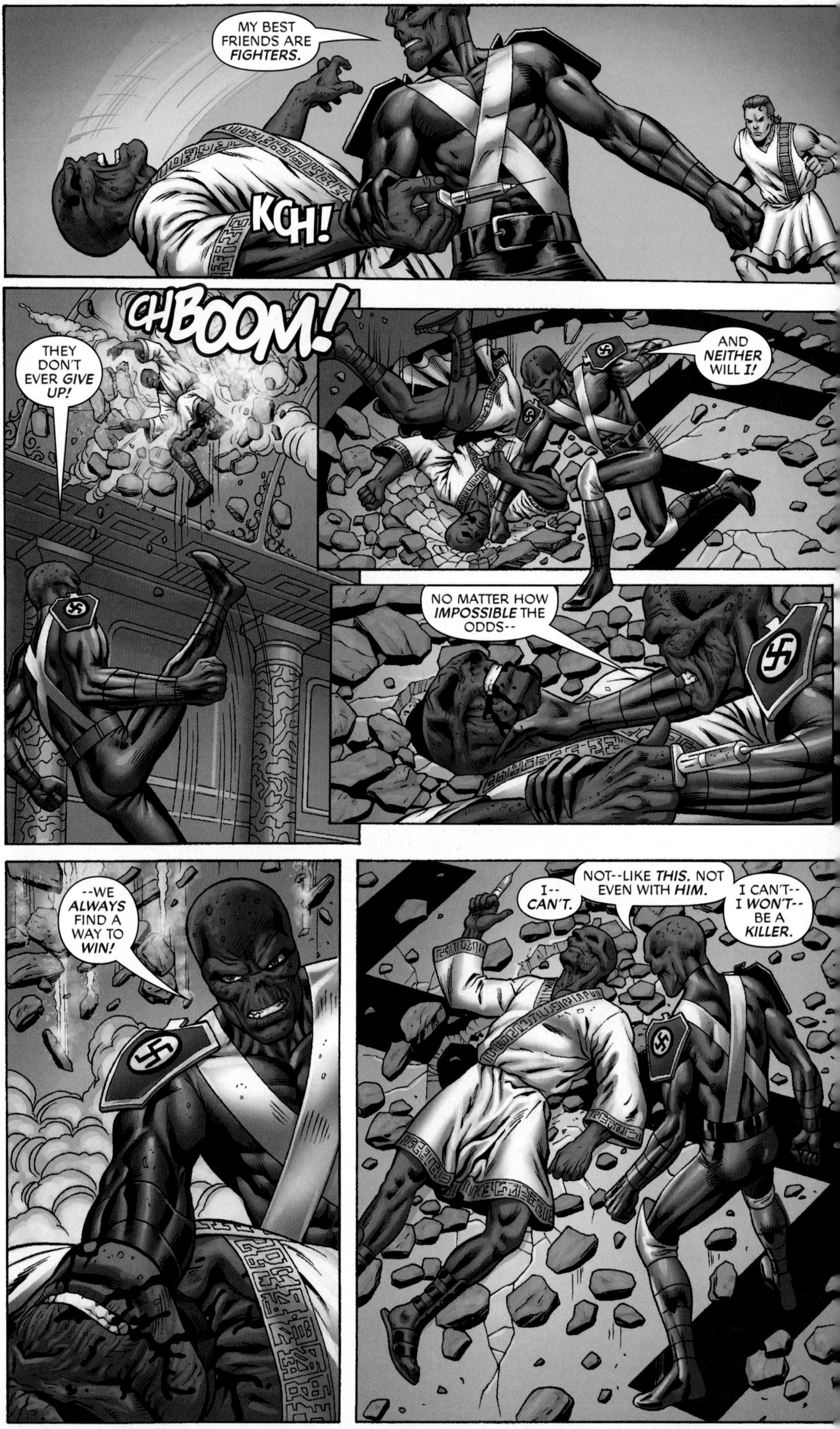
MY BEST FRIENDS ARE FIGHTERS.
KCH!
CHBOOM!
THEY DON'T EVER GIVE UP!
AND NEITHER WILL I!
NO MATTER HOW IMPOSSIBLE THE ODDS--
--WE ALWAYS FIND A WAY TO WIN!
I-- CAN'T.
NOT--LIKE THIS. NOT EVEN WITH HIM.
I CAN'T-- I WON'T-- BE A KILLER.

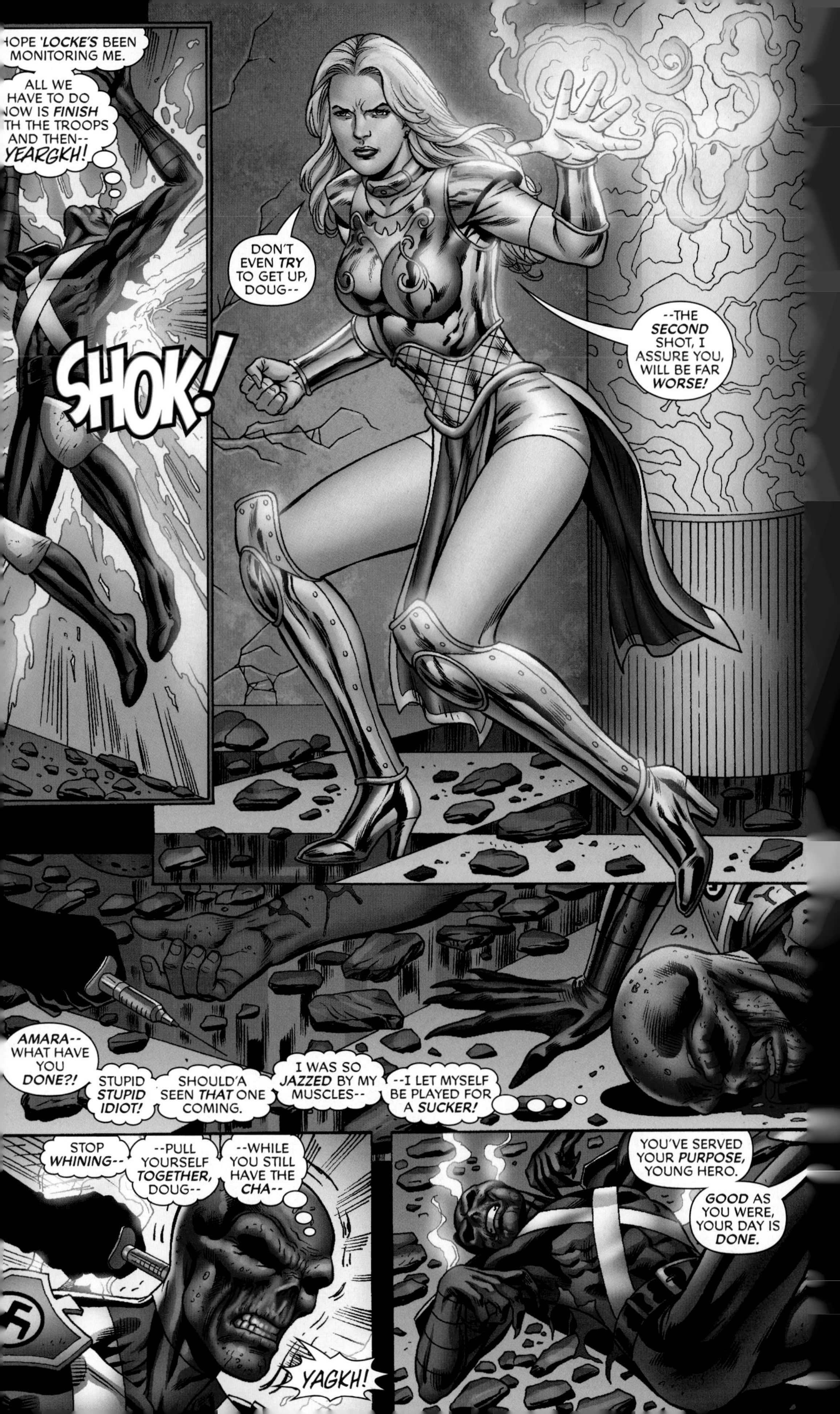

HOPE 'LOCKE'S BEEN MONITORING ME.
ALL WE HAVE TO DO NOW IS FINISH WITH THE TROOPS AND THEN-- YEARGKH!
SHOK!
DON'T EVEN TRY TO GET UP, DOUG--
--THE SECOND SHOT, I ASSURE YOU, WILL BE FAR WORSE!
AMARA-- WHAT HAVE YOU DONE?!
STUPID STUPID IDIOT!
SHOULD'A SEEN THAT ONE COMING.
I WAS SO JAZZED BY MY MUSCLES--
--I LET MYSELF BE PLAYED FOR A SUCKER!
STOP WHINING--
--PULL YOURSELF TOGETHER, DOUG--
--WHILE YOU STILL HAVE THE CHA--
YAGKH!
YOU'VE SERVED YOUR PURPOSE, YOUNG HERO.
GOOD AS YOU WERE, YOUR DAY IS DONE.

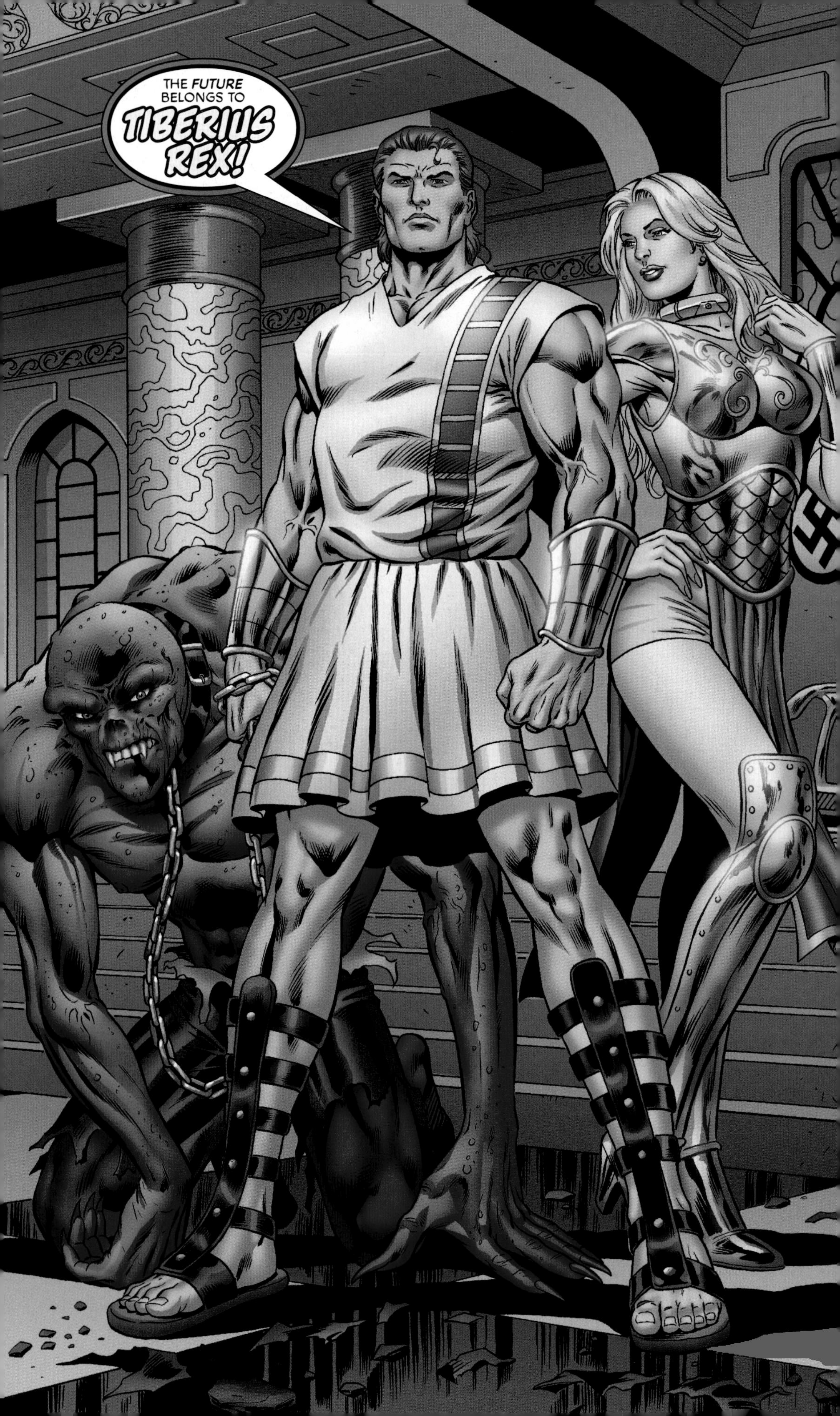
THE *FUTURE* BELONGS TO TIBERIUS REX!

#5

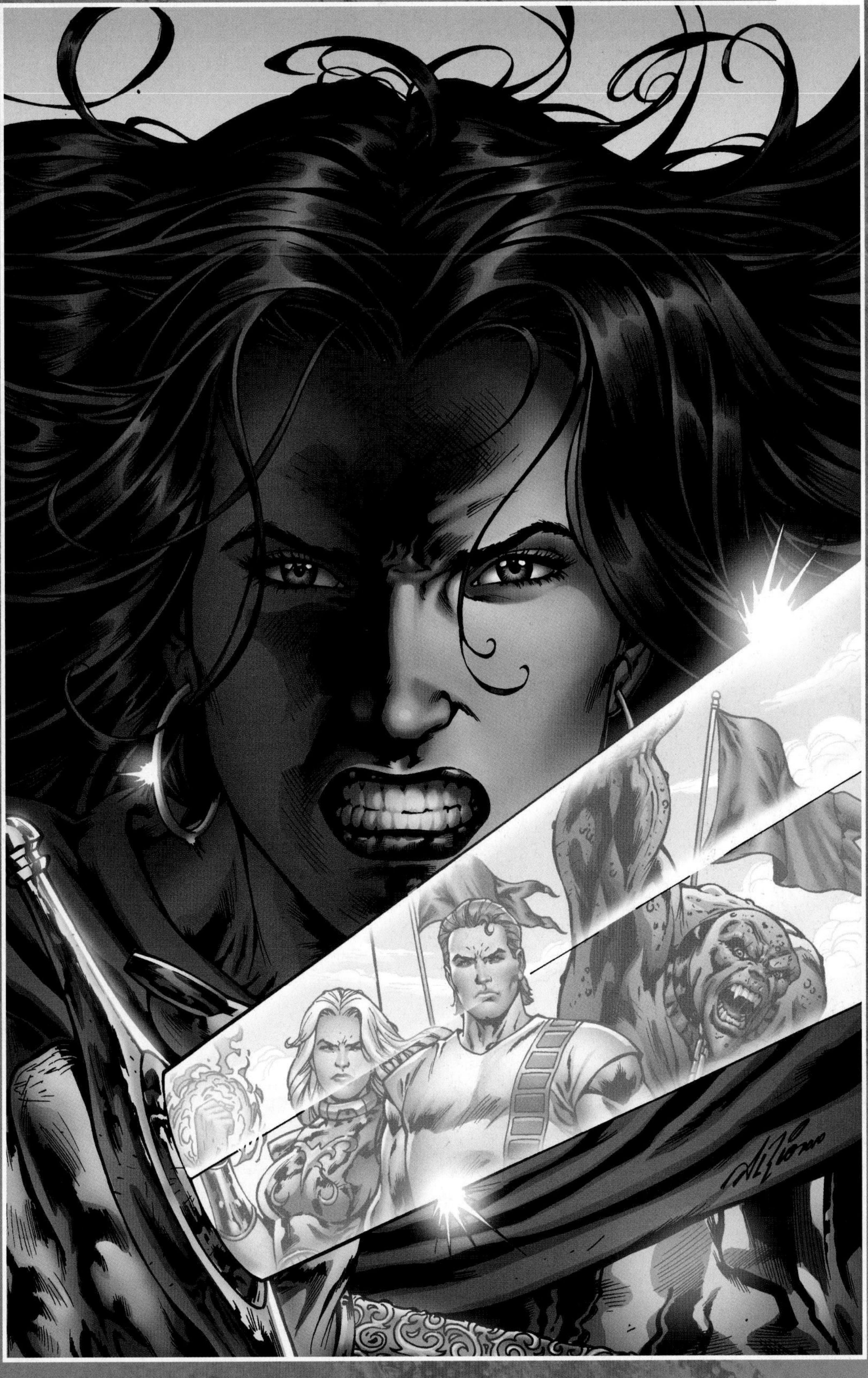

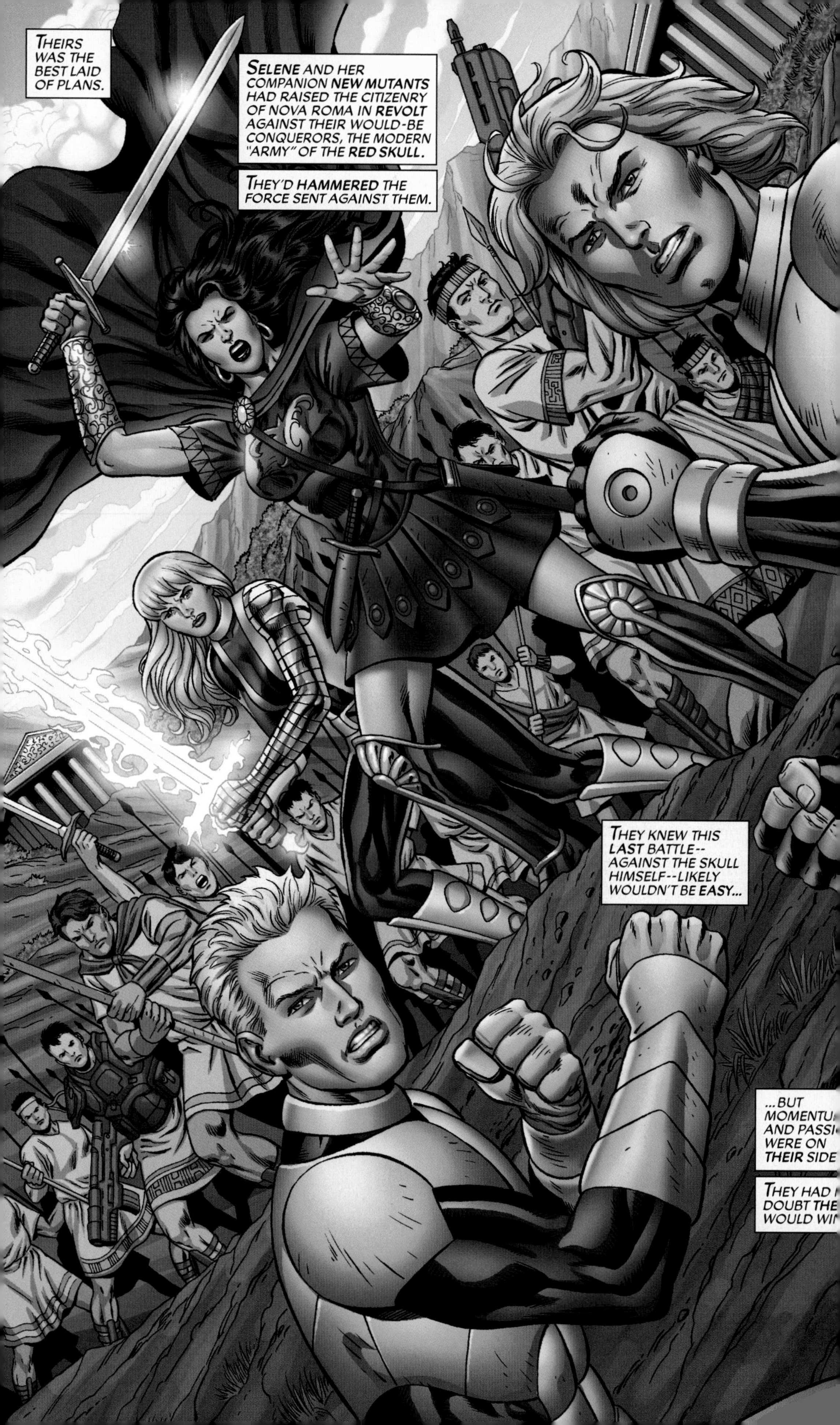
THEIRS WAS THE BEST LAID OF PLANS.
SELENE AND HER COMPANION NEW MUTANTS HAD RAISED THE CITIZENRY OF NOVA ROMA IN REVOLT AGAINST THEIR WOULD-BE CONQUERORS, THE MODERN "ARMY" OF THE RED SKULL.
THEY'D HAMMERED THE FORCE SENT AGAINST THEM.
THEY KNEW THIS LAST BATTLE--AGAINST THE SKULL HIMSELF--LIKELY WOULDN'T BE EASY...
...BUT MOMENTU AND PASSI WERE ON THEIR SIDE
THEY HAD DOUBT THE WOULD WI

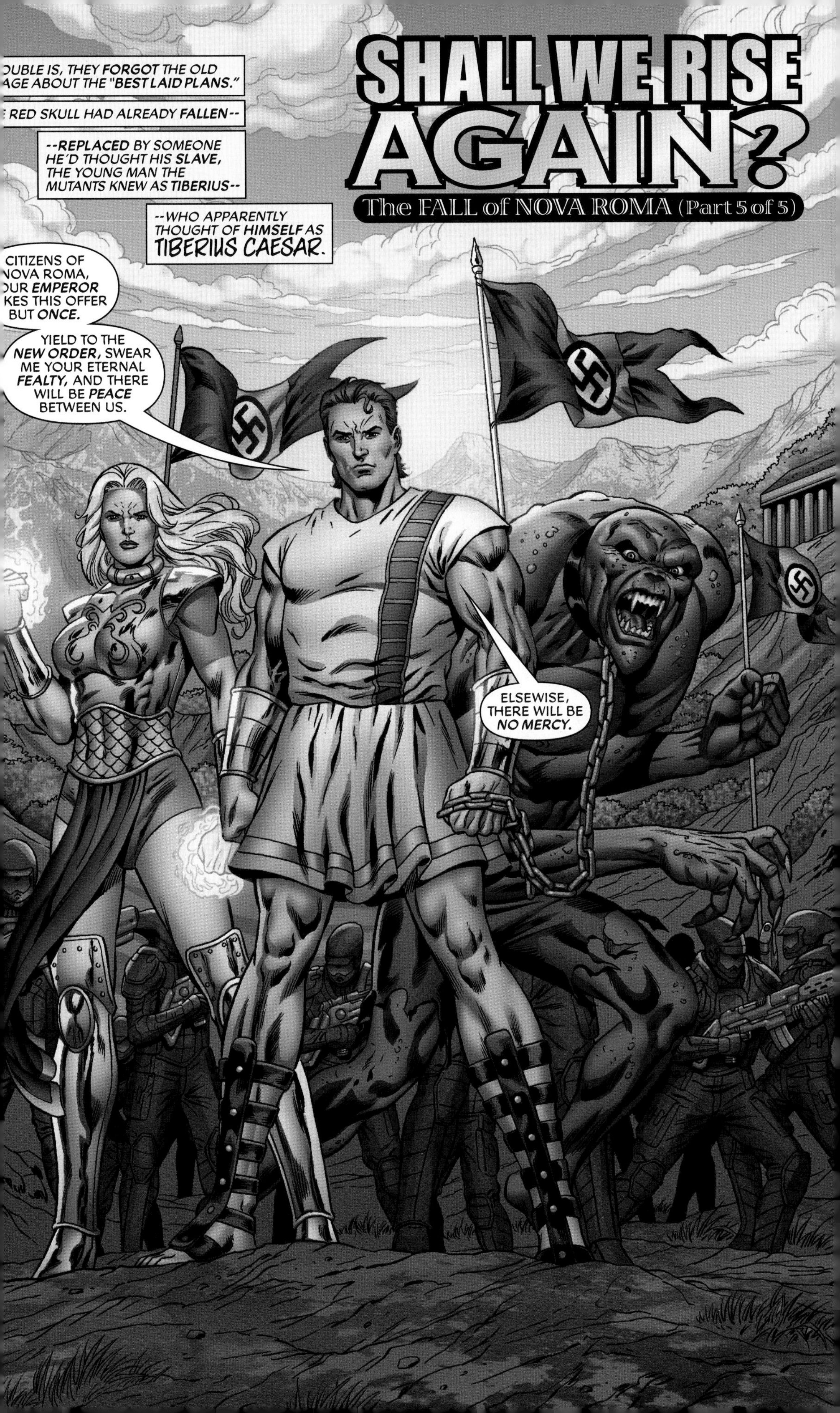
SHALL WE RISE AGAIN?
The FALL of NOVA ROMA (Part 5 of 5)
OUBLE IS, THEY FORGOT THE OLD AGE ABOUT THE "BEST LAID PLANS."
RED SKULL HAD ALREADY FALLEN--
--REPLACED BY SOMEONE HE'D THOUGHT HIS SLAVE, THE YOUNG MAN THE MUTANTS KNEW AS TIBERIUS--
--WHO APPARENTLY THOUGHT OF HIMSELF AS TIBERIUS CAESAR.
CITIZENS OF NOVA ROMA, OUR EMPEROR KES THIS OFFER BUT ONCE.
YIELD TO THE NEW ORDER, SWEAR ME YOUR ETERNAL FEALTY, AND THERE WILL BE PEACE BETWEEN US.
ELSEWISE, THERE WILL BE NO MERCY.

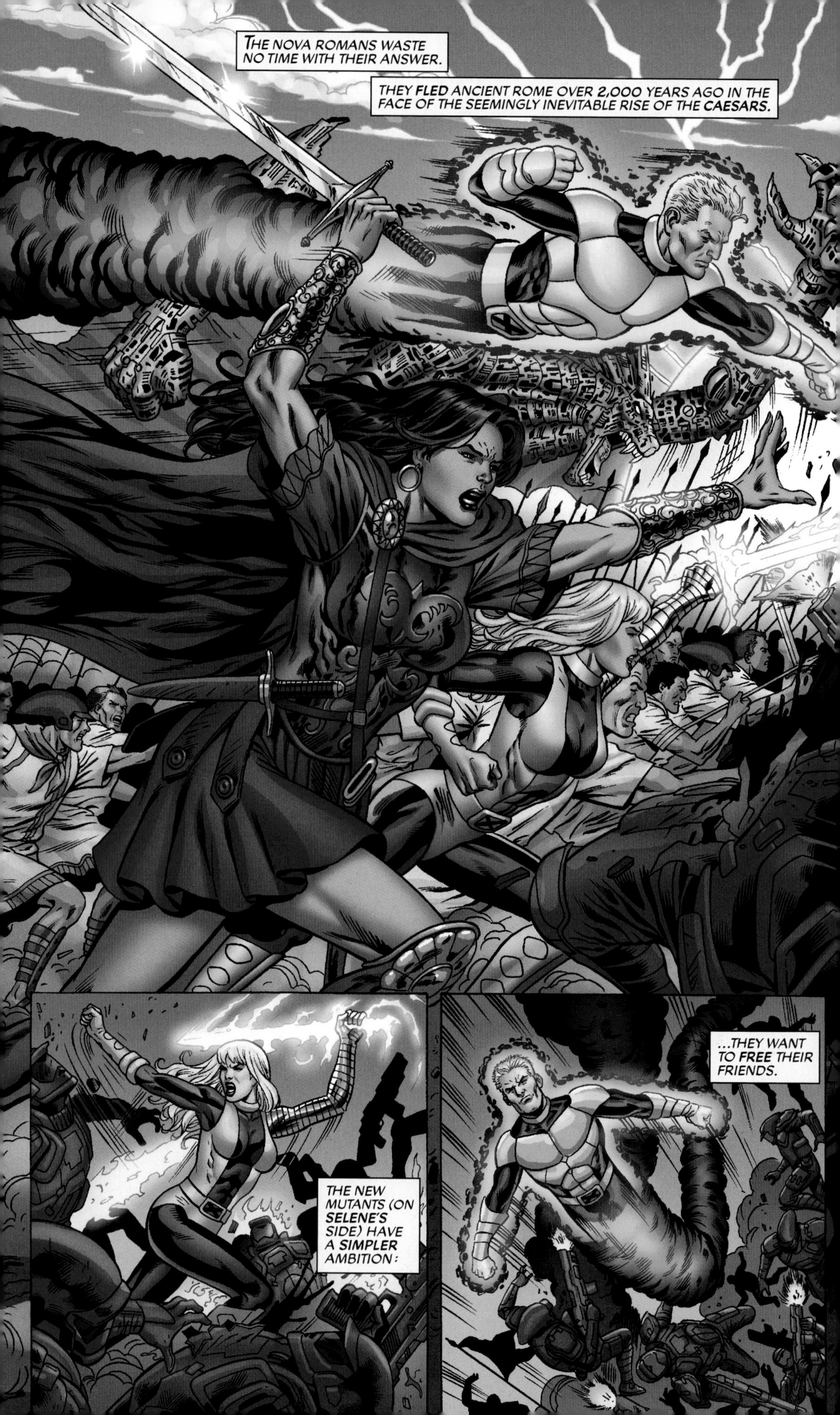
THE NOVA ROMANS WASTE NO TIME WITH THEIR ANSWER.
THEY FLED ANCIENT ROME OVER 2,000 YEARS AGO IN THE FACE OF THE SEEMINGLY INEVITABLE RISE OF THE CAESARS.
THE NEW MUTANTS (ON SELENE'S SIDE) HAVE A SIMPLER AMBITION:
...THEY WANT TO FREE THEIR FRIENDS.

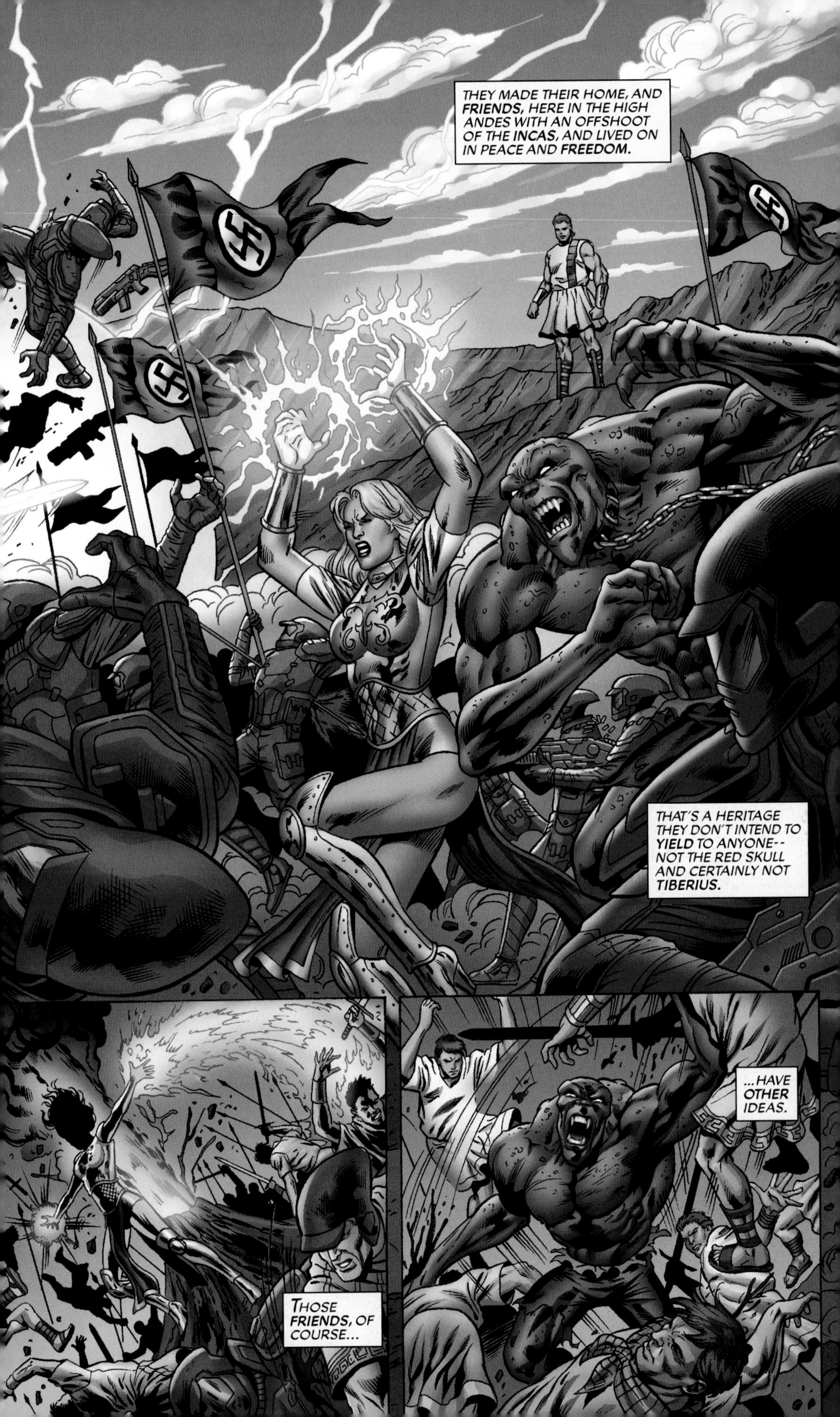

THEY MADE THEIR HOME, AND FRIENDS, HERE IN THE HIGH ANDES WITH AN OFFSHOOT OF THE INCAS, AND LIVED ON IN PEACE AND FREEDOM.
THAT'S A HERITAGE THEY DON'T INTEND TO YIELD TO ANYONE-- NOT THE RED SKULL AND CERTAINLY NOT TIBERIUS.
THOSE FRIENDS, OF COURSE...
...HAVE OTHER IDEAS.

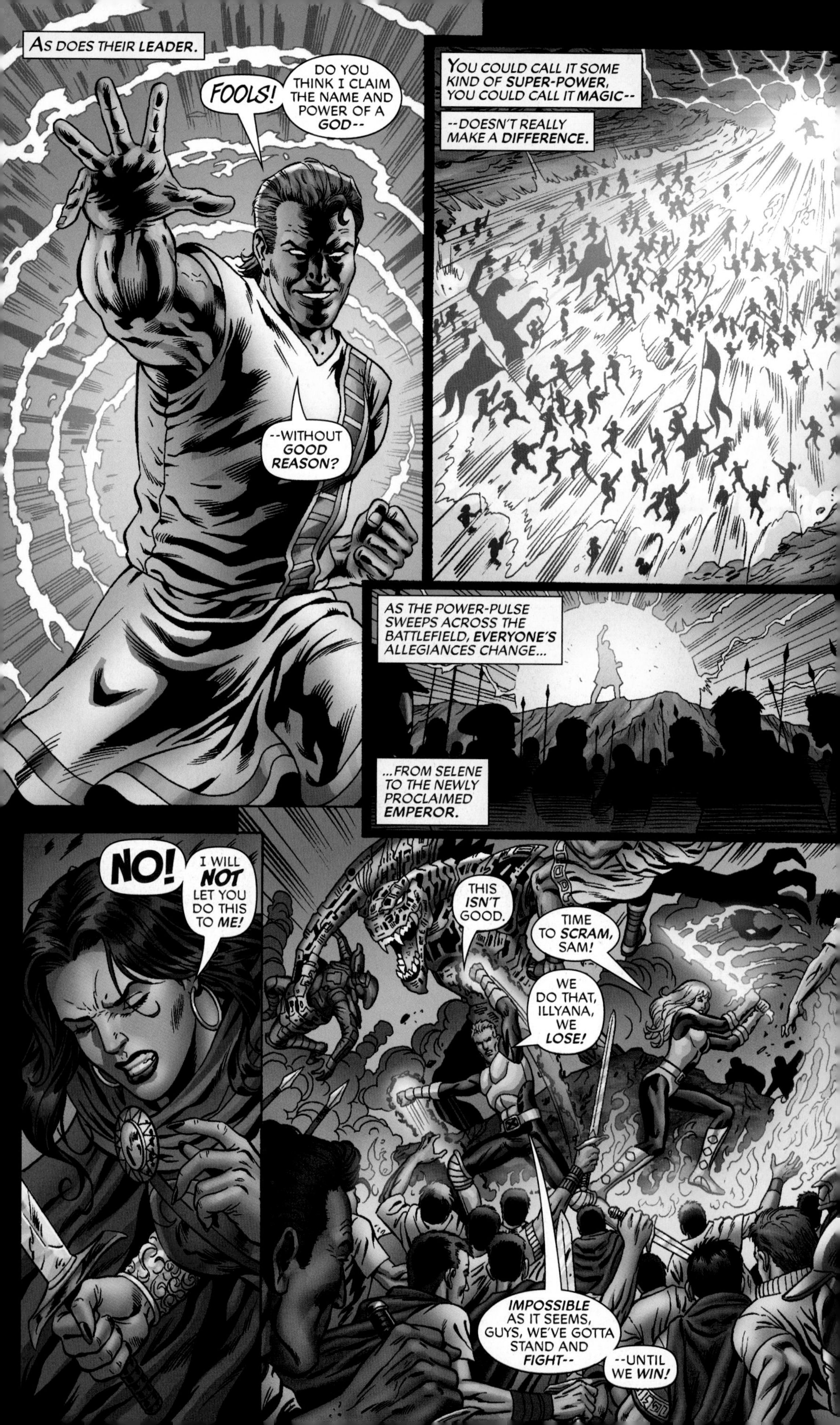
AS DOES THEIR LEADER.
FOOLS!
DO YOU THINK I CLAIM THE NAME AND POWER OF A GOD--
--WITHOUT GOOD REASON?
YOU COULD CALL IT SOME KIND OF SUPER-POWER, YOU COULD CALL IT MAGIC--
--DOESN'T REALLY MAKE A DIFFERENCE.
AS THE POWER-PULSE SWEEPS ACROSS THE BATTLEFIELD, EVERYONE'S ALLEGIANCES CHANGE...
...FROM SELENE TO THE NEWLY PROCLAIMED EMPEROR.
NO!
I WILL NOT LET YOU DO THIS TO ME!
THIS ISN'T GOOD.
TIME TO SCRAM, SAM!
WE DO THAT, ILLYANA, WE LOSE!
IMPOSSIBLE AS IT SEEMS, GUYS, WE'VE GOTTA STAND AND FIGHT--
--UNTIL WE WIN!

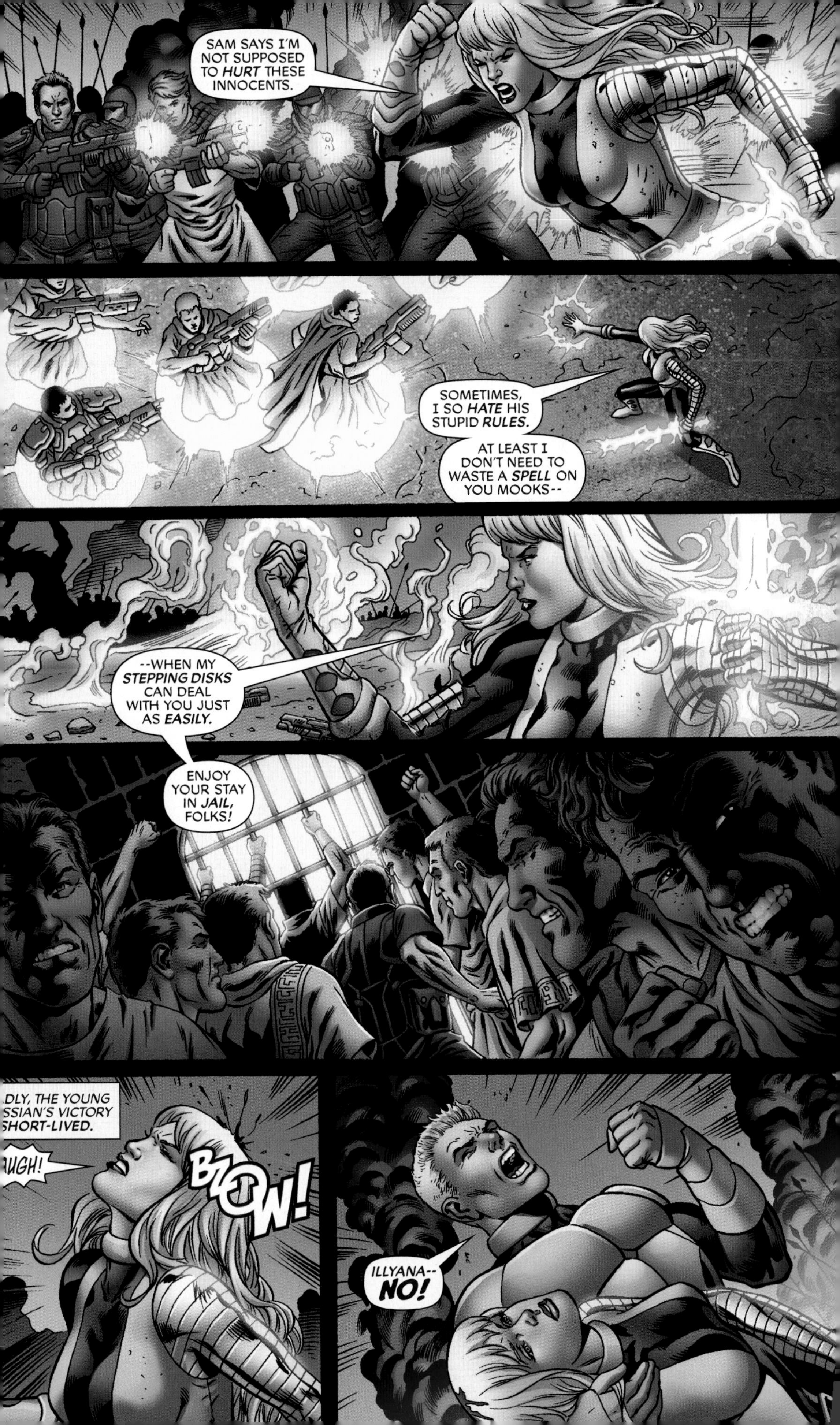
SAM SAYS I'M NOT SUPPOSED TO *HURT* THESE INNOCENTS.
SOMETIMES, I SO *HATE* HIS STUPID *RULES.*
AT LEAST I DON'T NEED TO WASTE A *SPELL* ON YOU MOOKS--
--WHEN MY *STEPPING DISKS* CAN DEAL WITH YOU JUST AS *EASILY.*
ENJOY YOUR STAY IN *JAIL,* FOLKS!
DLY, THE YOUNG SSIAN'S VICTORY SHORT-LIVED.
UGH!
BLOW!
ILLYANA-- NO!

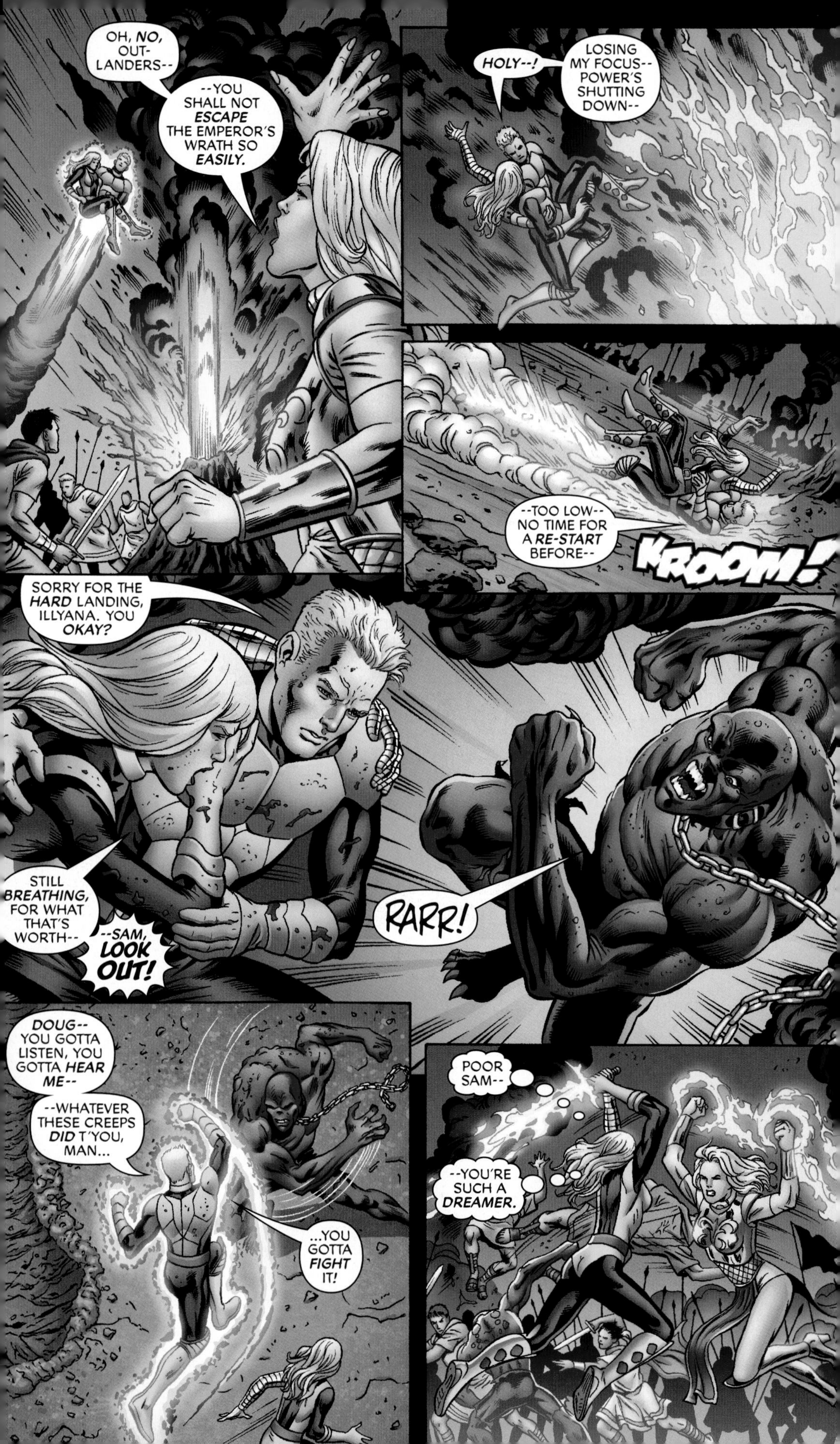
OH, NO, OUT-LANDERS--
--YOU SHALL NOT ESCAPE THE EMPEROR'S WRATH SO EASILY.
HOLY--!
LOSING MY FOCUS-- POWER'S SHUTTING DOWN--
--TOO LOW-- NO TIME FOR A RE-START BEFORE--
KROOM!
SORRY FOR THE HARD LANDING, ILLYANA. YOU OKAY?
STILL BREATHING, FOR WHAT THAT'S WORTH--
--SAM, LOOK OUT!
RARR!
DOUG-- YOU GOTTA LISTEN, YOU GOTTA HEAR ME--
--WHATEVER THESE CREEPS DID T'YOU, MAN...
...YOU GOTTA FIGHT IT!
POOR SAM--
--YOU'RE SUCH A DREAMER.

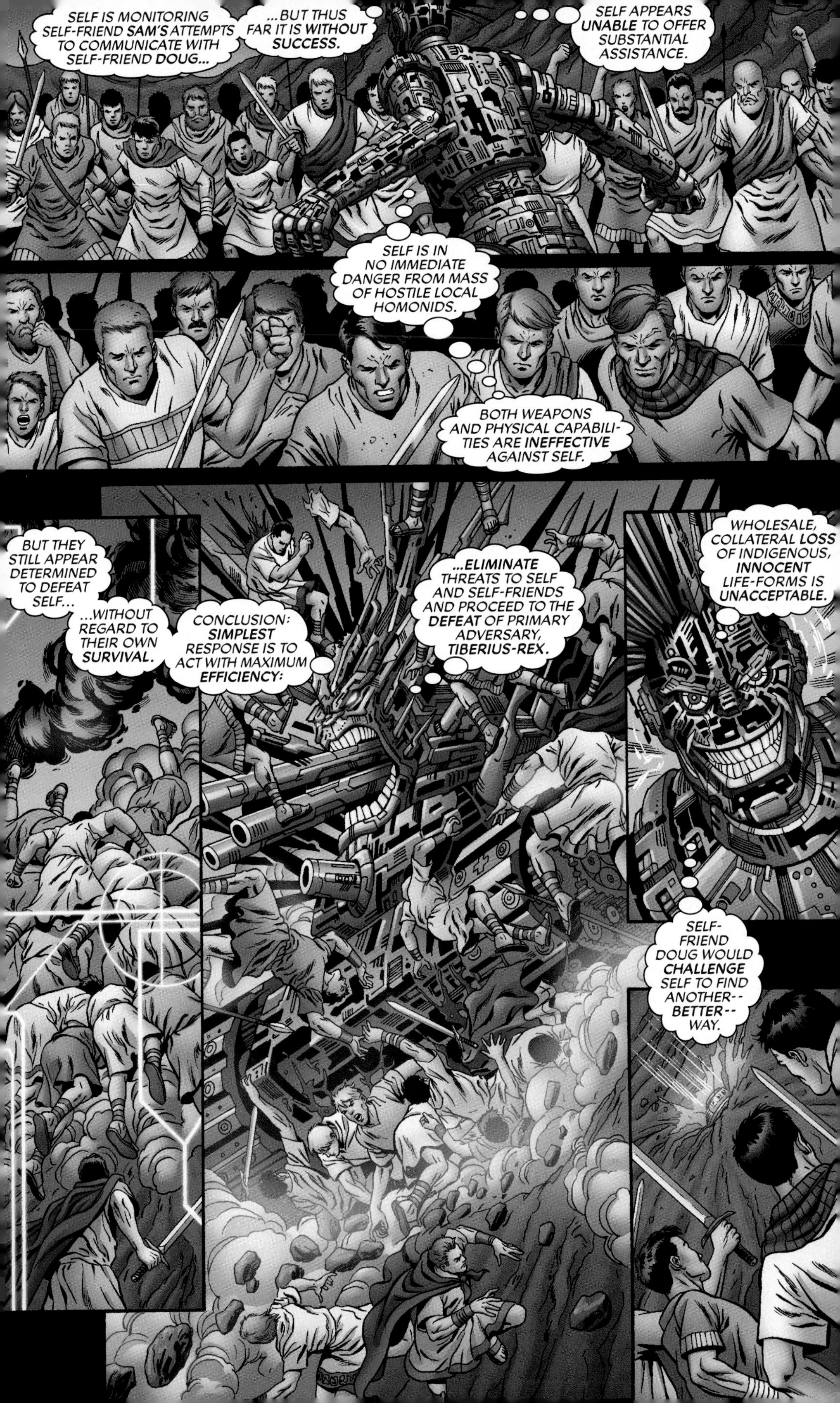

SELF IS MONITORING SELF-FRIEND SAM'S ATTEMPTS TO COMMUNICATE WITH SELF-FRIEND DOUG...
...BUT THUS FAR IT IS WITHOUT SUCCESS.
SELF APPEARS UNABLE TO OFFER SUBSTANTIAL ASSISTANCE.
SELF IS IN NO IMMEDIATE DANGER FROM MASS OF HOSTILE LOCAL HOMONIDS.
BOTH WEAPONS AND PHYSICAL CAPABILITIES ARE INEFFECTIVE AGAINST SELF.
BUT THEY STILL APPEAR DETERMINED TO DEFEAT SELF...
...WITHOUT REGARD TO THEIR OWN SURVIVAL.
CONCLUSION: SIMPLEST RESPONSE IS TO ACT WITH MAXIMUM EFFICIENCY:
...ELIMINATE THREATS TO SELF AND SELF-FRIENDS AND PROCEED TO THE DEFEAT OF PRIMARY ADVERSARY, TIBERIUS-REX.
WHOLESALE, COLLATERAL LOSS OF INDIGENOUS, INNOCENT LIFE-FORMS IS UNACCEPTABLE.
SELF-FRIEND DOUG WOULD CHALLENGE SELF TO FIND ANOTHER--BETTER--WAY.

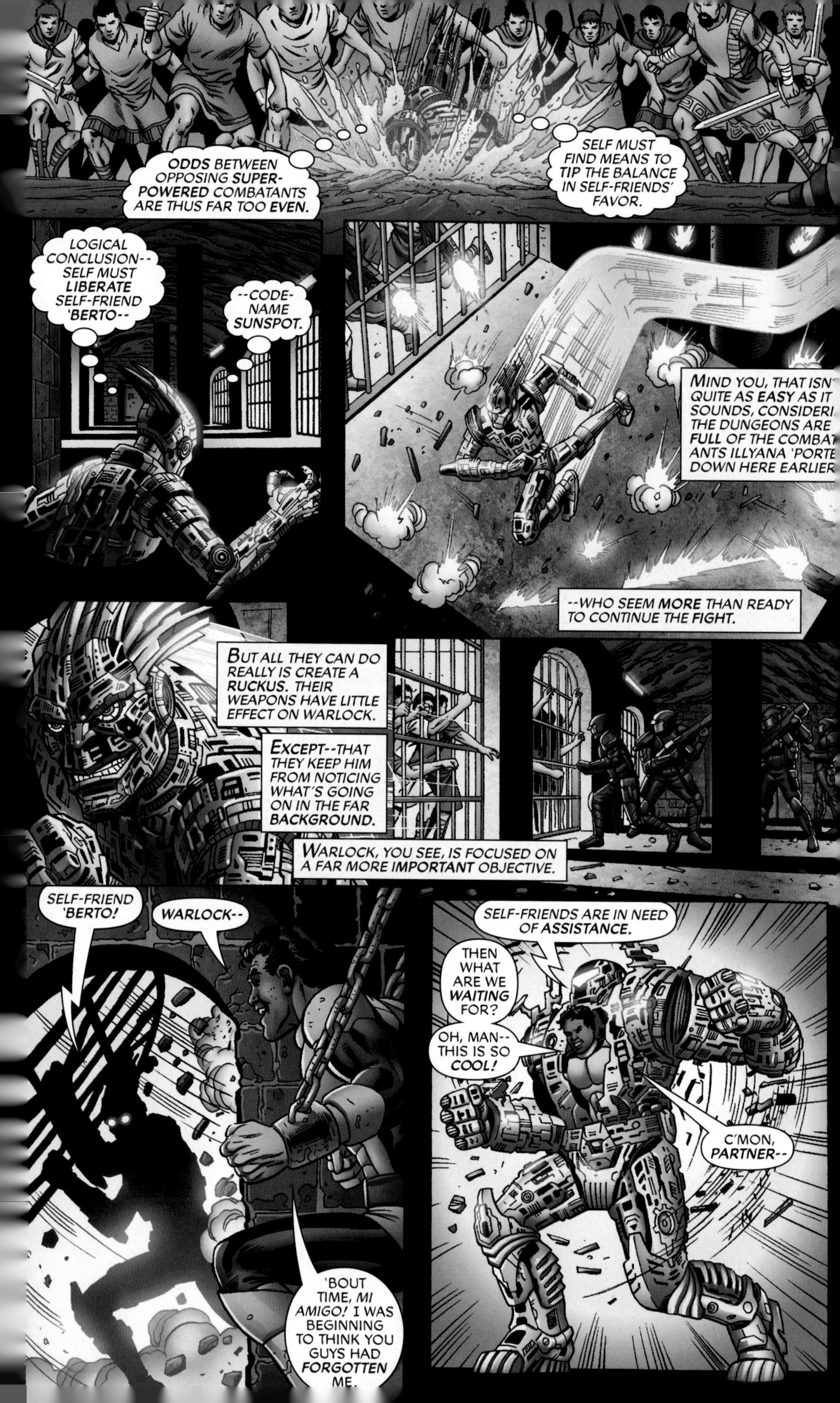
ODDS BETWEEN OPPOSING SUPER-POWERED COMBATANTS ARE THUS FAR TOO EVEN.
SELF MUST FIND MEANS TO TIP THE BALANCE IN SELF-FRIENDS' FAVOR.
LOGICAL CONCLUSION--SELF MUST LIBERATE SELF-FRIEND 'BERTO--
--CODE-NAME SUNSPOT.
MIND YOU, THAT ISN QUITE AS EASY AS IT SOUNDS, CONSIDERI THE DUNGEONS ARE FULL OF THE COMBAT ANTS ILLYANA 'PORTE DOWN HERE EARLIER
--WHO SEEM MORE THAN READY TO CONTINUE THE FIGHT.
BUT ALL THEY CAN DO REALLY IS CREATE A RUCKUS. THEIR WEAPONS HAVE LITTLE EFFECT ON WARLOCK.
EXCEPT--THAT THEY KEEP HIM FROM NOTICING WHAT'S GOING ON IN THE FAR BACKGROUND.
WARLOCK, YOU SEE, IS FOCUSED ON A FAR MORE IMPORTANT OBJECTIVE.
SELF-FRIEND 'BERTO!
WARLOCK--
'BOUT TIME, MI AMIGO! I WAS BEGINNING TO THINK YOU GUYS HAD FORGOTTEN ME.
SELF-FRIENDS ARE IN NEED OF ASSISTANCE.
THEN WHAT ARE WE WAITING FOR?
OH, MAN--THIS IS SO COOL!
C'MON, PARTNER--

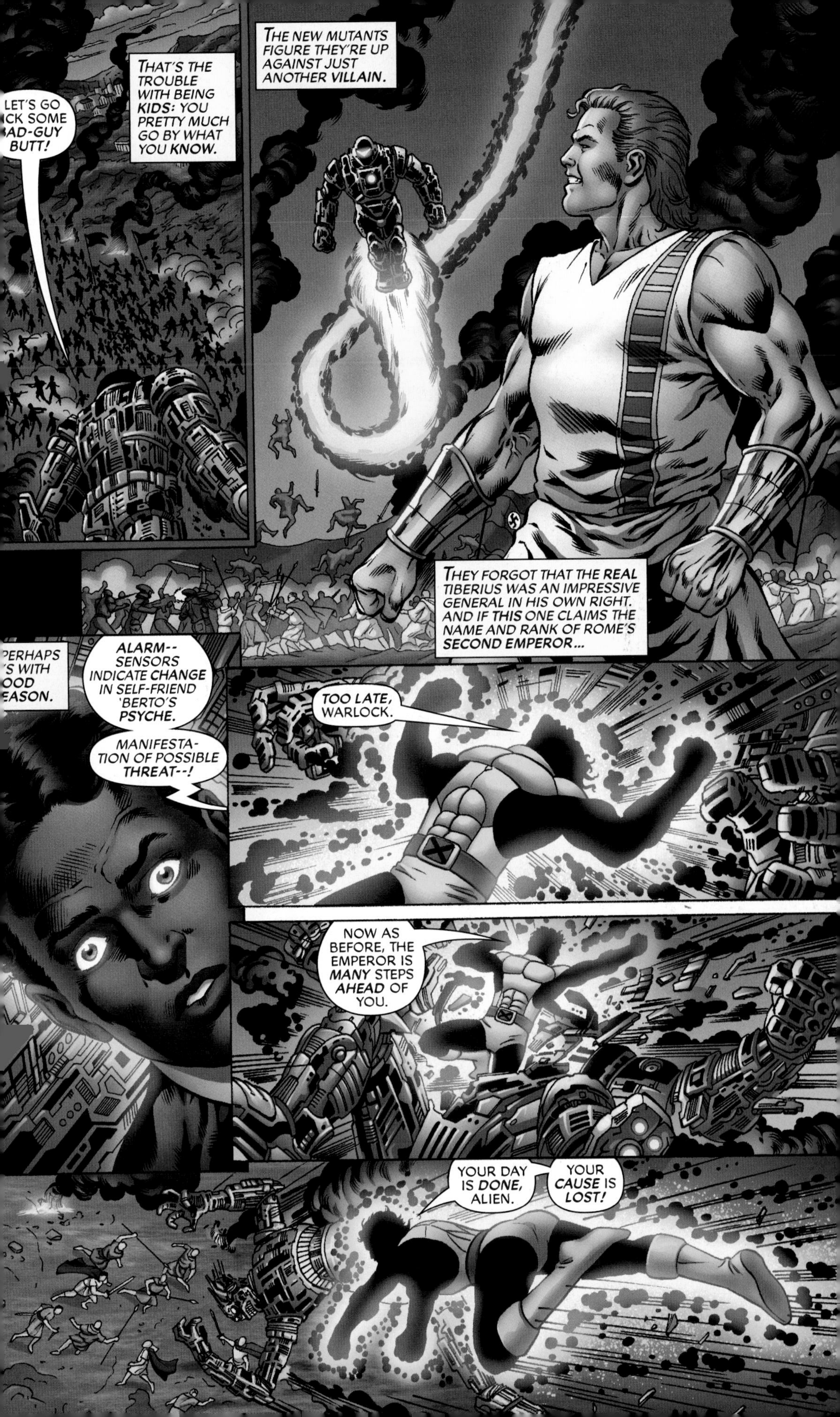

LET'S GO
CK SOME
AD-GUY
BUTT!
THAT'S THE TROUBLE WITH BEING KIDS: YOU PRETTY MUCH GO BY WHAT YOU KNOW.
THE NEW MUTANTS FIGURE THEY'RE UP AGAINST JUST ANOTHER VILLAIN.
THEY FORGOT THAT THE REAL TIBERIUS WAS AN IMPRESSIVE GENERAL IN HIS OWN RIGHT. AND IF THIS ONE CLAIMS THE NAME AND RANK OF ROME'S SECOND EMPEROR...
ERHAPS
'S WITH
OOD
EASON.
ALARM-- SENSORS INDICATE CHANGE IN SELF-FRIEND 'BERTO'S PSYCHE.
MANIFESTATION OF POSSIBLE THREAT--!
TOO LATE, WARLOCK.
NOW AS BEFORE, THE EMPEROR IS MANY STEPS AHEAD OF YOU.
YOUR DAY IS DONE, ALIEN.
YOUR CAUSE IS LOST!

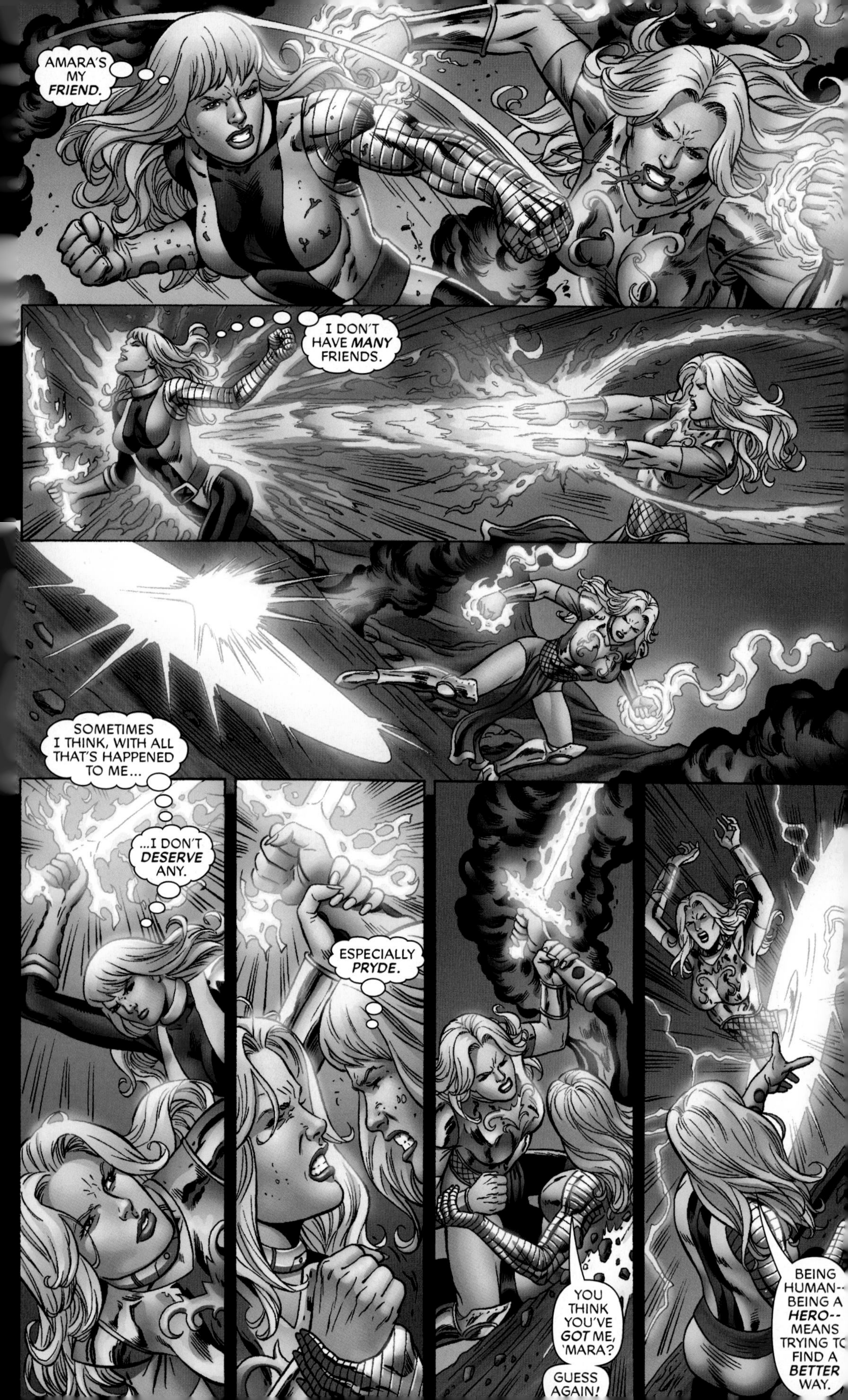
AMARA'S MY FRIEND.
I DON'T HAVE MANY FRIENDS.
SOMETIMES I THINK, WITH ALL THAT'S HAPPENED TO ME...
...I DON'T DESERVE ANY.
ESPECIALLY PRYDE.
YOU THINK YOU'VE GOT ME, 'MARA?
GUESS AGAIN!
BEING HUMAN-- BEING A HERO-- MEANS TRYING TO FIND A BETTER WAY.

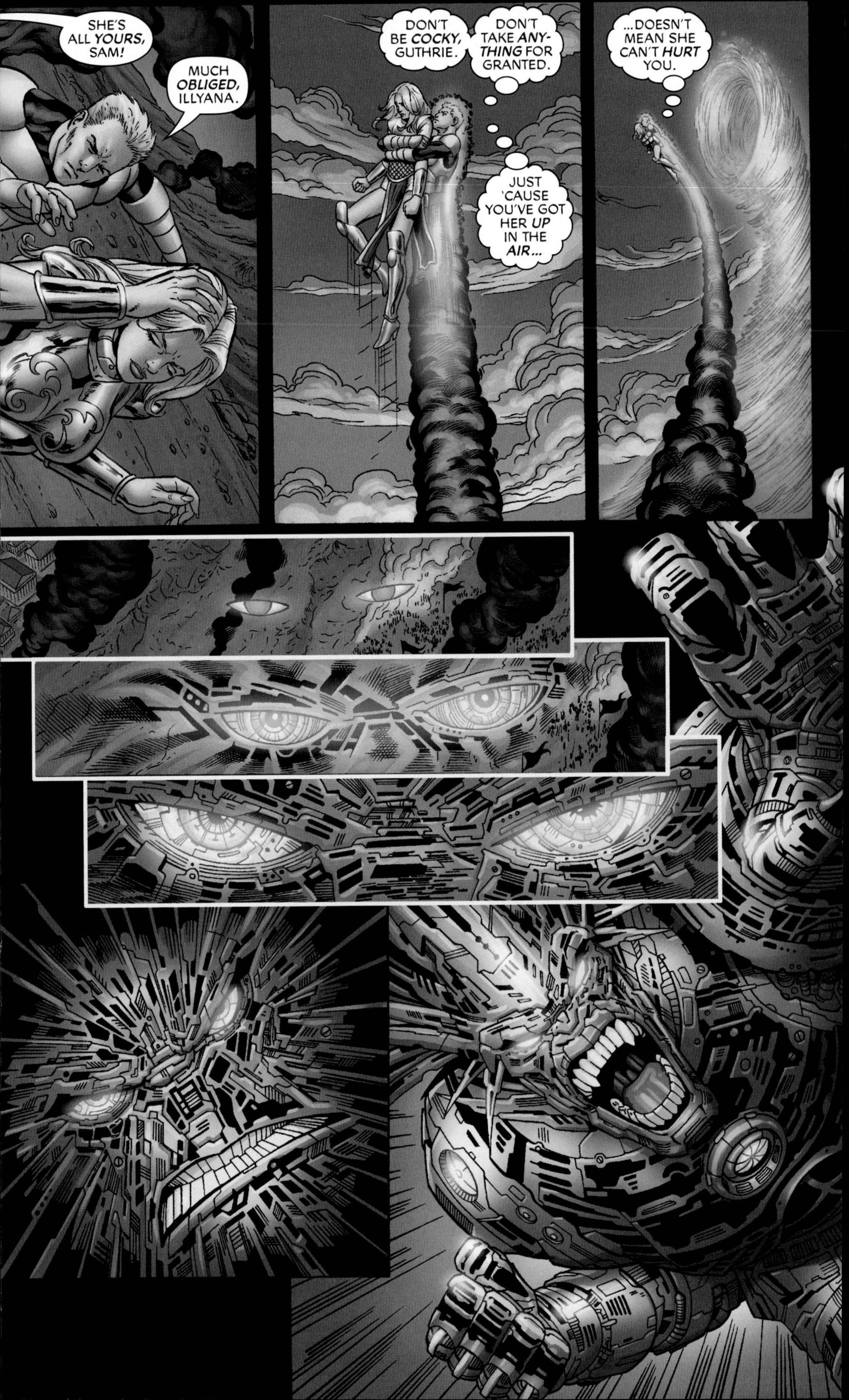
SHE'S ALL *YOURS,* SAM!
MUCH *OBLIGED,* ILLYANA.
DON'T BE *COCKY,* GUTHRIE.
DON'T TAKE *ANYTHING* FOR GRANTED.
JUST 'CAUSE YOU'VE GOT HER *UP* IN THE *AIR...*
...DOESN'T MEAN SHE CAN'T *HURT* YOU.

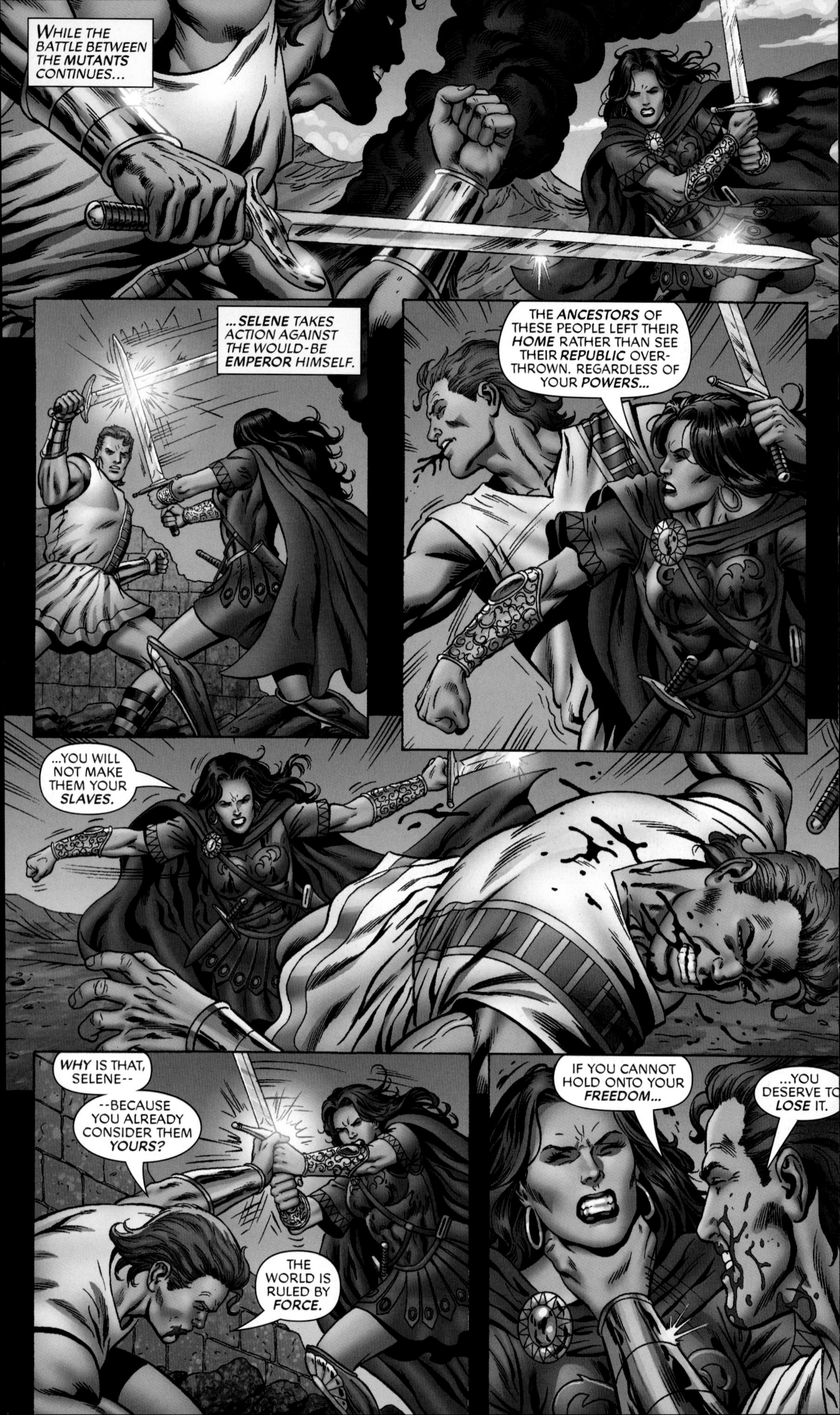
WHILE THE BATTLE BETWEEN THE MUTANTS CONTINUES...
...SELENE TAKES ACTION AGAINST THE WOULD-BE EMPEROR HIMSELF.
THE ANCESTORS OF THESE PEOPLE LEFT THEIR HOME RATHER THAN SEE THEIR REPUBLIC OVER-THROWN. REGARDLESS OF YOUR POWERS...
...YOU WILL NOT MAKE THEM YOUR SLAVES.
WHY IS THAT, SELENE--
--BECAUSE YOU ALREADY CONSIDER THEM YOURS?
THE WORLD IS RULED BY FORCE.
IF YOU CANNOT HOLD ONTO YOUR FREEDOM...
...YOU DESERVE TO LOSE IT.

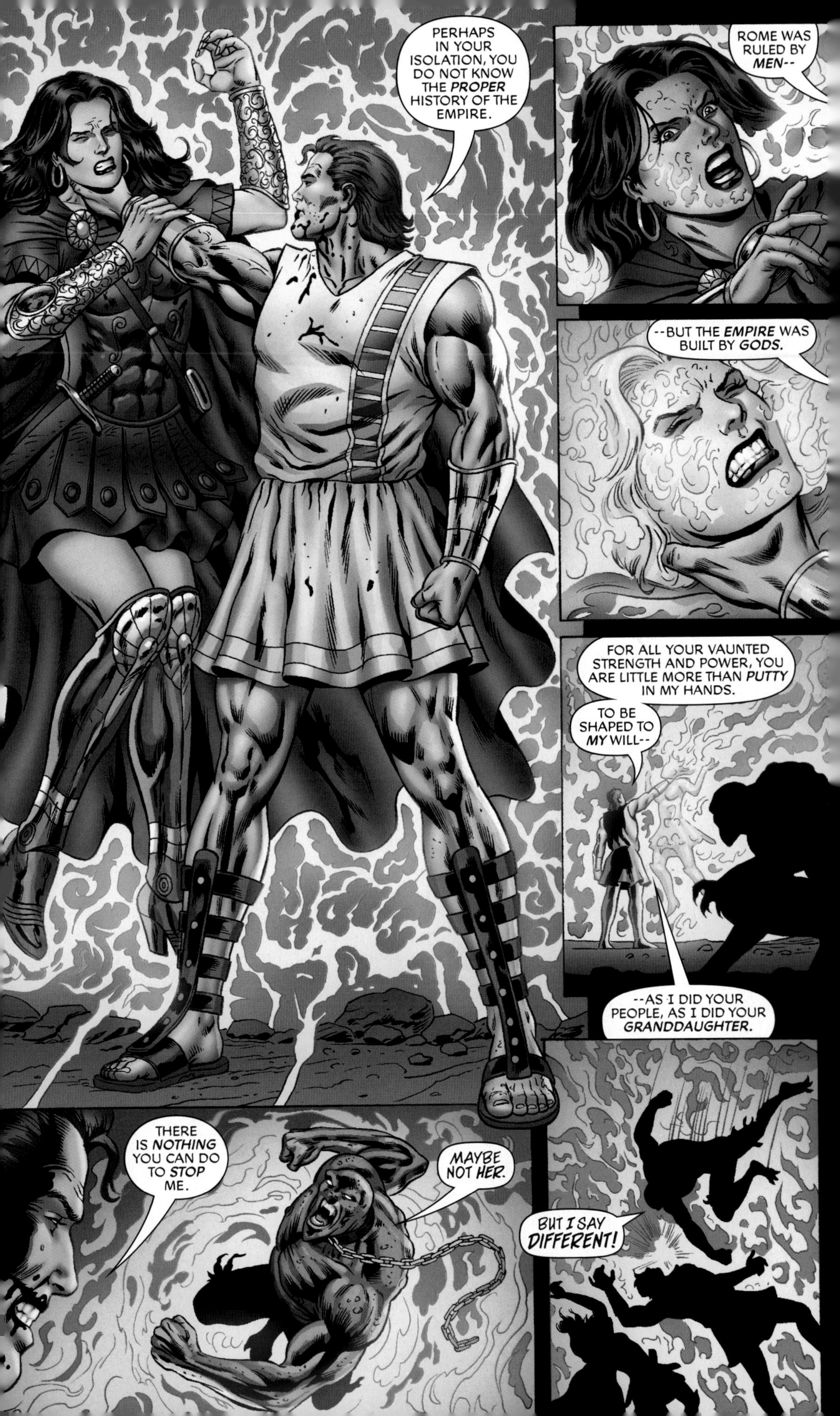
PERHAPS IN YOUR ISOLATION, YOU DO NOT KNOW THE *PROPER* HISTORY OF THE EMPIRE.
ROME WAS RULED BY *MEN*--
--BUT THE *EMPIRE* WAS BUILT BY *GODS*.
FOR ALL YOUR VAUNTED STRENGTH AND POWER, YOU ARE LITTLE MORE THAN *PUTTY* IN MY HANDS.
TO BE SHAPED TO *MY* WILL--
--AS I DID YOUR PEOPLE, AS I DID YOUR *GRANDDAUGHTER*.
THERE IS *NOTHING* YOU CAN DO TO *STOP* ME.
MAYBE NOT *HER*.
BUT I SAY *DIFFERENT!*

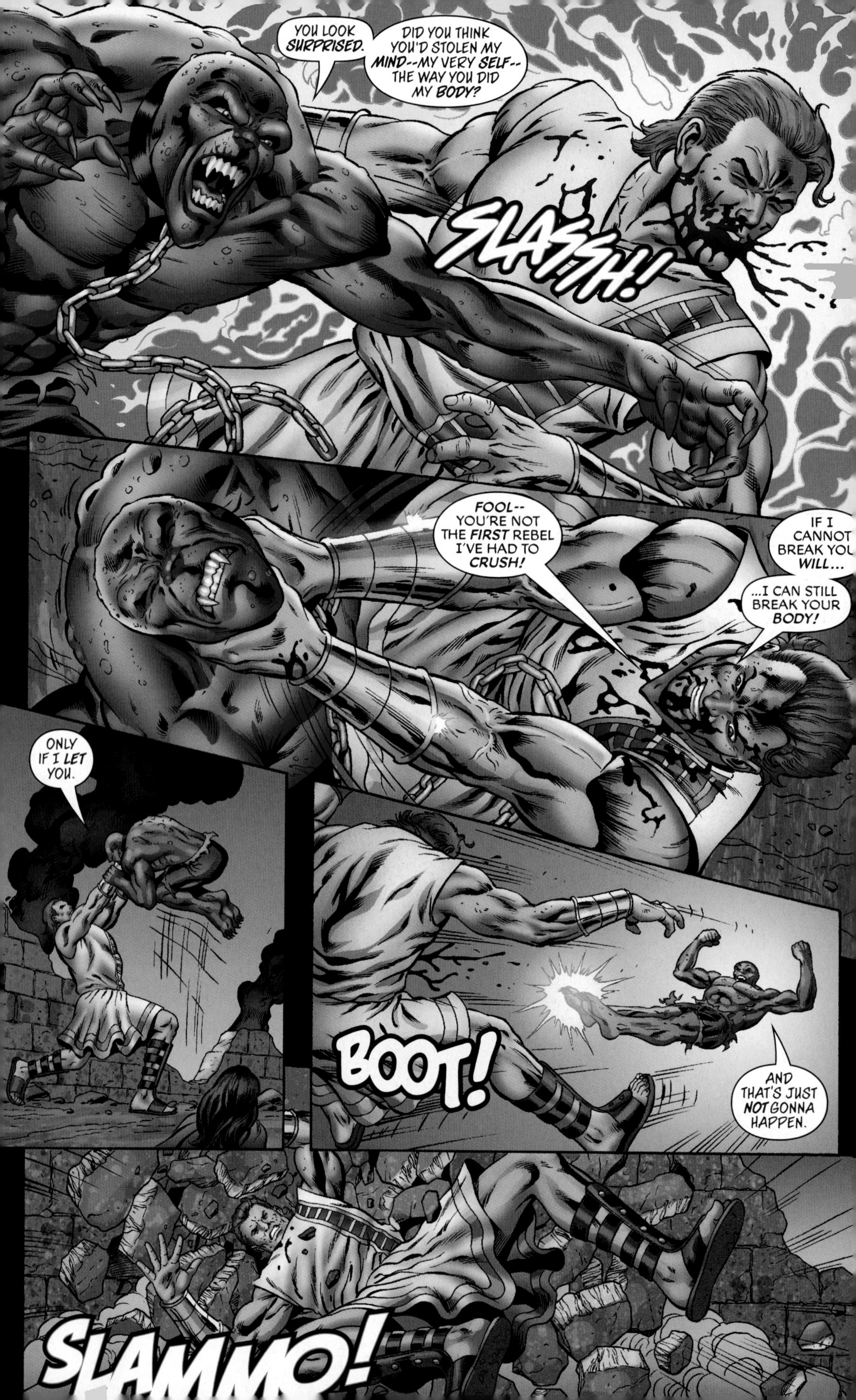

YOU LOOK SURPRISED.
DID YOU THINK YOU'D STOLEN MY MIND--MY VERY SELF--THE WAY YOU DID MY BODY?
SLASSH!
FOOL--YOU'RE NOT THE FIRST REBEL I'VE HAD TO CRUSH!
IF I CANNOT BREAK YOU WILL...
...I CAN STILL BREAK YOUR BODY!
ONLY IF I LET YOU.
BOOT!
AND THAT'S JUST NOT GONNA HAPPEN.
SLAMMO!

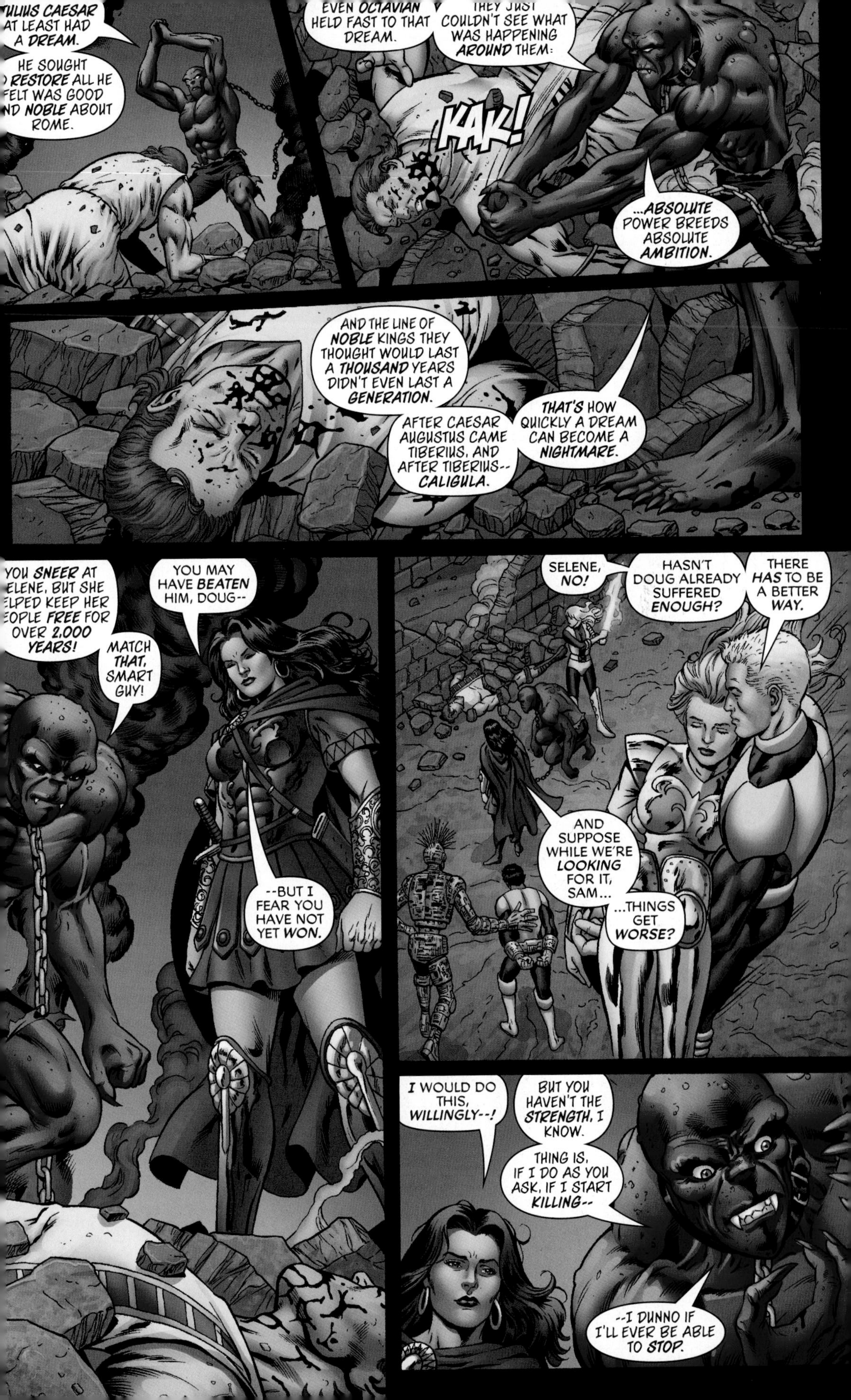

JULIUS CAESAR AT LEAST HAD A DREAM.
HE SOUGHT TO RESTORE ALL HE FELT WAS GOOD AND NOBLE ABOUT ROME.
EVEN OCTAVIAN HELD FAST TO THAT DREAM.
THEY JUST COULDN'T SEE WHAT WAS HAPPENING AROUND THEM:
KAK!
...ABSOLUTE POWER BREEDS ABSOLUTE AMBITION.
AND THE LINE OF NOBLE KINGS THEY THOUGHT WOULD LAST A THOUSAND YEARS DIDN'T EVEN LAST A GENERATION.
AFTER CAESAR AUGUSTUS CAME TIBERIUS, AND AFTER TIBERIUS--CALIGULA.
THAT'S HOW QUICKLY A DREAM CAN BECOME A NIGHTMARE.
YOU SNEER AT SELENE, BUT SHE HELPED KEEP HER PEOPLE FREE FOR OVER 2,000 YEARS!
MATCH THAT, SMART GUY!
YOU MAY HAVE BEATEN HIM, DOUG--
--BUT I FEAR YOU HAVE NOT YET WON.
SELENE, NO!
HASN'T DOUG ALREADY SUFFERED ENOUGH?
THERE HAS TO BE A BETTER WAY.
AND SUPPOSE WHILE WE'RE LOOKING FOR IT, SAM...
...THINGS GET WORSE?
I WOULD DO THIS, WILLINGLY--!
BUT YOU HAVEN'T THE STRENGTH, I KNOW.
THING IS, IF I DO AS YOU ASK, IF I START KILLING--
--I DUNNO IF I'LL EVER BE ABLE TO STOP.

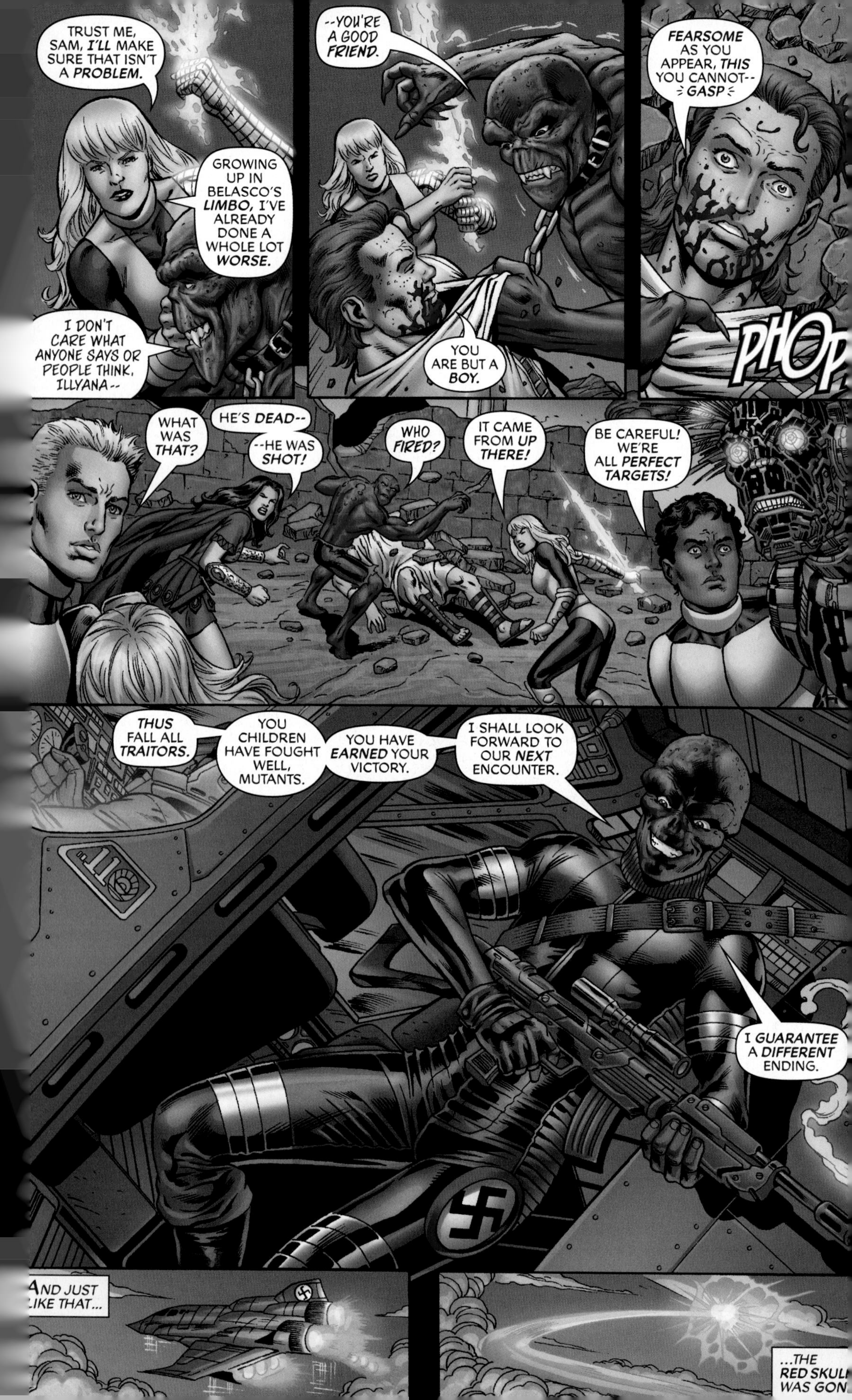

TRUST ME, SAM, I'LL MAKE SURE THAT ISN'T A PROBLEM.
GROWING UP IN BELASCO'S LIMBO, I'VE ALREADY DONE A WHOLE LOT WORSE.
I DON'T CARE WHAT ANYONE SAYS OR PEOPLE THINK, ILLYANA--
--YOU'RE A GOOD FRIEND.
YOU ARE BUT A BOY.
FEARSOME AS YOU APPEAR, THIS YOU CANNOT-- GASP
PHOP
WHAT WAS THAT?
HE'S DEAD--
--HE WAS SHOT!
WHO FIRED?
IT CAME FROM UP THERE!
BE CAREFUL! WE'RE ALL PERFECT TARGETS!
THUS FALL ALL TRAITORS.
YOU CHILDREN HAVE FOUGHT WELL, MUTANTS.
YOU HAVE EARNED YOUR VICTORY.
I SHALL LOOK FORWARD TO OUR NEXT ENCOUNTER.
I GUARANTEE A DIFFERENT ENDING.
AND JUST LIKE THAT...
...THE RED SKUL WAS GON

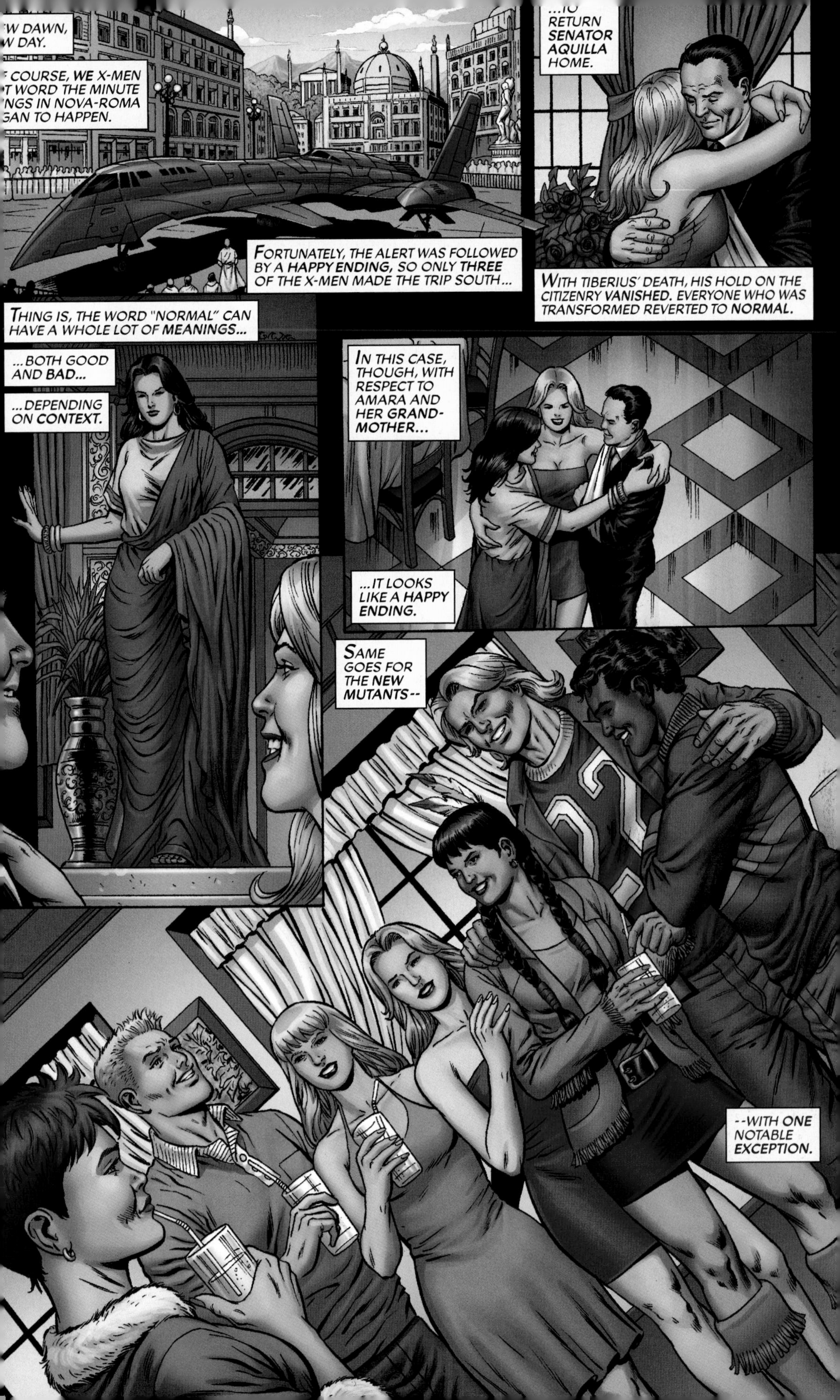

W DAWN,
W DAWN.
COURSE, WE X-MEN
T WORD THE MINUTE
NGS IN NOVA-ROMA
GAN TO HAPPEN.
FORTUNATELY, THE ALERT WAS FOLLOWED BY A HAPPY ENDING, SO ONLY THREE OF THE X-MEN MADE THE TRIP SOUTH...
...TO RETURN SENATOR AQUILLA HOME.
WITH TIBERIUS' DEATH, HIS HOLD ON THE CITIZENRY VANISHED. EVERYONE WHO WAS TRANSFORMED REVERTED TO NORMAL.
THING IS, THE WORD "NORMAL" CAN HAVE A WHOLE LOT OF MEANINGS...
...BOTH GOOD AND BAD...
...DEPENDING ON CONTEXT.
IN THIS CASE, THOUGH, WITH RESPECT TO AMARA AND HER GRAND-MOTHER...
...IT LOOKS LIKE A HAPPY ENDING.
SAME GOES FOR THE NEW MUTANTS--
--WITH ONE NOTABLE EXCEPTION.

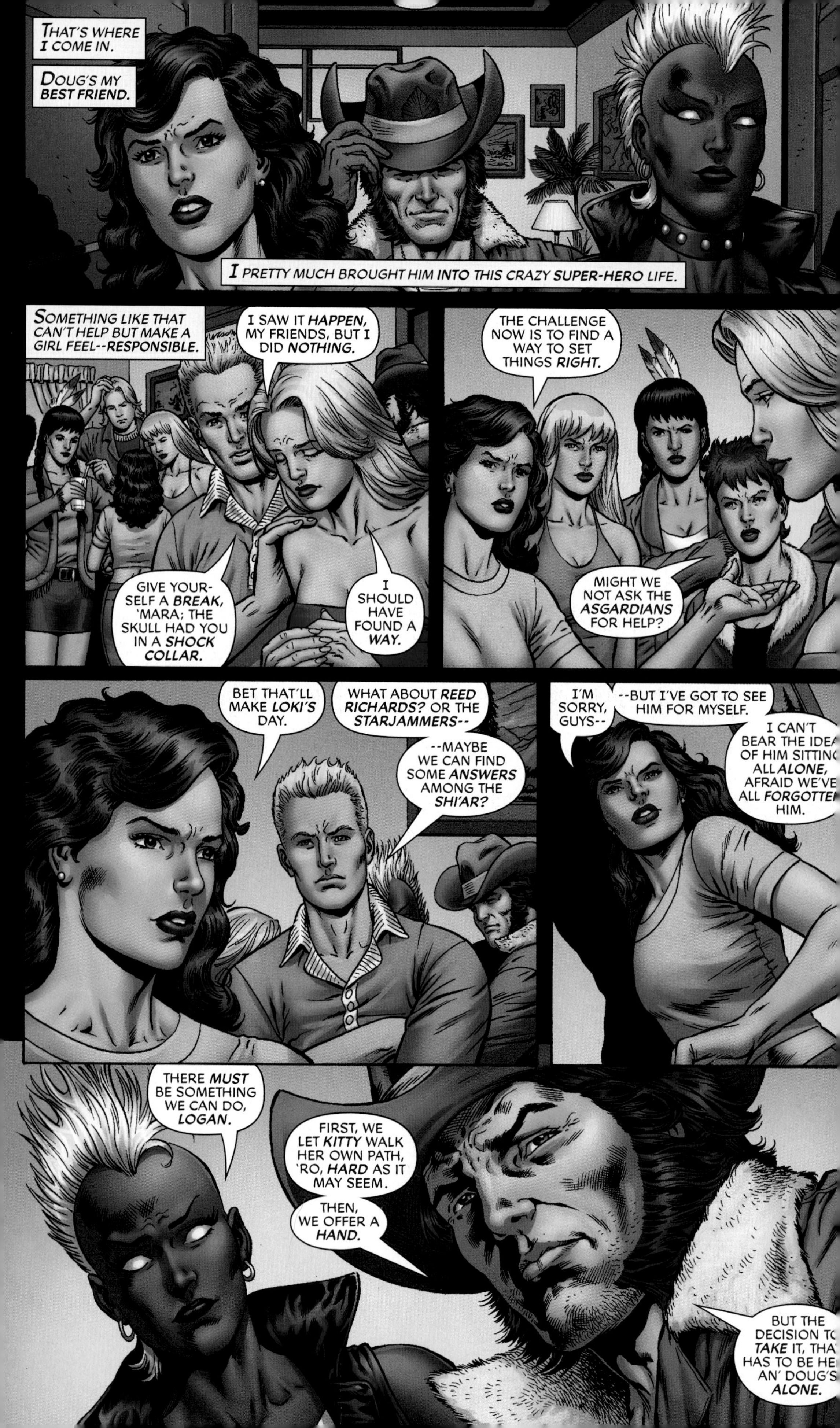
THAT'S WHERE I COME IN.
DOUG'S MY BEST FRIEND.
I PRETTY MUCH BROUGHT HIM INTO THIS CRAZY SUPER-HERO LIFE.
SOMETHING LIKE THAT CAN'T HELP BUT MAKE A GIRL FEEL--RESPONSIBLE.
I SAW IT HAPPEN, MY FRIENDS, BUT I DID NOTHING.
GIVE YOURSELF A BREAK, 'MARA; THE SKULL HAD YOU IN A SHOCK COLLAR.
I SHOULD HAVE FOUND A WAY.
THE CHALLENGE NOW IS TO FIND A WAY TO SET THINGS RIGHT.
MIGHT WE NOT ASK THE ASGARDIANS FOR HELP?
BET THAT'LL MAKE LOKI'S DAY.
WHAT ABOUT REED RICHARDS? OR THE STARJAMMERS--
--MAYBE WE CAN FIND SOME ANSWERS AMONG THE SHI'AR?
I'M SORRY, GUYS--
--BUT I'VE GOT TO SEE HIM FOR MYSELF.
I CAN'T BEAR THE IDEA OF HIM SITTING ALL ALONE, AFRAID WE'VE ALL FORGOTTEN HIM.
THERE MUST BE SOMETHING WE CAN DO, LOGAN.
FIRST, WE LET KITTY WALK HER OWN PATH, 'RO, HARD AS IT MAY SEEM.
THEN, WE OFFER A HAND.
BUT THE DECISION TO TAKE IT, THAT HAS TO BE HER AN' DOUG'S ALONE.

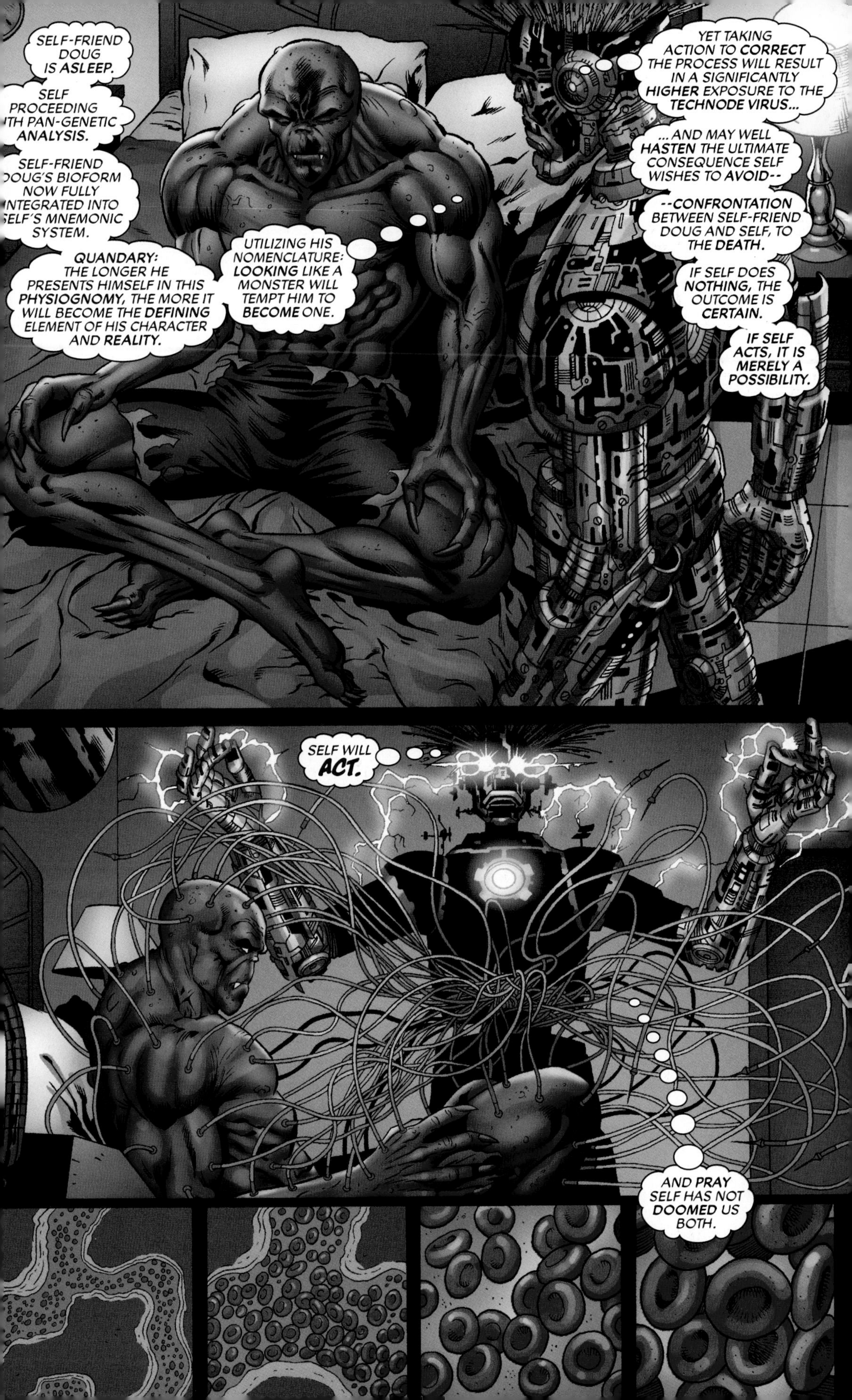
SELF-FRIEND DOUG IS ASLEEP.
SELF PROCEEDING WITH PAN-GENETIC ANALYSIS.
SELF-FRIEND DOUG'S BIOFORM NOW FULLY INTEGRATED INTO SELF'S MNEMONIC SYSTEM.
QUANDARY: THE LONGER HE PRESENTS HIMSELF IN THIS PHYSIOGNOMY, THE MORE IT WILL BECOME THE DEFINING ELEMENT OF HIS CHARACTER AND REALITY.
UTILIZING HIS NOMENCLATURE: LOOKING LIKE A MONSTER WILL TEMPT HIM TO BECOME ONE.
YET TAKING ACTION TO CORRECT THE PROCESS WILL RESULT IN A SIGNIFICANTLY HIGHER EXPOSURE TO THE TECHNODE VIRUS...
...AND MAY WELL HASTEN THE ULTIMATE CONSEQUENCE SELF WISHES TO AVOID--
--CONFRONTATION BETWEEN SELF-FRIEND DOUG AND SELF, TO THE DEATH.
IF SELF DOES NOTHING, THE OUTCOME IS CERTAIN.
IF SELF ACTS, IT IS MERELY A POSSIBILITY.
SELF WILL ACT.
AND PRAY SELF HAS NOT DOOMED US BOTH.

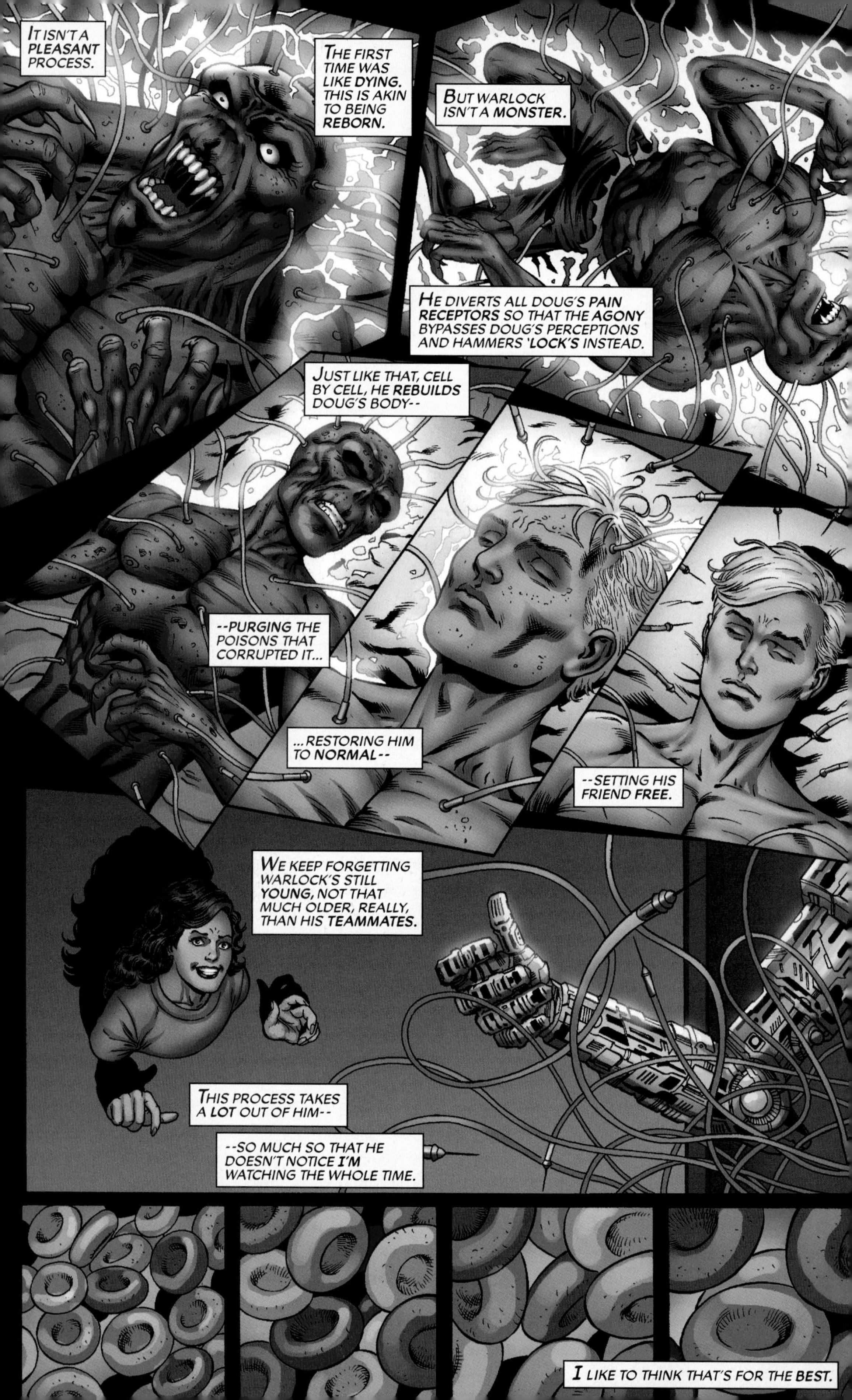
IT ISN'T A PLEASANT PROCESS.
THE FIRST TIME WAS LIKE DYING. THIS IS AKIN TO BEING REBORN.
BUT WARLOCK ISN'T A MONSTER.
HE DIVERTS ALL DOUG'S PAIN RECEPTORS SO THAT THE AGONY BYPASSES DOUG'S PERCEPTIONS AND HAMMERS 'LOCK'S INSTEAD.
JUST LIKE THAT, CELL BY CELL, HE REBUILDS DOUG'S BODY--
--PURGING THE POISONS THAT CORRUPTED IT...
...RESTORING HIM TO NORMAL--
--SETTING HIS FRIEND FREE.
WE KEEP FORGETTING WARLOCK'S STILL YOUNG, NOT THAT MUCH OLDER, REALLY, THAN HIS TEAMMATES.
THIS PROCESS TAKES A LOT OUT OF HIM--
--SO MUCH SO THAT HE DOESN'T NOTICE I'M WATCHING THE WHOLE TIME.
I LIKE TO THINK THAT'S FOR THE BEST.

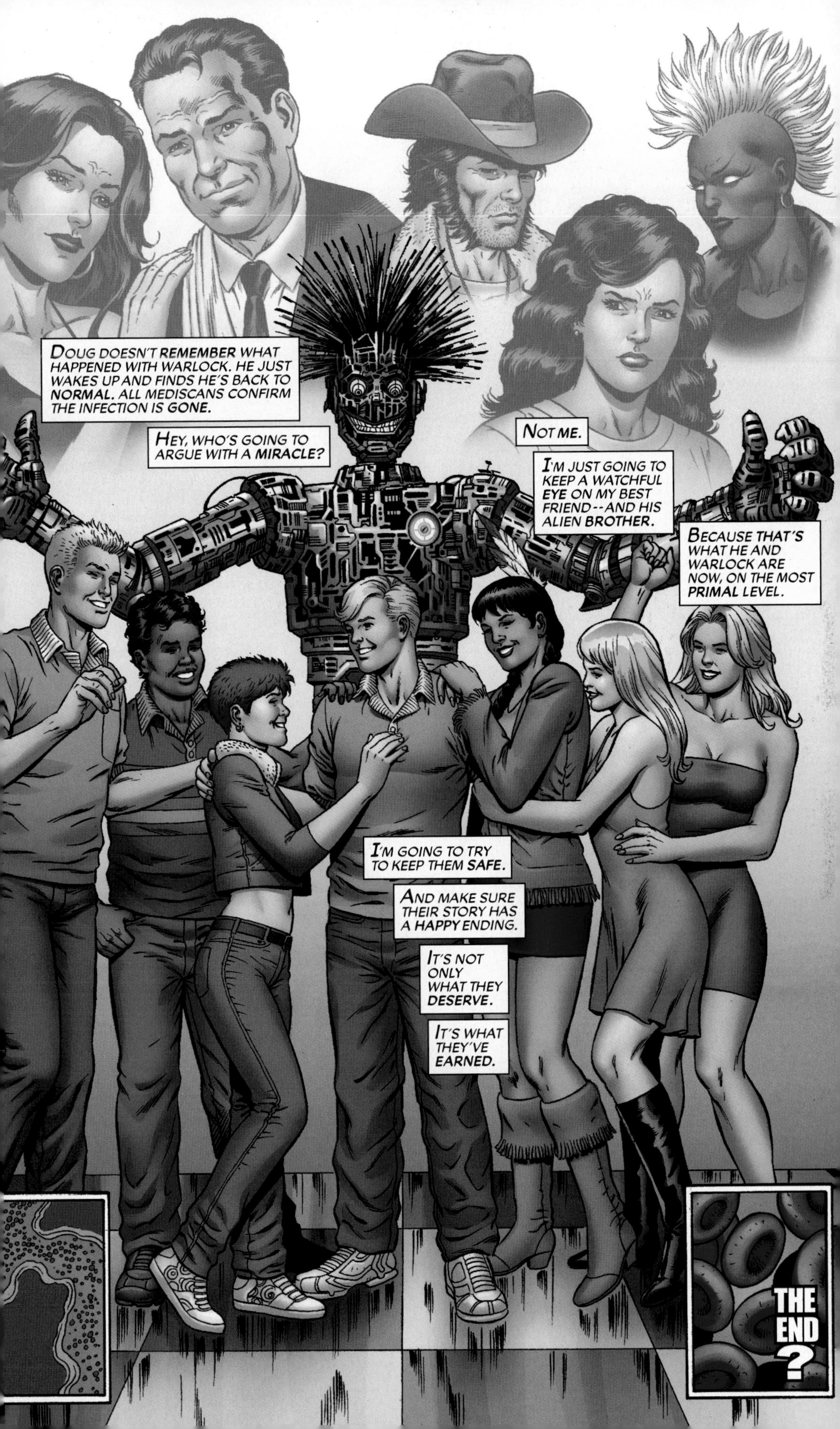
DOUG DOESN'T REMEMBER WHAT HAPPENED WITH WARLOCK. HE JUST WAKES UP AND FINDS HE'S BACK TO NORMAL. ALL MEDISCANS CONFIRM THE INFECTION IS GONE.
HEY, WHO'S GOING TO ARGUE WITH A MIRACLE?
NOT ME.
I'M JUST GOING TO KEEP A WATCHFUL EYE ON MY BEST FRIEND--AND HIS ALIEN BROTHER.
BECAUSE THAT'S WHAT HE AND WARLOCK ARE NOW, ON THE MOST PRIMAL LEVEL.
I'M GOING TO TRY TO KEEP THEM SAFE.
AND MAKE SURE THEIR STORY HAS A HAPPY ENDING.
IT'S NOT ONLY WHAT THEY DESERVE.
IT'S WHAT THEY'VE EARNED.
THE END?

They were a ragtag group of kids from across the world, plucked from their adolescent lives just as their mutant powers were on the cusp of manifesting. Following in the footsteps of Cyclops, Wolverine, Storm, and other X-Men, they were Professor Xavier's New Mutants. In the beginning there were five.

Rahne Sinclair, aka Wolfsbane, able to transform into a feral wolf form.

Dani Moonstar, aka Mirage, able to pull nightmare visions from her foe's psyche and make them seem real.

Robert da Costa, aka Sunspot, able to process the radiant power of the sun into super-strength.

Sam Guthrie, aka Cannonball, able to power through the air with intense force.

Xi'an "Shan" Coy Minh, aka Karma, able to possess others with the powers of her mind.

Each of these young mutants possessed formidable powers, but had only the slightest ability to harness them. Professor Xavier, and at times the big league X-Men, made it their job to teach them the ropes, running them through Danger Room scenarios and trying to keep them out of harm's way. But sometimes, trouble would find the New Mutants, and they'd have to learn on their own...

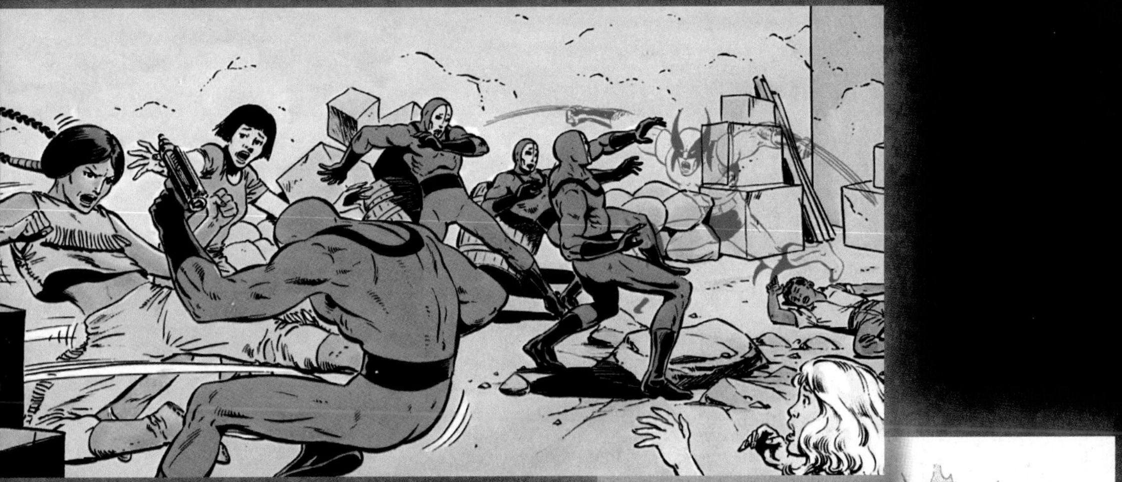

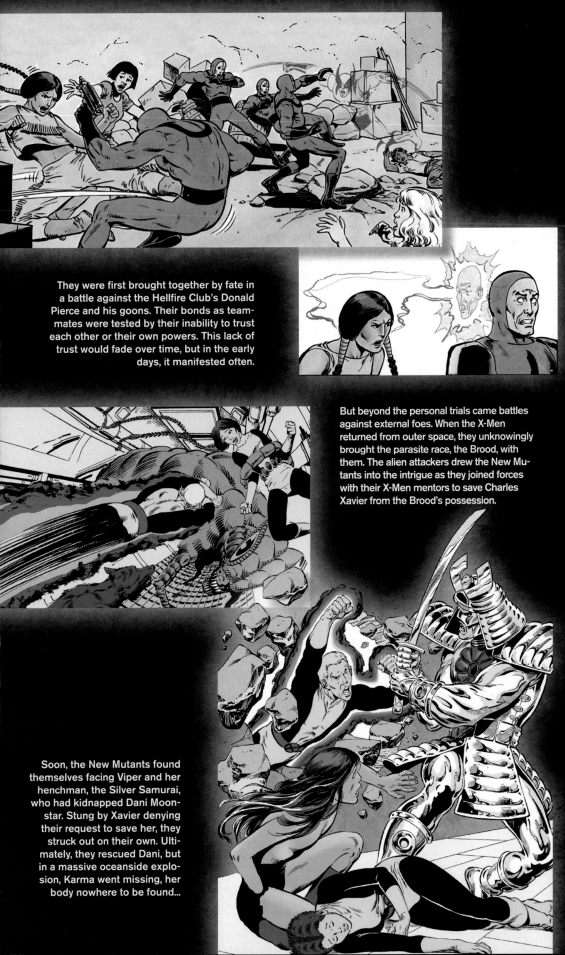

They were first brought together by fate in a battle against the Hellfire Club's Donald Pierce and his goons. Their bonds as teammates were tested by their inability to trust each other or their own powers. This lack of trust would fade over time, but in the early days, it manifested often.

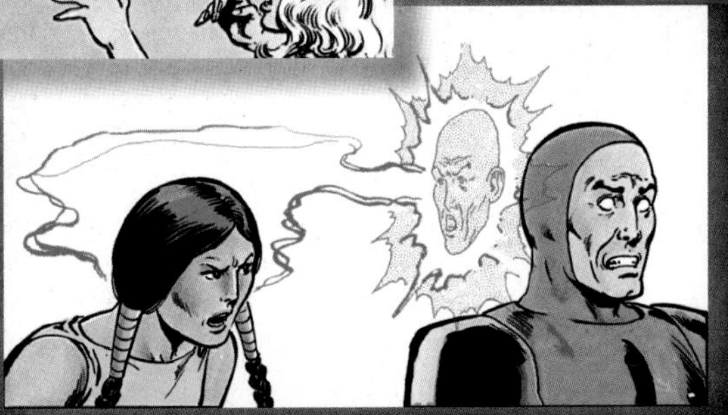

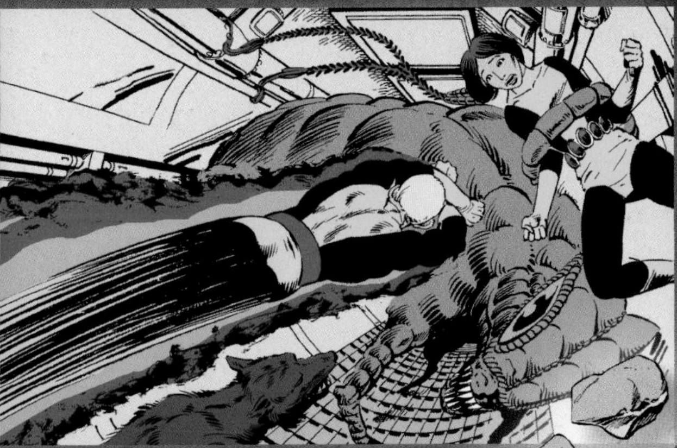

But beyond the personal trials came battles against external foes. When the X-Men returned from outer space, they unknowingly brought the parasite race, the Brood, with them. The alien attackers drew the New Mutants into the intrigue as they joined forces with their X-Men mentors to save Charles Xavier from the Brood's possession.

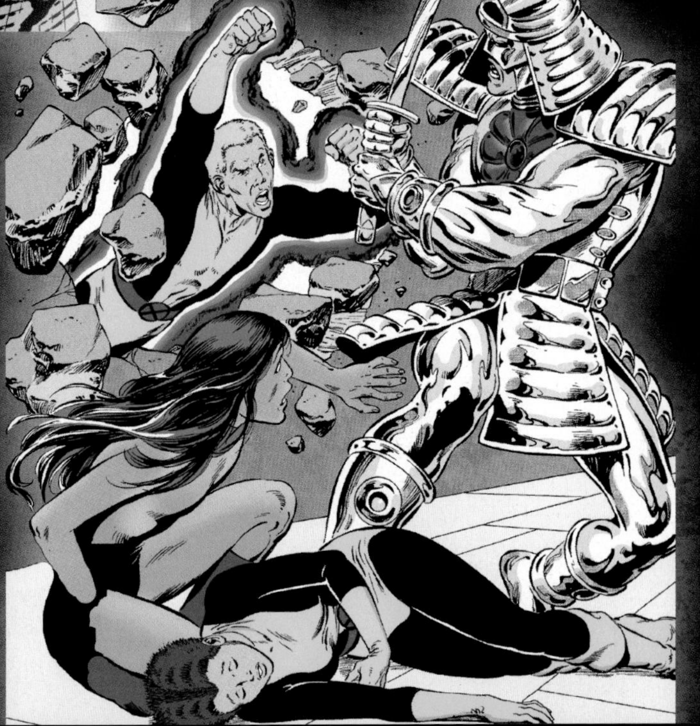

Soon, the New Mutants found themselves facing Viper and her henchman, the Silver Samurai, who had kidnapped Dani Moonstar. Stung by Xavier denying their request to save her, they struck out on their own. Ultimately, they rescued Dani, but in a massive oceanside explosion, Karma went missing, her body nowhere to be found...

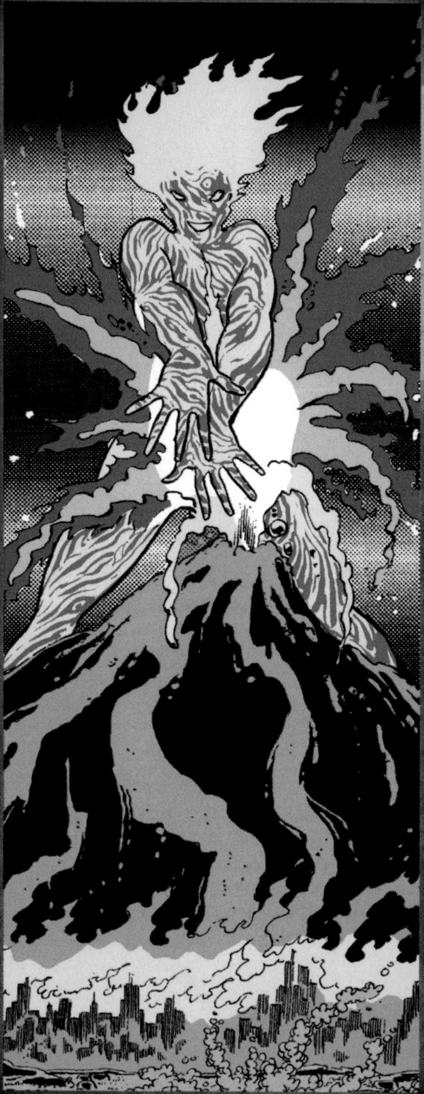

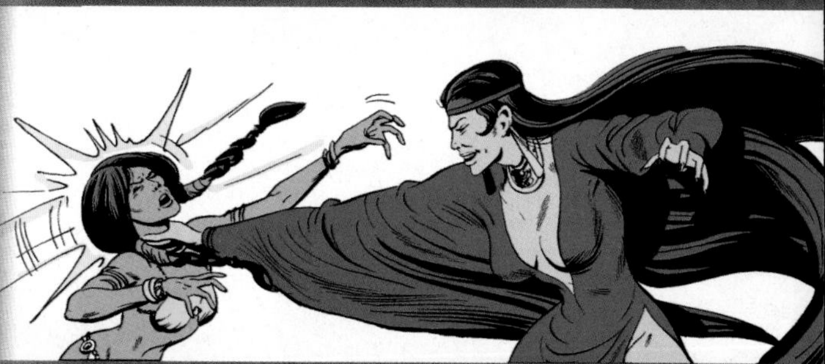

With Karma missing and presumed dead, Professor Xavier sent the team for some R&R, coordinating a cruise up the Amazon with Roberto's mother. What was supposed to be a soothing vacation of fun and fraternity became a hellish ordeal as the New Mutants were taken captive by the centurions of Nova Roma, a hidden city-state deep inside the Amazon jungle. It was in Nova Roma that the New Mutants gained a new member, Amara Aquilla, later codenamed Magma for her power to trigger seismic activity and lava flow, but it was there that they also gained a new foe, the evil Selene, a centuries-old psychic vampire.

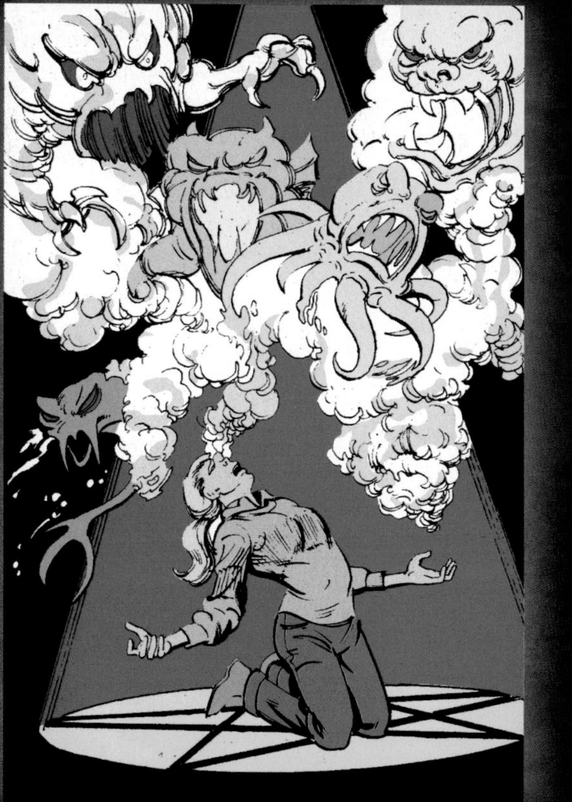

They overcame Selene and left Nova Roma with Amara in peace, and soon they would add yet another member to the mix. This time, it was Illyana Rasputin, aka Magik, younger sister of the X-Men's Colossus and recent refugee from the time-bending Limbo and its overlord, Belasco. In that stygian place, the little girl had aged several years in the space of moments – and returned to her native dimension with magical powers and the potent weapon, the Soulsword. Illyana's transition to the team roster would not be a smooth one, but eventually she would earn her teammates trust.

The New Mutants soon faced their villainous counterparts in the Hellions, a team of students with superpowers from Emma Frost's Massachusetts Academy. The X-Men's Kitty Pryde had been kidnapped and brainwashed, a fate that soon befell most of the New Mutants who rode to her rescue. Dani and Illyana managed to tele-port to Limbo just in time to escape the same fate, which allowed them to eventually free their friends after a battle royal with the Hellions.

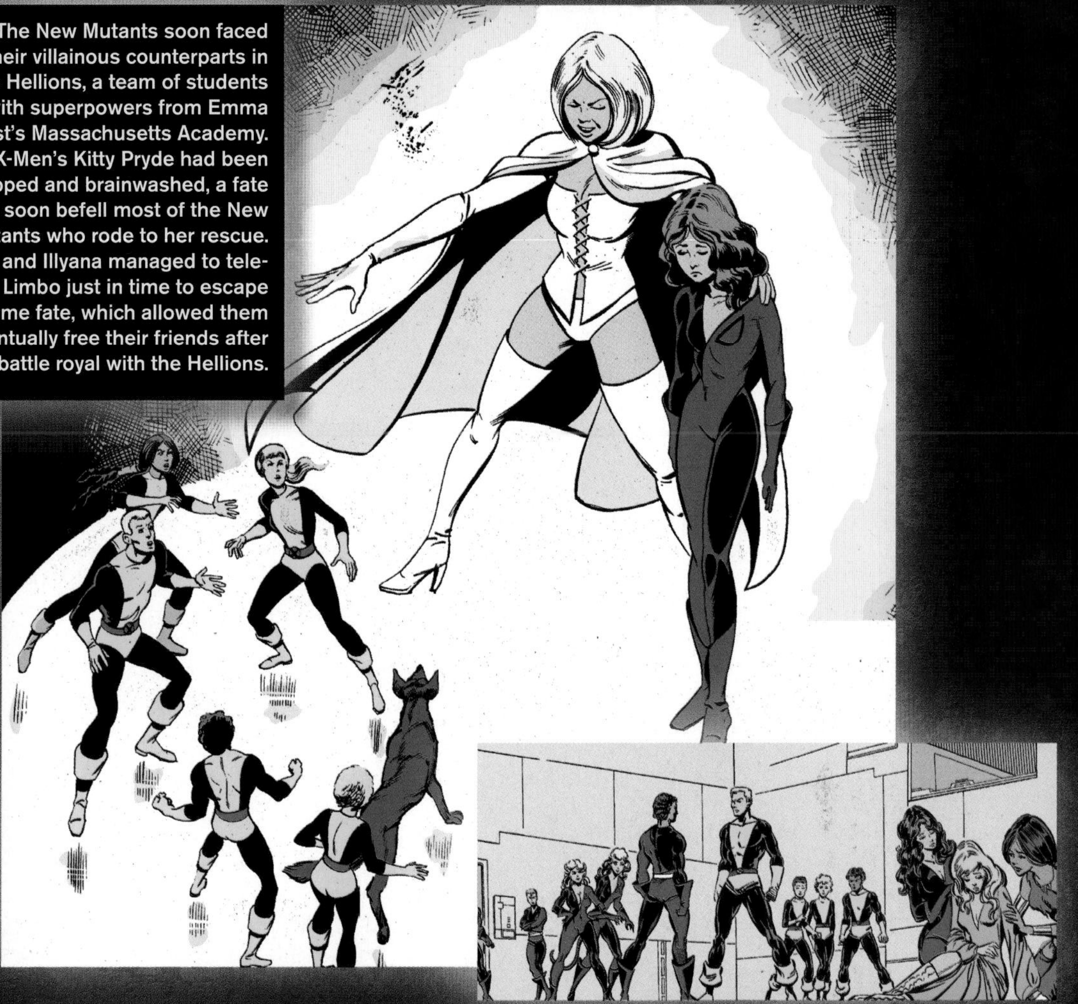

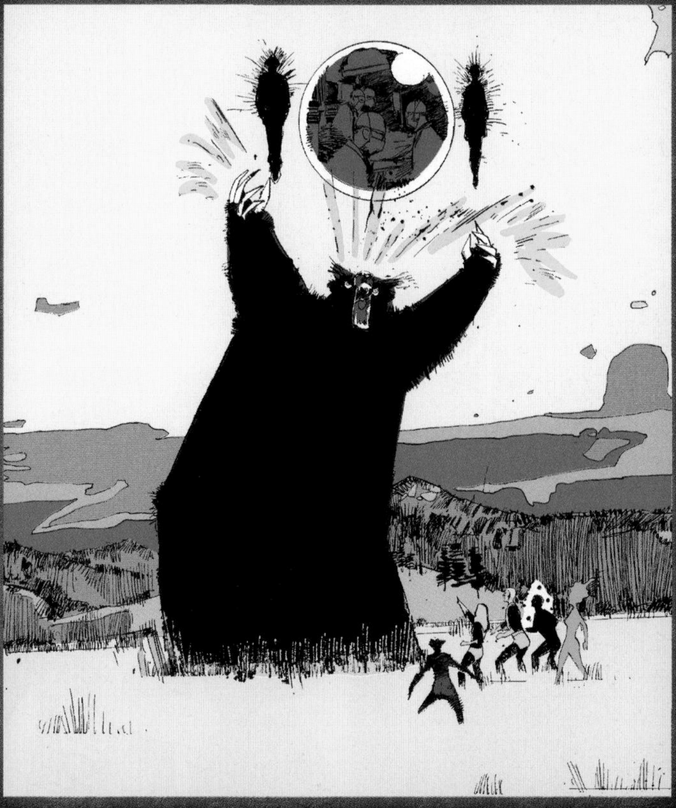

Dani's Cheyenne heritage had always been a great source of pride for her, but it came back to her in a terrible way in the form of the Demon Bear – a monstrous spirit form that had claimed the lives of her mother and father. Her initial bout with the Demon Bear sent her to the hospital with grave injuries. A mystical show-down between the Bear and her New Mutants teammates resulted in the spirit's defeat, and the resurrection of her parents.

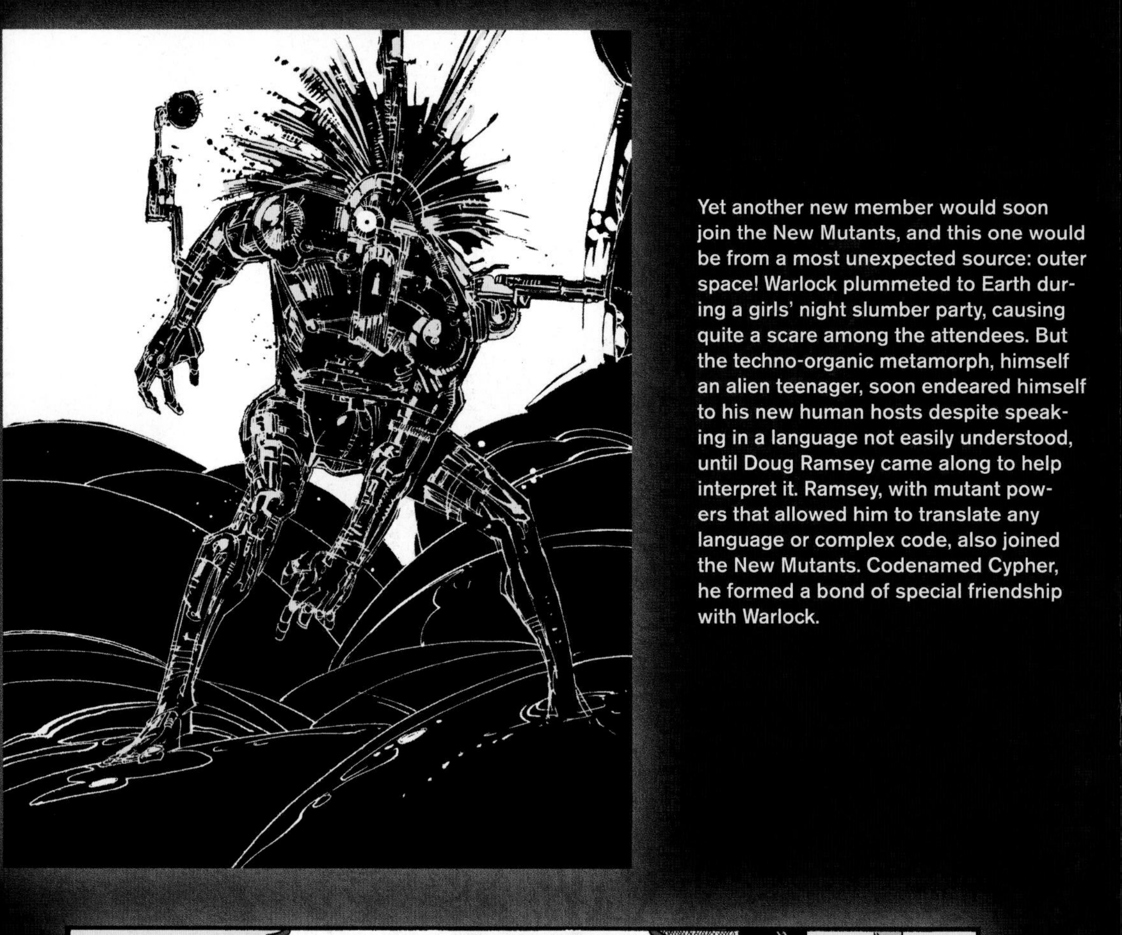

Yet another new member would soon join the New Mutants, and this one would be from a most unexpected source: outer space! Warlock plummeted to Earth during a girls' night slumber party, causing quite a scare among the attendees. But the techno-organic metamorph, himself an alien teenager, soon endeared himself to his new human hosts despite speaking in a language not easily understood, until Doug Ramsey came along to help interpret it. Ramsey, with mutant powers that allowed him to translate any language or complex code, also joined the New Mutants. Codenamed Cypher, he formed a bond of special friendship with Warlock.

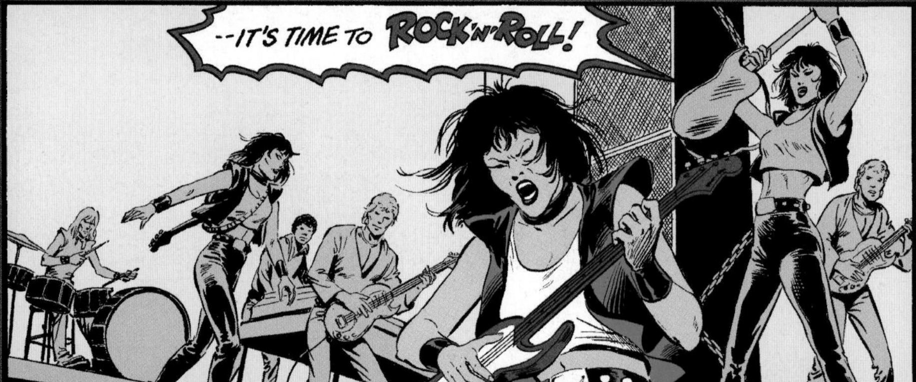
--IT'S TIME TO ROCK'N'ROLL!

The next adventure for the New Mutants would take them all the way to outer space! The team thought they were attending a Manhattan concert by chart-topping rocker Lila Cheney, but little did they know they would be sucked into the galaxy by the interstellar teleporter. Cheney, who used her mutant powers as an adventurer and thief, kindled a romance with Sam, which brought her a bit more down to earth – and to abandon plans to steal the Earth itself!

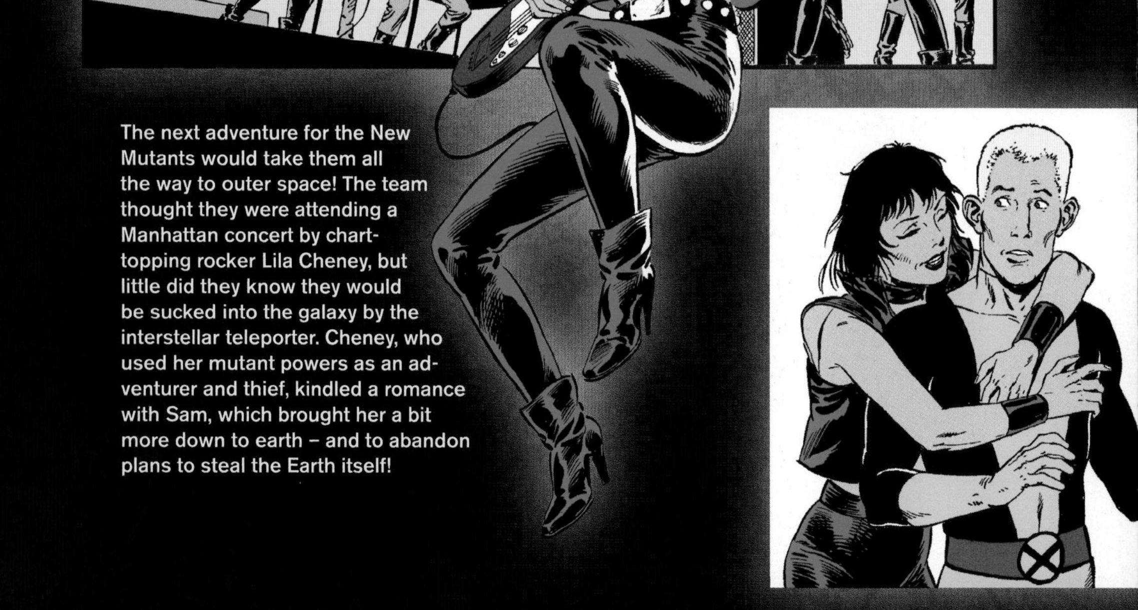

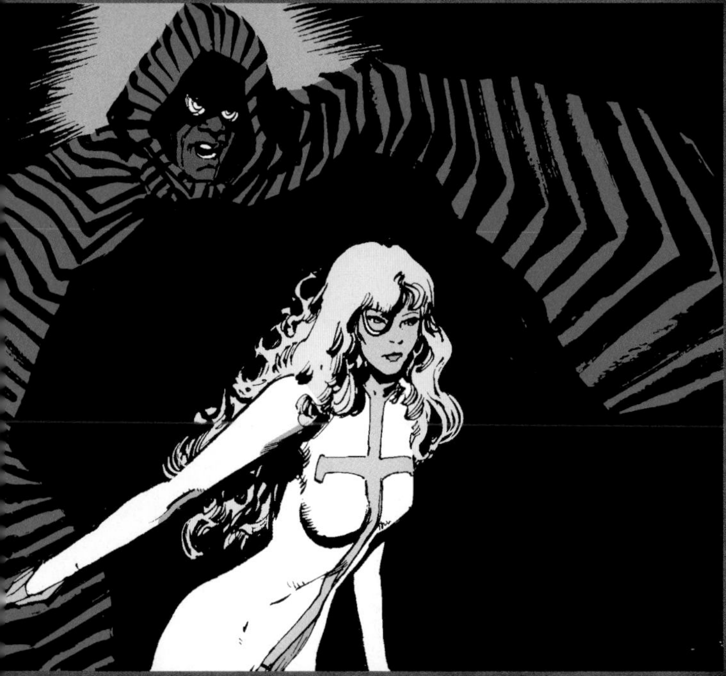

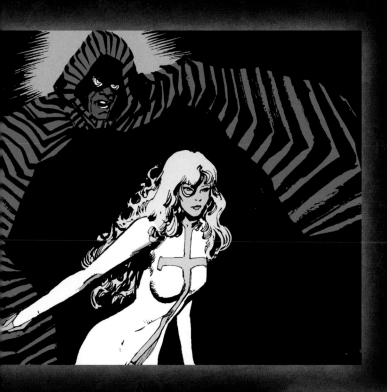

Upon their return to Earth, the New Mutants met up with a pair of homeless teenagers, Cloak and Dagger. In a strange stroke of fortune, their powers over darkness and light were swapped with Rahne and Roberto, a malady which was eventually solved after an overwhelming effort by Charles Xavier and their friends. Despite entreaties from Xavier, Cloak and Dagger refused acceptance to his school, and they returned to the streets to help fellow runaways and troubled youths.

But perhaps the most troubled youth of all was young David Haller, autistic son of research scientist Moira MacTaggart and Charles Xavier. Never having known he had a son, Xavier was doubly surprised when it was revealed that David had taken the form of Legion, a mind-warped schizophrenic whose multiple personalities were all fighting for control inside his mind – with devastating results for those targeted by his psychic abilities. Dani Moonstar was able to help Legion order his mind and restore mental calm, but it would only be a temporary respite in David's sanity...

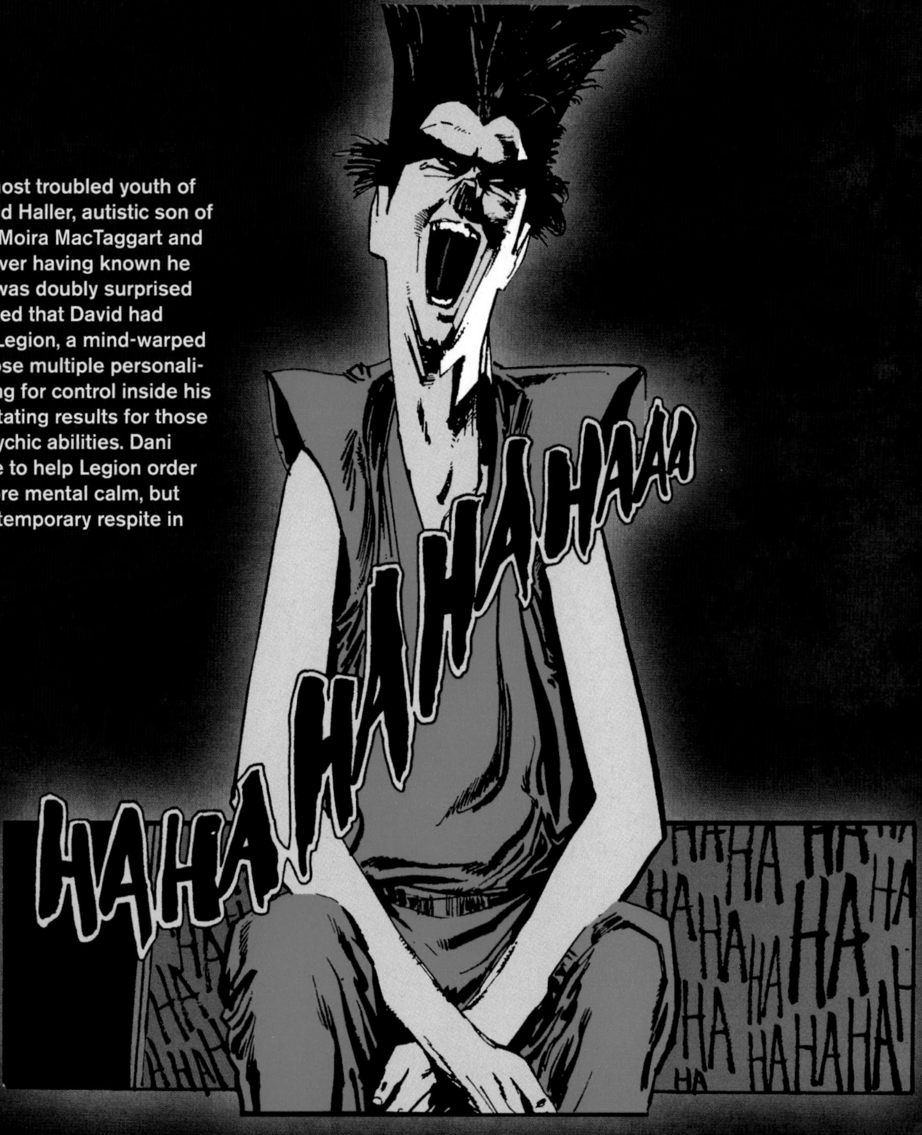
HAHAHAHAHAHAAA

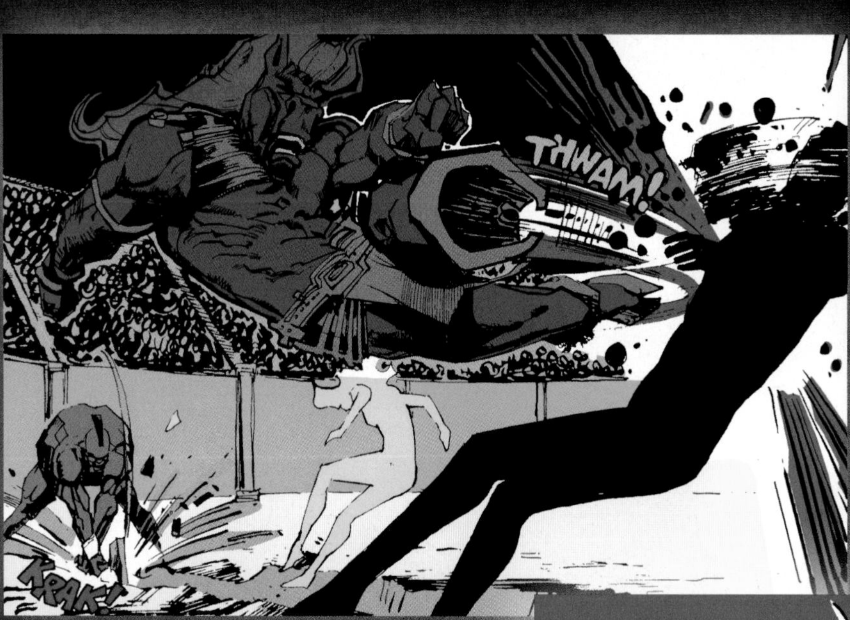
THWAM!
KRAK!

More New Mutants ac
tion followed when th
teens got caught up i
the seamy underworl
competition of the
Gladiators, in which a
assortment of super-
powered combatants
were forced to fight
each other in brutal
battles for the enterta
ment of Los Angeles'
elite. Roberto and Am
ara were taken captiv
and forced into battle
the arena.

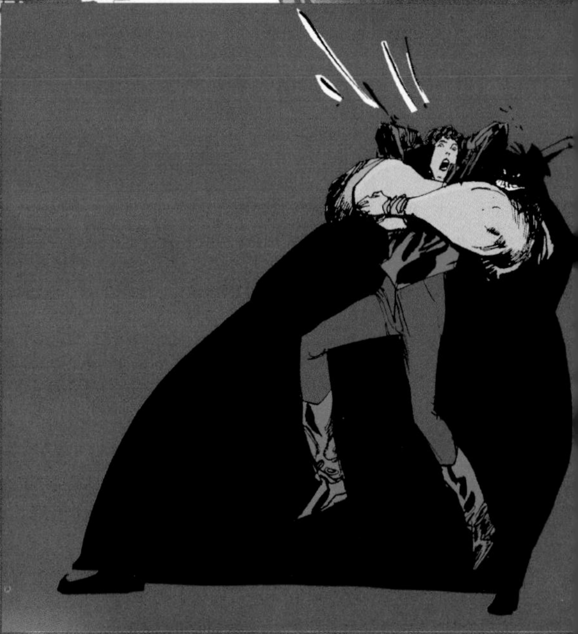

In perhaps the most shocking moment in their lives as the New Mutants, the team learned the identity of the Gladiators' ringleader: Karma! Horribly transformed into a massively corpulent beast by the astral form of Amahl Farouk, Xavier's former enemy, Karma was rehabilitated and returned to the fold with the New Mutants.

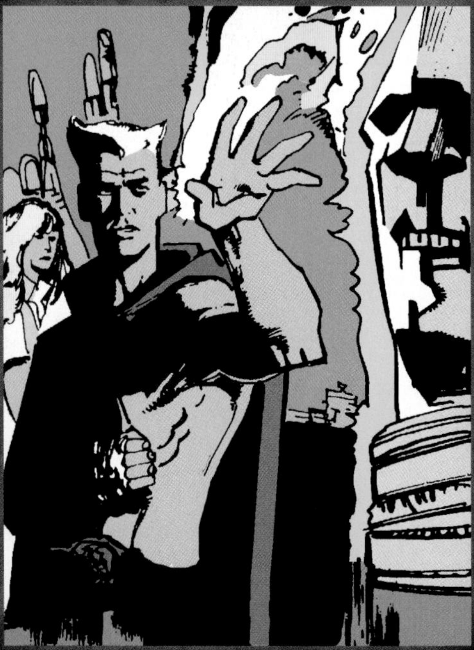

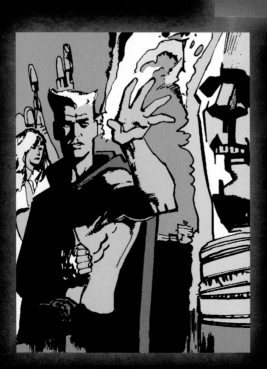

Karma wouldn't be the only personality returned to the world of the X-Men. Magneto had come to the campus to take over for the missing and presumed dead Xavier. Vowing to change his villainous ways to honor the wishes of the New Mutants' mentor, Magneto earned the respect of his young charges through hard work and counsel.

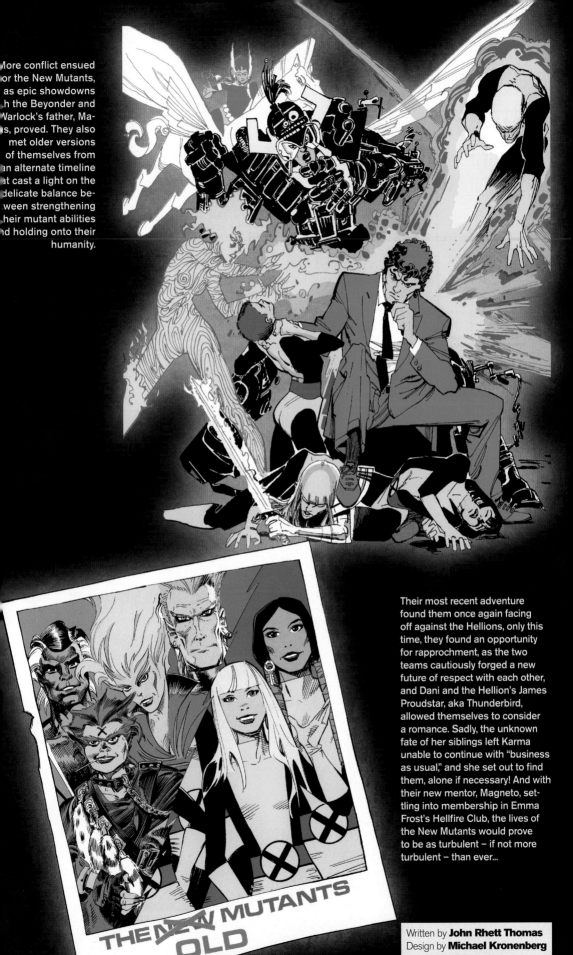

/lore conflict ensued or the New Mutants, as epic showdowns h the Beyonder and Warlock's father, Ma- s, proved. They also met older versions of themselves from n alternate timeline t cast a light on the delicate balance be- ween strengthening heir mutant abilities d holding onto their humanity.

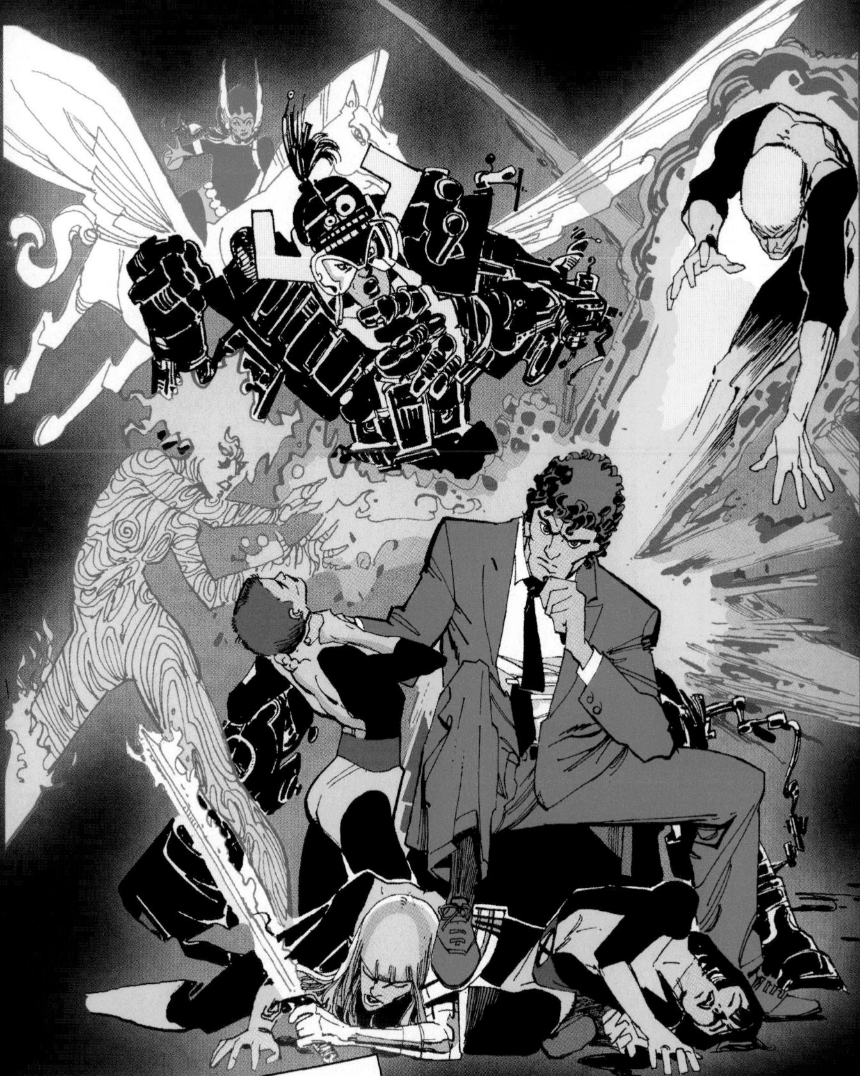

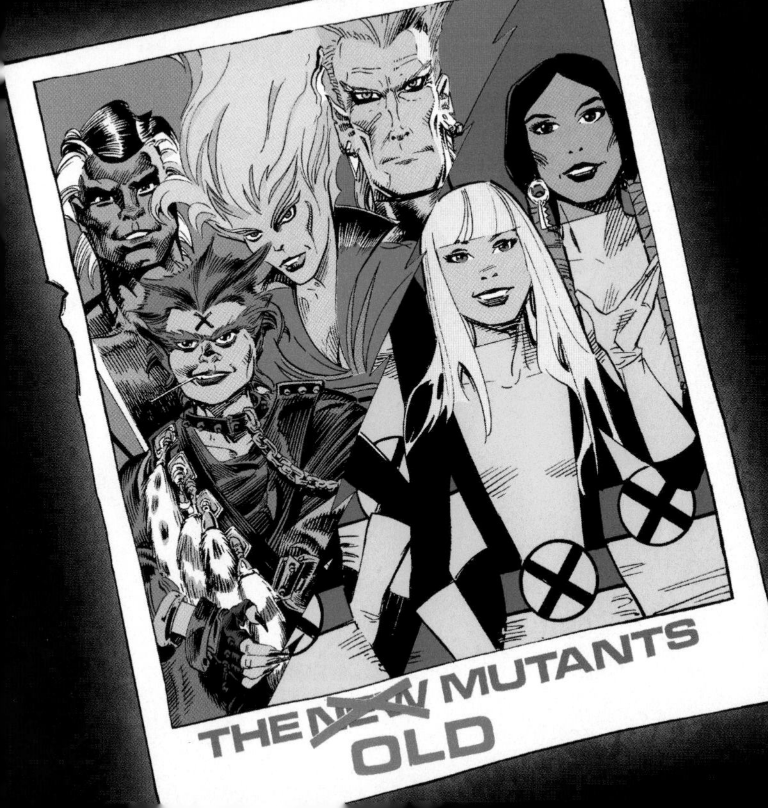
THE ~~NEW~~ MUTANTS
OLD

Their most recent adventure found them once again facing off against the Hellions, only this time, they found an opportunity for rapprochment, as the two teams cautiously forged a new future of respect with each other, and Dani and the Hellion's James Proudstar, aka Thunderbird, allowed themselves to consider a romance. Sadly, the unknown fate of her siblings left Karma unable to continue with "business as usual," and she set out to find them, alone if necessary! And with their new mentor, Magneto, settling into membership in Emma Frost's Hellfire Club, the lives of the New Mutants would prove to be as turbulent – if not more turbulent – than ever...

Written by **John Rhett Thomas**
Design by **Michael Kronenberg**

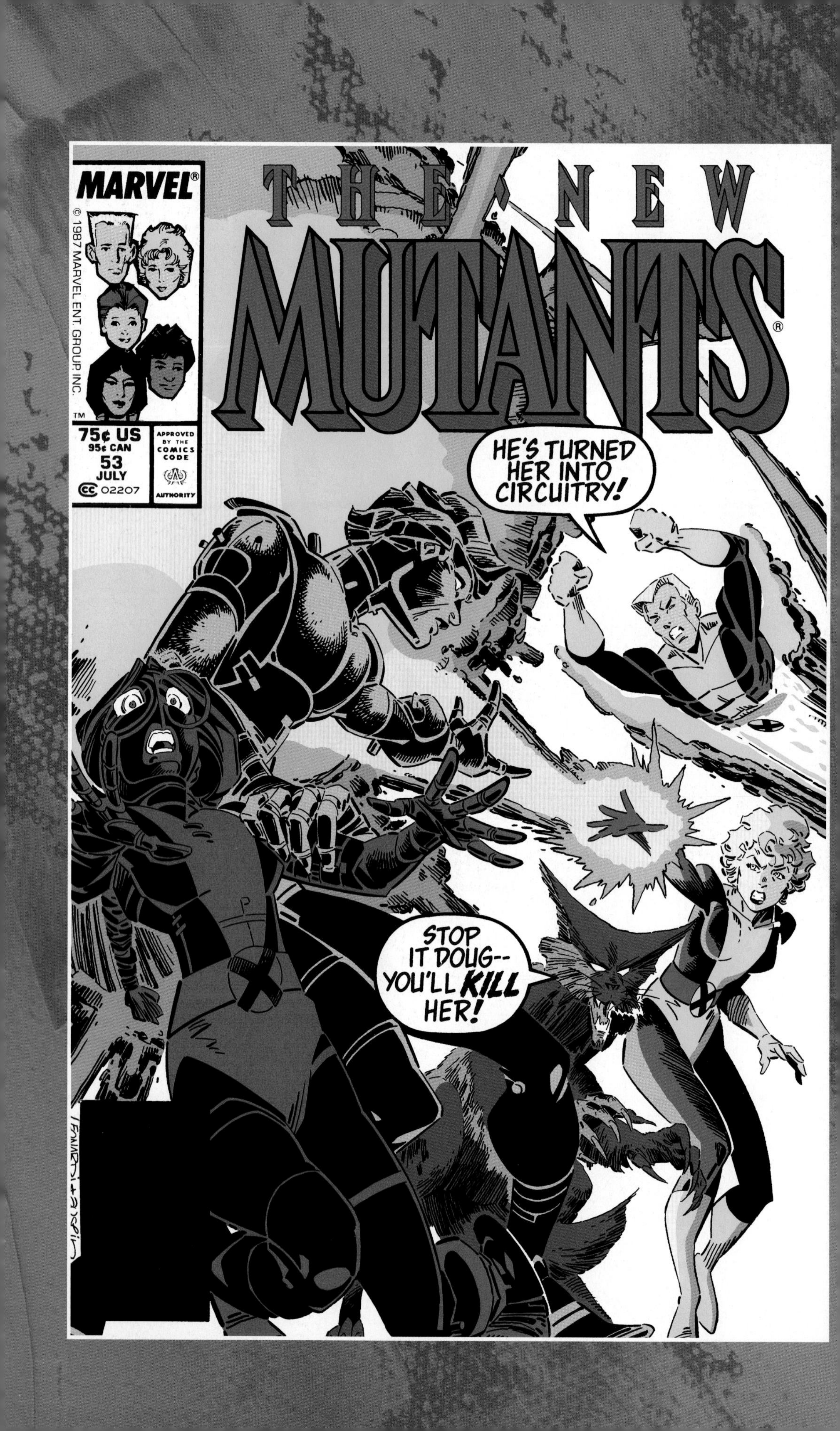
MARVEL
THE NEW MUTANTS
© 1987 MARVEL ENT. GROUP, INC.
75¢ US
95¢ CAN
53
JULY
02207
APPROVED BY THE COMICS CODE AUTHORITY
HE'S TURNED HER INTO CIRCUITRY!
STOP IT DOUG-- YOU'LL KILL HER!

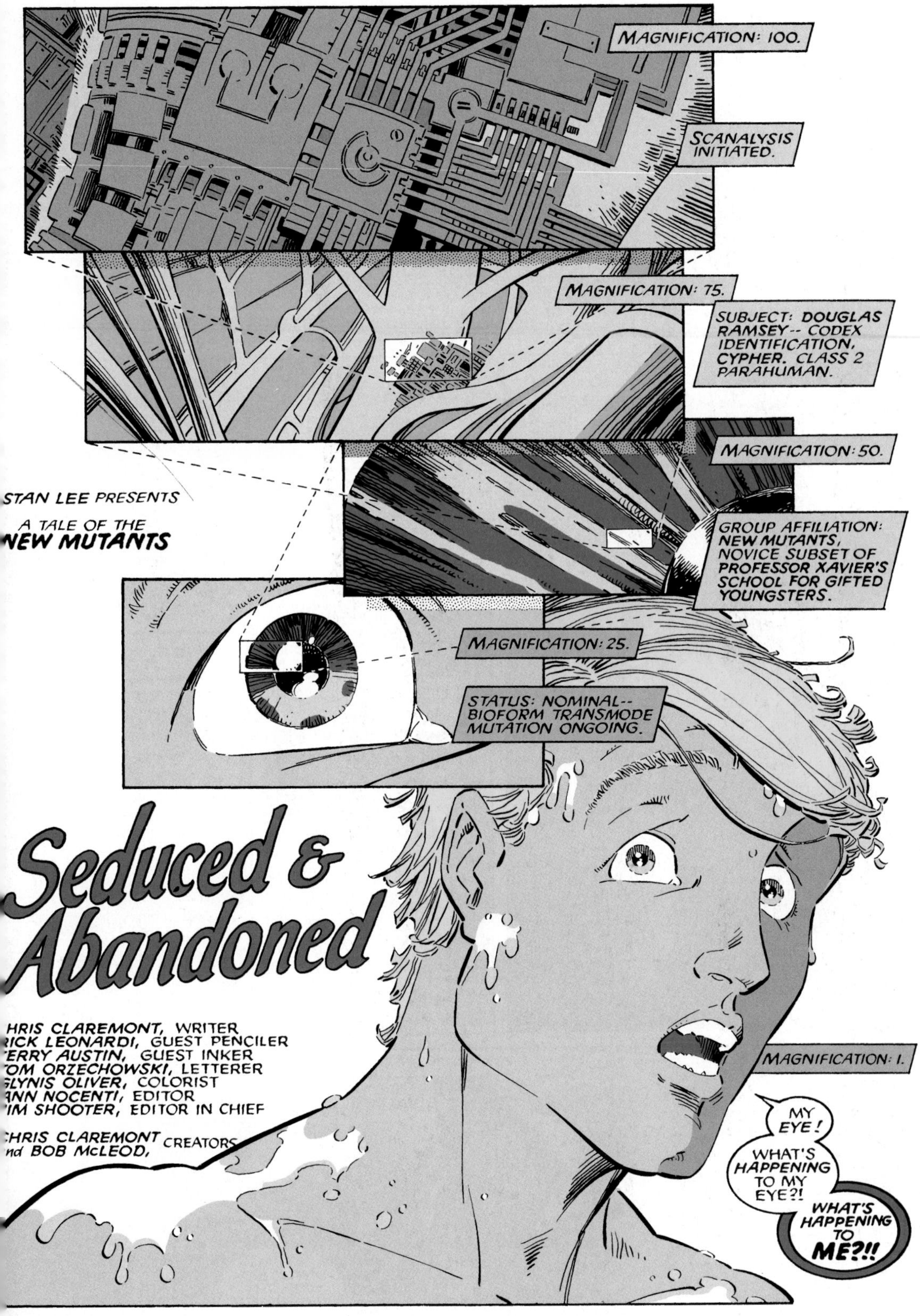
MAGNIFICATION: 100.
SCANALYSIS INITIATED.
MAGNIFICATION: 75.
SUBJECT: DOUGLAS RAMSEY-- CODEX IDENTIFICATION, CYPHER. CLASS 2 PARAHUMAN.
MAGNIFICATION: 50.
STAN LEE PRESENTS
A TALE OF THE NEW MUTANTS
GROUP AFFILIATION: NEW MUTANTS, NOVICE SUBSET OF PROFESSOR XAVIER'S SCHOOL FOR GIFTED YOUNGSTERS.
MAGNIFICATION: 25.
STATUS: NOMINAL-- BIOFORM TRANSMODE MUTATION ONGOING.
Seduced & Abandoned
HRIS CLAREMONT, WRITER
ICK LEONARDI, GUEST PENCILER
ERRY AUSTIN, GUEST INKER
OM ORZECHOWSKI, LETTERER
LYNIS OLIVER, COLORIST
NN NOCENTI, EDITOR
IM SHOOTER, EDITOR IN CHIEF
HRIS CLAREMONT nd BOB McLEOD, CREATORS
MAGNIFICATION: 1.
MY EYE!
WHAT'S HAPPENING TO MY EYE?!
WHAT'S HAPPENING TO ME?!!

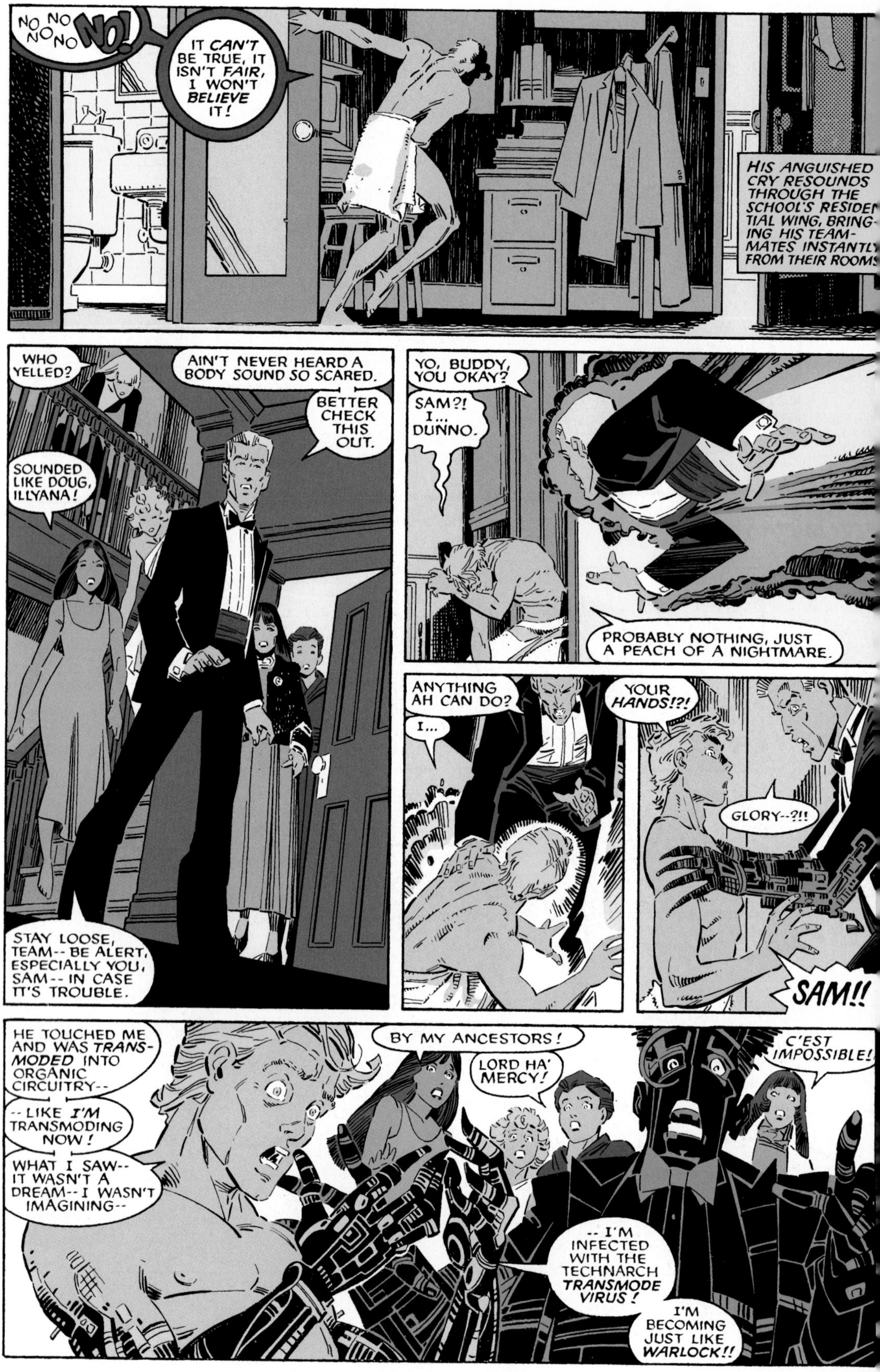
NO NO NO NO NO!
IT CAN'T BE TRUE, IT ISN'T FAIR, I WON'T BELIEVE IT!
HIS ANGUISHED CRY RESOUNDS THROUGH THE SCHOOL'S RESIDENTIAL WING, BRINGING HIS TEAMMATES INSTANTLY FROM THEIR ROOMS
WHO YELLED?
AIN'T NEVER HEARD A BODY SOUND SO SCARED.
BETTER CHECK THIS OUT.
SOUNDED LIKE DOUG, ILLYANA!
STAY LOOSE, TEAM-- BE ALERT, ESPECIALLY YOU, SAM-- IN CASE IT'S TROUBLE.
YO, BUDDY, YOU OKAY?
SAM?! I... DUNNO.
PROBABLY NOTHING, JUST A PEACH OF A NIGHTMARE.
ANYTHING AH CAN DO?
I...
YOUR HANDS!?!
GLORY--?!!
SAM!!
HE TOUCHED ME AND WAS TRANSMODED INTO ORGANIC CIRCUITRY--
--LIKE I'M TRANSMODING NOW!
WHAT I SAW-- IT WASN'T A DREAM-- I WASN'T IMAGINING--
BY MY ANCESTORS!
LORD HA' MERCY!
C'EST IMPOSSIBLE!
-- I'M INFECTED WITH THE TECHNARCH TRANSMODE VIRUS!
I'M BECOMING JUST LIKE WARLOCK!!

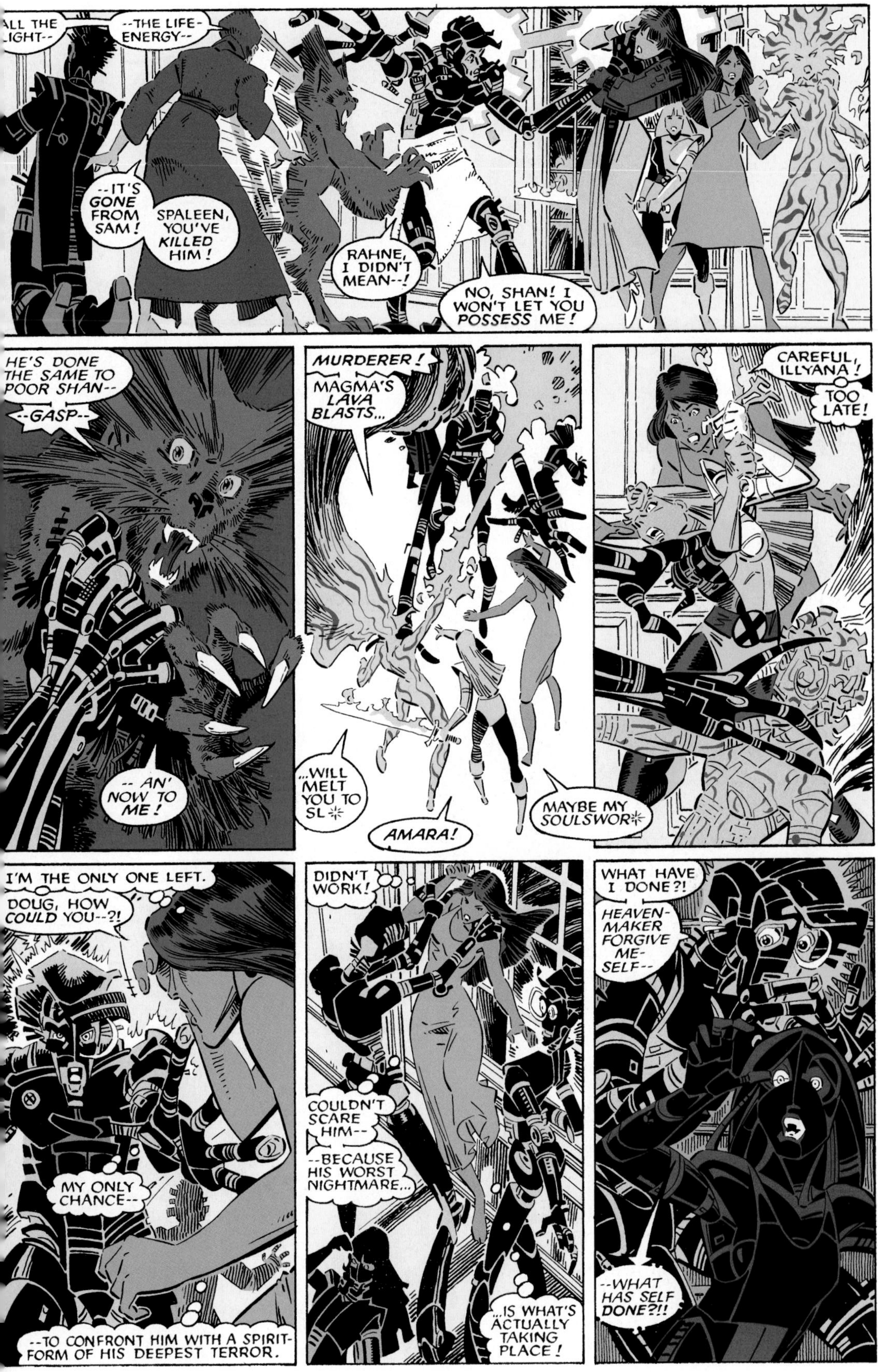
ALL THE LIGHT--
--THE LIFE-ENERGY--
--IT'S GONE FROM SAM!
SPALEEN, YOU'VE KILLED HIM!
RAHNE, I DIDN'T MEAN--!
NO, SHAN! I WON'T LET YOU POSSESS ME!
HE'S DONE THE SAME TO POOR SHAN--
--GASP--
-- AN' NOW TO ME!
MURDERER!
MAGMA'S LAVA BLASTS...
...WILL MELT YOU TO SL
AMARA!
CAREFUL, ILLYANA!
TOO LATE!
MAYBE MY SOULSWOR
I'M THE ONLY ONE LEFT.
DOUG, HOW COULD YOU--?!
MY ONLY CHANCE--
--TO CONFRONT HIM WITH A SPIRIT-FORM OF HIS DEEPEST TERROR.
DIDN'T WORK!
COULDN'T SCARE HIM--
--BECAUSE HIS WORST NIGHTMARE...
...IS WHAT'S ACTUALLY TAKING PLACE!
WHAT HAVE I DONE?!
HEAVEN-MAKER FORGIVE ME-SELF--
--WHAT HAS SELF DONE?!!

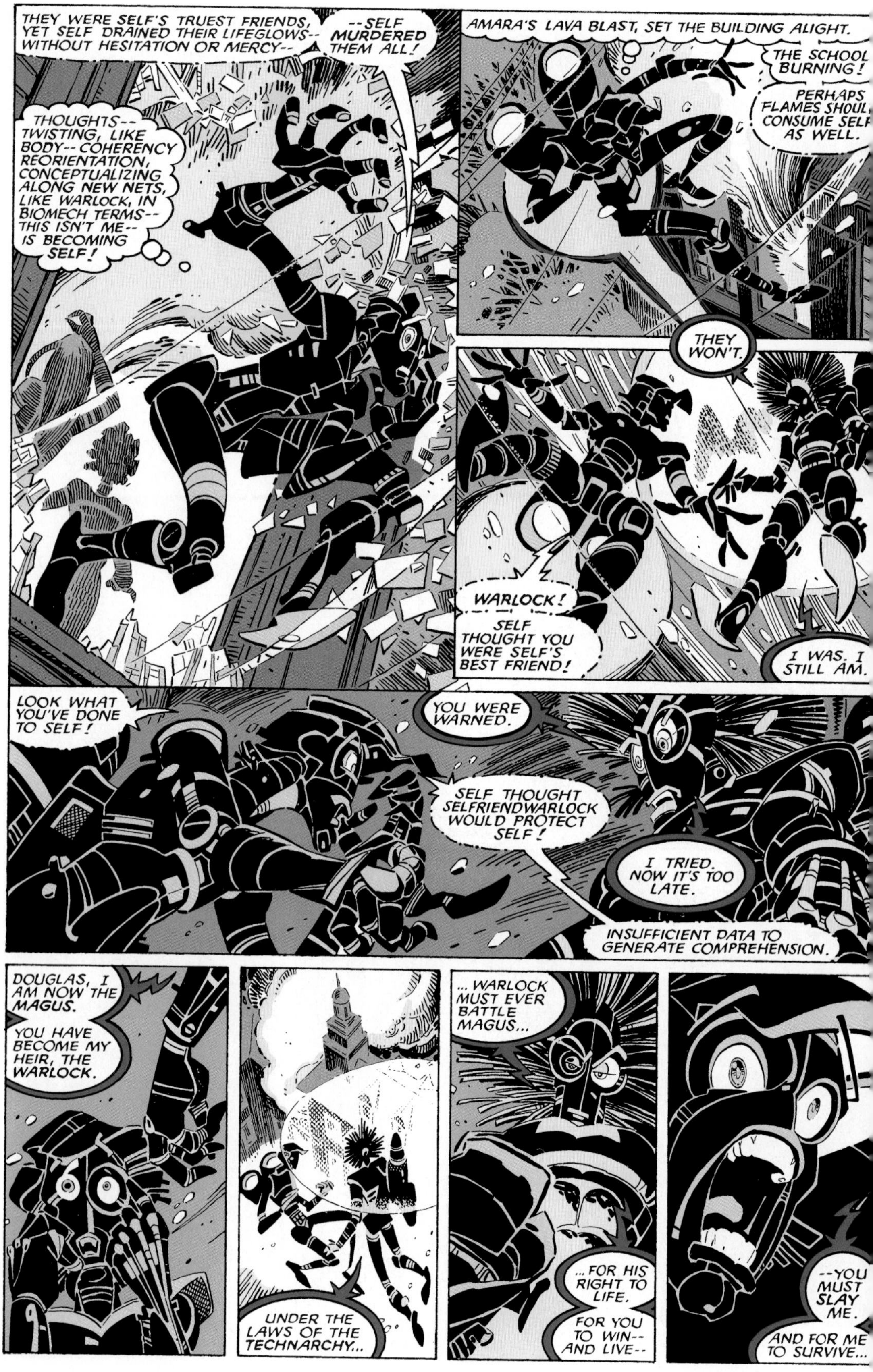
THEY WERE SELF'S TRUEST FRIENDS, YET SELF DRAINED THEIR LIFEGLOWS-- WITHOUT HESITATION OR MERCY--
--SELF MURDERED THEM ALL!
THOUGHTS-- TWISTING, LIKE BODY-- COHERENCY REORIENTATION, CONCEPTUALIZING ALONG NEW NETS, LIKE WARLOCK, IN BIOMECH TERMS-- THIS ISN'T ME-- IS BECOMING SELF!
AMARA'S LAVA BLAST, SET THE BUILDING ALIGHT.
THE SCHOOL BURNING!
PERHAPS FLAMES SHOULD CONSUME SELF AS WELL.
THEY WON'T.
WARLOCK!
SELF THOUGHT YOU WERE SELF'S BEST FRIEND!
I WAS. I STILL AM.
LOOK WHAT YOU'VE DONE TO SELF!
YOU WERE WARNED.
SELF THOUGHT SELFRIENDWARLOCK WOULD PROTECT SELF!
I TRIED. NOW IT'S TOO LATE.
INSUFFICIENT DATA TO GENERATE COMPREHENSION.
DOUGLAS, I AM NOW THE MAGUS.
YOU HAVE BECOME MY HEIR, THE WARLOCK.
UNDER THE LAWS OF THE TECHNARCHY...
...WARLOCK MUST EVER BATTLE MAGUS...
...FOR HIS RIGHT TO LIFE.
FOR YOU TO WIN-- AND LIVE--
--YOU MUST SLAY ME.
AND FOR ME TO SURVIVE...

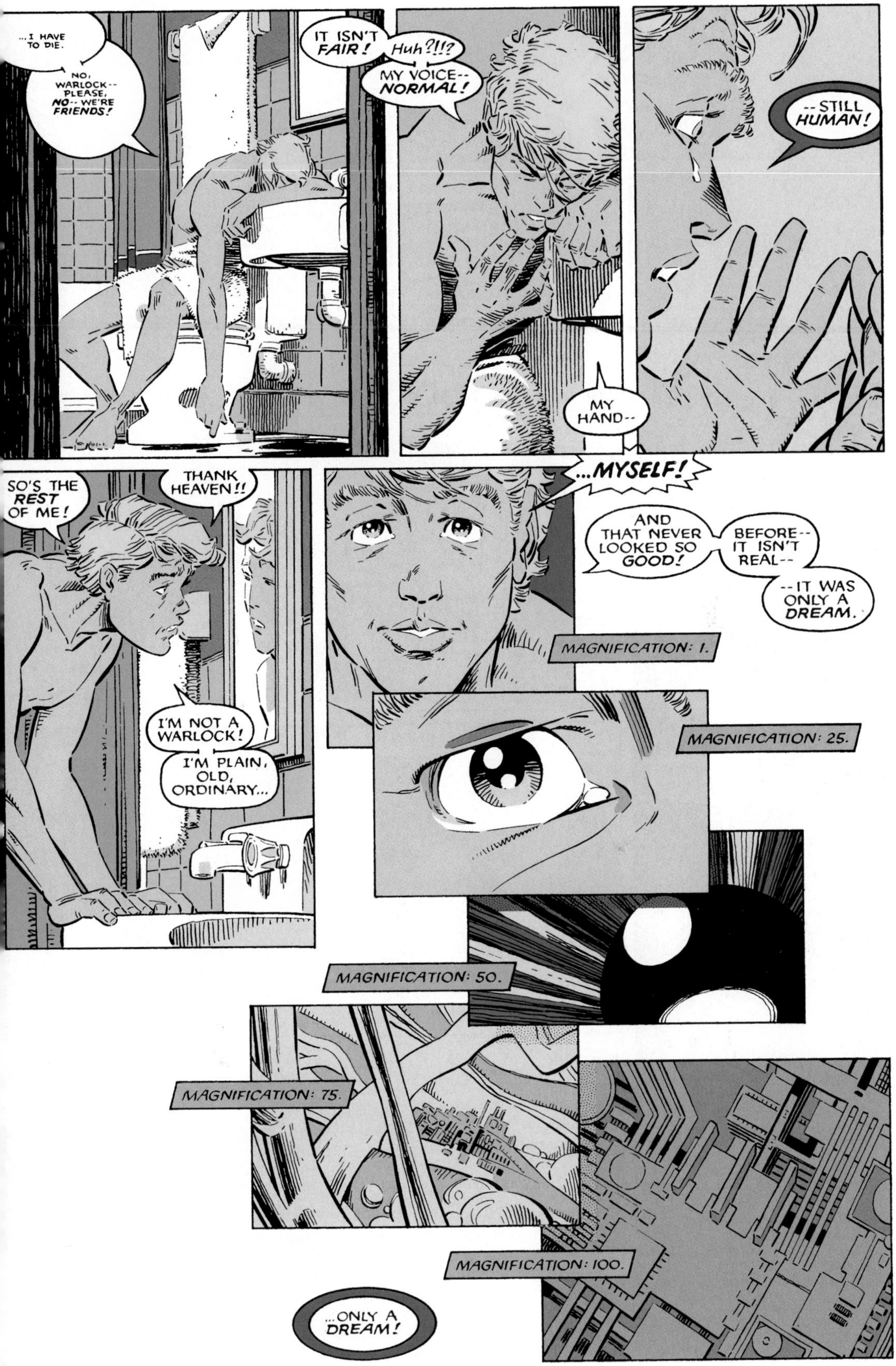
...I HAVE TO DIE.
NO, WARLOCK-- PLEASE, NO-- WE'RE FRIENDS!
IT ISN'T FAIR!
Huh?!!?
MY VOICE-- NORMAL!
MY HAND--
--STILL HUMAN!
SO'S THE REST OF ME!
THANK HEAVEN!!
I'M NOT A WARLOCK!
I'M PLAIN, OLD, ORDINARY...
...MYSELF!
AND THAT NEVER LOOKED SO GOOD!
BEFORE-- IT ISN'T REAL--
--IT WAS ONLY A DREAM.
MAGNIFICATION: 1.
MAGNIFICATION: 25.
MAGNIFICATION: 50.
MAGNIFICATION: 75.
MAGNIFICATION: 100.
...ONLY A DREAM!

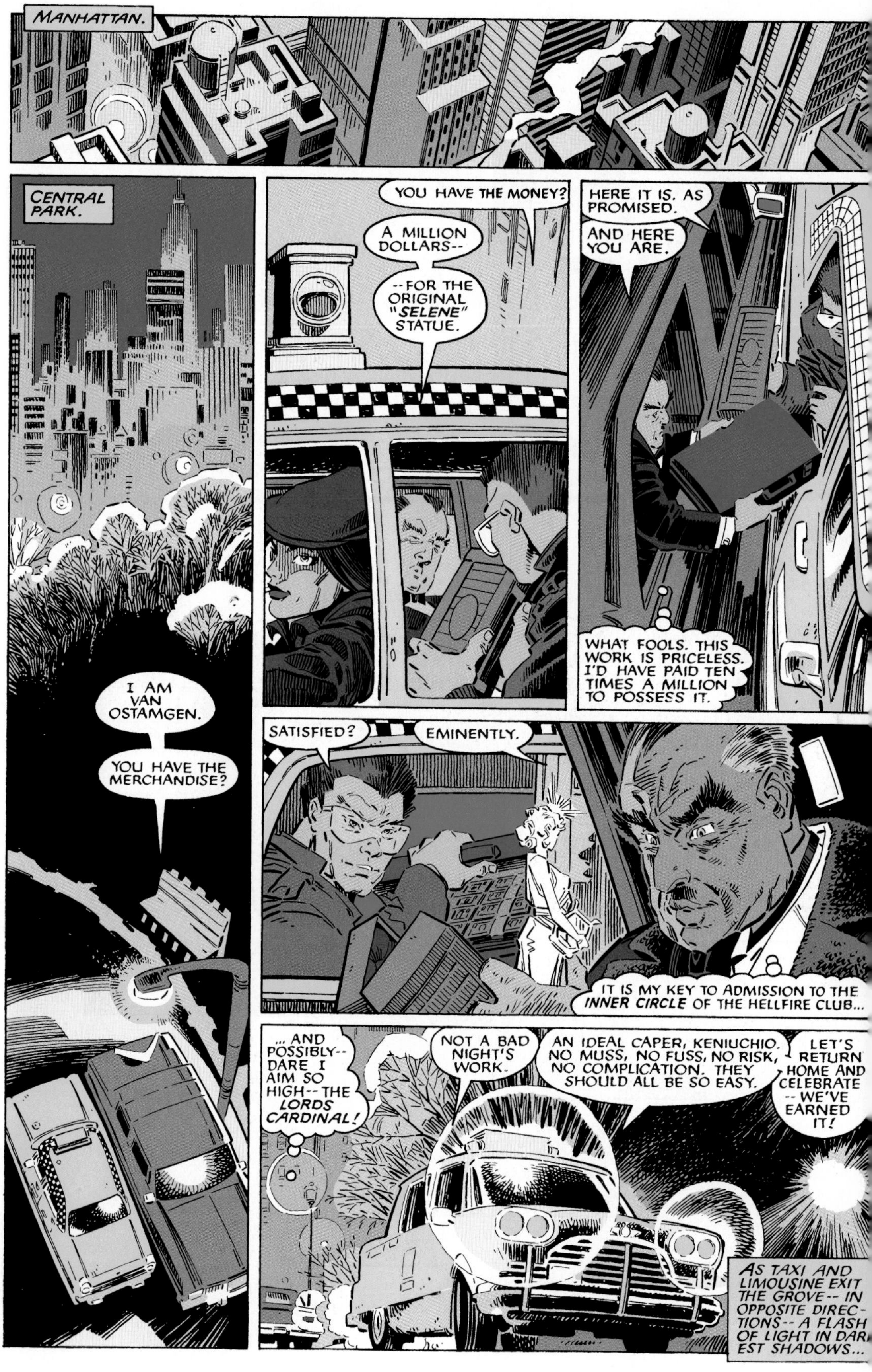
MANHATTAN.
CENTRAL PARK.
YOU HAVE THE MONEY?
A MILLION DOLLARS--
--FOR THE ORIGINAL "SELENE" STATUE.
HERE IT IS. AS PROMISED.
AND HERE YOU ARE.
WHAT FOOLS. THIS WORK IS PRICELESS. I'D HAVE PAID TEN TIMES A MILLION TO POSSESS IT.
I AM VAN OSTAMGEN.
YOU HAVE THE MERCHANDISE?
SATISFIED?
EMINENTLY.
IT IS MY KEY TO ADMISSION TO THE INNER CIRCLE OF THE HELLFIRE CLUB...
...AND POSSIBLY-- DARE I AIM SO HIGH-- THE LORDS CARDINAL!
NOT A BAD NIGHT'S WORK.
AN IDEAL CAPER, KENIUCHIO. NO MUSS, NO FUSS, NO RISK, NO COMPLICATION. THEY SHOULD ALL BE SO EASY.
LET'S RETURN HOME AND CELEBRATE --WE'VE EARNED IT!
AS TAXI AND LIMOUSINE EXIT THE GROVE-- IN OPPOSITE DIRECTIONS-- A FLASH OF LIGHT IN DAR EST SHADOWS...

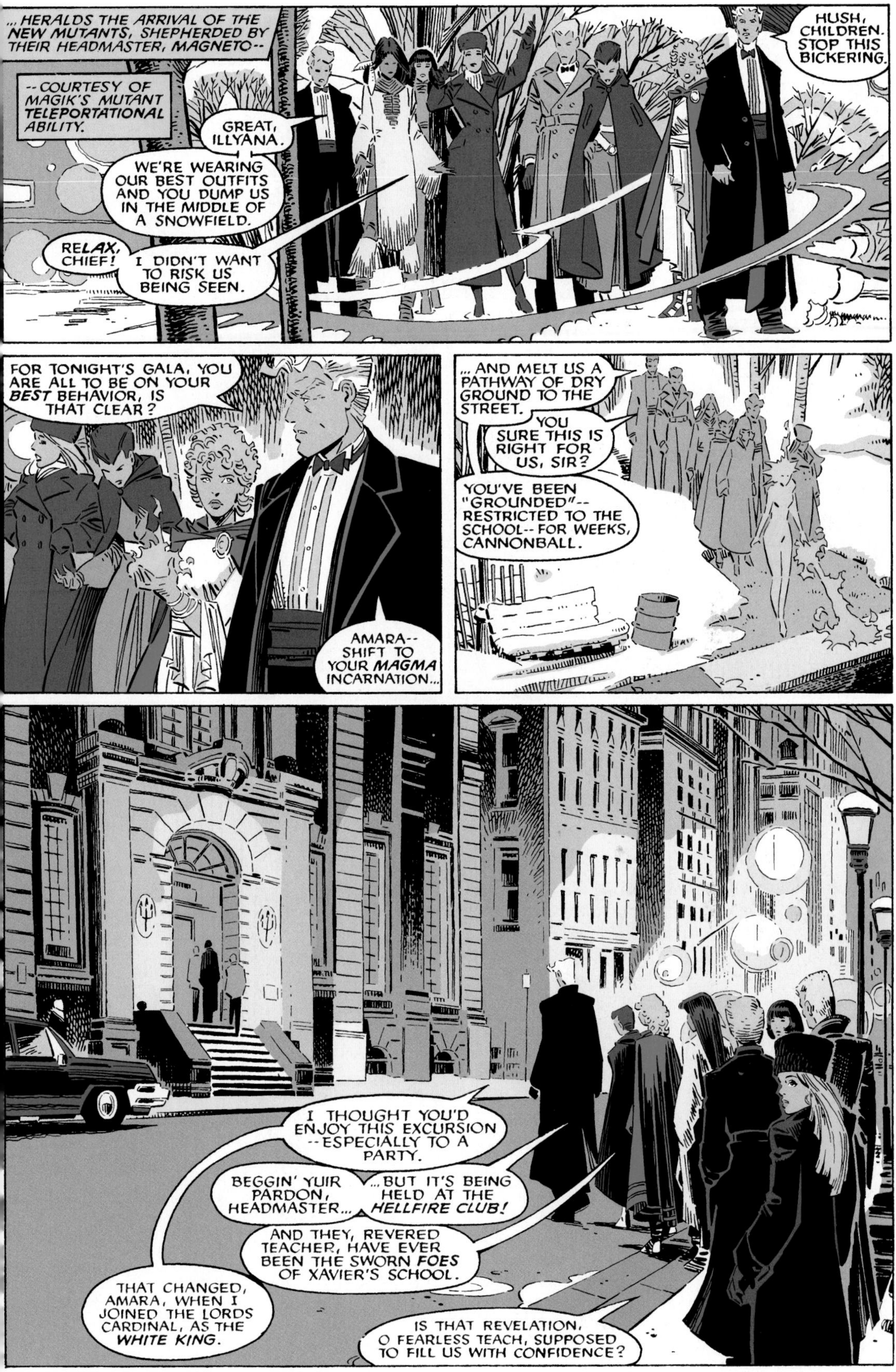

...HERALDS THE ARRIVAL OF THE NEW MUTANTS, SHEPHERDED BY THEIR HEADMASTER, MAGNETO--
--COURTESY OF MAGIK'S MUTANT TELEPORTATIONAL ABILITY.
GREAT, ILLYANA.
WE'RE WEARING OUR BEST OUTFITS AND YOU DUMP US IN THE MIDDLE OF A SNOWFIELD.
RELAX, CHIEF!
I DIDN'T WANT TO RISK US BEING SEEN.
HUSH, CHILDREN. STOP THIS BICKERING.
FOR TONIGHT'S GALA, YOU ARE ALL TO BE ON YOUR BEST BEHAVIOR, IS THAT CLEAR?
AMARA-- SHIFT TO YOUR MAGMA INCARNATION...
...AND MELT US A PATHWAY OF DRY GROUND TO THE STREET.
YOU SURE THIS IS RIGHT FOR US, SIR?
YOU'VE BEEN "GROUNDED"-- RESTRICTED TO THE SCHOOL-- FOR WEEKS, CANNONBALL.
I THOUGHT YOU'D ENJOY THIS EXCURSION --ESPECIALLY TO A PARTY.
BEGGIN' YUIR PARDON, HEADMASTER...
...BUT IT'S BEING HELD AT THE HELLFIRE CLUB!
AND THEY, REVERED TEACHER, HAVE EVER BEEN THE SWORN FOES OF XAVIER'S SCHOOL.
THAT CHANGED, AMARA, WHEN I JOINED THE LORDS CARDINAL, AS THE WHITE KING.
IS THAT REVELATION, O FEARLESS TEACH, SUPPOSED TO FILL US WITH CONFIDENCE?

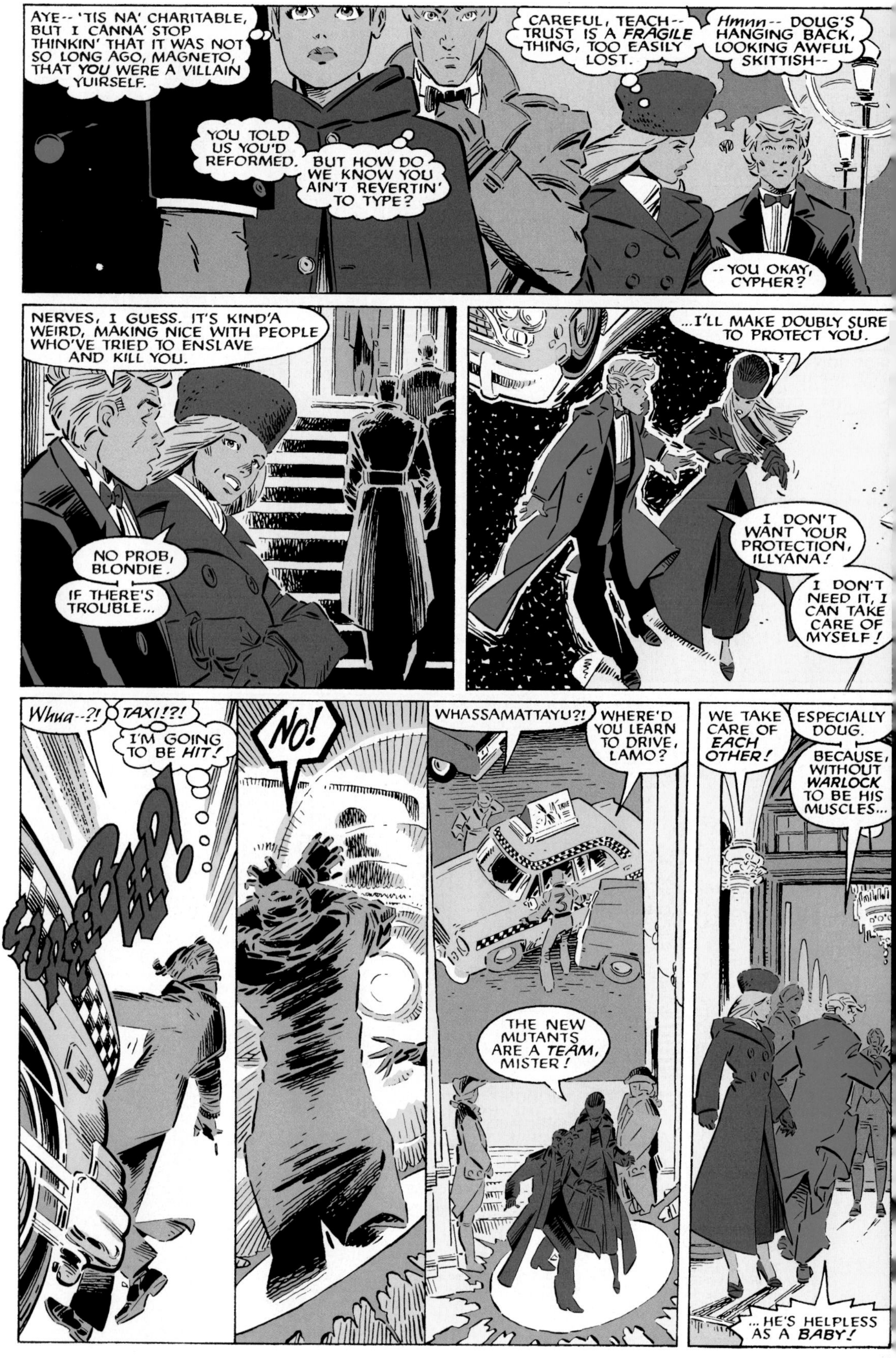
AYE-- 'TIS NA' CHARITABLE, BUT I CANNA' STOP THINKIN' THAT IT WAS NOT SO LONG AGO, MAGNETO, THAT YOU WERE A VILLAIN YUIRSELF.
YOU TOLD US YOU'D REFORMED.
BUT HOW DO WE KNOW YOU AIN'T REVERTIN' TO TYPE?
CAREFUL, TEACH-- TRUST IS A FRAGILE THING, TOO EASILY LOST.
Hmnn-- DOUG'S HANGING BACK, LOOKING AWFUL SKITTISH--
--YOU OKAY, CYPHER?
NERVES, I GUESS. IT'S KIND'A WEIRD, MAKING NICE WITH PEOPLE WHO'VE TRIED TO ENSLAVE AND KILL YOU.
NO PROB, BLONDIE.
IF THERE'S TROUBLE...
...I'LL MAKE DOUBLY SURE TO PROTECT YOU.
I DON'T WANT YOUR PROTECTION, ILLYANA!
I DON'T NEED IT, I CAN TAKE CARE OF MYSELF!
Whua--?!
TAXI!?!
I'M GOING TO BE HIT!
SKREEBEEP!
NO!
WHASSAMATTAYU?!
WHERE'D YOU LEARN TO DRIVE, LAMO?
THE NEW MUTANTS ARE A TEAM, MISTER!
WE TAKE CARE OF EACH OTHER!
ESPECIALLY DOUG.
BECAUSE, WITHOUT WARLOCK TO BE HIS MUSCLES...
...HE'S HELPLESS AS A BABY!

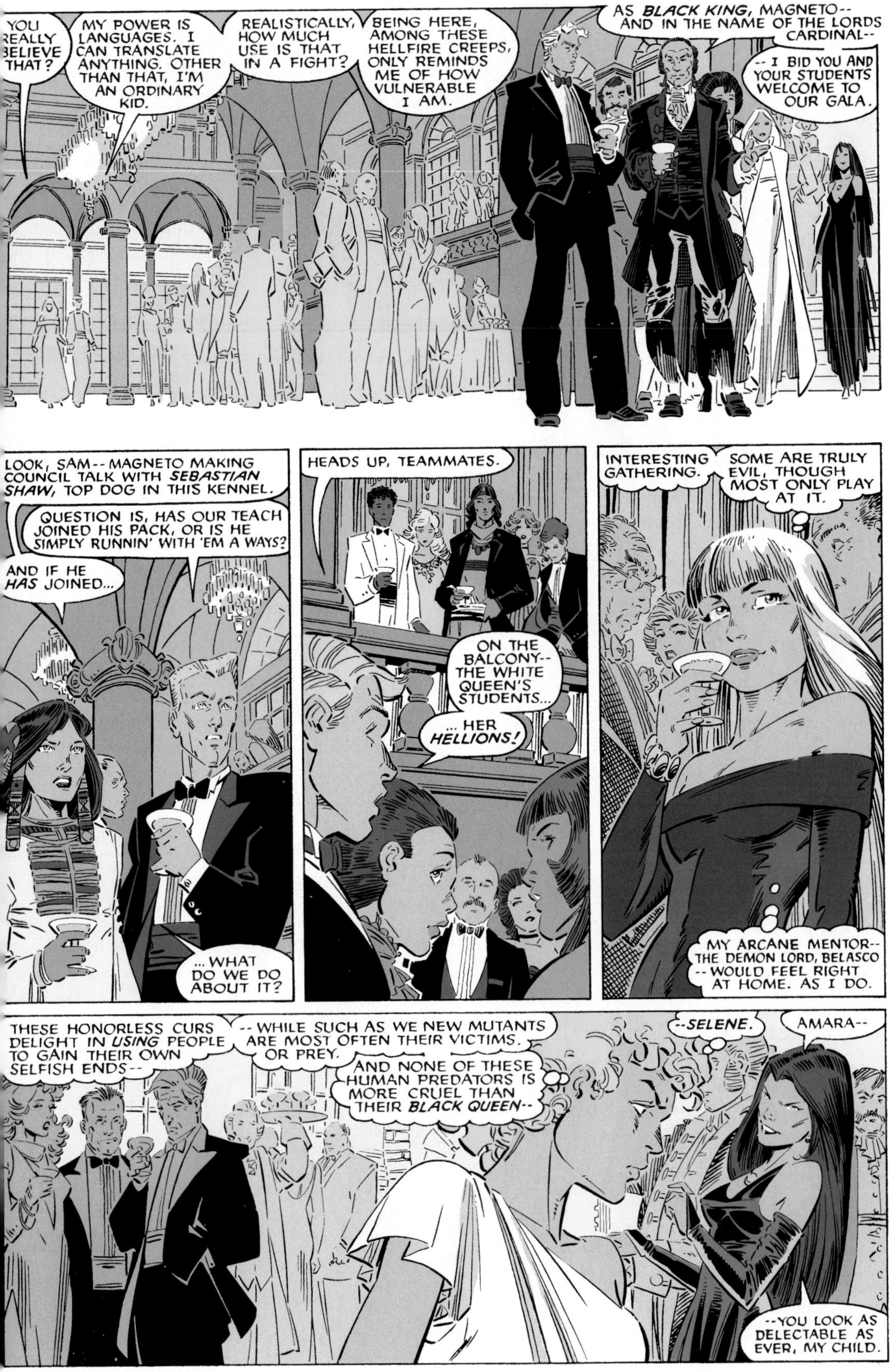
YOU REALLY BELIEVE THAT?
MY POWER IS LANGUAGES. I CAN TRANSLATE ANYTHING. OTHER THAN THAT, I'M AN ORDINARY KID.
REALISTICALLY, HOW MUCH USE IS THAT IN A FIGHT?
BEING HERE, AMONG THESE HELLFIRE CREEPS, ONLY REMINDS ME OF HOW VULNERABLE I AM.
AS BLACK KING, MAGNETO-- AND IN THE NAME OF THE LORDS CARDINAL--
-- I BID YOU AND YOUR STUDENTS WELCOME TO OUR GALA.
LOOK, SAM-- MAGNETO MAKING COUNCIL TALK WITH SEBASTIAN SHAW, TOP DOG IN THIS KENNEL.
QUESTION IS, HAS OUR TEACH JOINED HIS PACK, OR IS HE SIMPLY RUNNIN' WITH 'EM A WAYS?
AND IF HE HAS JOINED...
... WHAT DO WE DO ABOUT IT?
HEADS UP, TEAMMATES.
ON THE BALCONY-- THE WHITE QUEEN'S STUDENTS...
... HER HELLIONS!
INTERESTING GATHERING.
SOME ARE TRULY EVIL, THOUGH MOST ONLY PLAY AT IT.
MY ARCANE MENTOR-- THE DEMON LORD, BELASCO --WOULD FEEL RIGHT AT HOME. AS I DO.
THESE HONORLESS CURS DELIGHT IN USING PEOPLE TO GAIN THEIR OWN SELFISH ENDS--
-- WHILE SUCH AS WE NEW MUTANTS ARE MOST OFTEN THEIR VICTIMS. OR PREY.
AND NONE OF THESE HUMAN PREDATORS IS MORE CRUEL THAN THEIR BLACK QUEEN--
--SELENE.
AMARA--
--YOU LOOK AS DELECTABLE AS EVER, MY CHILD.

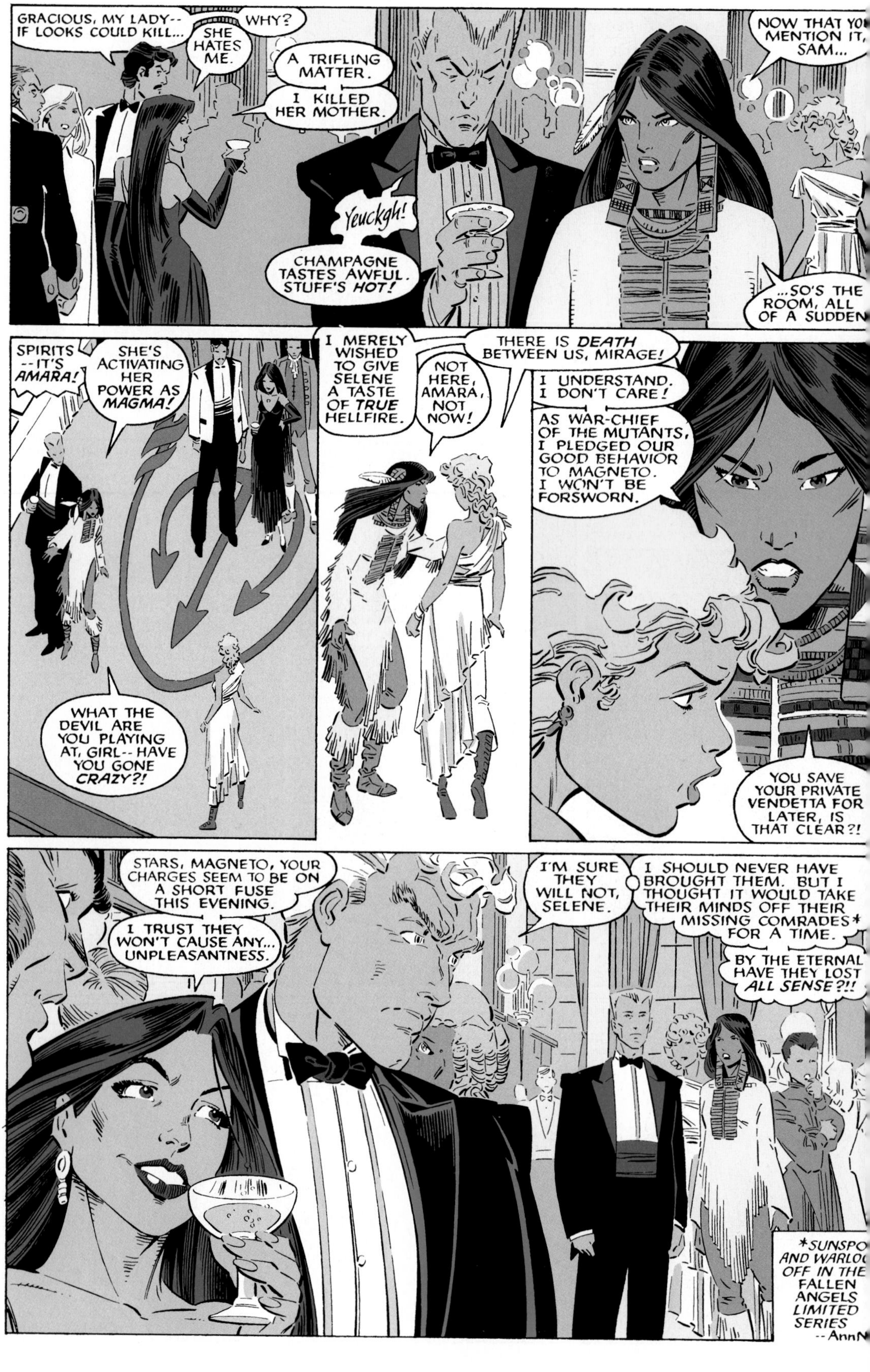
GRACIOUS, MY LADY-- IF LOOKS COULD KILL...
SHE HATES ME.
WHY?
A TRIFLING MATTER.
I KILLED HER MOTHER.
NOW THAT YO MENTION IT, SAM...
Yeuckgh!
CHAMPAGNE TASTES AWFUL. STUFF'S HOT!
...SO'S THE ROOM, ALL OF A SUDDEN
SPIRITS --IT'S AMARA!
SHE'S ACTIVATING HER POWER AS MAGMA!
WHAT THE DEVIL ARE YOU PLAYING AT, GIRL-- HAVE YOU GONE CRAZY?!
I MERELY WISHED TO GIVE SELENE A TASTE OF TRUE HELLFIRE.
NOT HERE, AMARA, NOT NOW!
THERE IS DEATH BETWEEN US, MIRAGE!
I UNDERSTAND. I DON'T CARE!
AS WAR-CHIEF OF THE MUTANTS, I PLEDGED OUR GOOD BEHAVIOR TO MAGNETO. I WON'T BE FORSWORN.
YOU SAVE YOUR PRIVATE VENDETTA FOR LATER, IS THAT CLEAR?!
STARS, MAGNETO, YOUR CHARGES SEEM TO BE ON A SHORT FUSE THIS EVENING.
I TRUST THEY WON'T CAUSE ANY... UNPLEASANTNESS.
I'M SURE THEY WILL NOT, SELENE.
I SHOULD NEVER HAVE BROUGHT THEM. BUT I THOUGHT IT WOULD TAKE THEIR MINDS OFF THEIR MISSING COMRADES* FOR A TIME.
BY THE ETERNAL HAVE THEY LOST ALL SENSE?!!
*SUNSPO AND WARLO OFF IN THE FALLEN ANGELS LIMITED SERIES --AnnN

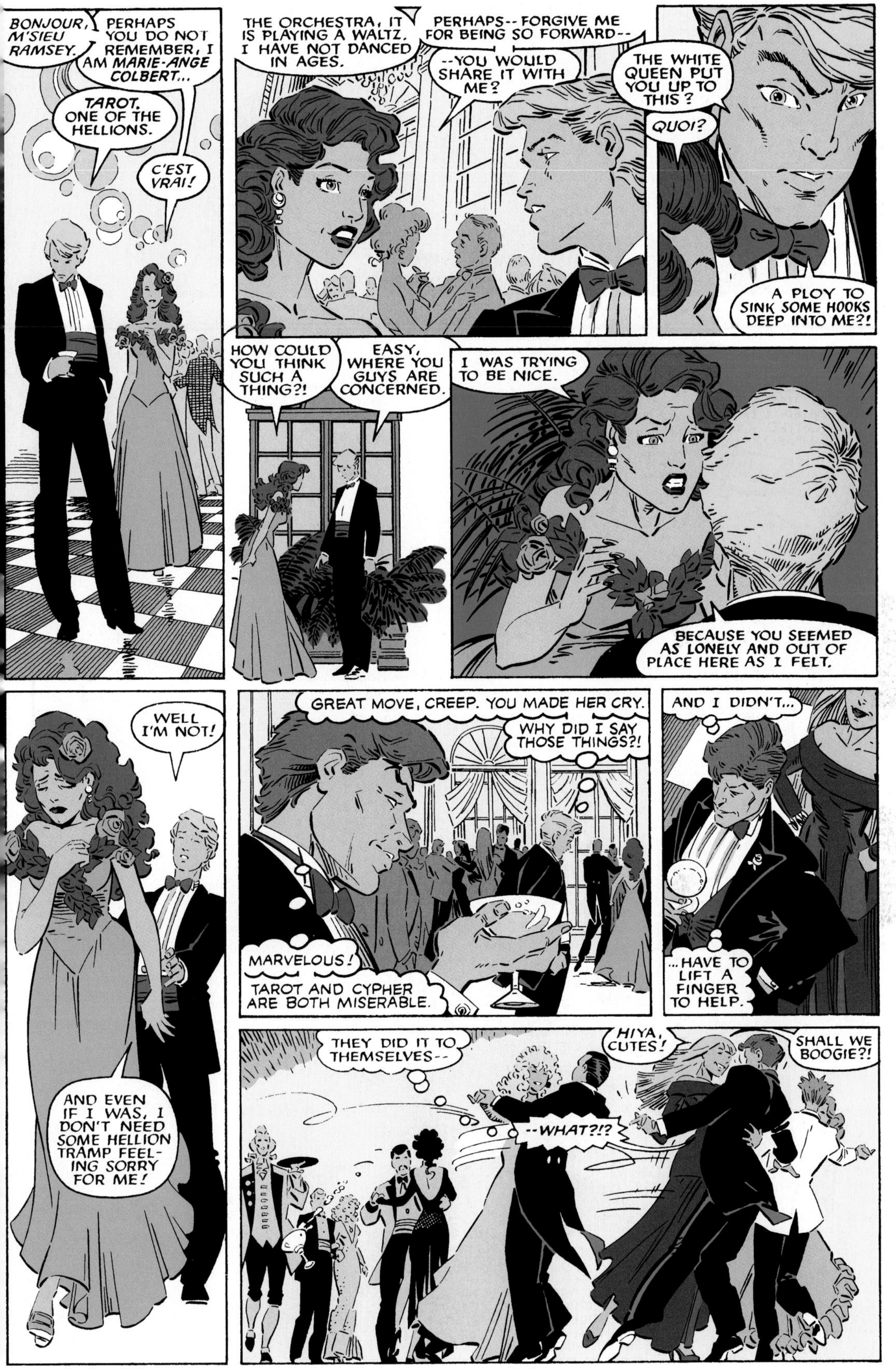
BONJOUR, M'SIEU RAMSEY.
PERHAPS YOU DO NOT REMEMBER, I AM MARIE-ANGE COLBERT...
TAROT. ONE OF THE HELLIONS.
C'EST VRAI!
THE ORCHESTRA, IT IS PLAYING A WALTZ. I HAVE NOT DANCED IN AGES.
PERHAPS-- FORGIVE ME FOR BEING SO FORWARD--
--YOU WOULD SHARE IT WITH ME?
THE WHITE QUEEN PUT YOU UP TO THIS?
QUOI?
A PLOY TO SINK SOME HOOKS DEEP INTO ME?!
HOW COULD YOU THINK SUCH A THING?!
EASY, WHERE YOU GUYS ARE CONCERNED.
I WAS TRYING TO BE NICE.
BECAUSE YOU SEEMED AS LONELY AND OUT OF PLACE HERE AS I FELT.
WELL I'M NOT!
AND EVEN IF I WAS, I DON'T NEED SOME HELLION TRAMP FEELING SORRY FOR ME!
GREAT MOVE, CREEP. YOU MADE HER CRY.
WHY DID I SAY THOSE THINGS?!
MARVELOUS!
TAROT AND CYPHER ARE BOTH MISERABLE.
AND I DIDN'T...
...HAVE TO LIFT A FINGER TO HELP.
THEY DID IT TO THEMSELVES--
HIYA, CUTES!
SHALL WE BOOGIE?!
--WHAT?!?

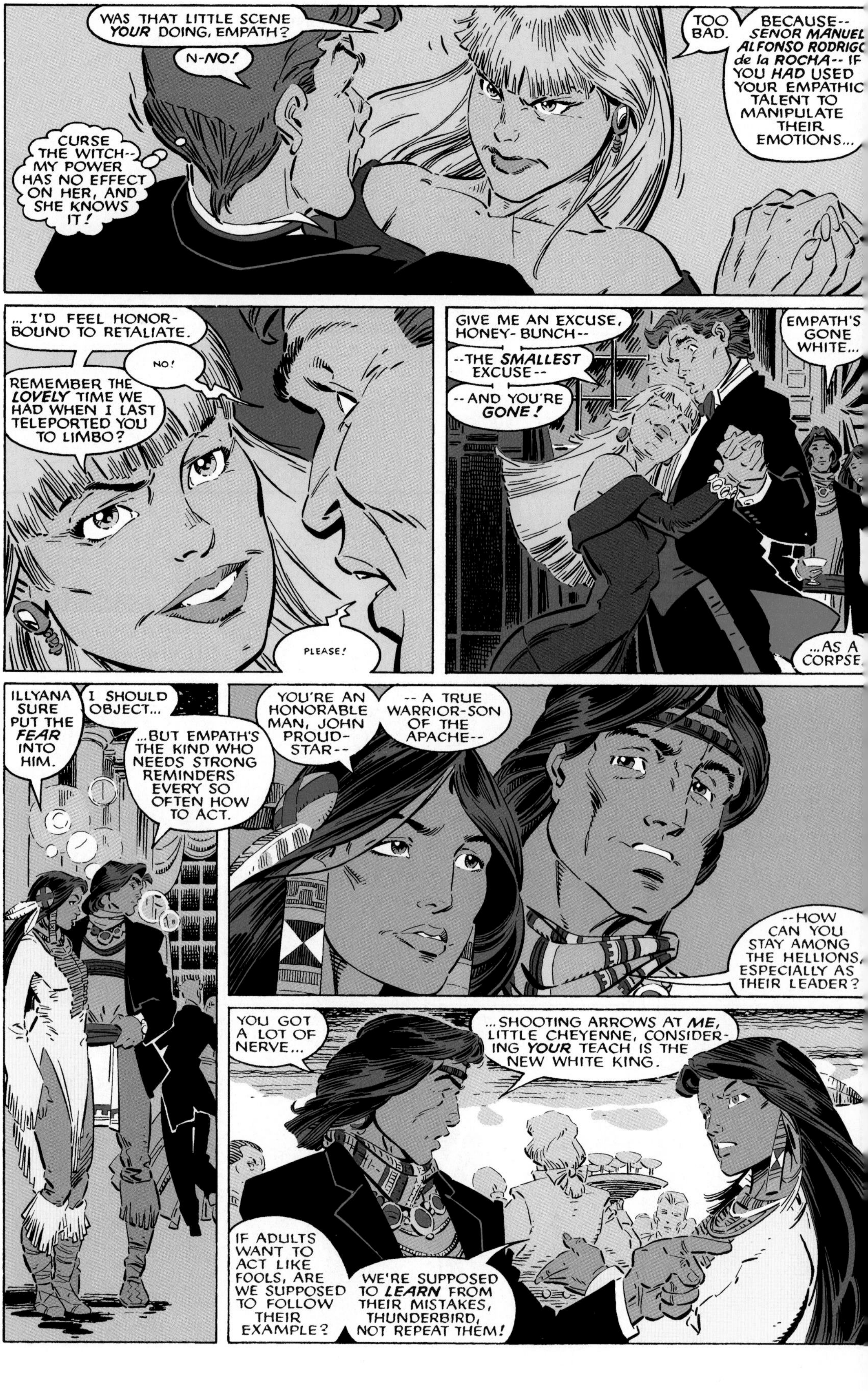
WAS THAT LITTLE SCENE YOUR DOING, EMPATH?
N-NO!
CURSE THE WITCH-- MY POWER HAS NO EFFECT ON HER, AND SHE KNOWS IT!
TOO BAD.
BECAUSE-- SENOR MANUEL ALFONSO RODRIGO de la ROCHA-- IF YOU HAD USED YOUR EMPATHIC TALENT TO MANIPULATE THEIR EMOTIONS...
... I'D FEEL HONOR-BOUND TO RETALIATE.
NO!
REMEMBER THE LOVELY TIME WE HAD WHEN I LAST TELEPORTED YOU TO LIMBO?
PLEASE!
GIVE ME AN EXCUSE, HONEY-BUNCH--
--THE SMALLEST EXCUSE--
--AND YOU'RE GONE!
EMPATH'S GONE WHITE...
...AS A CORPSE.
ILLYANA SURE PUT THE FEAR INTO HIM.
I SHOULD OBJECT...
...BUT EMPATH'S THE KIND WHO NEEDS STRONG REMINDERS EVERY SO OFTEN HOW TO ACT.
YOU'RE AN HONORABLE MAN, JOHN PROUDSTAR--
-- A TRUE WARRIOR-SON OF THE APACHE--
--HOW CAN YOU STAY AMONG THE HELLIONS, ESPECIALLY AS THEIR LEADER?
YOU GOT A LOT OF NERVE...
...SHOOTING ARROWS AT ME, LITTLE CHEYENNE, CONSIDERING YOUR TEACH IS THE NEW WHITE KING.
IF ADULTS WANT TO ACT LIKE FOOLS, ARE WE SUPPOSED TO FOLLOW THEIR EXAMPLE?
WE'RE SUPPOSED TO LEARN FROM THEIR MISTAKES, THUNDERBIRD, NOT REPEAT THEM!

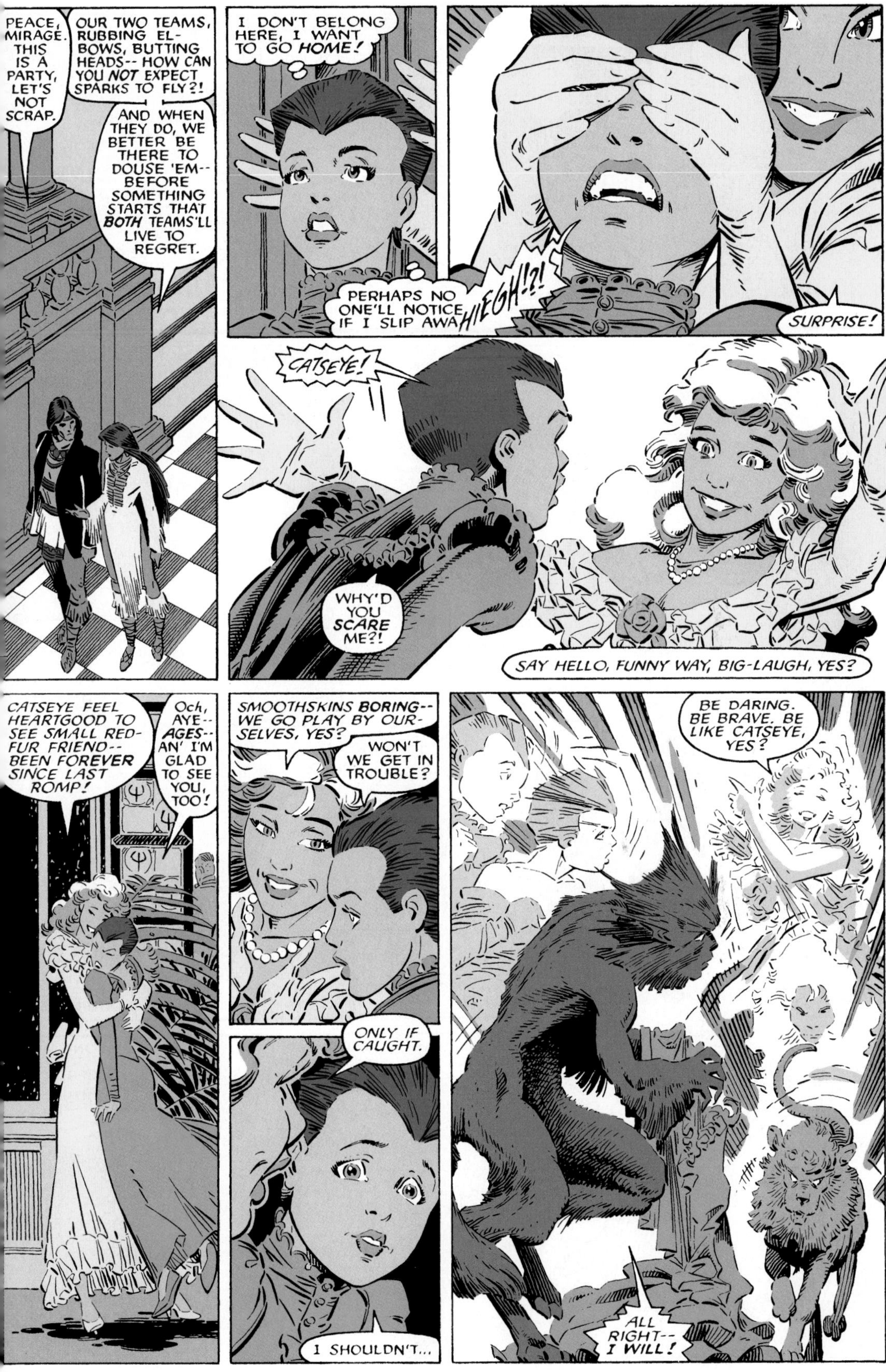
PEACE, MIRAGE. THIS IS A PARTY, LET'S NOT SCRAP.
OUR TWO TEAMS, RUBBING EL-BOWS, BUTTING HEADS-- HOW CAN YOU NOT EXPECT SPARKS TO FLY?!
AND WHEN THEY DO, WE BETTER BE THERE TO DOUSE 'EM-- BEFORE SOMETHING STARTS THAT BOTH TEAMS'LL LIVE TO REGRET.
I DON'T BELONG HERE, I WANT TO GO HOME!
PERHAPS NO ONE'LL NOTICE IF I SLIP AWA
HIEGH!?!
SURPRISE!
CATSEYE!
WHY'D YOU SCARE ME?!
SAY HELLO, FUNNY WAY, BIG-LAUGH, YES?
CATSEYE FEEL HEARTGOOD TO SEE SMALL RED-FUR FRIEND-- BEEN FOREVER SINCE LAST ROMP!
Och, AYE-- AGES-- AN' I'M GLAD TO SEE YOU, TOO!
SMOOTHSKINS BORING-- WE GO PLAY BY OUR-SELVES, YES?
WON'T WE GET IN TROUBLE?
ONLY IF CAUGHT.
I SHOULDN'T...
BE DARING. BE BRAVE. BE LIKE CATSEYE, YES?
ALL RIGHT-- I WILL!

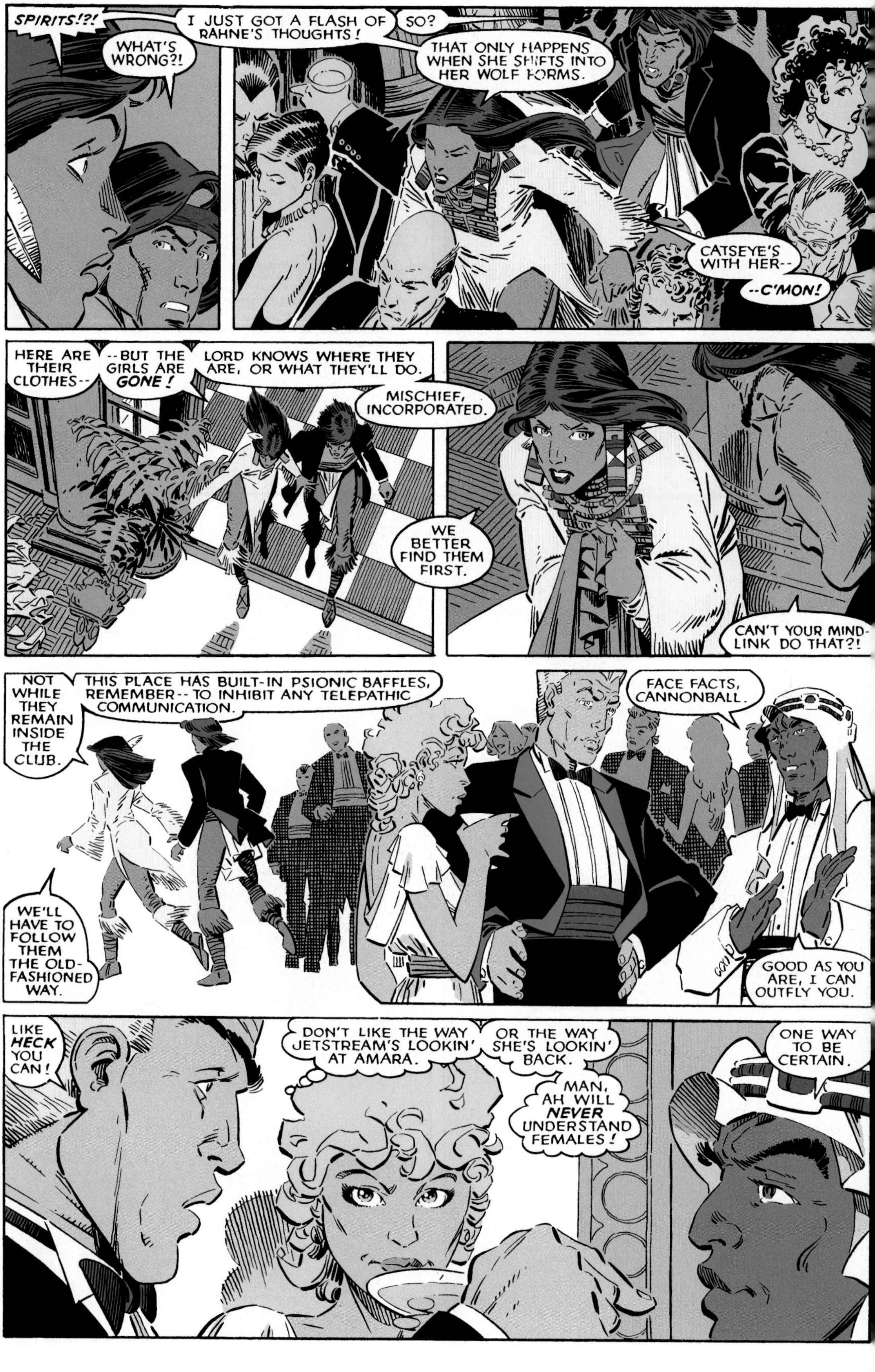
SPIRITS!?!
I JUST GOT A FLASH OF RAHNE'S THOUGHTS!
WHAT'S WRONG?!
SO?
THAT ONLY HAPPENS WHEN SHE SHIFTS INTO HER WOLF FORMS.
CATSEYE'S WITH HER--
--C'MON!
HERE ARE THEIR CLOTHES--
--BUT THE GIRLS ARE GONE!
LORD KNOWS WHERE THEY ARE, OR WHAT THEY'LL DO.
MISCHIEF, INCORPORATED.
WE BETTER FIND THEM FIRST.
CAN'T YOUR MIND-LINK DO THAT?!
NOT WHILE THEY REMAIN INSIDE THE CLUB.
THIS PLACE HAS BUILT-IN PSIONIC BAFFLES, REMEMBER-- TO INHIBIT ANY TELEPATHIC COMMUNICATION.
WE'LL HAVE TO FOLLOW THEM THE OLD-FASHIONED WAY.
FACE FACTS, CANNONBALL.
GOOD AS YOU ARE, I CAN OUTFLY YOU.
LIKE HECK YOU CAN!
DON'T LIKE THE WAY JETSTREAM'S LOOKIN' AT AMARA.
OR THE WAY SHE'S LOOKIN' BACK.
MAN, AH WILL NEVER UNDERSTAND FEMALES!
ONE WAY TO BE CERTAIN.

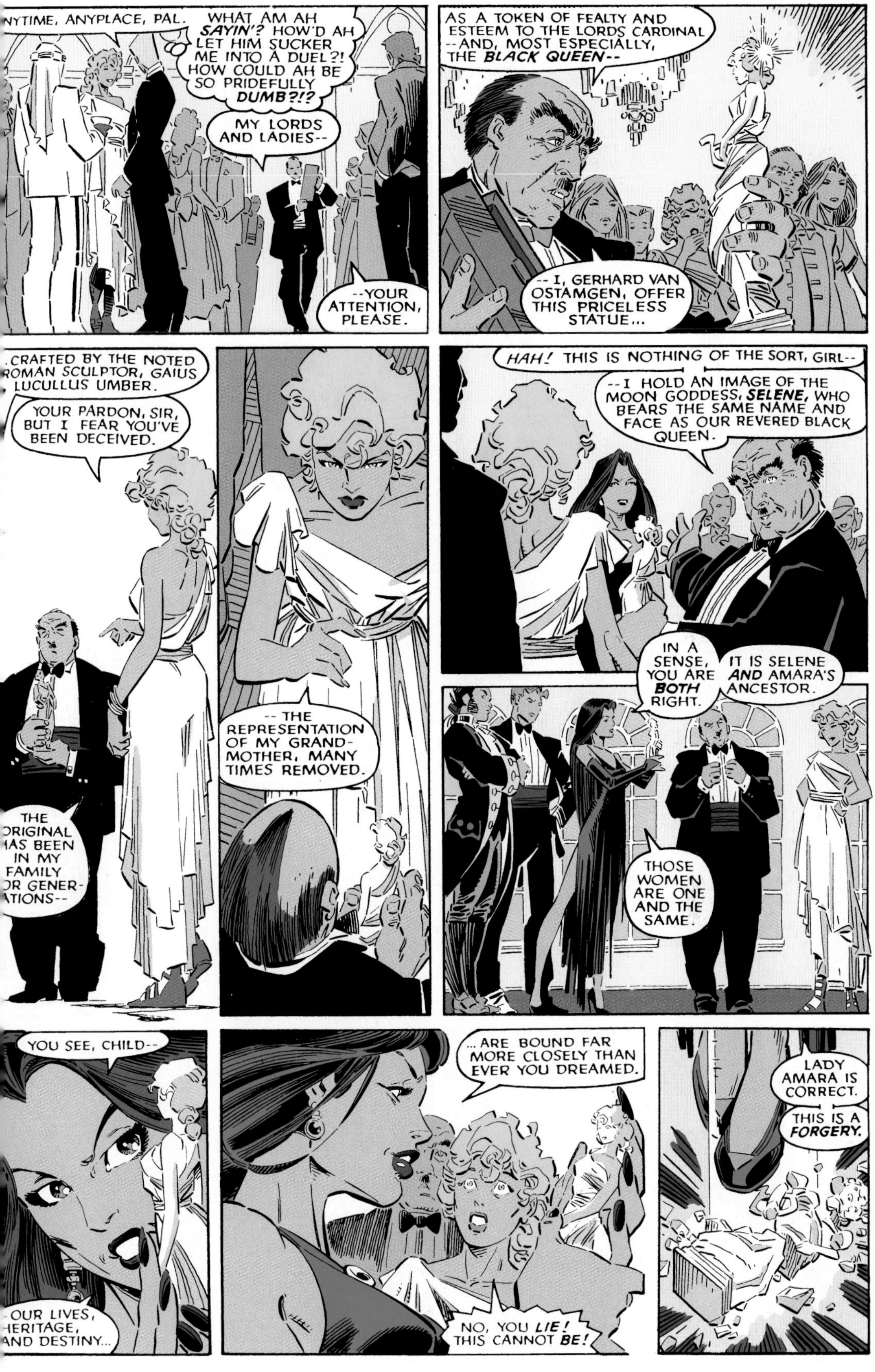

NYTIME, ANYPLACE, PAL.
WHAT AM AH *SAYIN'?* HOW'D AH LET HIM SUCKER ME INTO A DUEL?! HOW COULD AH BE SO PRIDEFULLY ***DUMB?!?***
MY LORDS AND LADIES--
--YOUR ATTENTION, PLEASE.
AS A TOKEN OF FEALTY AND ESTEEM TO THE LORDS CARDINAL --AND, MOST ESPECIALLY, THE ***BLACK QUEEN***--
-- I, GERHARD VAN OSTAMGEN, OFFER THIS PRICELESS STATUE...
..CRAFTED BY THE NOTED ROMAN SCULPTOR, GAIUS LUCULLUS UMBER.
YOUR PARDON, SIR, BUT I FEAR YOU'VE BEEN DECEIVED.
THE ORIGINAL HAS BEEN IN MY FAMILY FOR GENERATIONS--
-- THE REPRESENTATION OF MY GRANDMOTHER, MANY TIMES REMOVED.
*HAH!* THIS IS NOTHING OF THE SORT, GIRL--
--I HOLD AN IMAGE OF THE MOON GODDESS, ***SELENE,*** WHO BEARS THE SAME NAME AND FACE AS OUR REVERED BLACK QUEEN.
IN A SENSE, YOU ARE ***BOTH*** RIGHT.
IT IS SELENE ***AND*** AMARA'S ANCESTOR.
THOSE WOMEN ARE ONE AND THE SAME.
YOU SEE, CHILD--
--OUR LIVES, HERITAGE, AND DESTINY...
...ARE BOUND FAR MORE CLOSELY THAN EVER YOU DREAMED.
NO, YOU ***LIE!*** THIS CANNOT ***BE!***
LADY AMARA IS CORRECT.
THIS IS A ***FORGERY.***

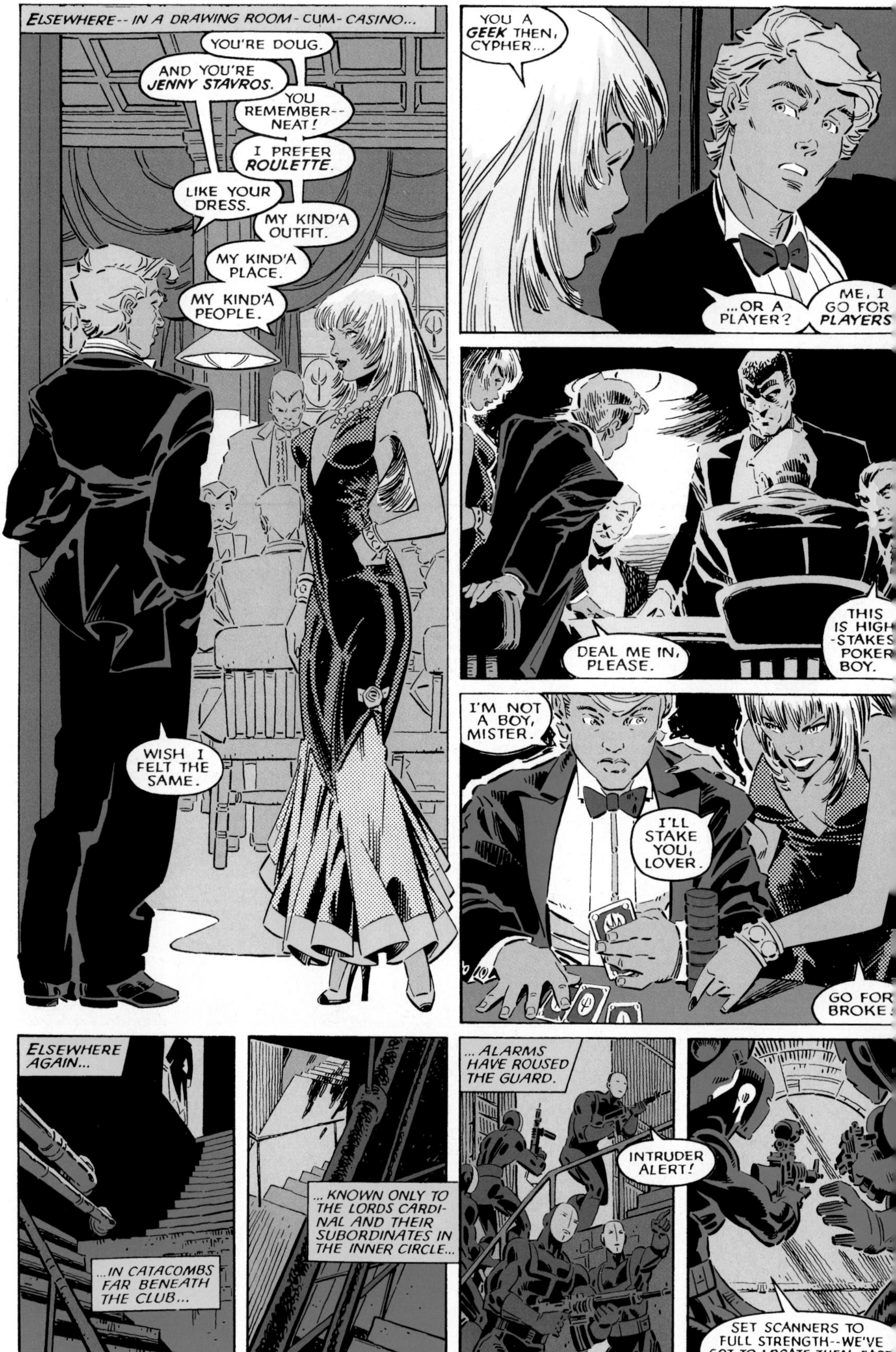
ELSEWHERE-- IN A DRAWING ROOM-CUM-CASINO...
YOU'RE DOUG.
AND YOU'RE JENNY STAVROS.
YOU REMEMBER-- NEAT!
I PREFER ROULETTE.
LIKE YOUR DRESS.
MY KIND'A OUTFIT.
MY KIND'A PLACE.
MY KIND'A PEOPLE.
WISH I FELT THE SAME.
YOU A GEEK THEN, CYPHER...
...OR A PLAYER?
ME, I GO FOR PLAYERS
DEAL ME IN, PLEASE.
THIS IS HIGH-STAKES POKER BOY.
I'M NOT A BOY, MISTER.
I'LL STAKE YOU, LOVER.
GO FOR BROKE.
ELSEWHERE AGAIN...
...IN CATACOMBS FAR BENEATH THE CLUB...
...KNOWN ONLY TO THE LORDS CARDINAL AND THEIR SUBORDINATES IN THE INNER CIRCLE...
...ALARMS HAVE ROUSED THE GUARD.
INTRUDER ALERT!
SET SCANNERS TO FULL STRENGTH--WE'VE GOT TO LOCATE THEM, FAST.

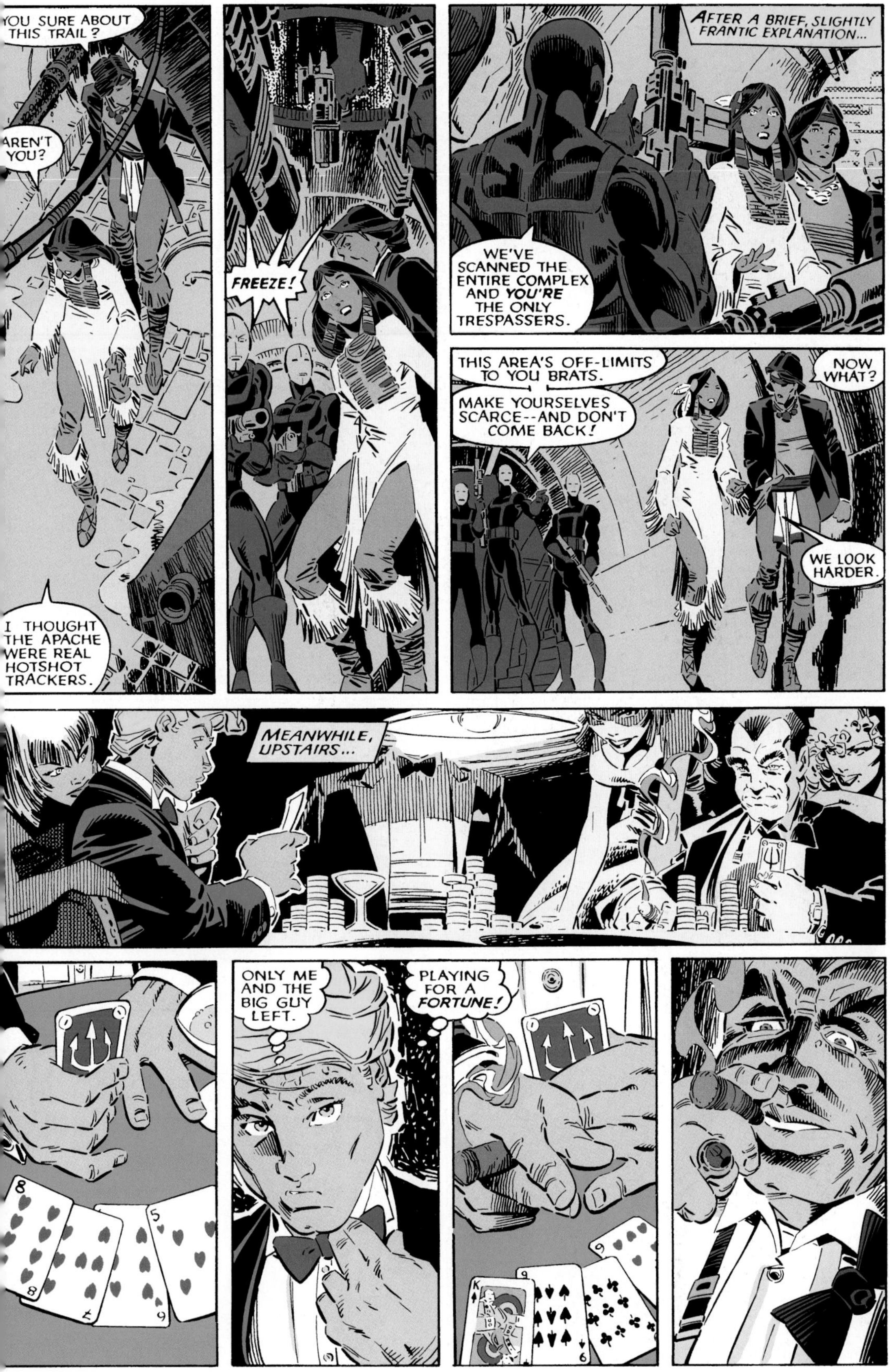

YOU SURE ABOUT THIS TRAIL?
AREN'T YOU?
I THOUGHT THE APACHE WERE REAL HOTSHOT TRACKERS.
FREEZE!
AFTER A BRIEF, SLIGHTLY FRANTIC EXPLANATION...
WE'VE SCANNED THE ENTIRE COMPLEX AND YOU'RE THE ONLY TRESPASSERS.
THIS AREA'S OFF-LIMITS TO YOU BRATS.
MAKE YOURSELVES SCARCE--AND DON'T COME BACK!
NOW WHAT?
WE LOOK HARDER.
MEANWHILE, UPSTAIRS...
ONLY ME AND THE BIG GUY LEFT.
PLAYING FOR A FORTUNE!

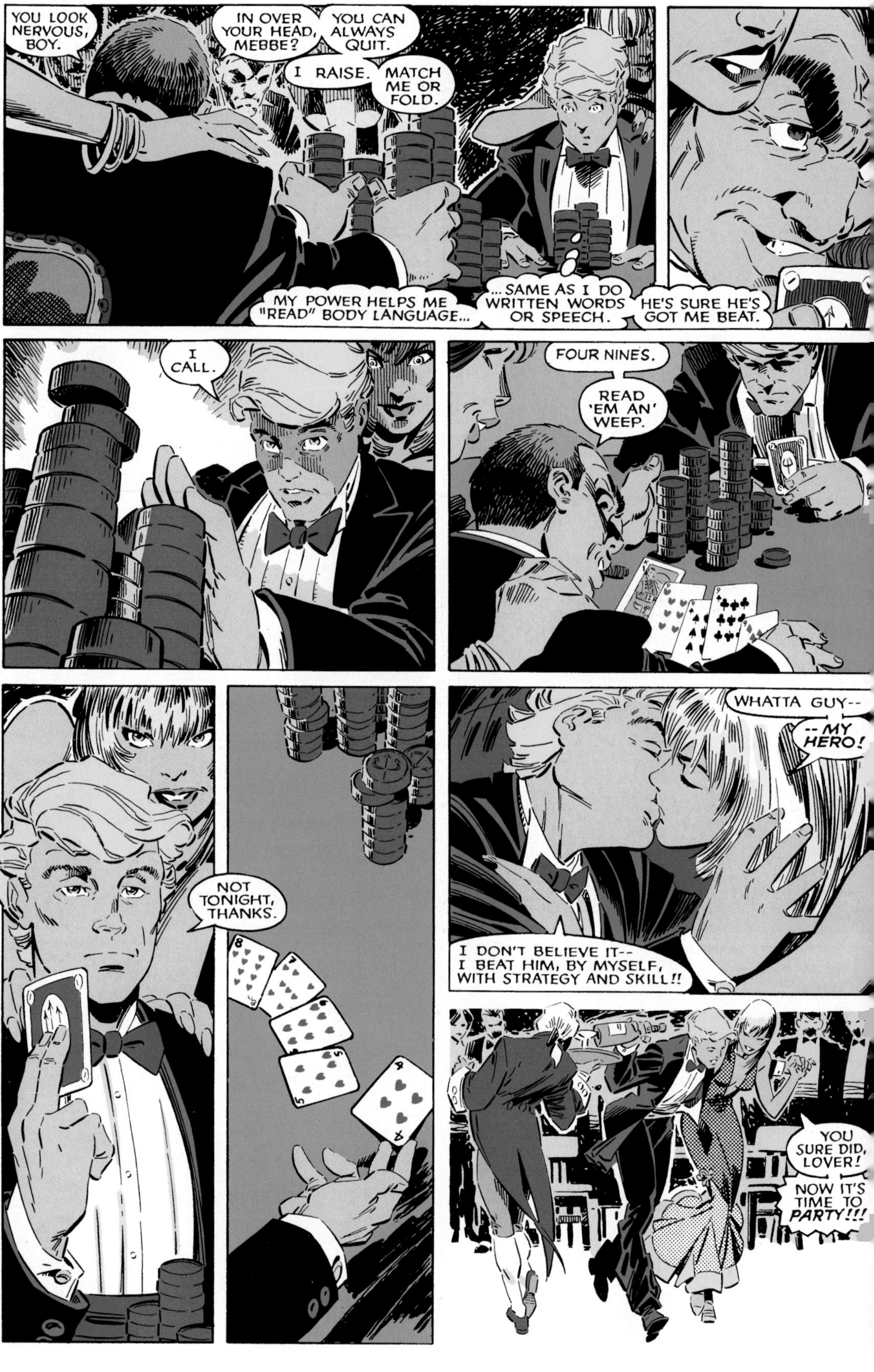
YOU LOOK NERVOUS, BOY.
IN OVER YOUR HEAD, MEBBE?
YOU CAN ALWAYS QUIT.
I RAISE.
MATCH ME OR FOLD.
MY POWER HELPS ME "READ" BODY LANGUAGE...
...SAME AS I DO WRITTEN WORDS OR SPEECH.
HE'S SURE HE'S GOT ME BEAT.
I CALL.
FOUR NINES.
READ 'EM AN' WEEP.
NOT TONIGHT, THANKS.
WHATTA GUY--
--MY HERO!
I DON'T BELIEVE IT-- I BEAT HIM, BY MYSELF, WITH STRATEGY AND SKILL!!
YOU SURE DID, LOVER!
NOW IT'S TIME TO PARTY!!!

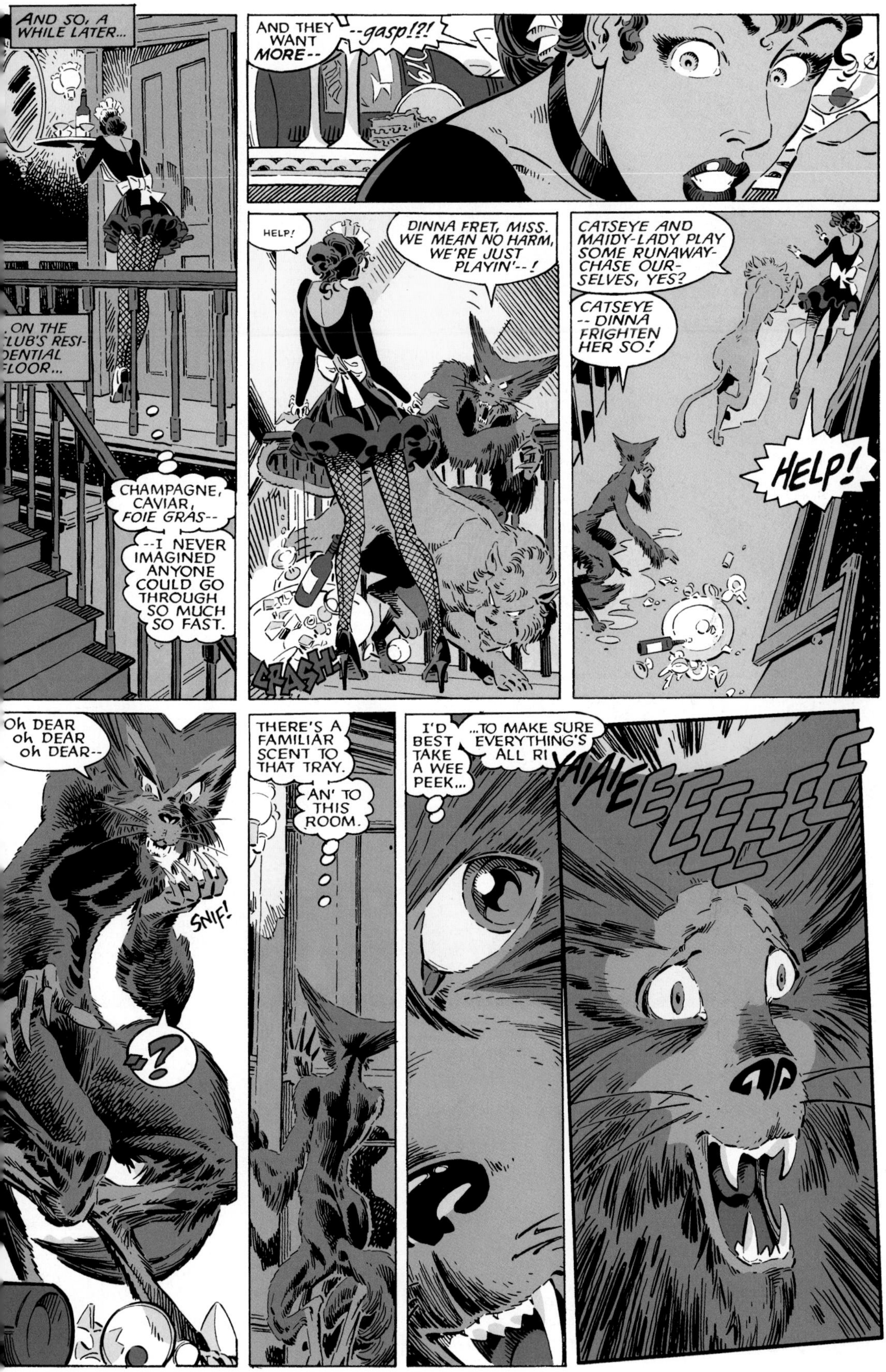
AND SO, A WHILE LATER...
...ON THE CLUB'S RESIDENTIAL FLOOR...
CHAMPAGNE, CAVIAR, FOIE GRAS--
--I NEVER IMAGINED ANYONE COULD GO THROUGH SO MUCH SO FAST.
AND THEY WANT MORE--
--gasp!?!
HELP!
DINNA FRET, MISS. WE MEAN NO HARM, WE'RE JUST PLAYIN'--!
CRASH!
CATSEYE AND MAIDY-LADY PLAY SOME RUNAWAY-CHASE OURSELVES, YES?
CATSEYE -- DINNA FRIGHTEN HER SO!
HELP!
Oh DEAR oh DEAR oh DEAR--
SNIF!
-?
THERE'S A FAMILIAR SCENT TO THAT TRAY.
AN' TO THIS ROOM.
I'D BEST TAKE A WEE PEEK...
...TO MAKE SURE EVERYTHING'S ALL RI
YAAAIEEEEEEEEEE

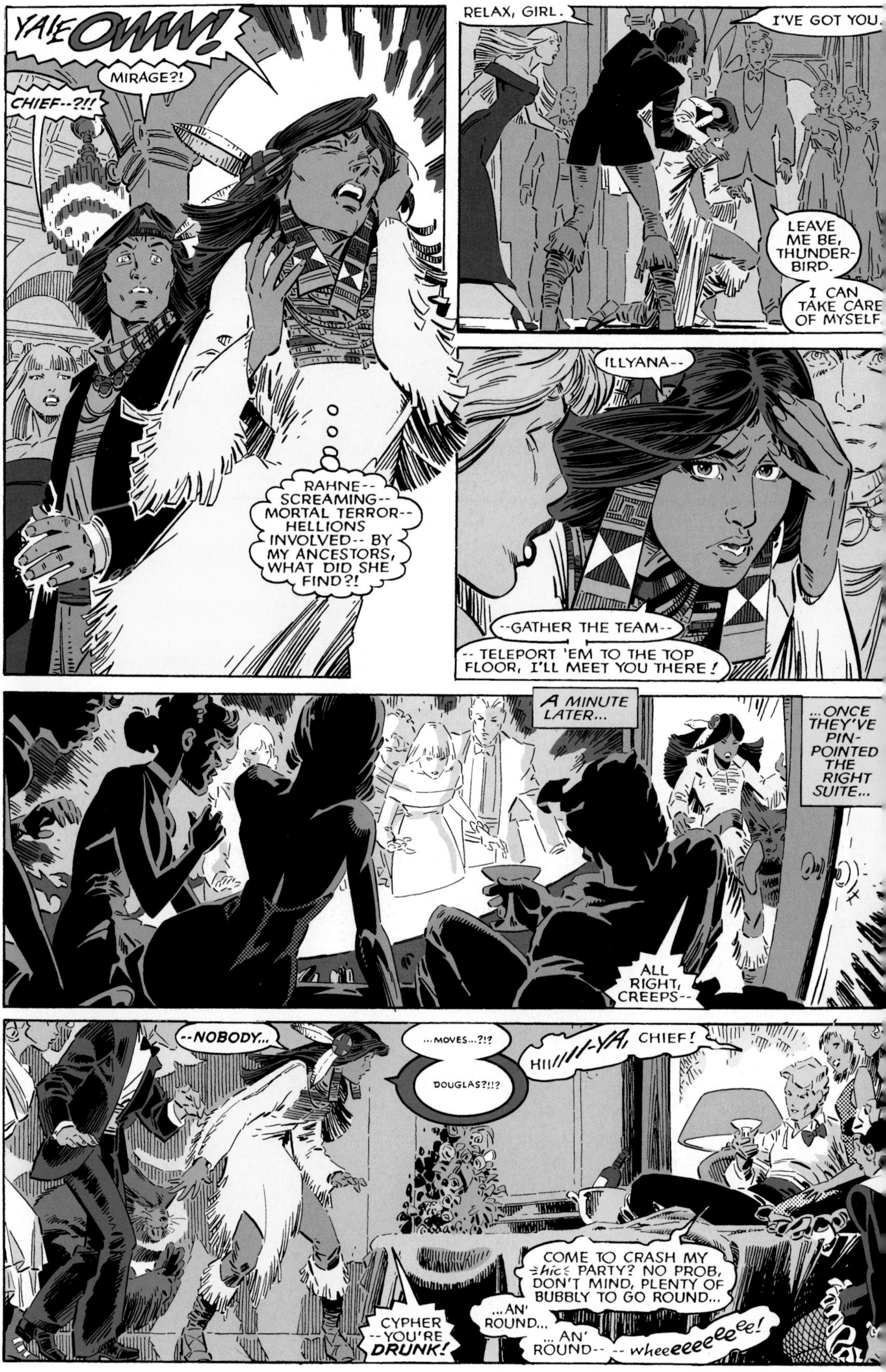
YA!EOWW!
MIRAGE?!
CHIEF--?!!
RAHNE-- SCREAMING-- MORTAL TERROR-- HELLIONS INVOLVED-- BY MY ANCESTORS, WHAT DID SHE FIND?!
RELAX, GIRL.
I'VE GOT YOU.
LEAVE ME BE, THUNDER-BIRD.
I CAN TAKE CARE OF MYSELF.
ILLYANA--
--GATHER THE TEAM--
-- TELEPORT 'EM TO THE TOP FLOOR, I'LL MEET YOU THERE!
A MINUTE LATER...
...ONCE THEY'VE PIN-POINTED THE RIGHT SUITE...
ALL RIGHT, CREEPS--
--NOBODY...
...MOVES...?!?
DOUGLAS?!!?
HIIIIII-YA, CHIEF!
COME TO CRASH MY hic PARTY? NO PROB, DON'T MIND, PLENTY OF BUBBLY TO GO ROUND...
...AN' ROUND...
... AN' ROUND--
-- wheeeeeeeee!
CYPHER --YOU'RE DRUNK!

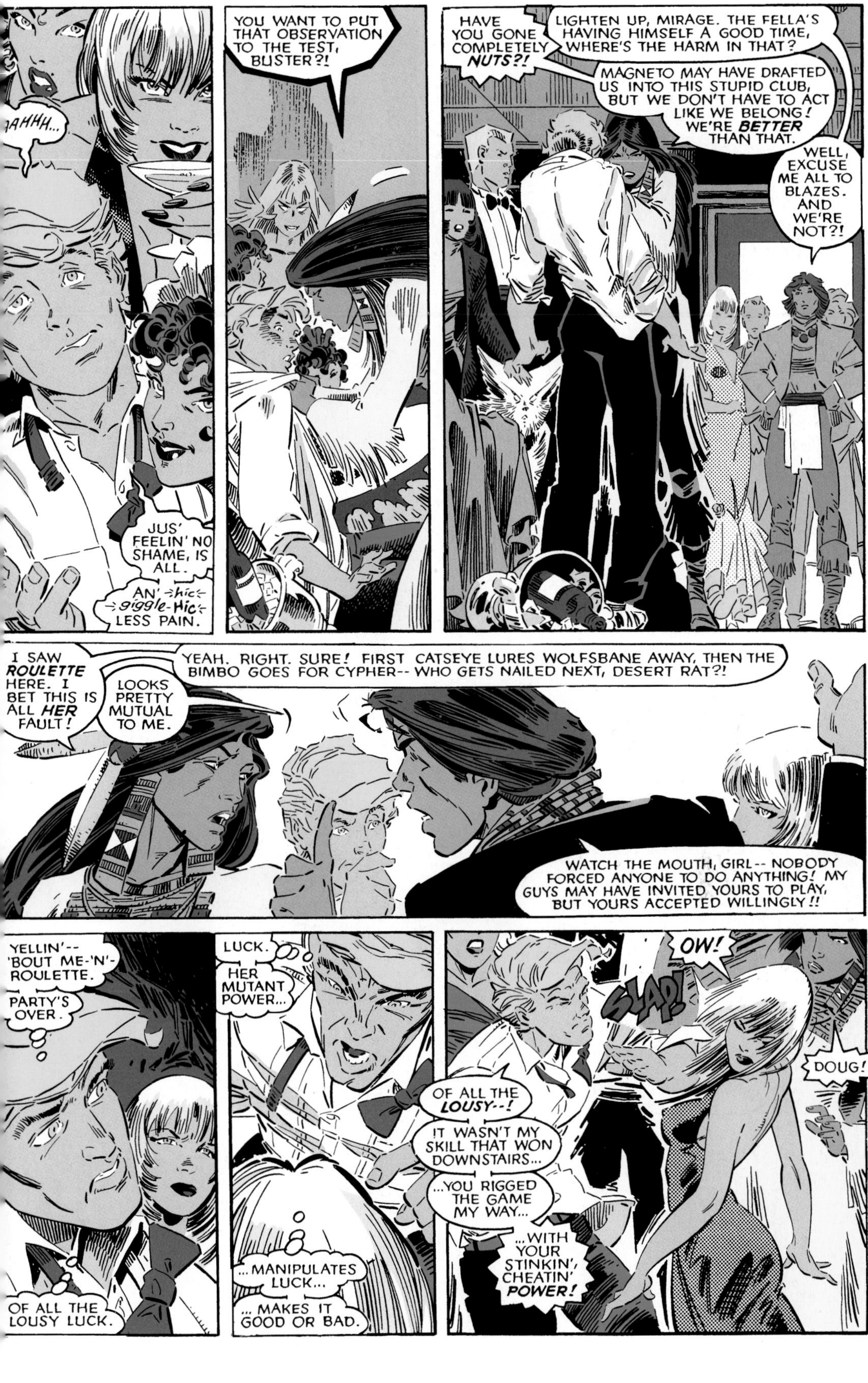

AHHH...
JUS' FEELIN' NO SHAME, IS ALL.
AN' -hic- -giggle- Hic- LESS PAIN.
YOU WANT TO PUT THAT OBSERVATION TO THE TEST, BUSTER?!
HAVE YOU GONE COMPLETELY NUTS?!
LIGHTEN UP, MIRAGE. THE FELLA'S HAVING HIMSELF A GOOD TIME, WHERE'S THE HARM IN THAT?
MAGNETO MAY HAVE DRAFTED US INTO THIS STUPID CLUB, BUT WE DON'T HAVE TO ACT LIKE WE BELONG! WE'RE BETTER THAN THAT.
WELL, EXCUSE ME ALL TO BLAZES. AND WE'RE NOT?!
I SAW ROULETTE HERE. I BET THIS IS ALL HER FAULT!
LOOKS PRETTY MUTUAL TO ME.
YEAH. RIGHT. SURE! FIRST CATSEYE LURES WOLFSBANE AWAY, THEN THE BIMBO GOES FOR CYPHER-- WHO GETS NAILED NEXT, DESERT RAT?!
WATCH THE MOUTH, GIRL-- NOBODY FORCED ANYONE TO DO ANYTHING! MY GUYS MAY HAVE INVITED YOURS TO PLAY, BUT YOURS ACCEPTED WILLINGLY!!
YELLIN'-- 'BOUT ME-'N'-ROULETTE.
PARTY'S OVER.
OF ALL THE LOUSY LUCK.
LUCK.
HER MUTANT POWER...
...MANIPULATES LUCK...
...MAKES IT GOOD OR BAD.
OW!
SLAP!
DOUG!
OF ALL THE LOUSY--!
IT WASN'T MY SKILL THAT WON DOWNSTAIRS...
...YOU RIGGED THE GAME MY WAY...
...WITH YOUR STINKIN', CHEATIN' POWER!

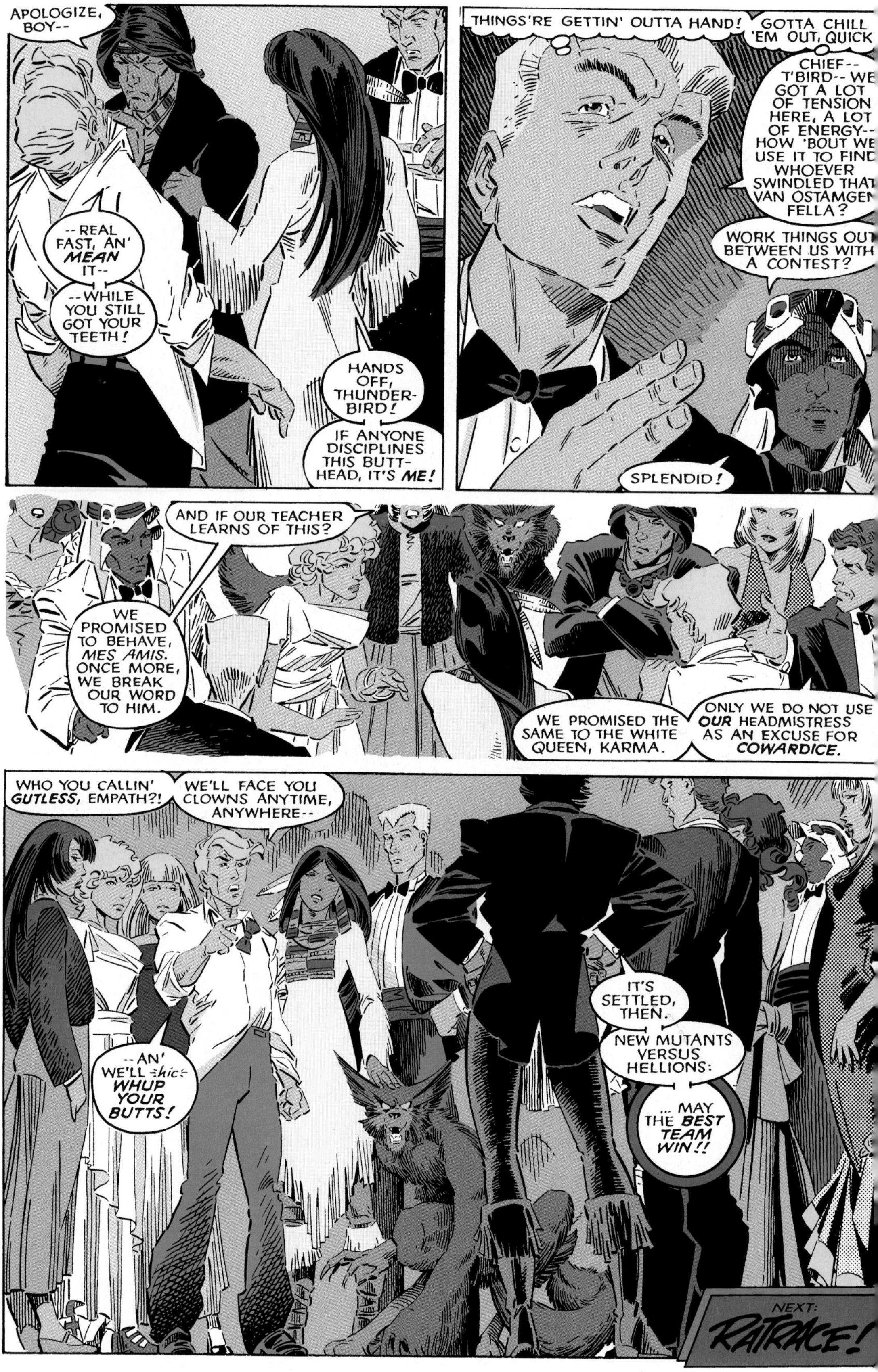
APOLOGIZE, BOY--
--REAL FAST, AN' MEAN IT--
--WHILE YOU STILL GOT YOUR TEETH!
HANDS OFF, THUNDERBIRD!
IF ANYONE DISCIPLINES THIS BUTT-HEAD, IT'S ME!
THINGS'RE GETTIN' OUTTA HAND!
GOTTA CHILL 'EM OUT, QUICK
CHIEF-- T'BIRD-- WE GOT A LOT OF TENSION HERE, A LOT OF ENERGY-- HOW 'BOUT WE USE IT TO FIND WHOEVER SWINDLED THAT VAN OSTAMGEN FELLA?
WORK THINGS OUT BETWEEN US WITH A CONTEST?
SPLENDID!
AND IF OUR TEACHER LEARNS OF THIS?
WE PROMISED TO BEHAVE, MES AMIS. ONCE MORE, WE BREAK OUR WORD TO HIM.
WE PROMISED THE SAME TO THE WHITE QUEEN, KARMA.
ONLY WE DO NOT USE OUR HEADMISTRESS AS AN EXCUSE FOR COWARDICE.
WHO YOU CALLIN' GUTLESS, EMPATH?!
WE'LL FACE YOU CLOWNS ANYTIME, ANYWHERE--
--AN' WE'LL -hic- WHUP YOUR BUTTS!
IT'S SETTLED, THEN.
NEW MUTANTS VERSUS HELLIONS:
... MAY THE BEST TEAM WIN!!
NEXT: RATRACE!

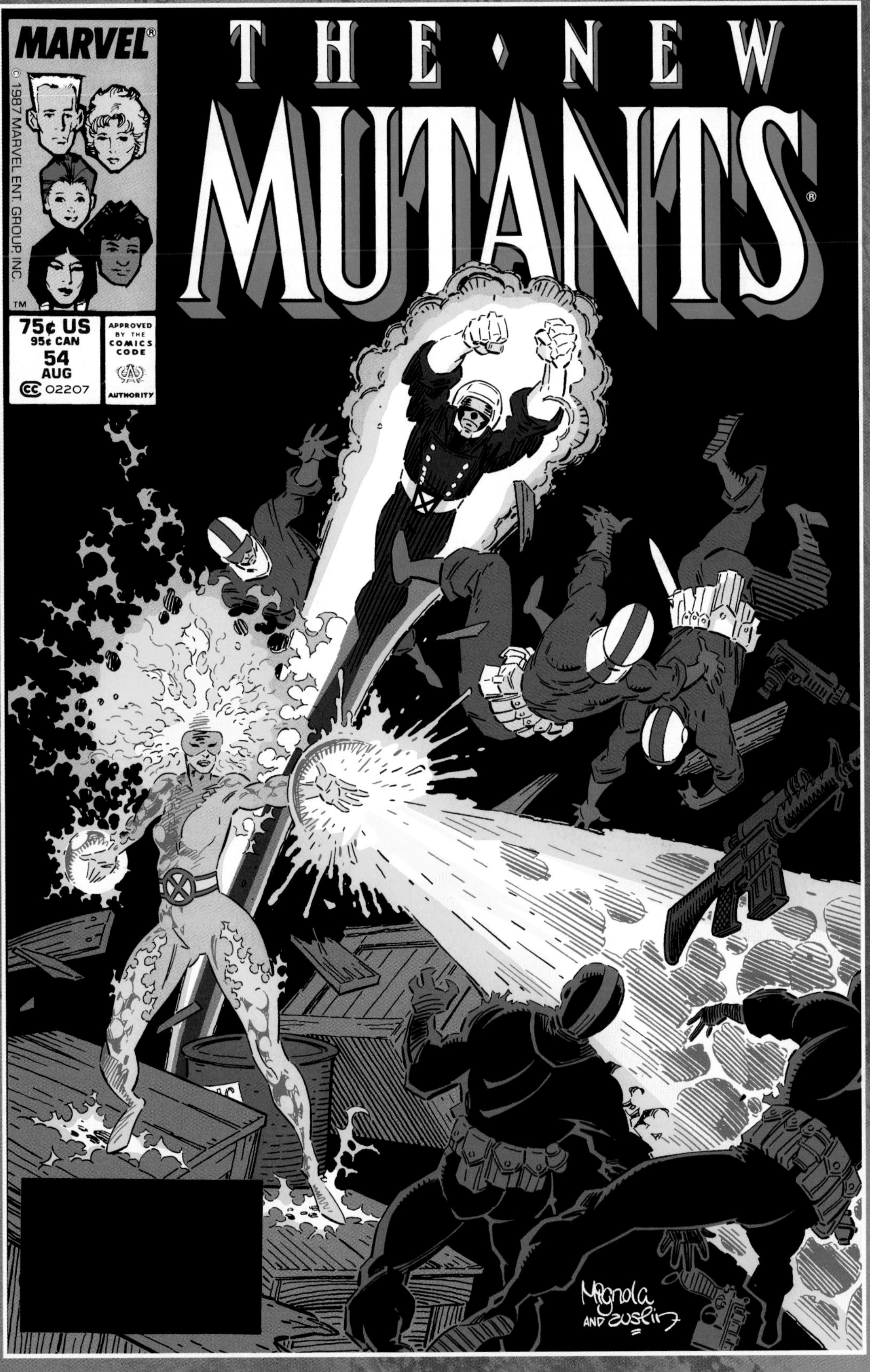
MARVEL®
© 1987 MARVEL ENT. GROUP INC.
TM
THE NEW MUTANTS®
75¢ US
95¢ CAN
54
AUG
CC 02207
APPROVED BY THE COMICS CODE AUTHORITY

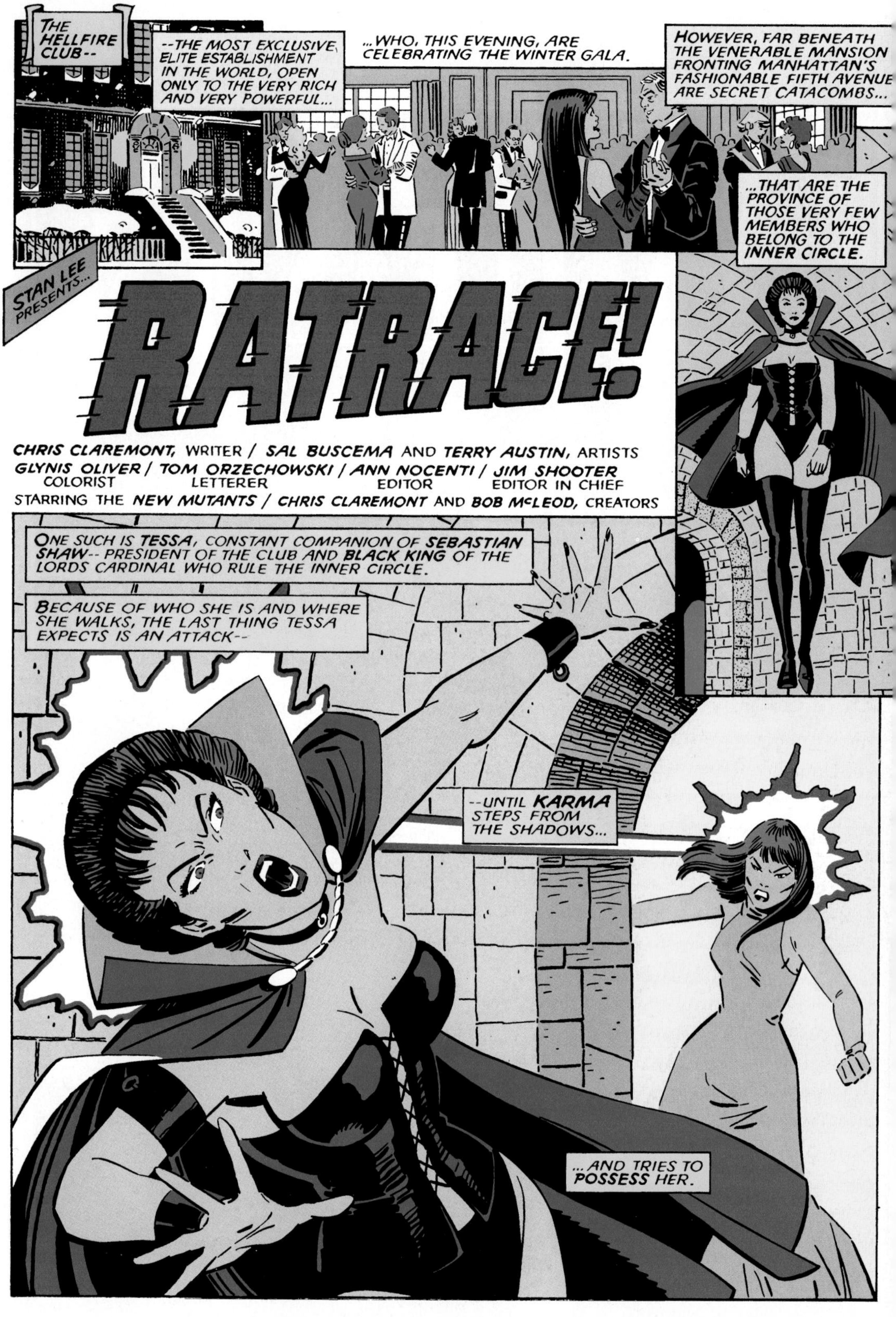

THE HELLFIRE CLUB--
--THE MOST EXCLUSIVE ELITE ESTABLISHMENT IN THE WORLD, OPEN ONLY TO THE VERY RICH AND VERY POWERFUL...
...WHO, THIS EVENING, ARE CELEBRATING THE WINTER GALA.
HOWEVER, FAR BENEATH THE VENERABLE MANSION FRONTING MANHATTAN'S FASHIONABLE FIFTH AVENUE ARE SECRET CATACOMBS...
...THAT ARE THE PROVINCE OF THOSE VERY FEW MEMBERS WHO BELONG TO THE INNER CIRCLE.
STAN LEE PRESENTS...
RATRACE!
CHRIS CLAREMONT, WRITER / SAL BUSCEMA AND TERRY AUSTIN, ARTISTS
GLYNIS OLIVER / TOM ORZECHOWSKI / ANN NOCENTI / JIM SHOOTER
COLORIST LETTERER EDITOR EDITOR IN CHIEF
STARRING THE NEW MUTANTS / CHRIS CLAREMONT AND BOB McLEOD, CREATORS
ONE SUCH IS TESSA, CONSTANT COMPANION OF SEBASTIAN SHAW-- PRESIDENT OF THE CLUB AND BLACK KING OF THE LORDS CARDINAL WHO RULE THE INNER CIRCLE.
BECAUSE OF WHO SHE IS AND WHERE SHE WALKS, THE LAST THING TESSA EXPECTS IS AN ATTACK--
--UNTIL KARMA STEPS FROM THE SHADOWS...
...AND TRIES TO POSSESS HER.

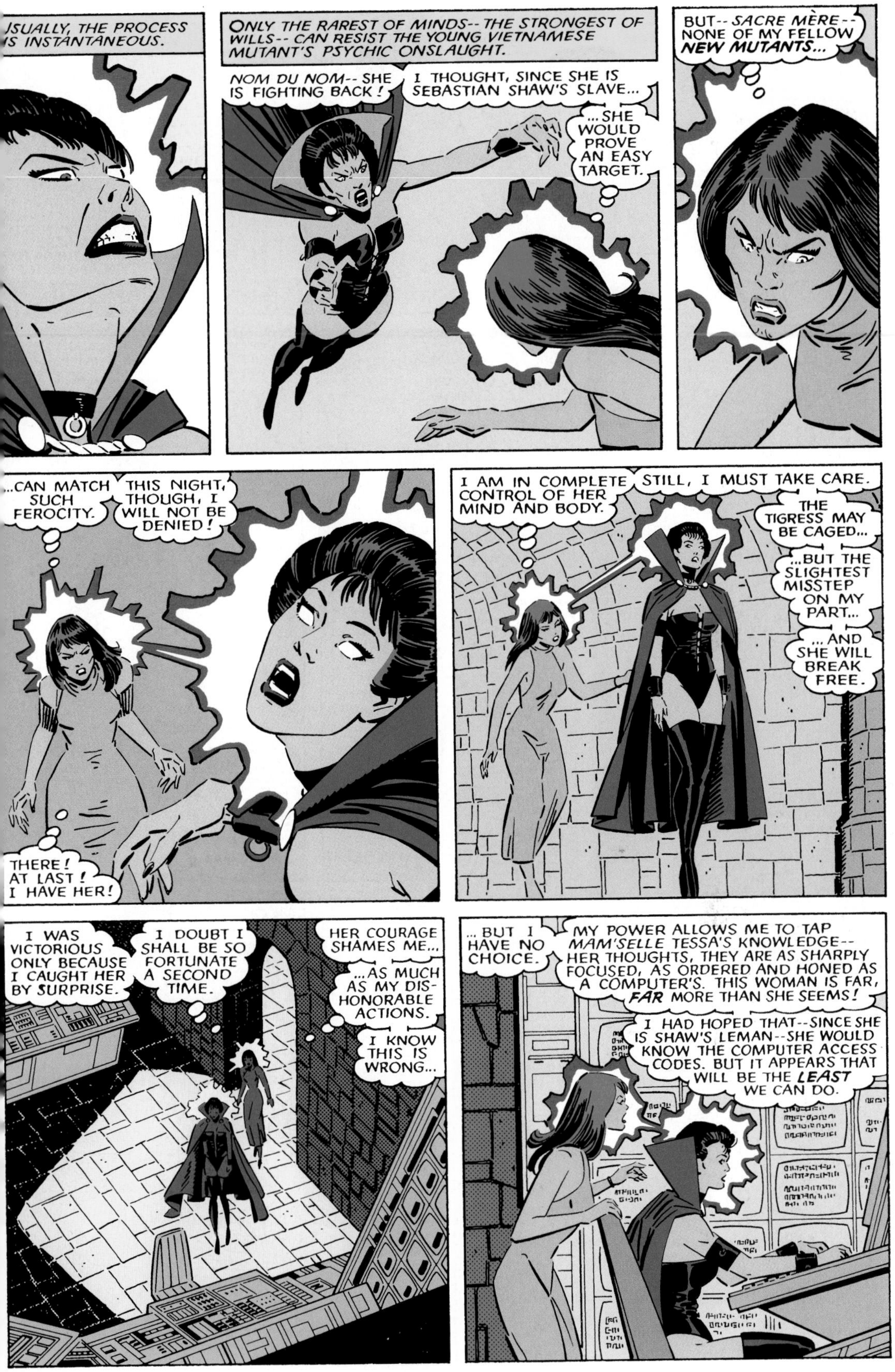
USUALLY, THE PROCESS IS INSTANTANEOUS.
ONLY THE RAREST OF MINDS-- THE STRONGEST OF WILLS-- CAN RESIST THE YOUNG VIETNAMESE MUTANT'S PSYCHIC ONSLAUGHT.
NOM DU NOM-- SHE IS FIGHTING BACK!
I THOUGHT, SINCE SHE IS SEBASTIAN SHAW'S SLAVE...
...SHE WOULD PROVE AN EASY TARGET.
BUT-- SACRE MÈRE-- NONE OF MY FELLOW NEW MUTANTS...
...CAN MATCH SUCH FEROCITY.
THIS NIGHT, THOUGH, I WILL NOT BE DENIED!
THERE! AT LAST! I HAVE HER!
I AM IN COMPLETE CONTROL OF HER MIND AND BODY.
STILL, I MUST TAKE CARE.
THE TIGRESS MAY BE CAGED...
...BUT THE SLIGHTEST MISSTEP ON MY PART...
...AND SHE WILL BREAK FREE.
I WAS VICTORIOUS ONLY BECAUSE I CAUGHT HER BY SURPRISE.
I DOUBT I SHALL BE SO FORTUNATE A SECOND TIME.
HER COURAGE SHAMES ME...
...AS MUCH AS MY DISHONORABLE ACTIONS.
I KNOW THIS IS WRONG...
...BUT I HAVE NO CHOICE.
MY POWER ALLOWS ME TO TAP MAM'SELLE TESSA'S KNOWLEDGE-- HER THOUGHTS, THEY ARE AS SHARPLY FOCUSED, AS ORDERED AND HONED AS A COMPUTER'S. THIS WOMAN IS FAR, FAR MORE THAN SHE SEEMS!
I HAD HOPED THAT--SINCE SHE IS SHAW'S LEMAN--SHE WOULD KNOW THE COMPUTER ACCESS CODES. BUT IT APPEARS THAT WILL BE THE LEAST WE CAN DO.

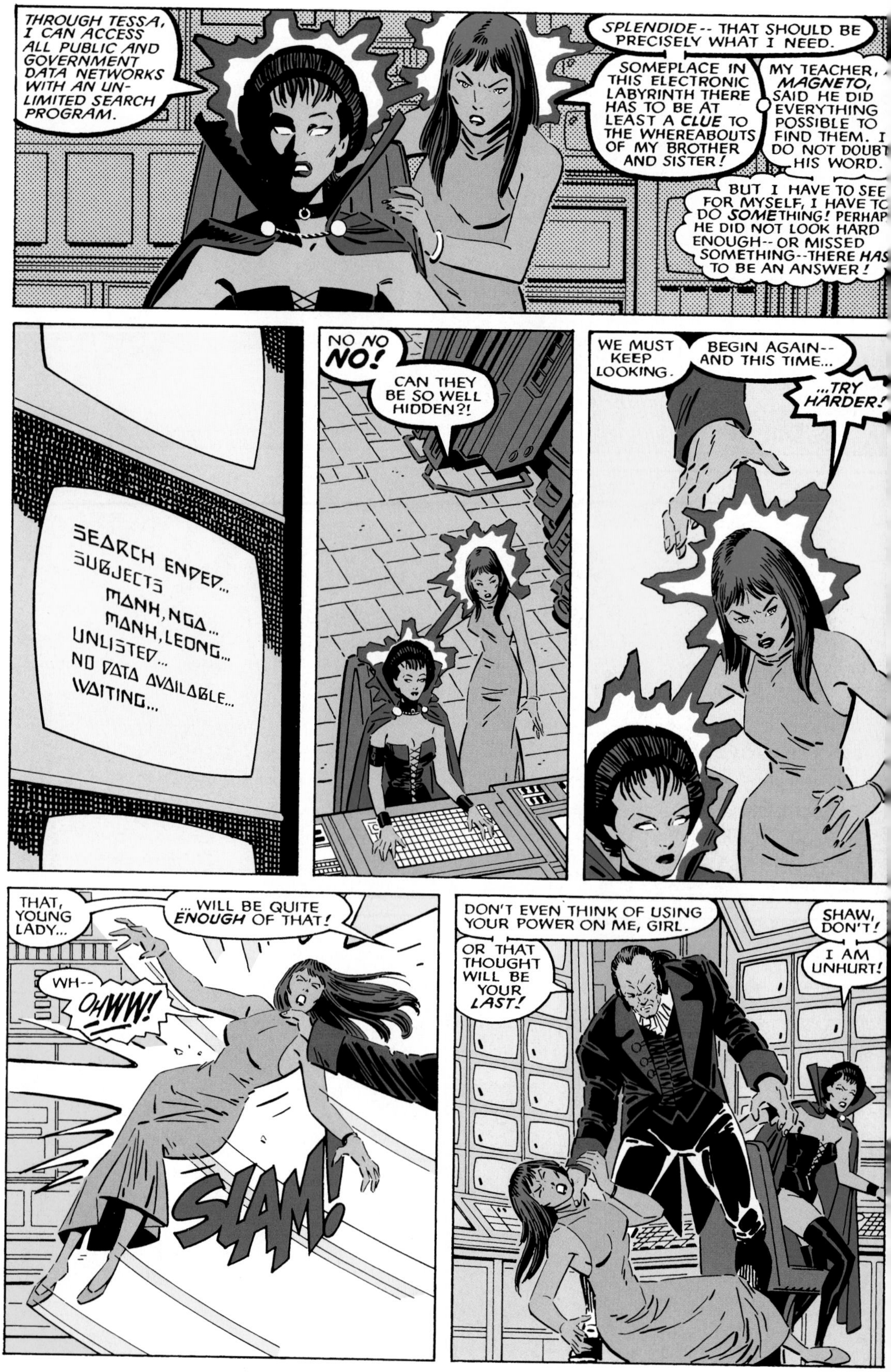

THROUGH TESSA, I CAN ACCESS ALL PUBLIC AND GOVERNMENT DATA NETWORKS WITH AN UNLIMITED SEARCH PROGRAM.
SPLENDIDE -- THAT SHOULD BE PRECISELY WHAT I NEED.
SOMEPLACE IN THIS ELECTRONIC LABYRINTH THERE HAS TO BE AT LEAST A CLUE TO THE WHEREABOUTS OF MY BROTHER AND SISTER!
MY TEACHER, MAGNETO, SAID HE DID EVERYTHING POSSIBLE TO FIND THEM. I DO NOT DOUBT HIS WORD.
BUT I HAVE TO SEE FOR MYSELF, I HAVE TO DO SOMETHING! PERHAP HE DID NOT LOOK HARD ENOUGH-- OR MISSED SOMETHING--THERE HAS TO BE AN ANSWER!
SEARCH ENDED... SUBJECTS MANH, NGA... MANH, LEONG... UNLISTED... NO DATA AVAILABLE... WAITING...
NO NO NO!
CAN THEY BE SO WELL HIDDEN?!
WE MUST KEEP LOOKING.
BEGIN AGAIN-- AND THIS TIME...
...TRY HARDER!
THAT, YOUNG LADY...
... WILL BE QUITE ENOUGH OF THAT!
WH--
OHWW!
SLAM!
DON'T EVEN THINK OF USING YOUR POWER ON ME, GIRL.
OR THAT THOUGHT WILL BE YOUR LAST!
SHAW, DON'T!
I AM UNHURT!

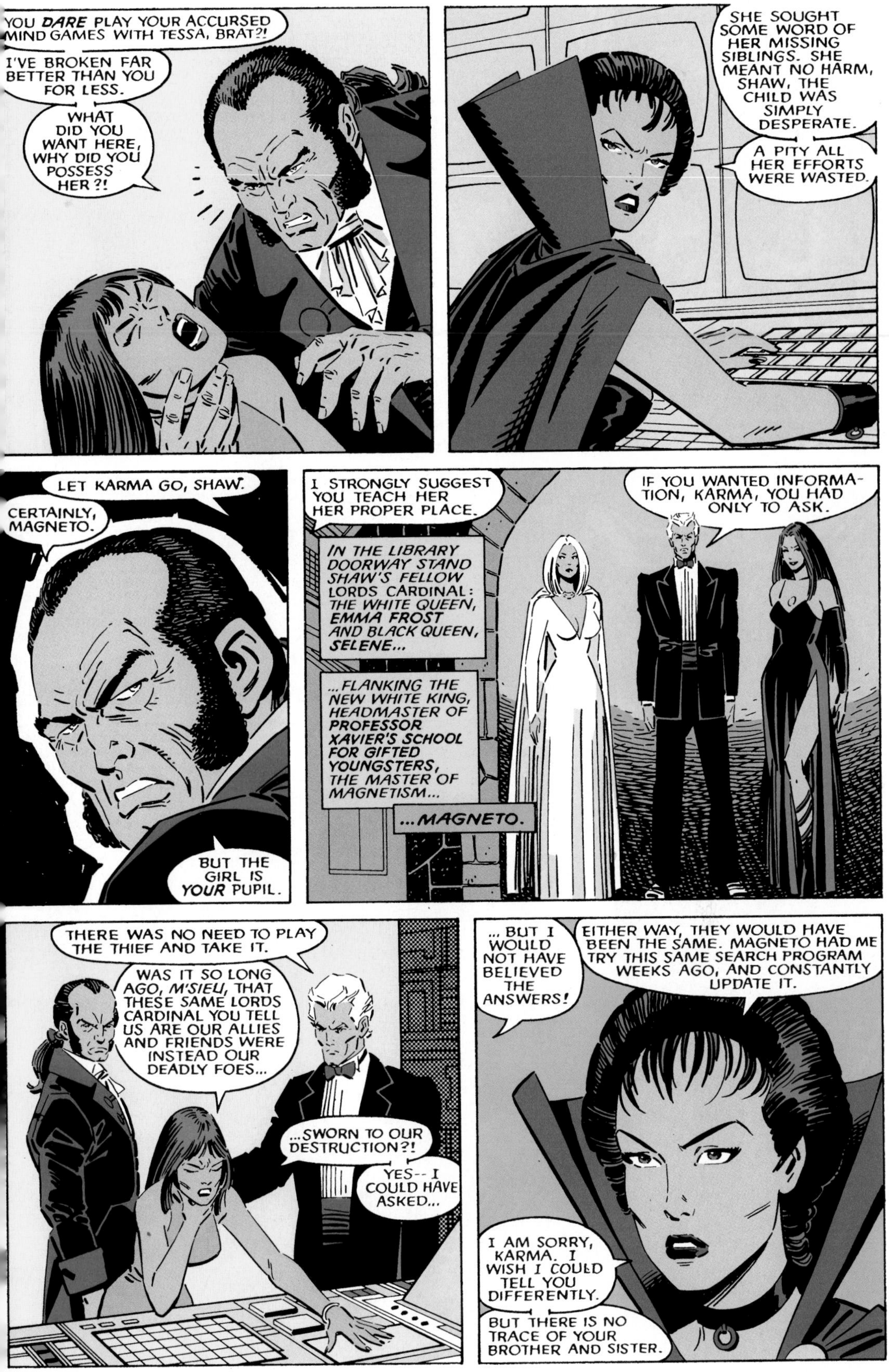

YOU *DARE* PLAY YOUR ACCURSED MIND GAMES WITH TESSA, BRAT?!
I'VE BROKEN FAR BETTER THAN YOU FOR LESS.
WHAT DID YOU WANT HERE, WHY DID YOU POSSESS HER?!
SHE SOUGHT SOME WORD OF HER MISSING SIBLINGS. SHE MEANT NO HARM, SHAW, THE CHILD WAS SIMPLY DESPERATE.
A PITY ALL HER EFFORTS WERE WASTED.
LET KARMA GO, SHAW.
CERTAINLY, MAGNETO.
BUT THE GIRL IS *YOUR* PUPIL.
I STRONGLY SUGGEST YOU TEACH HER HER PROPER PLACE.
*IN THE LIBRARY DOORWAY STAND SHAW'S FELLOW LORDS CARDINAL: THE WHITE QUEEN, **EMMA FROST** AND BLACK QUEEN, **SELENE**...*
*...FLANKING THE NEW WHITE KING, HEADMASTER OF **PROFESSOR XAVIER'S SCHOOL FOR GIFTED YOUNGSTERS**, THE MASTER OF MAGNETISM...*
***...MAGNETO.***
IF YOU WANTED INFORMATION, KARMA, YOU HAD ONLY TO ASK.
THERE WAS NO NEED TO PLAY THE THIEF AND TAKE IT.
WAS IT SO LONG AGO, *M'SIEU*, THAT THESE SAME LORDS CARDINAL YOU TELL US ARE OUR ALLIES AND FRIENDS WERE INSTEAD OUR DEADLY FOES...
...SWORN TO OUR DESTRUCTION?!
YES-- I COULD HAVE ASKED...
... BUT I WOULD NOT HAVE BELIEVED THE ANSWERS!
EITHER WAY, THEY WOULD HAVE BEEN THE SAME. MAGNETO HAD ME TRY THIS SAME SEARCH PROGRAM WEEKS AGO, AND CONSTANTLY UPDATE IT.
I AM SORRY, KARMA. I WISH I COULD TELL YOU DIFFERENTLY.
BUT THERE IS NO TRACE OF YOUR BROTHER AND SISTER.

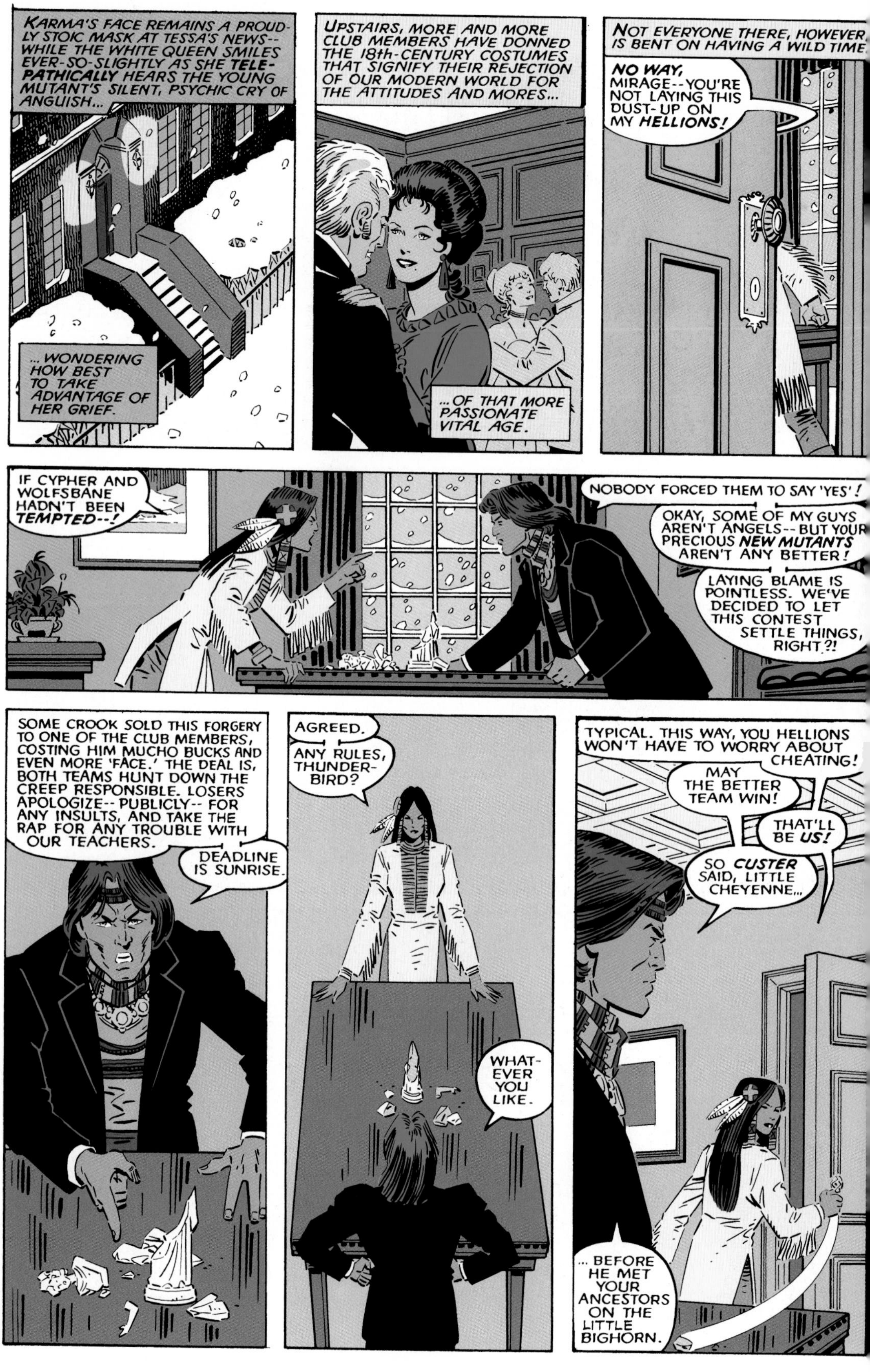
KARMA'S FACE REMAINS A PROUDLY STOIC MASK AT TESSA'S NEWS--WHILE THE WHITE QUEEN SMILES EVER-SO-SLIGHTLY AS SHE TELEPATHICALLY HEARS THE YOUNG MUTANT'S SILENT, PSYCHIC CRY OF ANGUISH...
...WONDERING HOW BEST TO TAKE ADVANTAGE OF HER GRIEF.
UPSTAIRS, MORE AND MORE CLUB MEMBERS HAVE DONNED THE 18th-CENTURY COSTUMES THAT SIGNIFY THEIR REJECTION OF OUR MODERN WORLD FOR THE ATTITUDES AND MORES...
...OF THAT MORE PASSIONATE VITAL AGE.
NOT EVERYONE THERE, HOWEVER, IS BENT ON HAVING A WILD TIME.
NO WAY, MIRAGE--YOU'RE NOT LAYING THIS DUST-UP ON MY HELLIONS!
IF CYPHER AND WOLFSBANE HADN'T BEEN TEMPTED--!
NOBODY FORCED THEM TO SAY 'YES'!
OKAY, SOME OF MY GUYS AREN'T ANGELS--BUT YOUR PRECIOUS NEW MUTANTS AREN'T ANY BETTER!
LAYING BLAME IS POINTLESS. WE'VE DECIDED TO LET THIS CONTEST SETTLE THINGS, RIGHT?!
SOME CROOK SOLD THIS FORGERY TO ONE OF THE CLUB MEMBERS, COSTING HIM MUCHO BUCKS AND EVEN MORE 'FACE.' THE DEAL IS, BOTH TEAMS HUNT DOWN THE CREEP RESPONSIBLE. LOSERS APOLOGIZE--PUBLICLY--FOR ANY INSULTS, AND TAKE THE RAP FOR ANY TROUBLE WITH OUR TEACHERS.
DEADLINE IS SUNRISE.
AGREED.
ANY RULES, THUNDERBIRD?
WHATEVER YOU LIKE.
TYPICAL. THIS WAY, YOU HELLIONS WON'T HAVE TO WORRY ABOUT CHEATING!
MAY THE BETTER TEAM WIN!
THAT'LL BE US!
SO CUSTER SAID, LITTLE CHEYENNE...
...BEFORE HE MET YOUR ANCESTORS ON THE LITTLE BIGHORN.

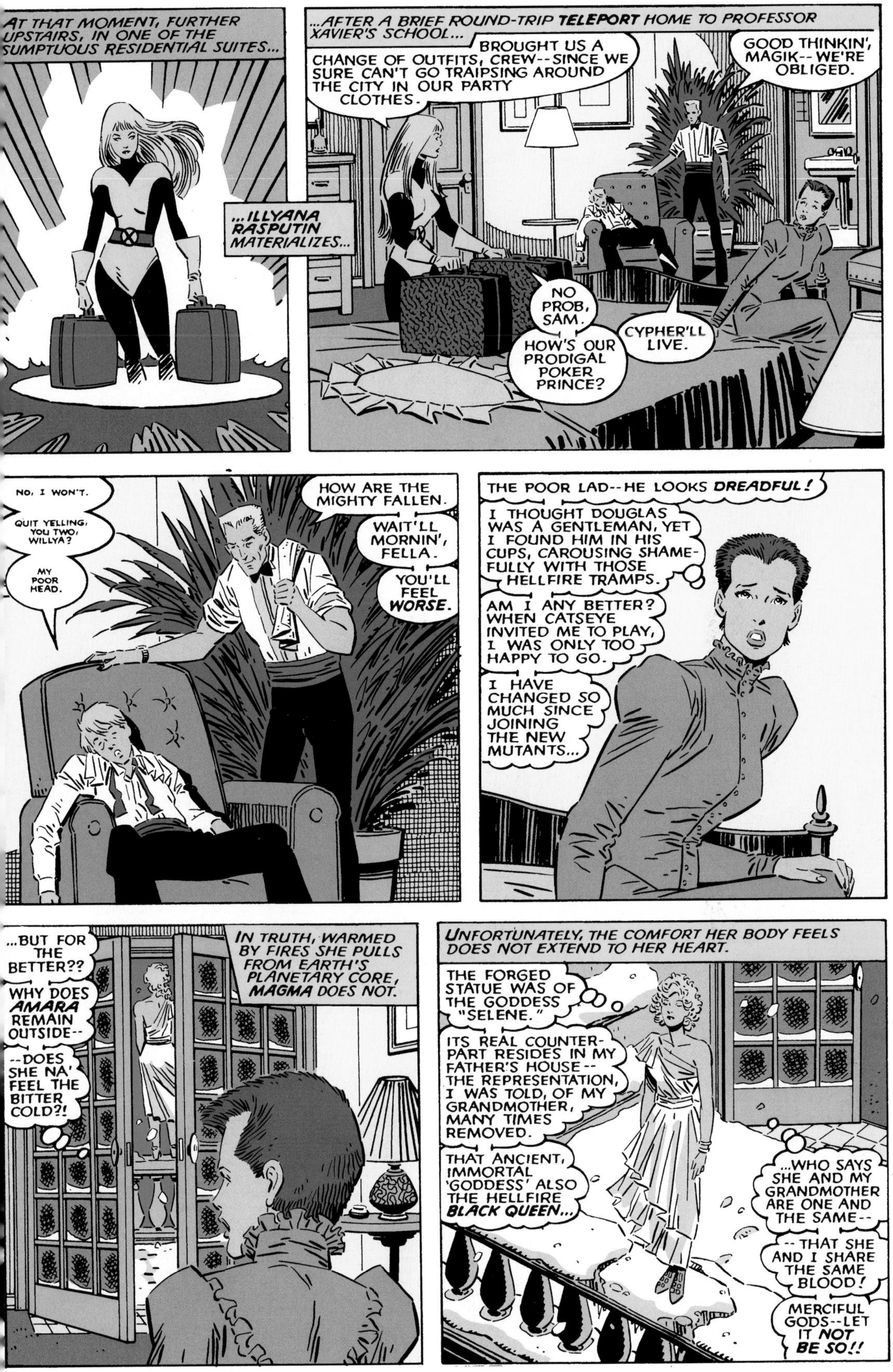

AT THAT MOMENT, FURTHER UPSTAIRS, IN ONE OF THE SUMPTUOUS RESIDENTIAL SUITES...
...ILLYANA RASPUTIN MATERIALIZES...
...AFTER A BRIEF ROUND-TRIP TELEPORT HOME TO PROFESSOR XAVIER'S SCHOOL...
BROUGHT US A CHANGE OF OUTFITS, CREW--SINCE WE SURE CAN'T GO TRAIPSING AROUND THE CITY IN OUR PARTY CLOTHES.
GOOD THINKIN', MAGIK-- WE'RE OBLIGED.
NO PROB, SAM.
HOW'S OUR PRODIGAL POKER PRINCE?
CYPHER'LL LIVE.
NO, I WON'T.
QUIT YELLING, YOU TWO, WILLYA?
MY POOR HEAD.
HOW ARE THE MIGHTY FALLEN.
WAIT'LL MORNIN', FELLA.
YOU'LL FEEL WORSE.
THE POOR LAD--HE LOOKS DREADFUL!
I THOUGHT DOUGLAS WAS A GENTLEMAN, YET I FOUND HIM IN HIS CUPS, CAROUSING SHAMEFULLY WITH THOSE HELLFIRE TRAMPS.
AM I ANY BETTER? WHEN CATSEYE INVITED ME TO PLAY, I WAS ONLY TOO HAPPY TO GO.
I HAVE CHANGED SO MUCH SINCE JOINING THE NEW MUTANTS...
...BUT FOR THE BETTER??
WHY DOES AMARA REMAIN OUTSIDE--
--DOES SHE NA' FEEL THE BITTER COLD?!
IN TRUTH, WARMED BY FIRES SHE PULLS FROM EARTH'S PLANETARY CORE, MAGMA DOES NOT.
UNFORTUNATELY, THE COMFORT HER BODY FEELS DOES NOT EXTEND TO HER HEART.
THE FORGED STATUE WAS OF THE GODDESS "SELENE."
ITS REAL COUNTERPART RESIDES IN MY FATHER'S HOUSE-- THE REPRESENTATION, I WAS TOLD, OF MY GRANDMOTHER, MANY TIMES REMOVED.
THAT ANCIENT, IMMORTAL 'GODDESS' ALSO THE HELLFIRE BLACK QUEEN...
...WHO SAYS SHE AND MY GRANDMOTHER ARE ONE AND THE SAME--
-- THAT SHE AND I SHARE THE SAME BLOOD!
MERCIFUL GODS--LET IT NOT BE SO!!

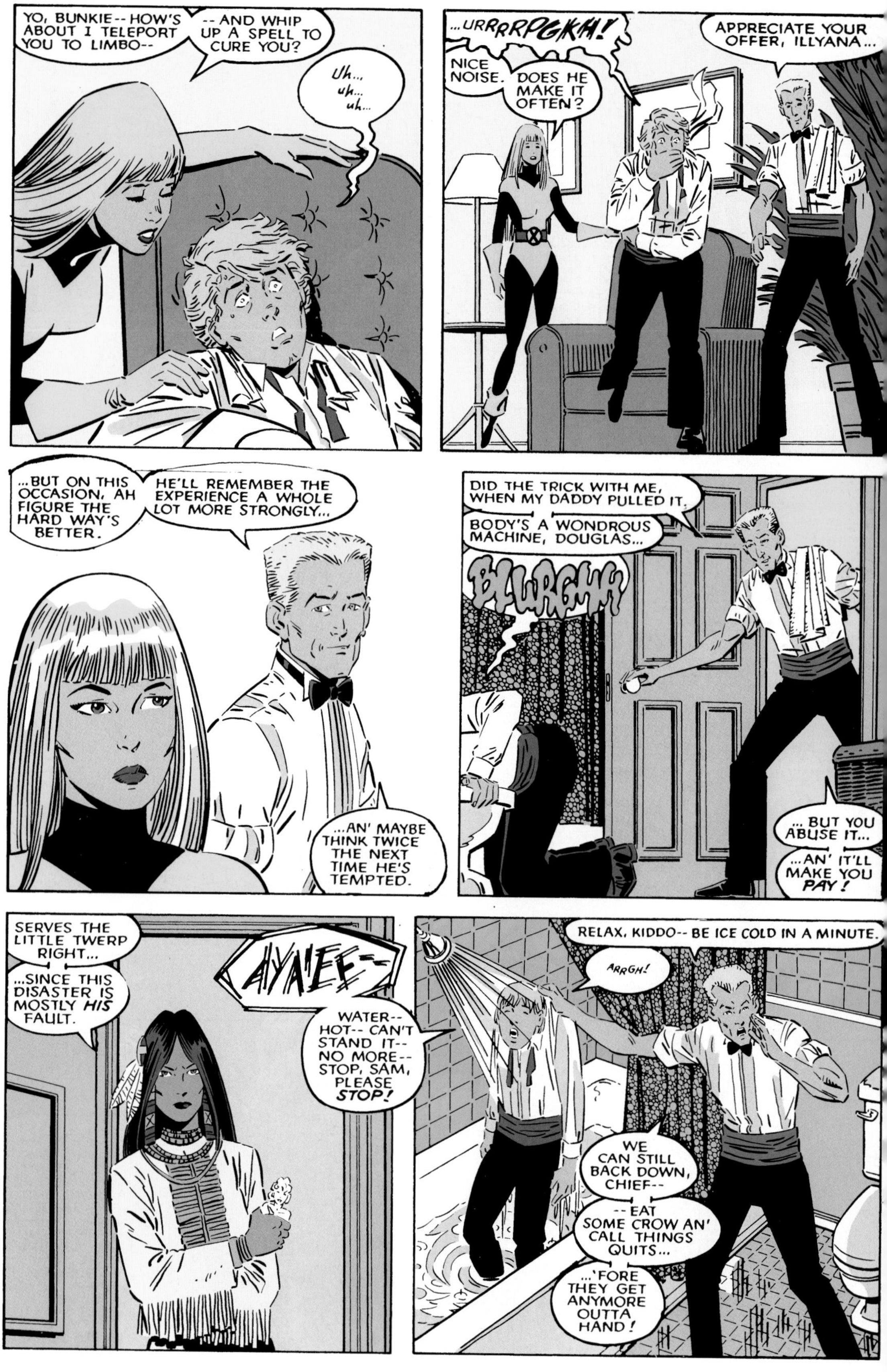
YO, BUNKIE-- HOW'S ABOUT I TELEPORT YOU TO LIMBO--
-- AND WHIP UP A SPELL TO CURE YOU?
Uh... uh... uh...
...URRRRPGKH!
NICE NOISE.
DOES HE MAKE IT OFTEN?
APPRECIATE YOUR OFFER, ILLYANA...
...BUT ON THIS OCCASION, AH FIGURE THE HARD WAY'S BETTER.
HE'LL REMEMBER THE EXPERIENCE A WHOLE LOT MORE STRONGLY...
...AN' MAYBE THINK TWICE THE NEXT TIME HE'S TEMPTED.
DID THE TRICK WITH ME, WHEN MY DADDY PULLED IT.
BODY'S A WONDROUS MACHINE, DOUGLAS...
BLURGHH
... BUT YOU ABUSE IT...
...AN' IT'LL MAKE YOU PAY!
SERVES THE LITTLE TWERP RIGHT...
...SINCE THIS DISASTER IS MOSTLY HIS FAULT.
AYAIEE--
WATER-- HOT-- CAN'T STAND IT-- NO MORE-- STOP, SAM, PLEASE STOP!
RELAX, KIDDO-- BE ICE COLD IN A MINUTE.
ARRGH!
WE CAN STILL BACK DOWN, CHIEF--
-- EAT SOME CROW AN' CALL THINGS QUITS...
...'FORE THEY GET ANYMORE OUTTA HAND!

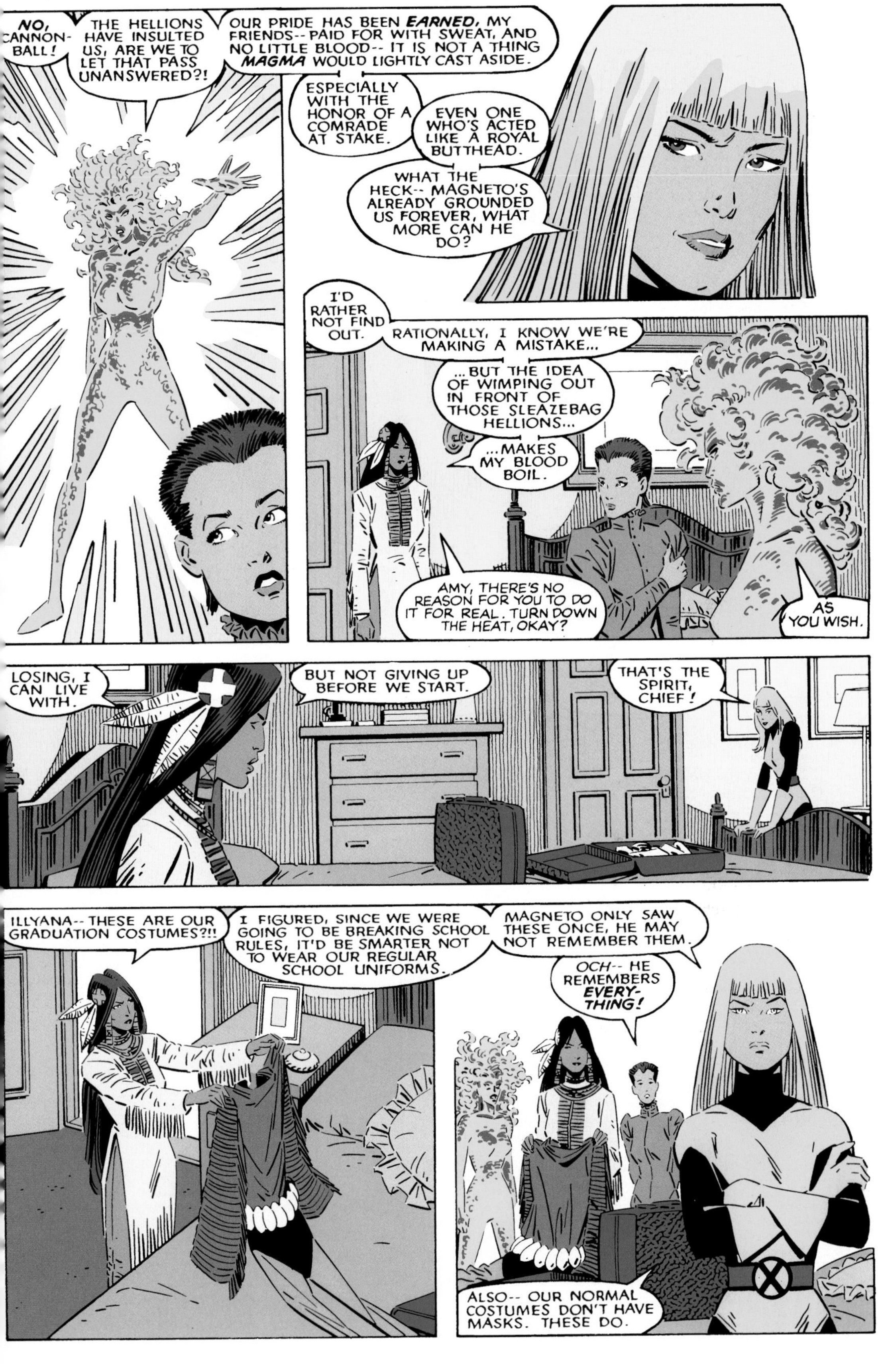
NO, CANNONBALL!
THE HELLIONS HAVE INSULTED US, ARE WE TO LET THAT PASS UNANSWERED?!
OUR PRIDE HAS BEEN EARNED, MY FRIENDS-- PAID FOR WITH SWEAT, AND NO LITTLE BLOOD-- IT IS NOT A THING MAGMA WOULD LIGHTLY CAST ASIDE.
ESPECIALLY WITH THE HONOR OF A COMRADE AT STAKE.
EVEN ONE WHO'S ACTED LIKE A ROYAL BUTTHEAD.
WHAT THE HECK-- MAGNETO'S ALREADY GROUNDED US FOREVER, WHAT MORE CAN HE DO?
I'D RATHER NOT FIND OUT.
RATIONALLY, I KNOW WE'RE MAKING A MISTAKE...
...BUT THE IDEA OF WIMPING OUT IN FRONT OF THOSE SLEAZEBAG HELLIONS...
...MAKES MY BLOOD BOIL.
AMY, THERE'S NO REASON FOR YOU TO DO IT FOR REAL. TURN DOWN THE HEAT, OKAY?
AS YOU WISH.
LOSING, I CAN LIVE WITH.
BUT NOT GIVING UP BEFORE WE START.
THAT'S THE SPIRIT, CHIEF!
ILLYANA-- THESE ARE OUR GRADUATION COSTUMES?!!
I FIGURED, SINCE WE WERE GOING TO BE BREAKING SCHOOL RULES, IT'D BE SMARTER NOT TO WEAR OUR REGULAR SCHOOL UNIFORMS.
MAGNETO ONLY SAW THESE ONCE, HE MAY NOT REMEMBER THEM.
OCH-- HE REMEMBERS EVERYTHING!
ALSO-- OUR NORMAL COSTUMES DON'T HAVE MASKS. THESE DO.

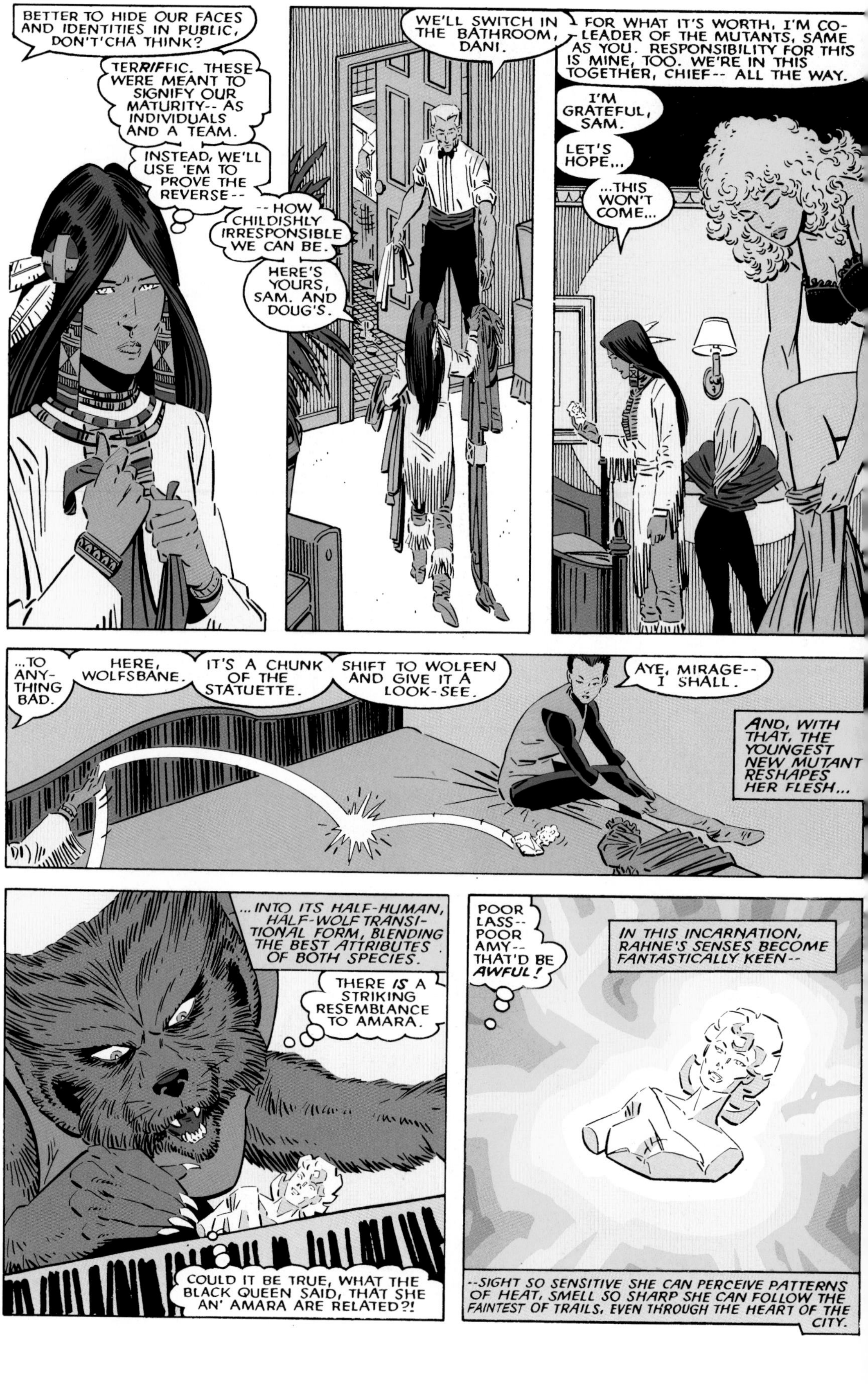
BETTER TO HIDE OUR FACES AND IDENTITIES IN PUBLIC, DON'T'CHA THINK?
TERRIFFIC. THESE WERE MEANT TO SIGNIFY OUR MATURITY-- AS INDIVIDUALS AND A TEAM.
INSTEAD, WE'LL USE 'EM TO PROVE THE REVERSE--
--HOW CHILDISHLY IRRESPONSIBLE WE CAN BE.
HERE'S YOURS, SAM. AND DOUG'S.
WE'LL SWITCH IN THE BATHROOM, DANI.
FOR WHAT IT'S WORTH, I'M CO-LEADER OF THE MUTANTS, SAME AS YOU. RESPONSIBILITY FOR THIS IS MINE, TOO. WE'RE IN THIS TOGETHER, CHIEF-- ALL THE WAY.
I'M GRATEFUL, SAM.
LET'S HOPE...
...THIS WON'T COME...
...TO ANYTHING BAD.
HERE, WOLFSBANE.
IT'S A CHUNK OF THE STATUETTE.
SHIFT TO WOLFEN AND GIVE IT A LOOK-SEE.
AYE, MIRAGE-- I SHALL.
AND, WITH THAT, THE YOUNGEST NEW MUTANT RESHAPES HER FLESH...
...INTO ITS HALF-HUMAN, HALF-WOLF TRANSITIONAL FORM, BLENDING THE BEST ATTRIBUTES OF BOTH SPECIES.
THERE IS A STRIKING RESEMBLANCE TO AMARA.
COULD IT BE TRUE, WHAT THE BLACK QUEEN SAID, THAT SHE AN' AMARA ARE RELATED?!
POOR LASS-- POOR AMY-- THAT'D BE AWFUL!
IN THIS INCARNATION, RAHNE'S SENSES BECOME FANTASTICALLY KEEN--
--SIGHT SO SENSITIVE SHE CAN PERCEIVE PATTERNS OF HEAT, SMELL SO SHARP SHE CAN FOLLOW THE FAINTEST OF TRAILS, EVEN THROUGH THE HEART OF THE CITY.

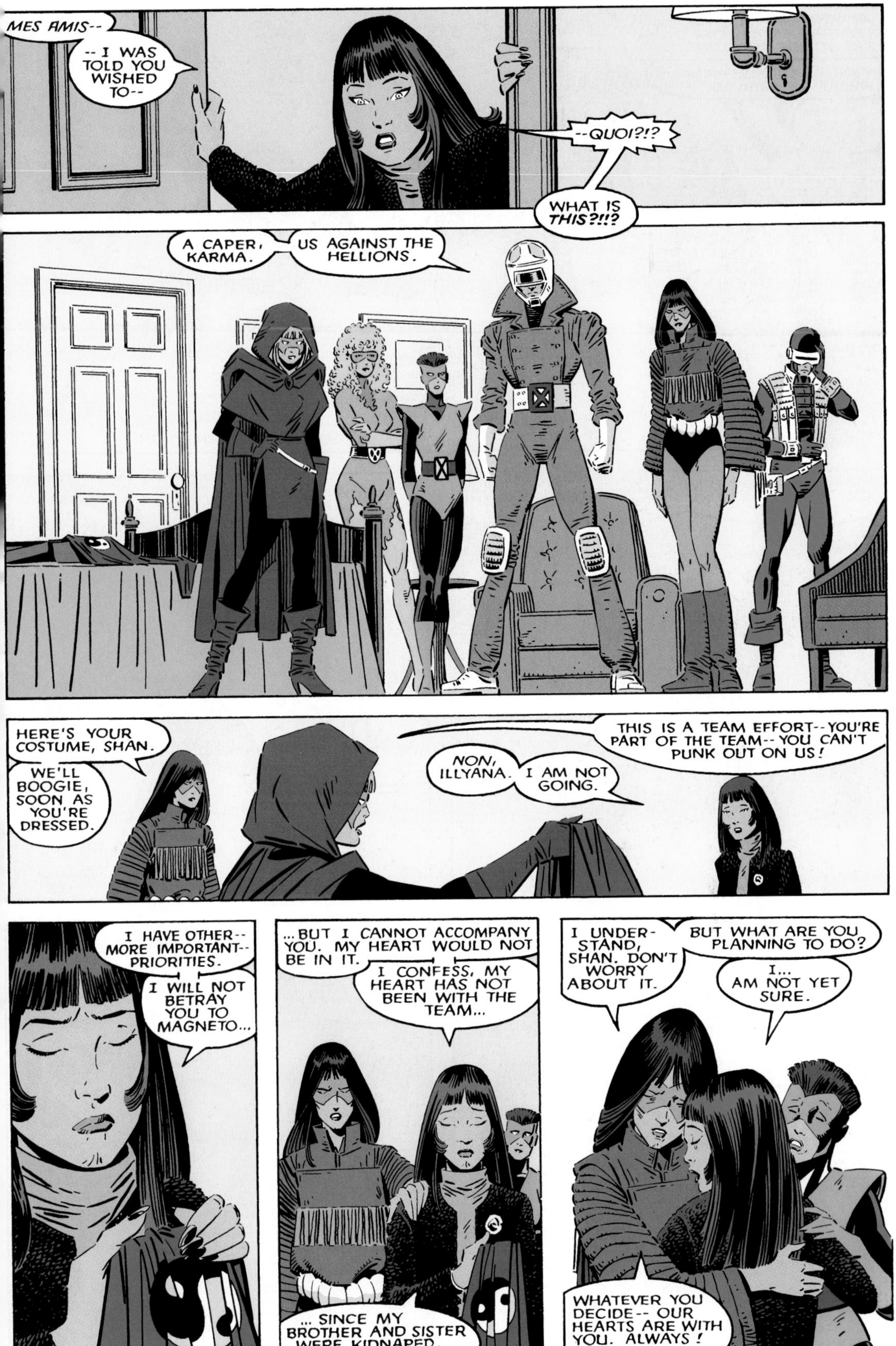
MES AMIS--
--I WAS TOLD YOU WISHED TO--
--QUOI?!?
WHAT IS THIS?!!?
A CAPER, KARMA.
US AGAINST THE HELLIONS.
HERE'S YOUR COSTUME, SHAN.
WE'LL BOOGIE, SOON AS YOU'RE DRESSED.
THIS IS A TEAM EFFORT--YOU'RE PART OF THE TEAM--YOU CAN'T PUNK OUT ON US!
NON, ILLYANA.
I AM NOT GOING.
I HAVE OTHER--MORE IMPORTANT--PRIORITIES.
I WILL NOT BETRAY YOU TO MAGNETO...
...BUT I CANNOT ACCOMPANY YOU. MY HEART WOULD NOT BE IN IT.
I CONFESS, MY HEART HAS NOT BEEN WITH THE TEAM...
...SINCE MY BROTHER AND SISTER WERE KIDNAPED.
I UNDER-STAND, SHAN. DON'T WORRY ABOUT IT.
BUT WHAT ARE YOU PLANNING TO DO?
I... AM NOT YET SURE.
WHATEVER YOU DECIDE--OUR HEARTS ARE WITH YOU. ALWAYS!

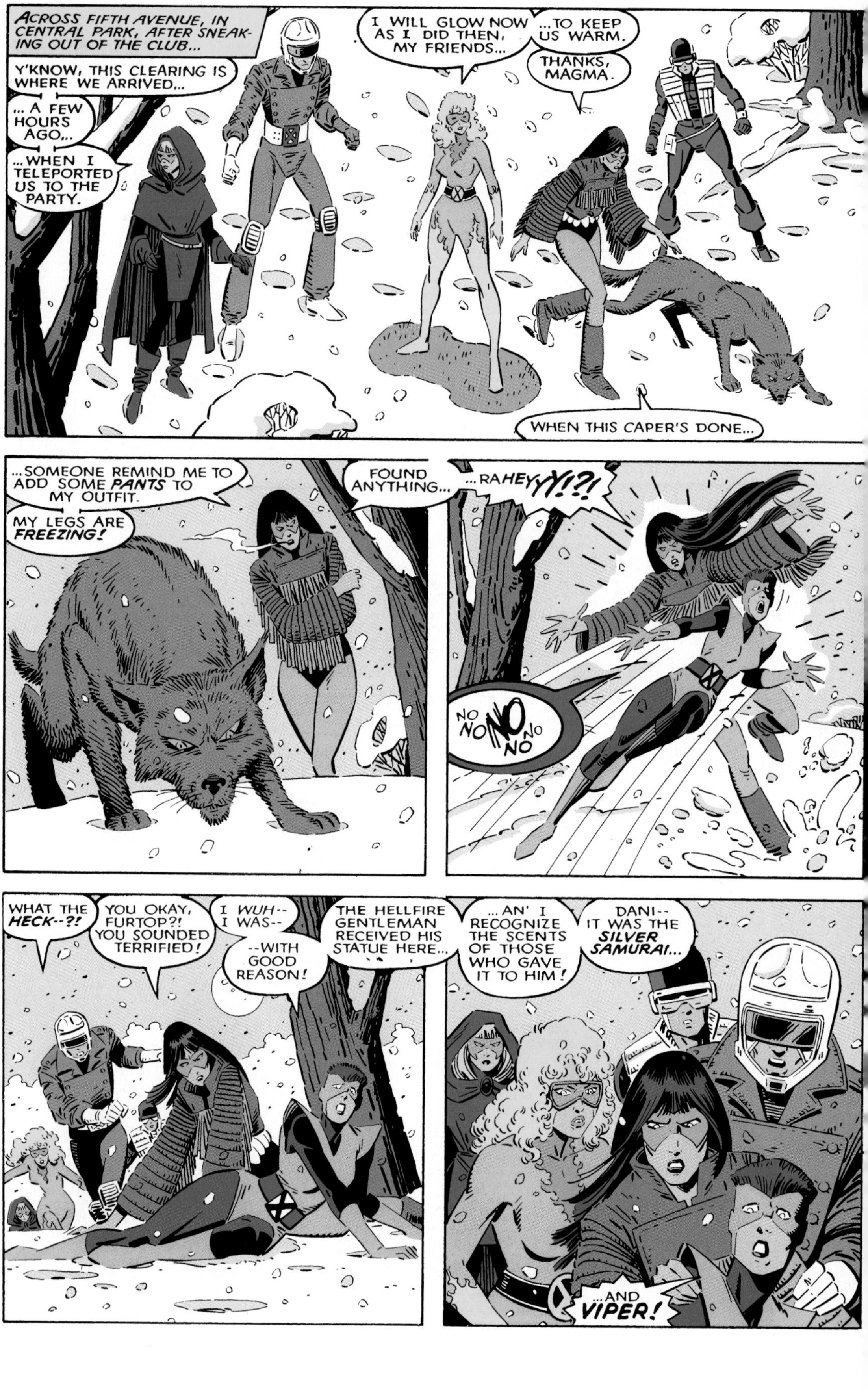
ACROSS FIFTH AVENUE, IN CENTRAL PARK, AFTER SNEAKING OUT OF THE CLUB...
Y'KNOW, THIS CLEARING IS WHERE WE ARRIVED...
...A FEW HOURS AGO...
...WHEN I TELEPORTED US TO THE PARTY.
I WILL GLOW NOW AS I DID THEN, MY FRIENDS...
...TO KEEP US WARM.
THANKS, MAGMA.
WHEN THIS CAPER'S DONE...
...SOMEONE REMIND ME TO ADD SOME PANTS TO MY OUTFIT.
MY LEGS ARE FREEZING!
FOUND ANYTHING...
...RAHEYYY!?!
NO NO NO NO NO NO
WHAT THE HECK--?!
YOU OKAY, FURTOP?! YOU SOUNDED TERRIFIED!
I WUH-- I WAS--
--WITH GOOD REASON!
THE HELLFIRE GENTLEMAN RECEIVED HIS STATUE HERE...
...AN' I RECOGNIZE THE SCENTS OF THOSE WHO GAVE IT TO HIM!
DANI-- IT WAS THE SILVER SAMURAI...
...AND VIPER!

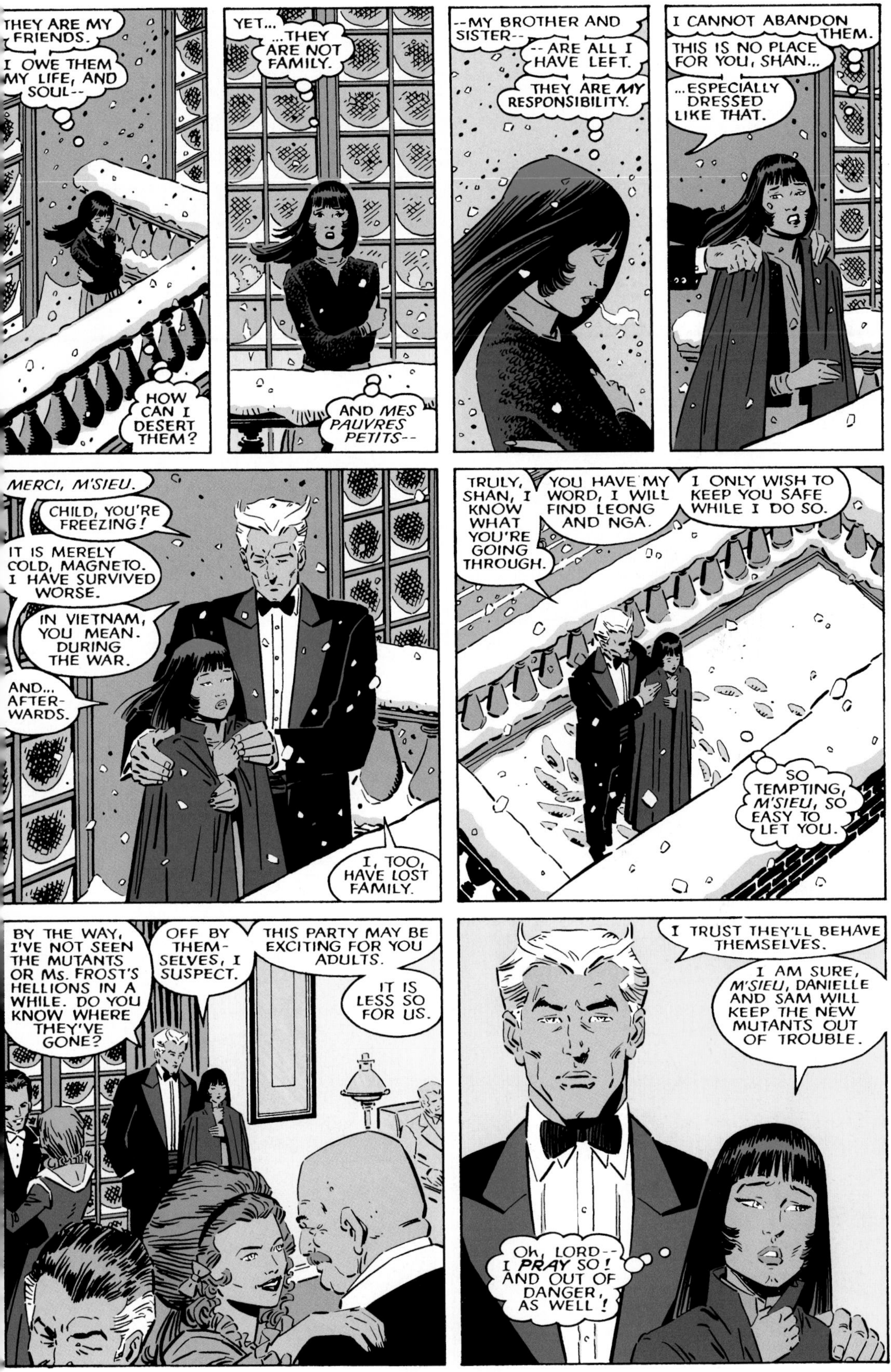
THEY ARE MY FRIENDS.
I OWE THEM MY LIFE, AND SOUL--
HOW CAN I DESERT THEM?
YET...
...THEY ARE NOT FAMILY.
AND MES PAUVRES PETITS--
--MY BROTHER AND SISTER--
--ARE ALL I HAVE LEFT.
THEY ARE MY RESPONSIBILITY.
I CANNOT ABANDON THEM.
THIS IS NO PLACE FOR YOU, SHAN...
...ESPECIALLY DRESSED LIKE THAT.
MERCI, M'SIEU.
CHILD, YOU'RE FREEZING!
IT IS MERELY COLD, MAGNETO. I HAVE SURVIVED WORSE.
IN VIETNAM, YOU MEAN. DURING THE WAR.
AND... AFTER-WARDS.
I, TOO, HAVE LOST FAMILY.
TRULY, SHAN, I KNOW WHAT YOU'RE GOING THROUGH.
YOU HAVE MY WORD, I WILL FIND LEONG AND NGA.
I ONLY WISH TO KEEP YOU SAFE WHILE I DO SO.
SO TEMPTING, M'SIEU, SO EASY TO LET YOU.
BY THE WAY, I'VE NOT SEEN THE MUTANTS OR Ms. FROST'S HELLIONS IN A WHILE. DO YOU KNOW WHERE THEY'VE GONE?
OFF BY THEM-SELVES, I SUSPECT.
THIS PARTY MAY BE EXCITING FOR YOU ADULTS.
IT IS LESS SO FOR US.
I TRUST THEY'LL BEHAVE THEMSELVES.
I AM SURE, M'SIEU, DANIELLE AND SAM WILL KEEP THE NEW MUTANTS OUT OF TROUBLE.
Oh, LORD-- I PRAY SO! AND OUT OF DANGER, AS WELL!

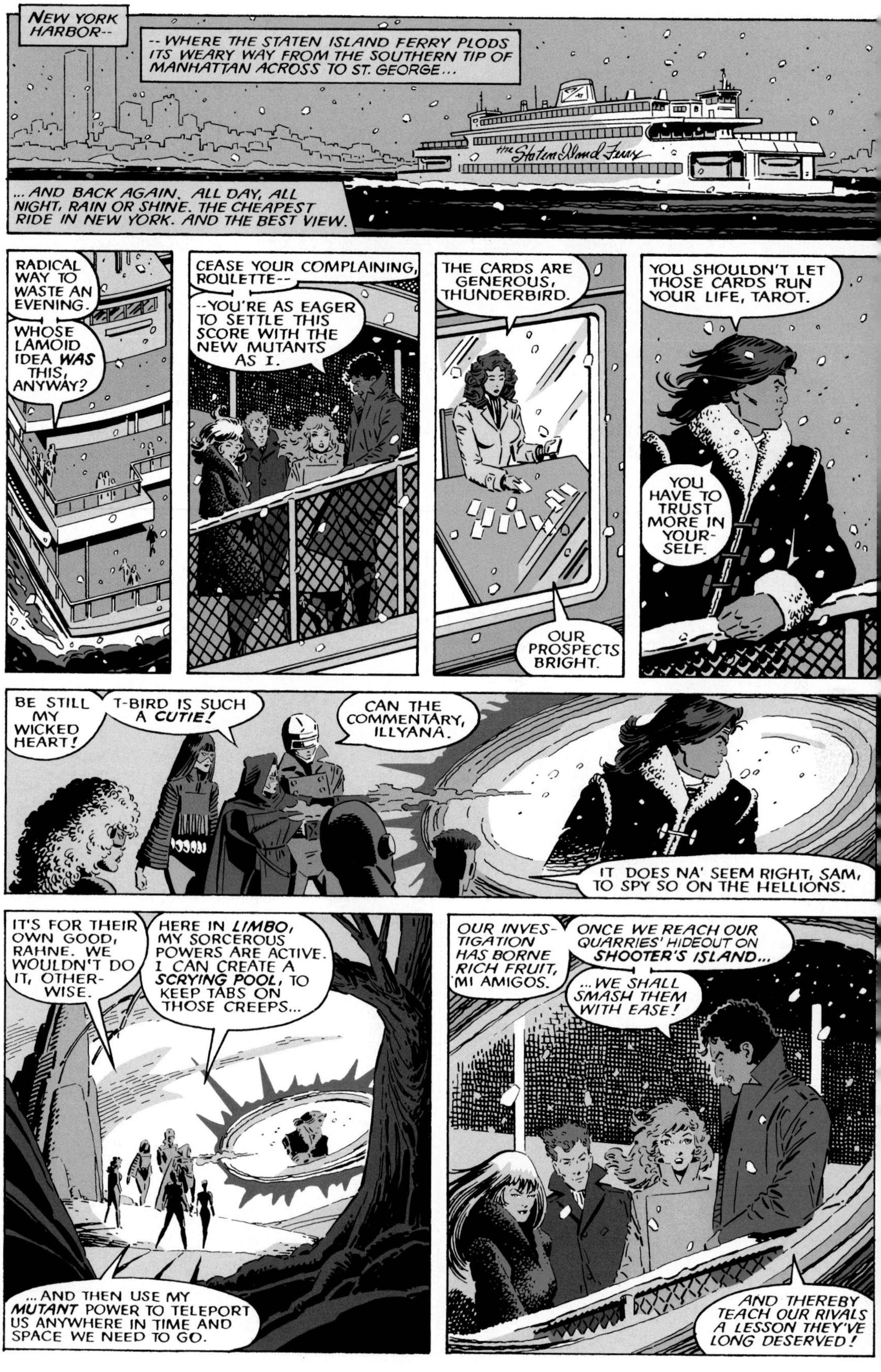
NEW YORK HARBOR--
--WHERE THE STATEN ISLAND FERRY PLODS ITS WEARY WAY FROM THE SOUTHERN TIP OF MANHATTAN ACROSS TO ST. GEORGE...
the Staten Island Ferry
...AND BACK AGAIN. ALL DAY, ALL NIGHT, RAIN OR SHINE. THE CHEAPEST RIDE IN NEW YORK. AND THE BEST VIEW.
RADICAL WAY TO WASTE AN EVENING.
WHOSE LAMOID IDEA WAS THIS, ANYWAY?
CEASE YOUR COMPLAINING, ROULETTE--
--YOU'RE AS EAGER TO SETTLE THIS SCORE WITH THE NEW MUTANTS AS I.
THE CARDS ARE GENEROUS, THUNDERBIRD.
OUR PROSPECTS BRIGHT.
YOU SHOULDN'T LET THOSE CARDS RUN YOUR LIFE, TAROT.
YOU HAVE TO TRUST MORE IN YOURSELF.
BE STILL MY WICKED HEART!
T-BIRD IS SUCH A CUTIE!
CAN THE COMMENTARY, ILLYANA.
IT DOES NA' SEEM RIGHT, SAM, TO SPY SO ON THE HELLIONS.
IT'S FOR THEIR OWN GOOD, RAHNE. WE WOULDN'T DO IT, OTHERWISE.
HERE IN LIMBO, MY SORCEROUS POWERS ARE ACTIVE. I CAN CREATE A SCRYING POOL, TO KEEP TABS ON THOSE CREEPS...
...AND THEN USE MY MUTANT POWER TO TELEPORT US ANYWHERE IN TIME AND SPACE WE NEED TO GO.
OUR INVESTIGATION HAS BORNE RICH FRUIT, MI AMIGOS.
ONCE WE REACH OUR QUARRIES' HIDEOUT ON SHOOTER'S ISLAND...
...WE SHALL SMASH THEM WITH EASE!
AND THEREBY TEACH OUR RIVALS A LESSON THEY'VE LONG DESERVED!

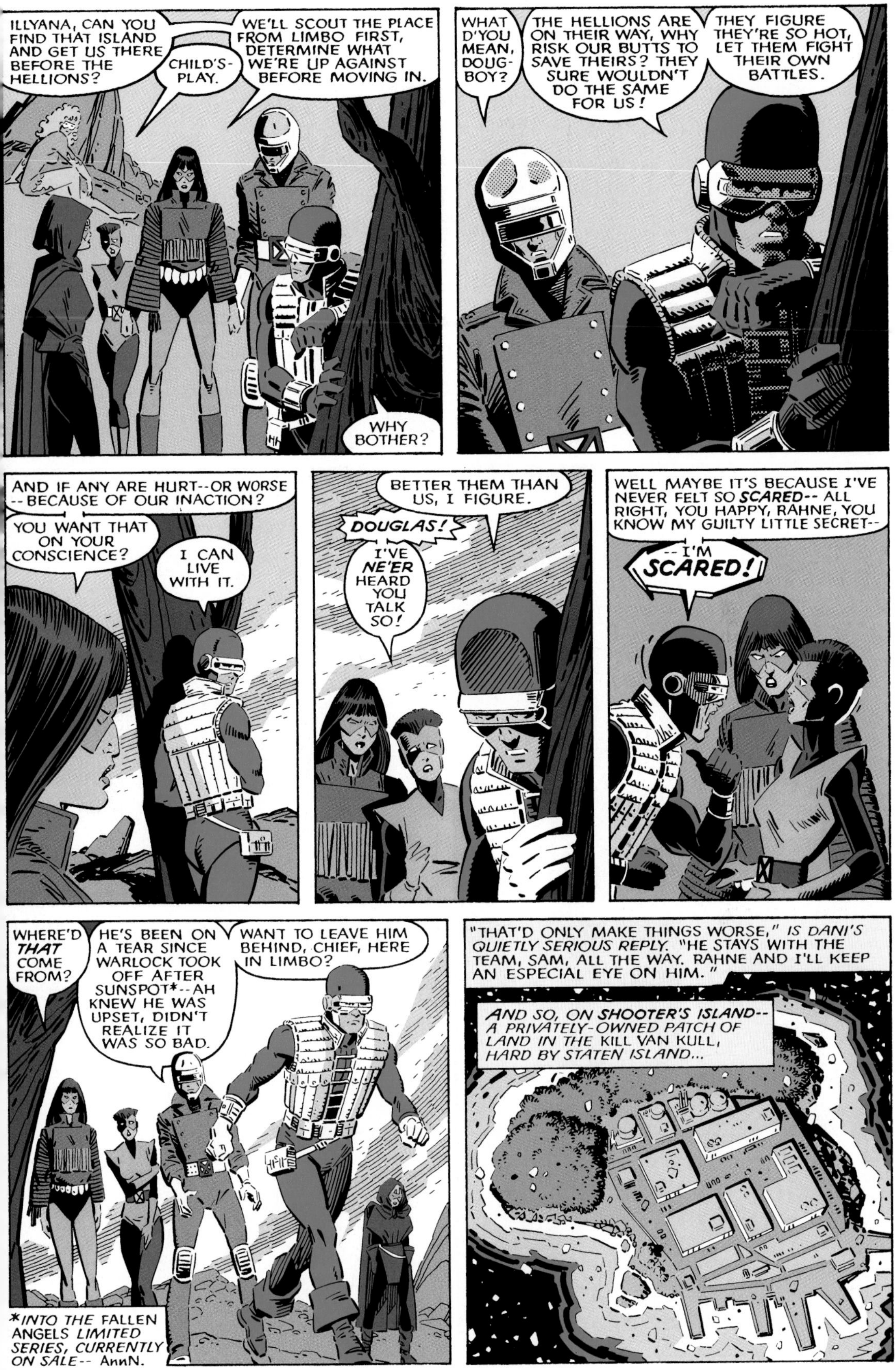
ILLYANA, CAN YOU FIND THAT ISLAND AND GET US THERE BEFORE THE HELLIONS?
CHILD'S-PLAY.
WE'LL SCOUT THE PLACE FROM LIMBO FIRST, DETERMINE WHAT WE'RE UP AGAINST BEFORE MOVING IN.
WHY BOTHER?
WHAT D'YOU MEAN, DOUG-BOY?
THE HELLIONS ARE ON THEIR WAY, WHY RISK OUR BUTTS TO SAVE THEIRS? THEY SURE WOULDN'T DO THE SAME FOR US!
THEY FIGURE THEY'RE SO HOT, LET THEM FIGHT THEIR OWN BATTLES.
AND IF ANY ARE HURT--OR WORSE --BECAUSE OF OUR INACTION?
YOU WANT THAT ON YOUR CONSCIENCE?
I CAN LIVE WITH IT.
BETTER THEM THAN US, I FIGURE.
DOUGLAS!
I'VE NE'ER HEARD YOU TALK SO!
WELL MAYBE IT'S BECAUSE I'VE NEVER FELT SO SCARED-- ALL RIGHT, YOU HAPPY, RAHNE, YOU KNOW MY GUILTY LITTLE SECRET--
--I'M SCARED!
WHERE'D THAT COME FROM?
HE'S BEEN ON A TEAR SINCE WARLOCK TOOK OFF AFTER SUNSPOT*--AH KNEW HE WAS UPSET, DIDN'T REALIZE IT WAS SO BAD.
WANT TO LEAVE HIM BEHIND, CHIEF, HERE IN LIMBO?
*INTO THE FALLEN ANGELS LIMITED SERIES, CURRENTLY ON SALE-- AnnN.
"THAT'D ONLY MAKE THINGS WORSE," IS DANI'S QUIETLY SERIOUS REPLY. "HE STAYS WITH THE TEAM, SAM, ALL THE WAY. RAHNE AND I'LL KEEP AN ESPECIAL EYE ON HIM."
AND SO, ON SHOOTER'S ISLAND-- A PRIVATELY-OWNED PATCH OF LAND IN THE KILL VAN KULL, HARD BY STATEN ISLAND...

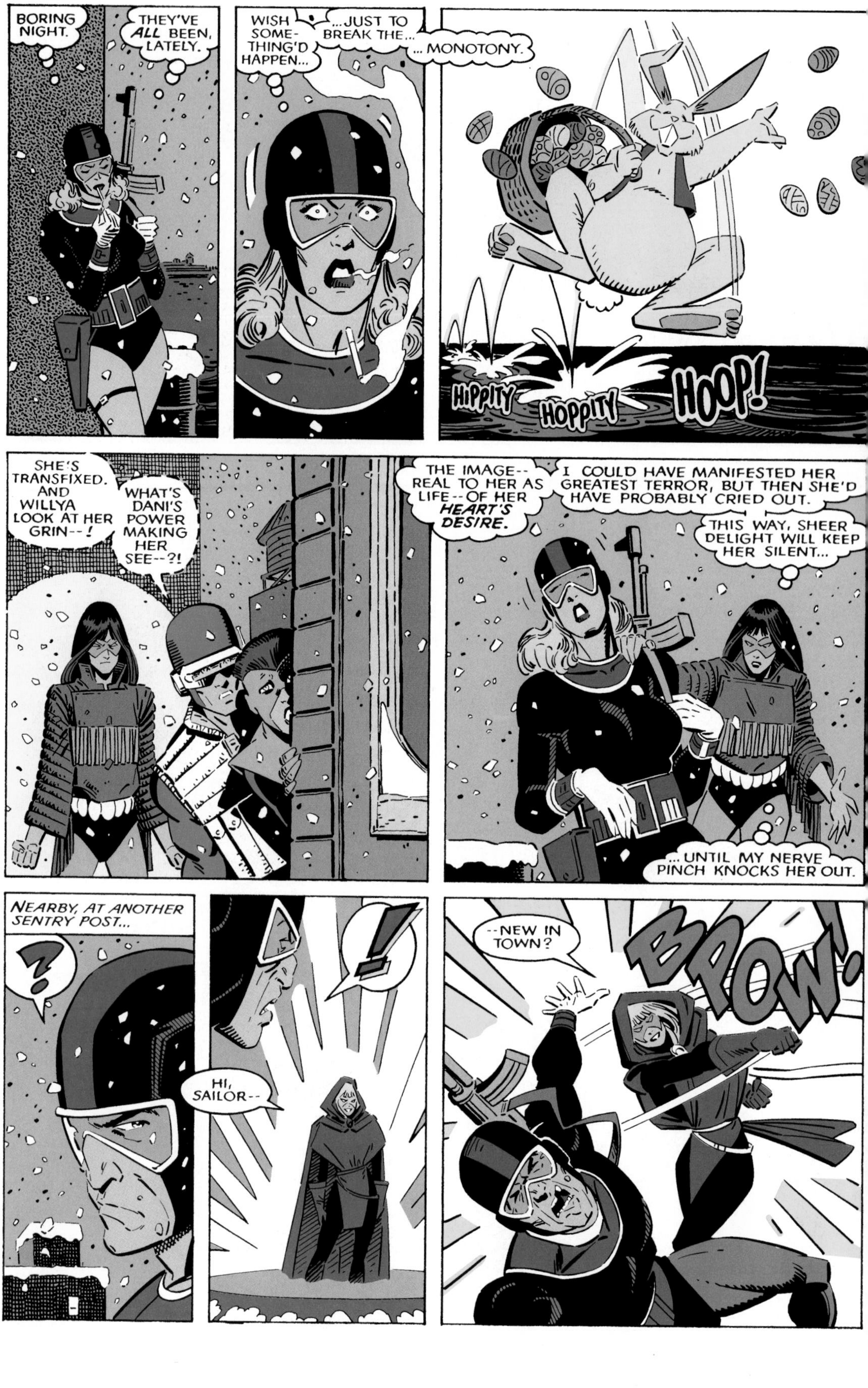
BORING NIGHT.
THEY'VE ALL BEEN, LATELY.
WISH SOME-THING'D HAPPEN...
...JUST TO BREAK THE...
...MONOTONY.
HIPPITY
HOPPITY
HOOP!
SHE'S TRANSFIXED. AND WILLYA LOOK AT HER GRIN--!
WHAT'S DANI'S POWER MAKING HER SEE--?!
THE IMAGE--REAL TO HER AS LIFE--OF HER HEART'S DESIRE.
I COULD HAVE MANIFESTED HER GREATEST TERROR, BUT THEN SHE'D HAVE PROBABLY CRIED OUT.
THIS WAY, SHEER DELIGHT WILL KEEP HER SILENT...
...UNTIL MY NERVE PINCH KNOCKS HER OUT.
NEARBY, AT ANOTHER SENTRY POST...
?
!
HI, SAILOR--
--NEW IN TOWN?
BPOW!

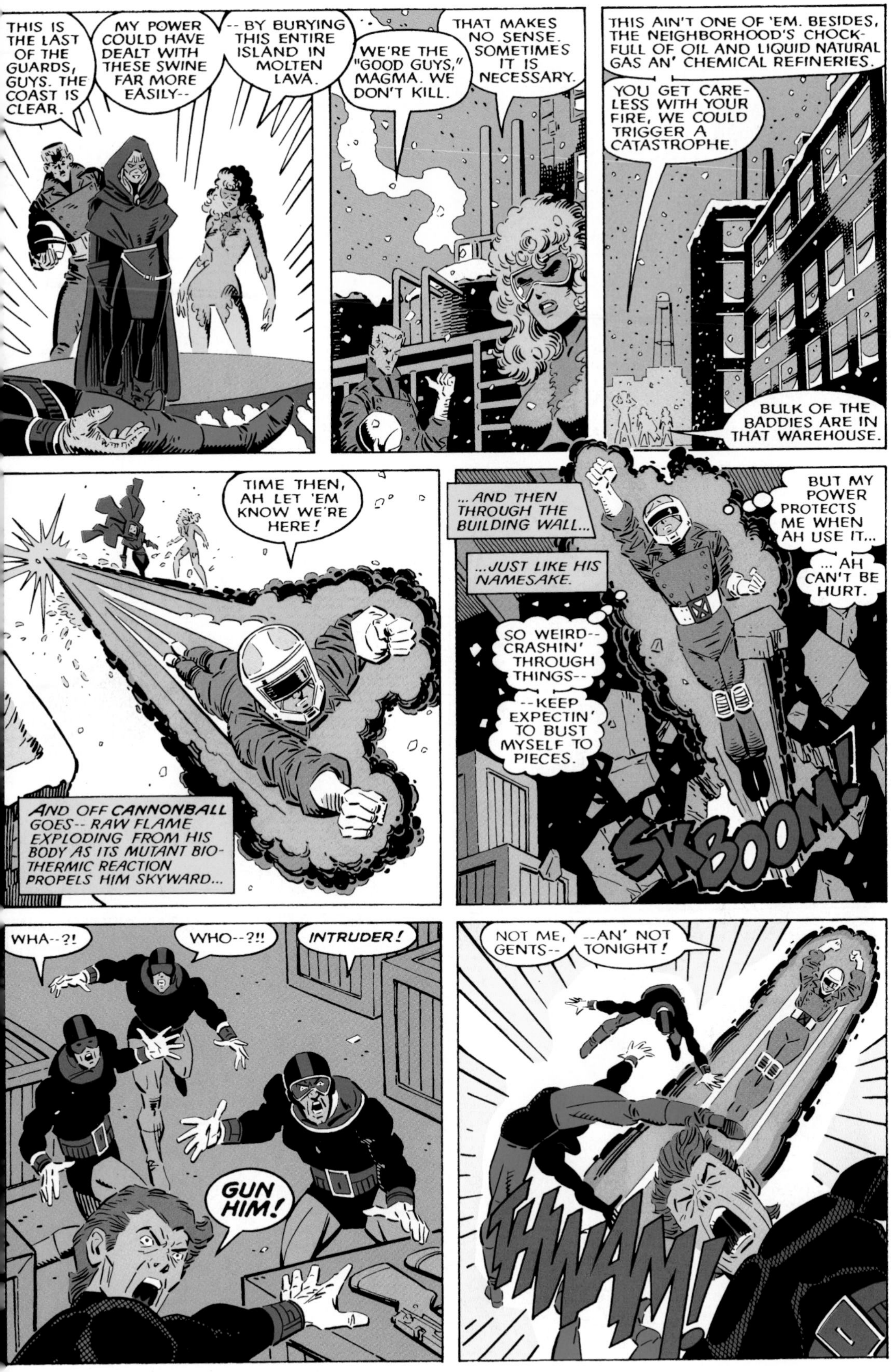

THIS IS THE LAST OF THE GUARDS, GUYS. THE COAST IS CLEAR.
MY POWER COULD HAVE DEALT WITH THESE SWINE FAR MORE EASILY--
--BY BURYING THIS ENTIRE ISLAND IN MOLTEN LAVA.
WE'RE THE "GOOD GUYS," MAGMA. WE DON'T KILL.
THAT MAKES NO SENSE. SOMETIMES IT IS NECESSARY.
THIS AIN'T ONE OF 'EM. BESIDES, THE NEIGHBORHOOD'S CHOCK-FULL OF OIL AND LIQUID NATURAL GAS AN' CHEMICAL REFINERIES.
YOU GET CARELESS WITH YOUR FIRE, WE COULD TRIGGER A CATASTROPHE.
BULK OF THE BADDIES ARE IN THAT WAREHOUSE.
TIME THEN, AH LET 'EM KNOW WE'RE HERE!
AND OFF CANNONBALL GOES-- RAW FLAME EXPLODING FROM HIS BODY AS ITS MUTANT BIO-THERMIC REACTION PROPELS HIM SKYWARD...
...AND THEN THROUGH THE BUILDING WALL...
...JUST LIKE HIS NAMESAKE.
BUT MY POWER PROTECTS ME WHEN AH USE IT...
...AH CAN'T BE HURT.
SO WEIRD-- CRASHIN' THROUGH THINGS--
--KEEP EXPECTIN' TO BUST MYSELF TO PIECES.
SKBOOM!
WHA--?!
WHO--?!!
INTRUDER!
GUN HIM!
NOT ME, GENTS--
--AN' NOT TONIGHT!
THWAM!

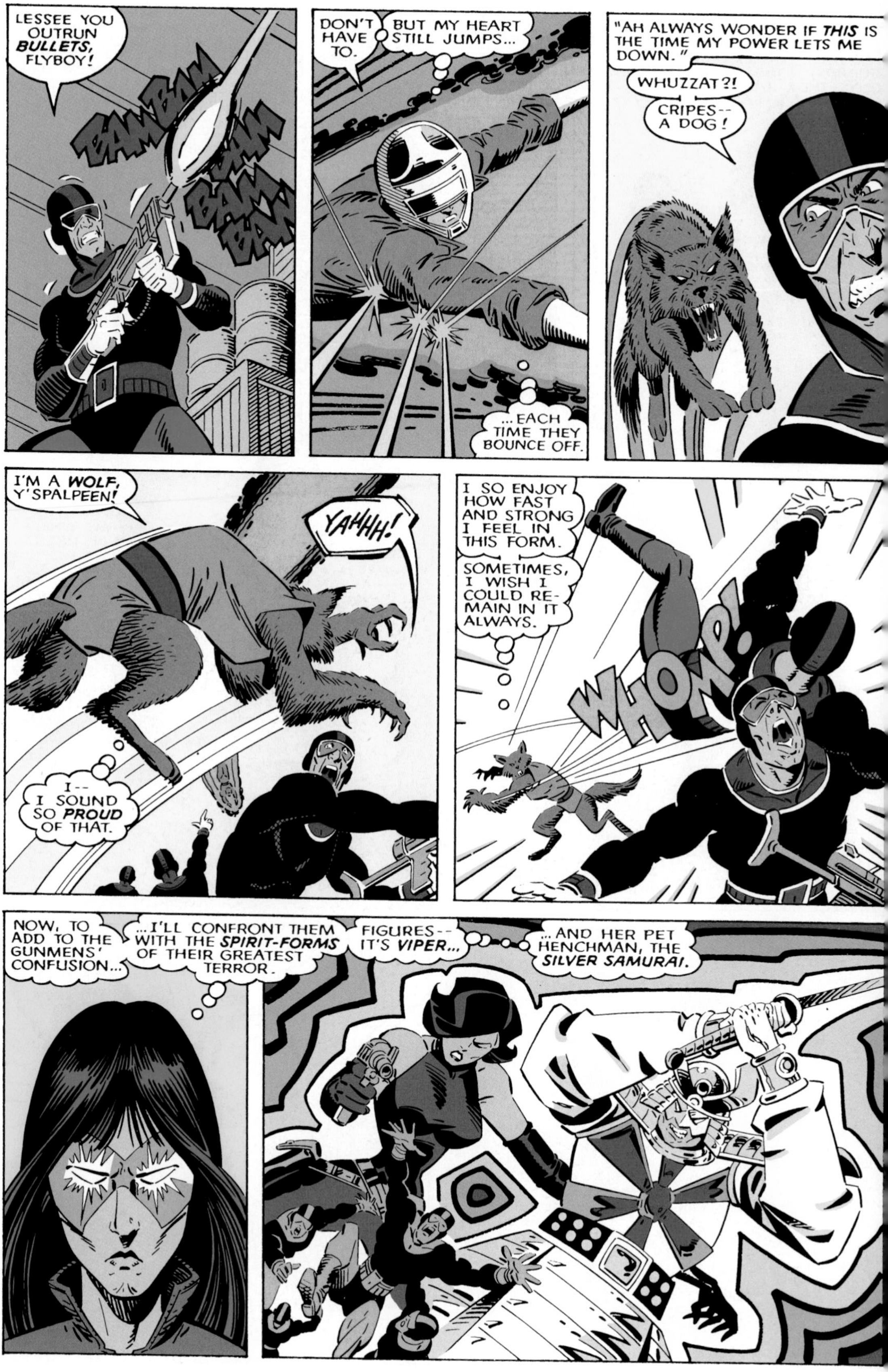
LESSEE YOU OUTRUN *BULLETS,* FLYBOY!
BAM BAM
BAM BAM
BAM BAM
DON'T HAVE TO.
BUT MY HEART STILL JUMPS...
...EACH TIME THEY BOUNCE OFF.
"AH ALWAYS WONDER IF *THIS* IS THE TIME MY POWER LETS ME DOWN."
WHUZZAT?!
CRIPES-- A DOG!
I'M A *WOLF,* Y'SPALPEEN!
YAHHH!
I-- I SOUND SO *PROUD* OF THAT.
I SO ENJOY HOW FAST AND STRONG I FEEL IN THIS FORM.
SOMETIMES, I WISH I COULD RE-MAIN IN IT ALWAYS.
WHOMP!
NOW, TO ADD TO THE GUNMENS' CONFUSION...
...I'LL CONFRONT THEM WITH THE *SPIRIT-FORMS* OF THEIR GREATEST TERROR.
FIGURES-- IT'S *VIPER*...
...AND HER PET HENCHMAN, THE *SILVER SAMURAI.*

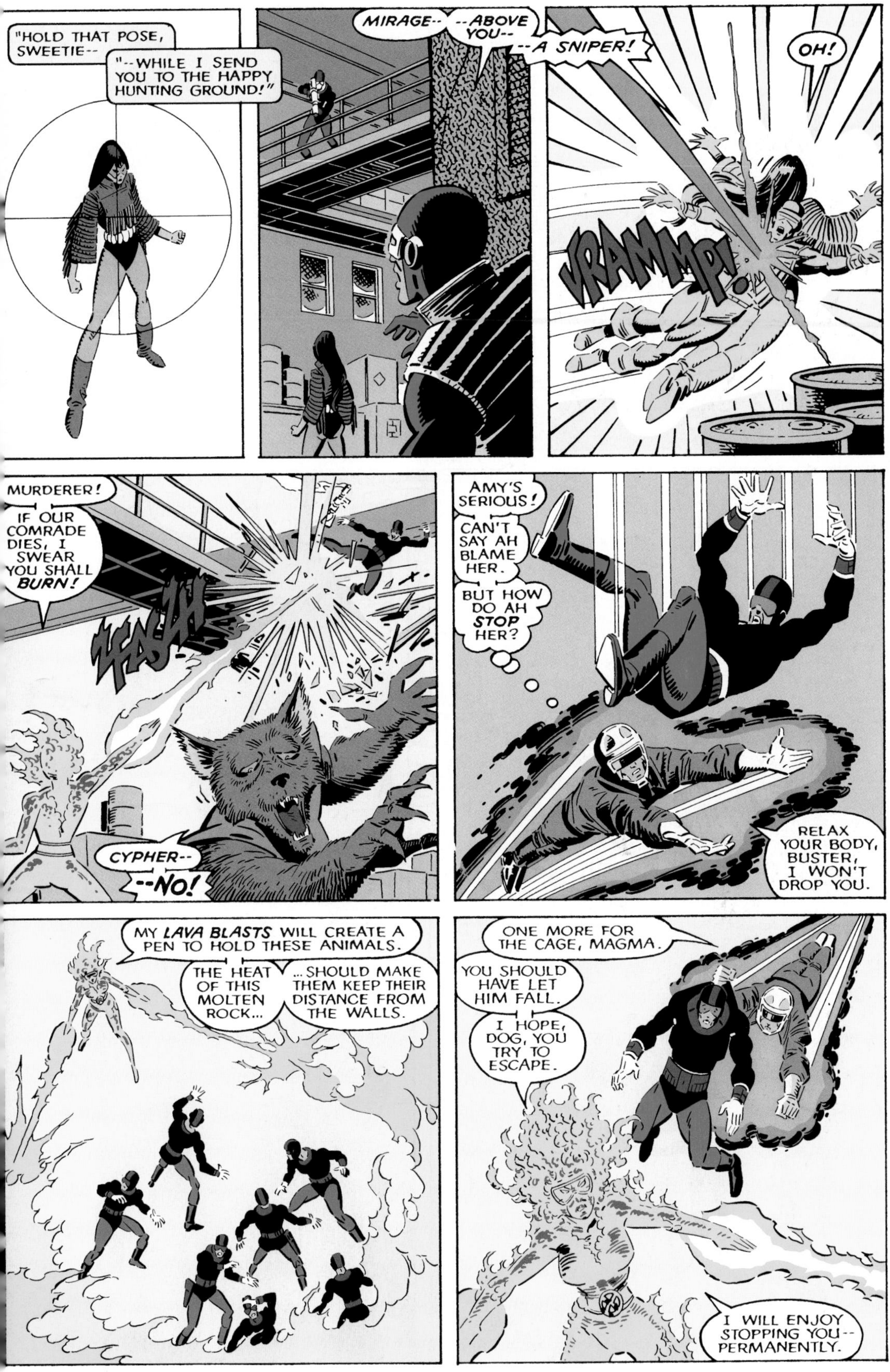
"HOLD THAT POSE, SWEETIE--
"--WHILE I SEND YOU TO THE HAPPY HUNTING GROUND!"
MIRAGE--
--ABOVE YOU--
--A SNIPER!
OH!
VRAMMP!
MURDERER!
IF OUR COMRADE DIES, I SWEAR YOU SHALL BURN!
CYPHER--
--NO!
AMY'S SERIOUS!
CAN'T SAY AH BLAME HER.
BUT HOW DO AH STOP HER?
RELAX YOUR BODY, BUSTER, I WON'T DROP YOU.
MY LAVA BLASTS WILL CREATE A PEN TO HOLD THESE ANIMALS.
THE HEAT OF THIS MOLTEN ROCK...
...SHOULD MAKE THEM KEEP THEIR DISTANCE FROM THE WALLS.
ONE MORE FOR THE CAGE, MAGMA.
YOU SHOULD HAVE LET HIM FALL.
I HOPE, DOG, YOU TRY TO ESCAPE.
I WILL ENJOY STOPPING YOU-- PERMANENTLY.

DOUGLAS--?!?

HE'S NA' MOVING-- BREATH'S SO SHALLOW--

MUST CALM MYSELF-- TRY TO USE MY WOLFEN SENSES TO LEARN HIS CONDITION!

DON'T HURT ME--I'M SORRY-- CALL THE COPS-- I'LL CONFESS-- I'LL PLEAD GUILTY--

--PLEASE, oh PLEASE-- I BEG YOU-- I DON'T WANNA FRY!

HEY, PAL--

--FORGET ABOUT MAGMA.

WORRY ABOUT ME.

IF IT HURTS THIS MUCH...

...I GUESS I'M NOT DEAD.

CYPHER!

MY NEW COSTUME, IT'S RUINED!

IT SAVED YUIR LIFE, YOU GREAT SILLY--

--AS YOU SAVED MIRAGE'S!

YAY, ME--

--OW! RAHNE!! DON'T HUG SO HARD!!!

SORRY.

CHEE DI INDUCTE STREN

WE GOT VIPER'S GOONS.

WHAT ABOUT HER?

WAS SHE NOT SUPPOSED TO BE HERE?

THAT'S WHAT I THOUGHT.

NO PROBLEM-- WE'LL SIMPLY "PERSUADE" ONE OF OUR PRISON- ERS TO LEAD US TO HER.

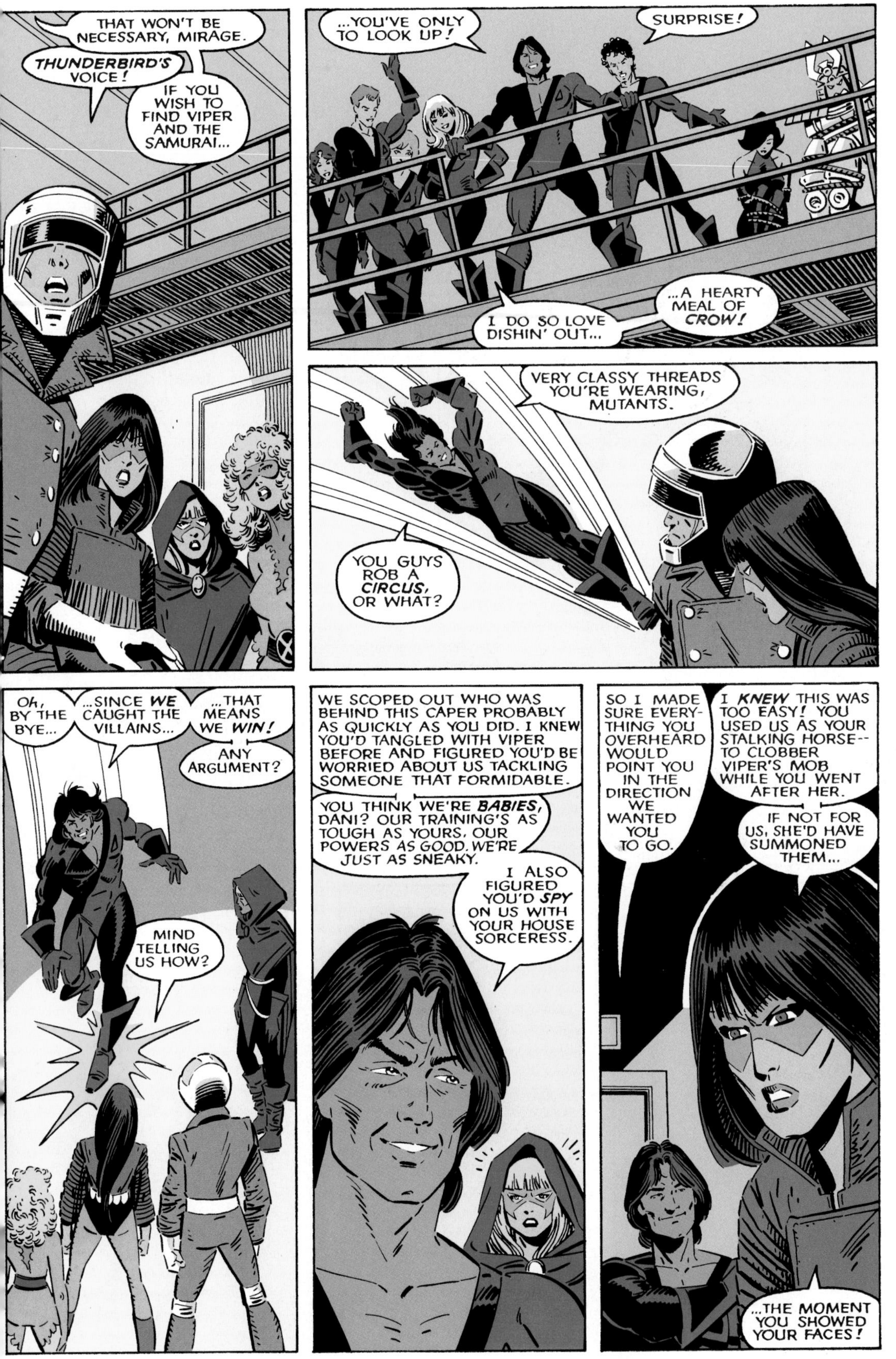
THAT WON'T BE NECESSARY, MIRAGE.
THUNDERBIRD'S VOICE!
IF YOU WISH TO FIND VIPER AND THE SAMURAI...
...YOU'VE ONLY TO LOOK UP!
SURPRISE!
I DO SO LOVE DISHIN' OUT...
...A HEARTY MEAL OF CROW!
VERY CLASSY THREADS YOU'RE WEARING, MUTANTS.
YOU GUYS ROB A CIRCUS, OR WHAT?
Oh, BY THE BYE...
...SINCE WE CAUGHT THE VILLAINS...
...THAT MEANS WE WIN!
ANY ARGUMENT?
MIND TELLING US HOW?
WE SCOPED OUT WHO WAS BEHIND THIS CAPER PROBABLY AS QUICKLY AS YOU DID. I KNEW YOU'D TANGLED WITH VIPER BEFORE AND FIGURED YOU'D BE WORRIED ABOUT US TACKLING SOMEONE THAT FORMIDABLE.
YOU THINK WE'RE BABIES, DANI? OUR TRAINING'S AS TOUGH AS YOURS. OUR POWERS AS GOOD. WE'RE JUST AS SNEAKY.
I ALSO FIGURED YOU'D SPY ON US WITH YOUR HOUSE SORCERESS.
SO I MADE SURE EVERYTHING YOU OVERHEARD WOULD POINT YOU IN THE DIRECTION WE WANTED YOU TO GO.
I KNEW THIS WAS TOO EASY! YOU USED US AS YOUR STALKING HORSE-- TO CLOBBER VIPER'S MOB WHILE YOU WENT AFTER HER.
IF NOT FOR US, SHE'D HAVE SUMMONED THEM...
...THE MOMENT YOU SHOWED YOUR FACES!

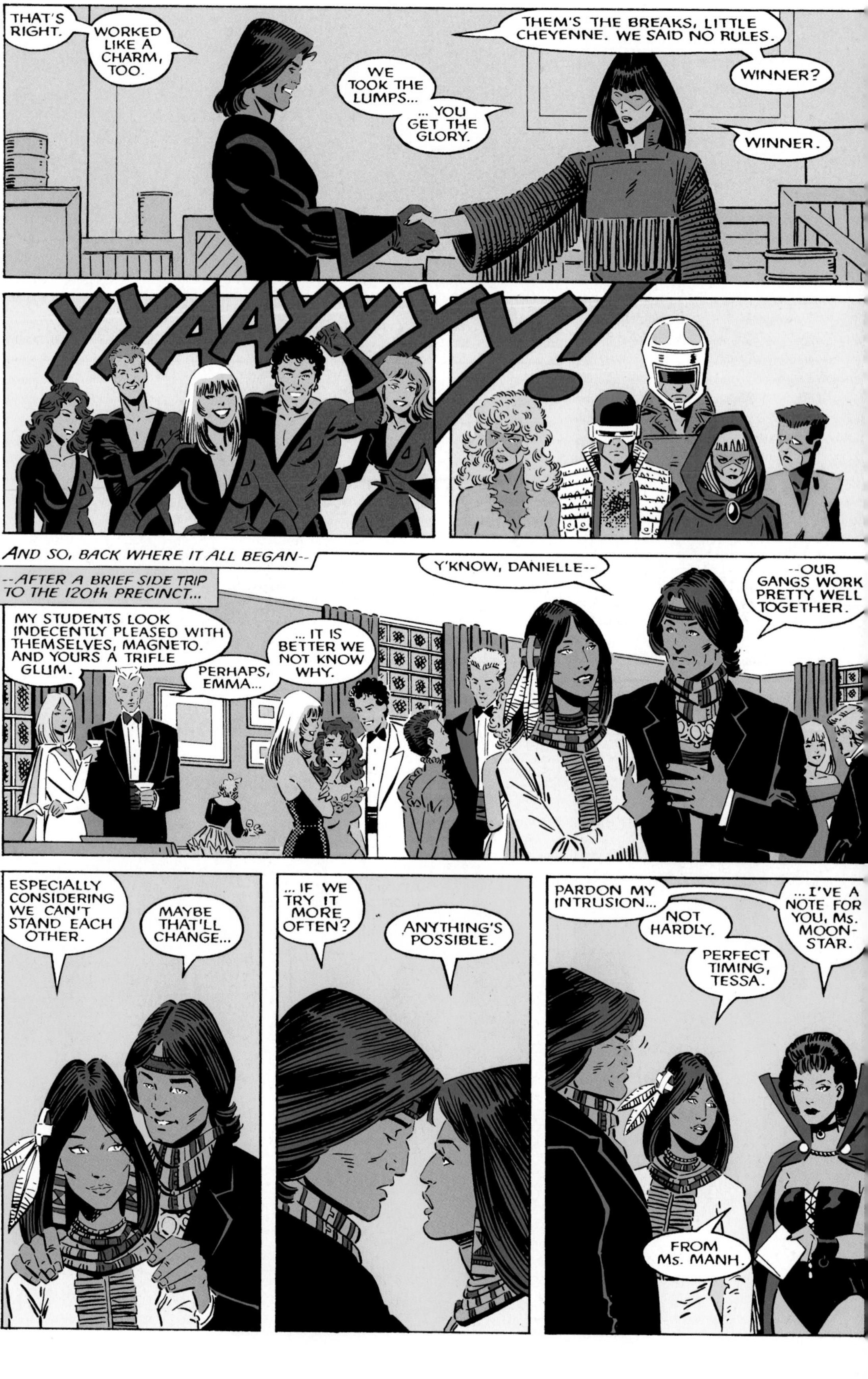
THAT'S RIGHT.
WORKED LIKE A CHARM, TOO.
WE TOOK THE LUMPS...
... YOU GET THE GLORY.
THEM'S THE BREAKS, LITTLE CHEYENNE. WE SAID NO RULES.
WINNER?
WINNER.
YYAAYYYY!
AND SO, BACK WHERE IT ALL BEGAN--
--AFTER A BRIEF SIDE TRIP TO THE 120th PRECINCT...
MY STUDENTS LOOK INDECENTLY PLEASED WITH THEMSELVES, MAGNETO. AND YOURS A TRIFLE GLUM.
PERHAPS, EMMA...
... IT IS BETTER WE NOT KNOW WHY.
Y'KNOW, DANIELLE--
--OUR GANGS WORK PRETTY WELL TOGETHER.
ESPECIALLY CONSIDERING WE CAN'T STAND EACH OTHER.
MAYBE THAT'LL CHANGE...
...IF WE TRY IT MORE OFTEN?
ANYTHING'S POSSIBLE.
PARDON MY INTRUSION...
NOT HARDLY.
...I'VE A NOTE FOR YOU, Ms. MOONSTAR.
PERFECT TIMING, TESSA.
FROM Ms. MANH.

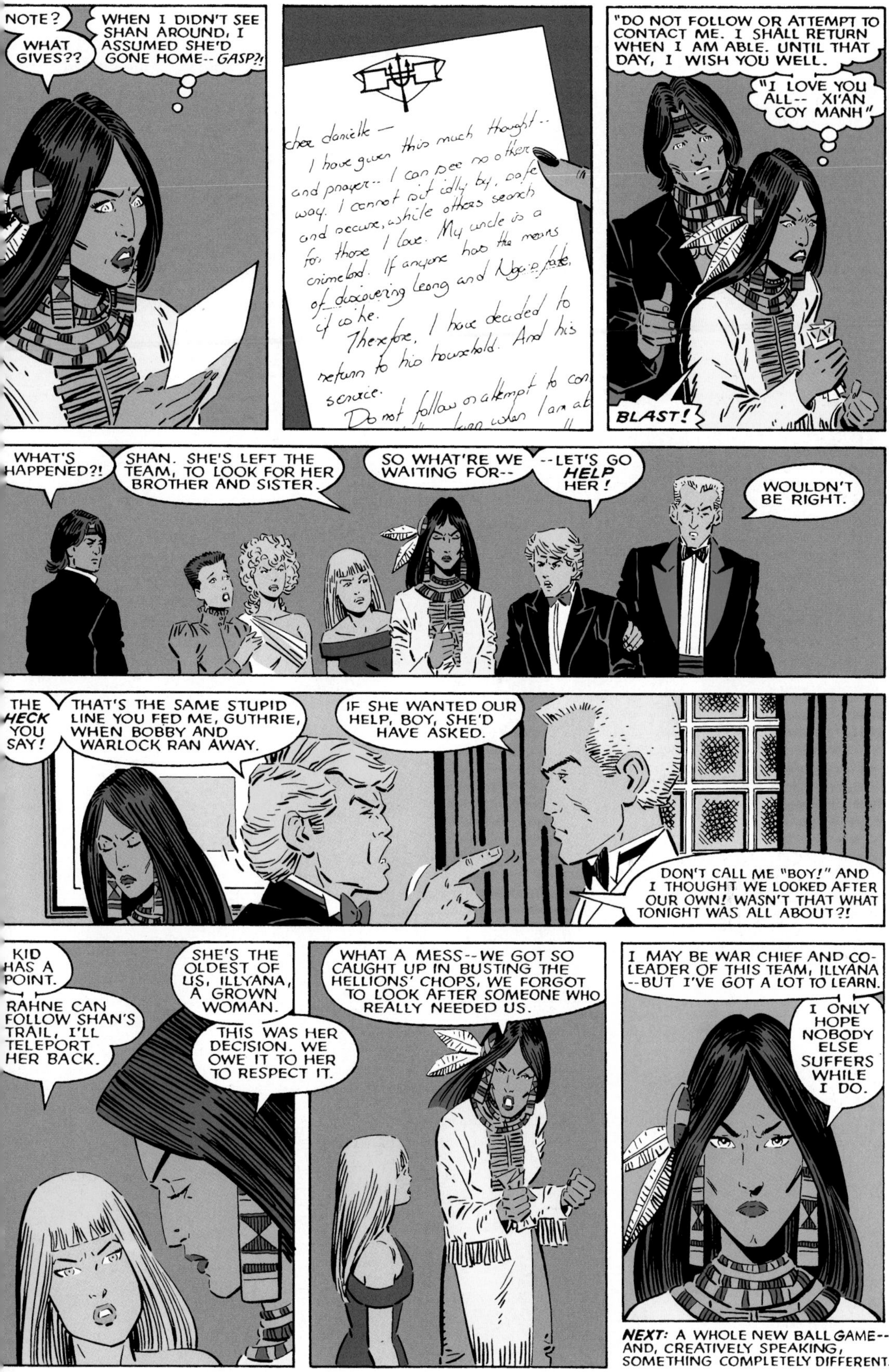
NOTE? WHAT GIVES??
WHEN I DIDN'T SEE SHAN AROUND, I ASSUMED SHE'D GONE HOME-- *GASP?!*
cher danielle —
I have given this much thought..
and prayer.. I can see no other
way. I cannot sit idly by, safe
and secure, while others search
for those I love. My uncle is a
crimelord. If anyone has the means
of discovering Leong and Ngoc's fate,
it is he.
Therefore, I have decided to
return to his household. And his
service.
Do not follow or attempt to con
"DO NOT FOLLOW OR ATTEMPT TO CONTACT ME. I SHALL RETURN WHEN I AM ABLE. UNTIL THAT DAY, I WISH YOU WELL.
"I LOVE YOU ALL-- XI'AN COY MANH"
BLAST!
WHAT'S HAPPENED?!
SHAN. SHE'S LEFT THE TEAM, TO LOOK FOR HER BROTHER AND SISTER.
SO WHAT'RE WE WAITING FOR--
--LET'S GO *HELP* HER!
WOULDN'T BE RIGHT.
THE *HECK* YOU SAY!
THAT'S THE SAME STUPID LINE YOU FED ME, GUTHRIE, WHEN BOBBY AND WARLOCK RAN AWAY.
IF SHE WANTED OUR HELP, BOY, SHE'D HAVE ASKED.
DON'T CALL ME "BOY!" AND I THOUGHT WE LOOKED AFTER OUR OWN! WASN'T THAT WHAT TONIGHT WAS ALL ABOUT?!
KID HAS A POINT.
RAHNE CAN FOLLOW SHAN'S TRAIL, I'LL TELEPORT HER BACK.
SHE'S THE OLDEST OF US, ILLYANA, A GROWN WOMAN.
THIS WAS HER DECISION. WE OWE IT TO HER TO RESPECT IT.
WHAT A MESS--WE GOT SO CAUGHT UP IN BUSTING THE HELLIONS' CHOPS, WE FORGOT TO LOOK AFTER SOMEONE WHO REALLY NEEDED US.
I MAY BE WAR CHIEF AND CO-LEADER OF THIS TEAM, ILLYANA --BUT I'VE GOT A LOT TO LEARN.
I ONLY HOPE NOBODY ELSE SUFFERS WHILE I DO.

***NEXT:*** A WHOLE NEW BALL GAME-- AND, CREATIVELY SPEAKING, SOMETHING COMPLETELY DIFFERENT!

# #1 VARIANT BY BILL SIENKIEWICZ

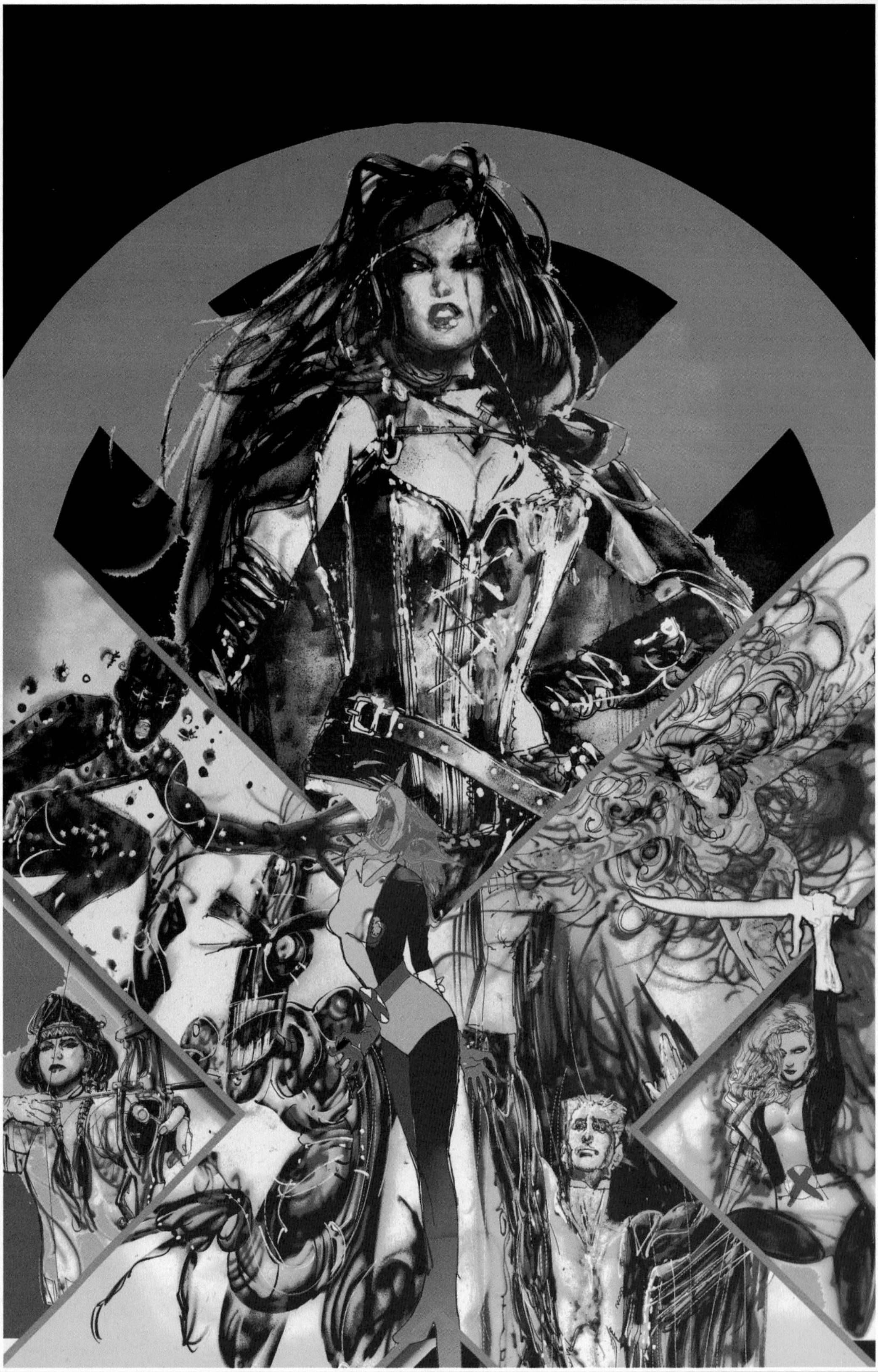

# #2 VARIANT BY BILL SIENKIEWICZ

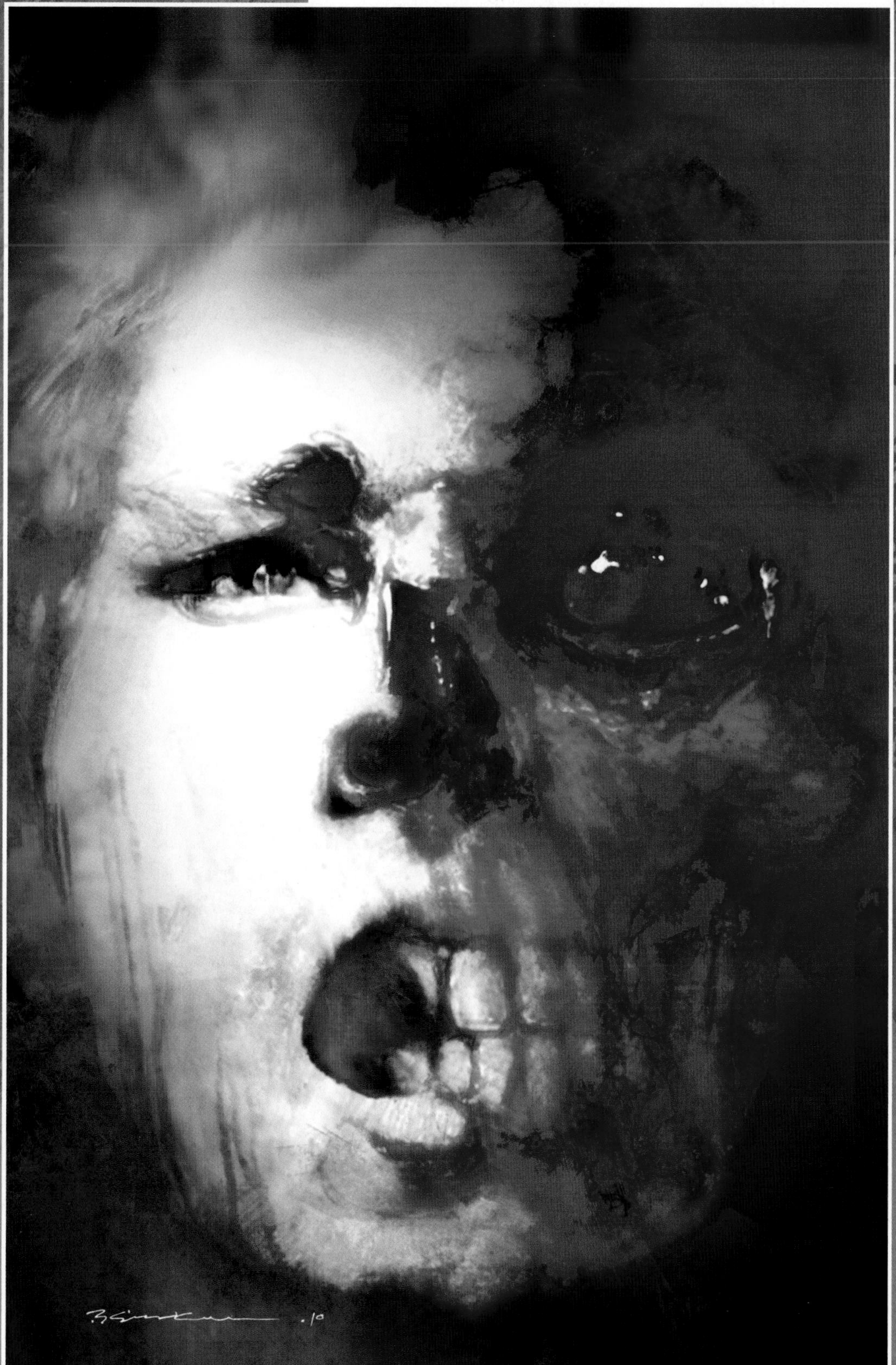

## #3 VARIANT BY BILL SIENKIEWICZ

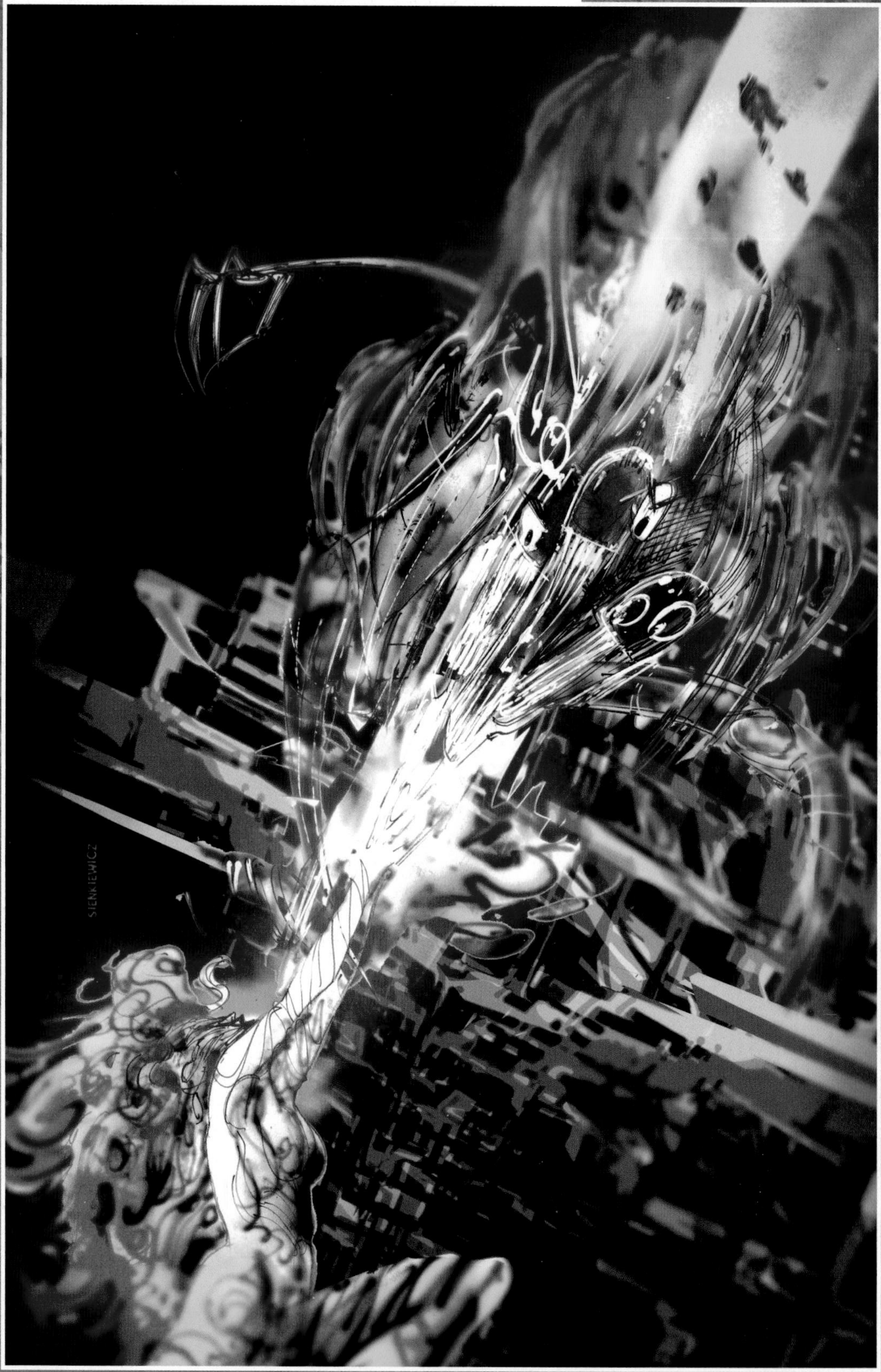
SIENKIEWICZ